The Completed Work of Christ in John 17:4

The Completed Work of Christ in John 17:4

An Interpretive Key for Reading the Fourth Gospel

ERIC C. REDMOND

☙PICKWICK *Publications* · Eugene, Oregon

THE COMPLETED WORK OF CHRIST IN JOHN 17:4
An Interpretive Key for Reading the Fourth Gospel

Copyright © 2025 Eric C. Redmond. All rights reserved. Except for brief quotations in critical publications or reviews, no part of this book may be reproduced in any manner without prior written permission from the publisher. Write: Permissions, Wipf and Stock Publishers, 199 W. 8th Ave., Suite 3, Eugene, OR 97401.

Pickwick Publications
An Imprint of Wipf and Stock Publishers
199 W. 8th Ave., Suite 3
Eugene, OR 97401

www.wipfandstock.com

PAPERBACK ISBN: 978-1-6667-7917-2
HARDCOVER ISBN: 978-1-6667-7918-9
EBOOK ISBN: 978-1-6667-7919-6

Cataloguing-in-Publication data:

Names: Redmond, Eric C., author.

Title: The completed work of Christ in John 17:4 : an interpretive key for reading the fourth gospel / Eric C. Redmond.

Description: Eugene, OR: Pickwick Publications, 2025. | Includes bibliographical references and index.

Identifiers: ISBN 978-1-6667-7917-2 (paperback). | ISBN 978-1-6667-7918-9 (hardcover). | ISBN 978-1-6667-7919-6 (ebook).

Subjects: LCSH: Bible.—John XVII, 4—Criticism, interpretation, etc. | Bible.—John—Criticism, interpretation, etc.

Classification: BS2615.2 2025 (print). | BS2615.2 (ebook).

09/29/25

To Pamela, my Autumn,
whose clear skies and crisp air invite me to wrap my scarf
and jump with her into life's piles of colorful leaves,
and whose love keeps winter in abeyance—
this is your dissertation for your degree,
for you have put hubby through,

and to Erice E. Doss,
who once was the youngest person I knew holding
a research doctorate, and you were
both inspiring and caring,

and to R. Guy Vickers,
who came to my high school and recruited me to Georgia Tech
to study engineering, and who said to the vast majority
of African American students on campus,
"Whatever you do, get your PhD,"

and to Rev. Wm. Dwight McKissick,
whose thoughts are far deeper than those of a great many with PhDs,
and whose heart is far bigger than the
collected knowledge of a score of scholars,

and to Christine S. Doerfler,
who believed in me from the time I was your student,
and gave me opportunities to grow and thrive,
and played your role in hope of this degree,
and whom I always will consider dear to me
and now can say, "We did it!"

Contents

List of Tables | ix
Acknowledgments | xi
List of Abbreviations | xiii
1 The Completed Event That Is Yet to Happen or Is Finished | 1
2 The Tale of Two Readings | 29
3 Making God Known Publicly and Privately | 91
4 The Book with Two Completions | 119
5 The Work of the Words and Works | 185
6 The Absentee Father | 203
Conclusion | 217
Bibliography | 235

Tables

Table 1. Summary of Primary-Proleptic Views | 88

Table 2. Summary of Primary-Reflective Views | 89

Table 3. Sir 38:6–8 LXX Compared to John 17:4 GNT | 111

Table 4. Ellis' Overview of Morphological Features of Greek Verbs | 153

Table 5. Morphological Features of ἐδόξασα | 154

Table 6. Morphological Features of τελειώσας | 155

Table 7. Morphological Features of ποιήσω | 156

Table 8. Tense and Aspect for μι-Conjugation verb δέδωκάς as a First Singular Active Indicative Verb | 157

Table 9. Morphological Diagramming of τελειόω Verbs in the NT | 164

Table 10. Morphological Diagramming of τελειόω Verbs in John and 1 John | 165

Table 11. Morphological Diagramming of τελέω in the NT | 167

Table 12. Morphological Diagramming of τελειόω in the NT | 168

Table 13. Morphological Diagramming of Τελειόω in the Fourth Gospel | 169

Table 14. Morphological Diagramming of Τελέω in the Fourth Gospel | 169

Table 15. Use of τελειόω in the NT | 176

Table 16. Use of τελέω in the NT in the Sense of Fulfillment | 179

Table 17. Use of τελέω in the NT in a Sense other than Fulfillment | 181

Table 18. Use of τελέω in John 19:28, 30 | 182

Table 19. πατήρ for God the Father Across the 21 Chapters of John 1:1–21:25 | 212

Table 20. πατήρ for God the Father Across John 1–12 Compared to John 13–21 | 213

Table 21. πατήρ for God the Father Across the 867 verses of John 1:1–21:25 | 213

Table 22. πατήρ for God the Father Across John 1–16 Compared to John 18–21 | 214

Acknowledgments

I WISH TO THANK many who made this dissertation and its corresponding degree possible, beginning with Dr. Mark Meyer, former colleague and friend, who invited me from another doctoral program to join this one. Dr. Doug Finkbeiner has been a joyous advisor and instructor. Each of my instructors in the program have shaped my scholarship and pedagogy in very meaningful ways. I have been most grateful to the staff of the libraries of Lancaster Bible College and Moody Bible Institute for tirelessly meeting my enormous number of ILL and document requests.

As always, my parents have been in my corner. Every year that I live, serve my own family, and serve the families of many others, my love and gratitude grow for all you continue to do. None on earth could ask for better parents. I am humbled by the shadow of faithfulness and grace cast by you.

The Five Cs—my children—have been pulling for Daddy the whole way. You have asked, encouraged, and prayed, taking on the role Mommy and I have had in your lives. It is a blessing to be your father and especially to see you grow toward Christ the Lord. God the Son is faithful toward you.

The body of Christ that is Reformation Alive Baptist Church—now Emmanuel Church, New Canaan Baptist Church, Mt. Pleasant Baptist Church, and Calvary Memorial Church—you each have loved me in ways that encouraged me through this project. So too have scores of friends who have been part of a dedicated team of prayer partners who interceded on my behalf in order to see the accomplishment of this paper and the degree, including a great number of former students. Thank you, Pastor Terry D. Streeter, for being a kind pastor over my soul, even at a distance. Thank you, Pastors Todd Wilson and Gerald Hiestand, for allowing grace as I raced to the finish line. Thank you, Sarah McCaffrey, for leading the dedicated prayer team with joy.

I work at a tremendous institution: Moody Bible Institute (MBI). What a blessing it is to have colleagues, students, and graduates constantly rooting for me, asking, "How close are you to finishing?" or "How's the paper coming?" and then adding, "I am praying." I thank MBI former President Dr. Paul Nyquist, former Provost Dr. Junias Venugopal, and Assistant Provost Dr. Larry Davidhizar for presenting me to the Bible Department as a faculty candidate a handful of years ago. Thank you, MBI, for giving me the necessary support to see the degree through to the end. Thank you, too, Dr. James Spencer—former Academic Dean and now serving with The Moody Center—for your friendship and support.

Of course, no one has given me greater support than my wife, Pamela, as is true for each work I do. This, like all my works, is dedicated to you first, among mortals. Only to God the Father, God the Son, and God the Holy Spirit do I give greater praise—praise that outstrips any I might give to another: praise that acknowledges the grace the Godhead has given to me by giving me you. I love you.

Abbreviations

ABR	*Australian Biblical Review*
act.	active
AD	*anno Domini*
AJBT	*American Journal of Biblical Theology*
aor.	aorist
Bar	Baruch
BBR	*Bulletin for Biblical Research*
BC	before Christ
BDAG	Walter Bauer, Frederick W. Danker, William F. Arndt, and F. Wilbur Gingrich. *Greek-English Lexicon of the New Testament and Other Early Christian Literature.* 3rd ed. Chicago: University of Chicago Press, 2000
BDB	Francis Brown, S. R. Driver, and Charles A. Briggs. *A Hebrew and English Lexicon of the Old Testament*
BHS	*Biblia Hebraica Stuttgartensia.* Edited by Karl Elliger and Wilhelm Rudolph. Stuttgart: Deutsche Bibelgesellschaft, 1983
Bib	*Biblica*
BSac	*Bibliotheca Sacra*
BT	*The Bible Translator*
CBQ	*Catholic Biblical Quarterly*
Chm	*Churchman*

Colloq	Colloquium
CSB	Christian Standard Bible
DBSJ	Detroit Baptist Seminary Journal
EDNT	*Exegetical Dictionary of the New Testament*. Edited by Horst Balz and Gerhard Schneider. Edited by Virgil P. Howard et al. 3 vols. Grand Rapids: Eerdmans, 1990–1993
1–2 Esd	1–2 Esdras
ESV	English Standard Version
EvQ	*Evangelical Quarterly*
ExAud	*Ex Auditu*
gen.	genitive
GNT	Good News Translation
HALOT	*The Hebrew and Aramaic Lexicon of the Old Testament*. Ludwig Koehler, Walter Baumgartner, and Johann J. Stamm. Translated and edited under the supervision of Mervyn E. J. Richardson. 4 vols. Leiden: Brill, 1994–1999
Heb.	Hebrew
HS	*Hebrew Studies*
HTR	*Harvard Theological Review*
ind.	indicative
inf.	infinitive
JBL	*Journal of Biblical Literature*
JCID	*Journal of the Christian Institute on Disability*
Jdt	Judith
JETS	*Journal of the Evangelical Theological Society*
JPC&C	*Journal of Pastoral Care & Counseling*
JPT	*Journal of Pentecostal Theology*
JSNT	*Journal for the Study of the New Testament*
JSNTSup	*Journal for the Study of the New Testament Supplement Series*

L&N	Louw, Johannes P., and Eugene A. Nida, eds. *Greek-English Lexicon of the New Testament: Based on Semantic Domains*. 2nd ed. New York: United Bible Societies, 1989
LSJ	H. G. Liddell, Robert Scott, H. Stuart Jones, and Roderick McKenzie, *Greek-English Lexicon*. Oxford: Clarendon, 1968
LXX	Septuagint
1–2 Macc	1–2 Maccabees
masc.	masculine
MT	Masoretic Text
NASB	New American Standard Bible
Neot	*Neotestamentica*
NET	New English Translation
NETS	*A New English Translation of the Septuagint*
NIDNTTE	*New International Dictionary of New Testament Theology and Exegesis*. 2nd ed. Edited by Moisés Silva. Grand Rapids: Zondervan, 2014
NIV	New International Version
NLT	New Living Translation
NovT	*Novum Testamentum*
NRSV	New Revised Standard Version
NTS	*New Testament Studies*
Odes	Odes of Solomon
part.	participle
pass.	passive
perf.	perfect
pl.	plural
P. Oxy.	*The Oxyrhynchus Papyri*
P. Petr.	*The Flinders Petrie Papyri*
Presb	*Presbyterion*
Pss. Sol.	Psalms of Solomon

PRSt	*Perspectives in Religious Studies*
RSV	Revised Standard Version
SBJT	*Southern Baptist Journal of Theology*
Sir	Sirach
SJT	*Scottish Journal of Theology*
subj.	subjunctive
TDNT	*Theological Dictionary of the New Testament.* Edited by Gerhard Kittel and Gerhard Friedrich. Translated by Geoffrey W. Bromiley. 10 vols. Grand Rapids: Eerdmans, 1964–1976
Them	*Themelios*
TTE	*The Theological Educator*
TynBul	*Tyndale Bulletin*
VE	*Vox Evangelica*
VTSup	Supplements to Vetus Testamentum
ZNW	*Zeitschrift für die neutestamentliche Wissenschaft und die Kunde der älteren Kirche*

1

The Completed Event That Is Yet to Happen or Is Finished

IN THE HISTORY OF the church, John 17 stands out as a uniquely significant chapter in the Gospel of John. Often identified as a high-priestly prayer of Christ,[1] it brings a climax to the Upper Room Discourse. The Discourse expands the private, intimate discussions between Christ and the disciples that are assumed in the Synoptic Gospels.[2]

JOHN 17 IN HISTORY OF INTERPRETATION

Puritan writer Thomas Manton confers upon John 17 a pneumatological superlative with respect to the emotional depth and lasting worth of Christ's prayer, saying,

> The Holy Ghost seemeth to put a mark of respect upon this prayer above other prayers which Christ conceived in the days of his flesh. Elsewhere the scripture telleth us that Christ prayed; but the form is not expressed, or else only brief hints are delivered, but this is expressed at large. This was, as it were, his dying blaze. Natural motion is swifter and stronger in the end; so was

1. Sixteenth-century Lutheran theologian, David Chytraeus (1530–1600), was the first to title the prayer of John 17 as "priestly prayer" (Beasley-Murray, *John*, 294; Carson, *The Gospel According to John*, 552; Moloney, *Johannine Studies, 1975–2017*, 451).

2. The episode of the Upper Room Discourse in the first three Gospels has discussions significantly shorter and different than that of John 14–16. See Matt 26:19–29; Mark 14:17–31; Luke 22:14–38.

> Christ's love hottest and strongest in the close of his life; and here you have the eruption and flame of it. He would now open to us the bottom of his heart, and give us a copy of his continual intercession. This prayer is a standing monument of Christ's affection to the church; it did not pass away with the external sound, or as soon as Christ ascended into heaven, and sat at the right hand of the Father; it retaineth a perpetual efficacy; the virtue remaineth, though the words be over.[3]

According to Manton, Christ's words express his love for his church in the greatest verbal form. In comparison to previous words from Christ, he presently ("now") bares his deepest, innermost being and emotions. Such words, too, are exemplary of the words of intercession Christ makes for his own before the Father in his present session in heaven (cf. Rom 8:34; Heb 7:25; 1 John 2:1). For Manton, Christ's words excel in efficacious power in a special way and seemingly are dissimilar from other words of Christ.

Only two centuries later, on the significance of John 17, Charles Spurgeon preaches,

> This chapter, which ought to be universally known as the Lord's Prayer, may be called the holy of holies of the word of God. Here we are admitted to that secret place where the Son of God speaks with the Father in closest fellowship of love. Here we look into the heart of Jesus, as he sets out in order his desires and requests before his Father on our behalf. Here inspiration lifts her veil, and we behold truth face to face.[4]

In the mind of this Baptist evangelist, the moniker "holy of holies" sets apart this chapter as the most important one in the entirety of Scripture. For Spurgeon, similar to the commentary by Manton, in John 17 lies an exceptional instance within the inspiration of the Scriptures, where special insight is given into the heart of Jesus. What has been secret to Jesus in the Gospel narratives thus far, the writer of the Fourth Gospel now unveils so that the full glory of Christ–that which would have been hidden behind the curtain in the holiest place within the tabernacle–is visible "face to face" in a mini beatific vision (cf. Exod 26:33–34; 33:11; 40:21; Num 14:14; 1 Cor 13:12; 2 Cor 3:1).

---

3. Manton, *The Complete Works of Thomas Manton, D.D*, 109.

4. Spurgeon, "Our Lord's Prayer for His Own People's Sanctification: A Sermon Delivered on Lord's-Day Morning, March 7th, 1886, No. 1890," *Metropolitan Tabernacle Pulpit: Sermons Preached and Revised During the Year 1886*, 145–46.

Within a century of Spurgeon, D. M. Lloyd-Jones builds upon Spurgeon's concept of the holiness of John 17, noting, "There have been those in the past who have felt that here we are dealing with something which is so sacred, because it is the very opening into our Lord's own heart, that the only right thing to do with this prayer is to read it."[5] Further, the significance of this chapter encompasses the earthly knowledge needed for the church's Christian discipleship. Lloyd-Jones continues,

> If we had nothing but John 17 we would surely have more than enough to sustain us, because here our Lord has given us an insight into our whole position, and into everything that is of importance and of value to us while we are in this world of time. We can do nothing better, therefore, than to look at this prayer, and to consider what he has to say.[6]

The importance of this chapter for Lloyd-Jones accounts, in part, for his preaching of forty-eight sermons on John 17.[7]

Later in the twentieth century, with less spiritual superlatives but equally important designation, Barnabas Lindars writes about the significance of John 17 to the Upper Room Discourse, "It fittingly concludes the account of the Last Supper, summing up as it does the whole purpose of John's presentation of the narrative, in which the meaning of discipleship has been the dominant theme."[8] Other commentators will follow Lindars in seeing a summing up of the theology of the Fourth Gospel within John 17.

For example, C. K. Barrett suggests, "The present prayer is a summary of Johannine Theology relative to the work of Christ."[9] D. A. Carson, similarly, notes, "In some respects the prayer is a summary of the entire Fourth Gospel to this point."[10] Andreas Köstenberger finds this

---

5. Lloyd-Jones, *The Assurance of Our Salvation*, 12.

6. Lloyd-Jones, *The Assurance of Our Salvation*, 13.

7. Christopher Catherwood, editor of the published version of the sermons, records that Lloyd-Jones preached the sermons from 1952–1953, (Lloyd-Jones, *Assurance*, 11).

8. Lindars, *The Gospel of John*, 516.

9. Barrett, *The Gospel According to St. John*, 417.

10. Carson, *John*, 551. Carson continues his thoughts on the summarizing and climaxing nature of John 17, positing, "Its principal themes include Jesus' obedience to his Father, the glorification of his Father through his death/exaltation, the revelation of God in Christ Jesus, the choosing of the disciples out of the world, their mission to the world, their unity modelled on the unity of the Father and the Son, and their final destiny in the presence of the Father and the Son. To cast this summary in the form of a prayer is not only to anticipate Jesus' being 'lifted up' on the cross, but to contribute to

chapter to be a capstone to some themes in John's Gospel. He writes, "Jesus's final prayer culminates John's portrayal of Jesus as the one sent from the Father who, after completing his mission, is about to return to the one who sent him."[11] J. Ramsey Michaels finds the author of John 17 "revisiting most of the themes of the preceding discourse."[12] The concept of John 17 as a summation of John's teaching to this point also agrees with John Calvin's understanding of the significance of John 17: "In short, this prayer of Christ is, as it were, the seal of the preceding teaching, both that it might be ratified in itself and that it might obtain full authority with the disciples."[13]

Doctrinally speaking, others find John 17 useful to support narrower concepts. Jim Dekker appeals, somewhat uniquely, to John 17 to support a theology of "generativity."[14] With another idea, Lindars notes, "It is not without reason that [John 17] has become the charter of the Ecumenical Movement in the twentieth century."[15] Reflective of Lindars' conclusions are ecumenical statements by The World Council of Churches,[16] the National Council of Churches in Christ in the USA,[17] and

---

the climax of the movement that brings Christ back to God—one of the central themes of the farewell discourse . . . John 17 is part of the crescendo to which such passages as 1:29, 34; 3:14–15; 6:51–58; 10:11; 11:49–52; 13:8 have been building, a crescendo that is climaxed in chs. 18–20 in the passion and triumph of Jesus the Messiah" (551).

11. Köstenberger, *John*, 483.

12. Michaels, *The Gospel of John*, 857.

13. Calvin, *Calvin's New Testament Commentaries: John 11–21 and 1 John*, 134.

14. Dekker, "Generativity, Covenant Witness, and Jesus' Final Discourse."

15. Lindars, *The Gospel of John*, 516.

16. "The ecumenical movement has its centre in the Triune God and not in human efforts, plans and desires. The committee affirms that the theological foundation of the search for the full visible unity of the church, and its common witness to the world is rooted in Scripture, namely in Christ's prayer for his disciples ('that they may all be one') as found in John 17:21. It is our understanding that the search for the goal of full visible unity of the church is also for the sake of the healing and transformation of the world. Common witness for justice and peace has always been central for the ecumenical movement. The theme of the forthcoming WCC Assembly at Busan resonates well with this conviction and trajectory: 'God of life, lead us to justice and peace.'" Continuation Committee on Ecumenism in the 21st Century, "Final Report," 10.

17. "The words 'ecumenism' and 'ecumenical' derive from the New Testament Greek *oikoumene*, typically used during the days of the Roman Empire to refer to the whole inhabited world (e.g., Lk 2:1 and Acts 11:28). In recent times these terms have most commonly come to signify a movement dedicated to renewing the unity of the Church. Common fellowship, shared service, and types of witness are prevalent themes. New Testament passages such as John 17:20–23 give a sense of purpose to the ecumenical movement. Here Christ teaches that our unity flows out of his own unity

the Roman Catholic Church.[18] Baptist theologian and Protestant Reformation scholar, Timothy George, appeals differently to John 17:21 in reference to his belief in "an ecumenism of conviction, not an ecumenism of accommodation."[19] Dissimilarly, Ernst Käsemann uses John 17 as his starting point to examine "the historical question of the historical situation out of which [the Fourth Gospel] grew."[20]

John 17 is a unique chapter in its placement and contents.[21] Nothing like John 17 appears in the Synoptic Gospels. In the life of Christ, in addition to his cries from the cross in the Synoptics (Matt 27:46; Mark 15:34; Luke 23:34, 46), Jesus offered only two prayers near and within the passion narrative—one in Gethsemane,[22] and one in John 17.

Yet, as Köstenberger notes, "It is by far the longest prayer of Jesus recorded in any Gospel and comes at a strategic time in Jesus' ministry,

---

with God. In prayer he says, 'I in them and you in me. May they be brought to complete unity to let the world know that you sent me and have loved them even as you have loved me' (17:23). Therefore, Christian unity is not merely a good idea or a sentimental aspiration but an imperative of the highest order. "Interfaith Relations and the Church: The Ecumenical Challenge: A Resource of the Interfaith Relations Committee of the National Council of Churches in Christ in the USA" (New York: National Council of Churches in Christ in the USA, n.d.), 2.

18. The ecumenical devotion reflected in Pope John Paul II's Encyclical Letter, *Ut Unum Sint*, is based on Jesus's high priestly prayer in ch. 17 of St. John's Gospel. Braaten and Jenson, "Introduction," in *Church Unity and the Papal Office: An Ecumenical Dialogue with John Paul II's Encyclical Ut Unum Sint*. See also the official statement of Vatican II, "Decree on Ecumenism: Unitatis Redintegratio: La Santa Sede, September 21, 1964," http://www.vatican.va/archive/hist_councils/ii_vatican_council/documents/vat-ii_decree_19641121_unitatis-redintegratio_en.htm.

19. Berry and Hottman, "Baptists and Ecumenism: An Interview with Timothy George," http://www.centerforbaptistrenewal.com/blog/2017/4/6/baptists-and-ecumenism-a-discussion-with-timothy-george. Elsewhere, George identified John 17:21 as, "the locus classicus of all ecumenical endeavors for the Orthodox, Catholics, and Protestants alike," (George, "Ecumenism After 50 Years").

20. Käsemann proposes "the glory of Christ" (Christology), "the community under the Word" (Ecclesiology), and "Christian unity" (Soteriology) as categories for his study—categories that do not approach John 17 as an exegetical and literary examination. Käsemann, *The Testament of Jesus*, 3. Instead, Käsemann's concern is the recreation or reconstruction of a historical setting of the Johannine writer, writers, or community that produced the Gospel of John.

21. Matthew Henry finds John 17 to be significant to the church in six ways, as: 1) a prayer after a sermon; 2) a prayer after Christ and his disciples had eaten the Passover and the Lord's supper together; 3) a family prayer, for Christ's disciples were his family; 4) a parting prayer; 5) a prayer that was a preface to his sacrifice, which Christ prayed as a priest; and 6) a prayer that was a specimen of his intercession. Henry, *Matthew Henry's Commentary on the Whole Bible*.

22. See Matt 26:36–44; Mark 14:22–40; Luke 22:39–46.

sandwiched, as it were, between his final instructions to his closest followers and his passion."[23] John 17 does indeed draw a conclusion to the Upper Room Discourse (John 13–16), and serves as a monologue between the narratives of the night of Jesus's betrayal (John 13:30, 38) and the day of his crucifixion (John 18:1, 28). It is the only prayer that gives details into Jesus's intercession for his disciples.

THE INTERPRETATION OF JOHN 17:4 IN HISTORY

Although John 17 as a whole is significant in the histories of interpretation, theology, and ministry, within treatments of John 17, John 17:4 receives varying discussions with respect to its role in formulating theological statements. G. C. Berkouwer utilizes John 17:4 within an explanation of the humility of Christ in relationship to the kingdom.[24] Ralph Smith finds support for the *pactum salutis*, covenant of redemption, or "counsel of peace" in the language of John 17:4.[25] Several theological writers use 17:4 in discussions about an eternal covenant.

Among systematic writers, Usher uses John 17:4 in support of the reason for the ascent of Christ.[26] Edgar Mullins finds the verse has sig-

---

23. Köstenberger, *John*, 482.

24. Berkouwer, *The Return of Christ*, 433. In words significant to later discussion within my work, Berkouwer writes, "Earlier, in His high priestly prayer, He says: 'I glorified thee on earth, having accomplished (*teleiōsas*) the work which thou gavest me to do' (John 17:4; cf. 13:1—'to the end'). Christ's purpose was to accomplish God's work (4:34; 5:36), to fulfil His charge, which was to lay down His life and to take it up again (10:18). This mandate ended when this work had been completed . . . The fact that Christ referred to this deed as complete even before His death indicates how certain and irreversible His passion really was. He saw the completed work on the basis of what became unalterable reality in the cross. It is the fulfilment, the culmination, full of the glory for which Christ prayed in the high priestly prayer (John 17:1; cf. 12:23f.). This is the Christ, the one sent by the Father, fulfilling His mandate. Everything in that work is directed to God" (433).

25. "The 'counsel of peace,'" writes Smith, "is the covenant made between the Father and the Son for the salvation of the elect. No doubt this notion connects the doctrine of the covenant with the doctrine of election and connects election with God's working in history." Smith, "Trinitarian Covenant in John 17," 1–13. See also Hodge, *Outlines of Theology*, 273; Beach, "The Doctrine of the Pactum Salutis in the Covenant Theology of Herman Witsius," 126; Berkhof, *Systematic Theology*, 266; Breckinridge, *The Knowledge of God, Subjectively Considered*, 62; Fesko, "John Owen on Union with Christ and Justification," 10; Helm, "Calvin and the Covenant: Unity and Continuity," 69–70; Pictet, *Christian Theology*, 281; Witsius, *The Economy of the Covenants between God and Man*, 143.

26. Usher, *A Body of Divinity*, 224.

nificance to Christ's self-awareness as the Messianic Son of God, saying, "Certainly there are moments when Christ is conscious of an eternal relation to God."[27]

Many use John 17:4 in support of Christ's obedience and/or subordination to the Father or cooperation with the will of God.[28] In support of both the doctrine of the Trinity and Christ's deity and singular personality, Berkhof appeals to John 17:4.[29] William Shedd found John 17:4 useful in the discussion of Christ's humiliation.[30] In a similar fashion, Berkouwer sees a reference to the completed nature of Christ's sacrifice in the verse.[31]

But other than these types of usages, John 17:4 is seemingly not important to theology derived from the New Testament. It is evident that the discussions of the systematic volumes do not steer toward the nature of the completed work of Christ of which Christ speaks in the verse. This may account for the paucity of the appearances of this verse in theological tomes. John 17:4 is not included in verses used to support doctrinal formations within major evangelical systematics of our day, or only one use of the verse appears in some systematics.[32]

---

27. Mullins, *The Christian Religion in Its Doctrinal Expression*, 189.

28. Barth, Bromiley, and Torrance, *Church Dogmatics: The Doctrine of God, Part 1*, 164; Barth, Bromiley, and Torrance, *Church Dogmatics: The Doctrine of Creation, Part 4*, 486; Berkouwer, *The Person of Christ*, 242, 249; Berkouwer, *The Work of Christ*, 315; Bloesch, *Jesus Christ: Savior & Lord*, 162; Boyce, *Abstract of Systematic Theology*, 153; Pope, *A Compendium of Christian Theology*, 152.

29. Berkhof, *Systematic Theology*, 323. Elsewhere Berkhof writes, "The work of representing the Trinity in the Counsel of Redemption, as the holy and righteous Being, whose right was violated . . ." (91).

30. Shedd, *Dogmatic Theology*, 676.

31. Berkouwer, *Faith and Justification*, 149.

32. Considering a selection of systematics, a reference to John 17:4 is not found in Akin, ed., *A Theology for the Church*, rev. ed. It is not a major passage of attention in Grudem, *Systematic Theology*. Erickson does not have any references in *The Word Became Flesh*. However, Erickson does have two references in his full systematic, *Christian Theology*, 3rd ed., one instance being used as support of Christ's perfect fellowship with the Father (471). There is one reference coupled with 17:5 in each of Bray, *God is Love*, 189, and Peterson, *Salvation Accomplished by the Son*, 253. Culver (*Systematic Theology: Biblical and Historical*) has two references (pp. 490 and 838), but without explanation or use in reference to the work of Christ. Frame makes reference to John 17:4 in outlining the unity of the church (Frame, *Salvation Belongs to the Lord*, 239–40). Reference to John 17:4 is absent from Wellum, *God the Son Incarnate*. Two recent articles discuss the imbalanced use of Scripture in works of systematic theology, noting the pride of place for the works of Paul, and the paucity of references to the OT; of the top 100 verses most frequently cited in works of systematic theology, only nine are from the OT.

Yet, I think John 17:4 may be one of the most significant verses within the Gospel of John. It contains a sweeping assertion by Jesus of completing "work," which is the second reference to a singular work of Jesus within the Fourth Gospel, following 4:34. The verse also speaks conclusively of Jesus bringing glory to the Father. It ties this glory exclusively to his incarnate life on earth and speaks of the glory and the completed work within some scope of the decree of God for the Son of God. Rather tersely in one verse, it brings together terms associated with multiple themes resonating throughout the Gospel of John. In keeping with others' proposals of seeing John 17 as a summing up of the teaching of John 1–16, I would suggest that a greater understanding of John 17:4 allows for a reader to have a greater understanding of the entirety of the Gospel of John.

In order to explore the scope of the research needed to demonstrate the significance of John 17:4, I examined the verse through a series of questions about this passage, its terms, and the associated thematic concepts that need to be answered:

1. Concerning "glory," what is the meaning of "glory" in the Fourth Gospel?[33] Is there an OT background to the term that has significance to John 17:4? How does "glory" relate to "work?"

See Lindgren, "Sorry, Old Testament: Most Theologians Don't Use You," and Brannan, "Writing a Systematic Theology? You Must Discuss These References." In response to the invitation of *Christianity Today* for scholars to weigh in on the data of the top 100 verses, Kevin Vanhoozer writes, "I hope that any biblically literate theologian knows, first, where to find the most important biblical statements pertaining to various doctrines" (Lindgren, "Sorry, Old Testament"). The statement suggests that there appears to be a hierarchy of Scripture verses when building a systematic theology. This would seem to diminish the *plenary* aspect of the evangelical doctrine of the inspiration of the Scriptures, or at least redefine what one means by the authority of Scripture—a corollary of the doctrine of inspiration. It would seem that if all Scripture is inspired by God and of equal authority, then every verse of *Scripture* should contribute to a systematic understanding of the doctrines of the *Scriptures*. Yet the task of systematic theologians then would require attention to the exegesis of every verse of Scripture and its usage in its immediate literary-historical and broader canonical contexts. Also, as Keener, Stackhouse, and Dyrness each note separately in their responses to the data of the top 100 verses within the same article, the inclusion of other verses may require reading Scriptures outside of the *loci classici* of Western Theologies (Lindgren, "Sorry, Old Testament"). John 17:4 does not seem to fit within the "most important biblical statements" or the *classici loci* of systematics.

33. As a noun, "glory" (δόξα) occurs in John nineteen times (1:14 [2x]; 2:11; 5:41, 44 [2x]; 7:18 [2x]; 8:50, 54; 9:24; 11:4, 40; 12:41, 43 [2x]; 17:5, 22, 24). As a verb, "glorify" (δοξάζω) occurs in John 23 times (7:39; 8:54 [2x]; 11:4; 12:16, 23, 28 [3x]; 13:31 [2x], 33 [3x]; 14:13; 15:8; 16:14; 17:1 [2x], 4, 5, 10; 21:19). It occurs in both noun and verb forms

2. Concerning "Father," what is the significance of the term "Father" in the Fourth Gospel?[34] Before John 17, what happens with the term "Father?" After John 17, what happens with the term for "Father?"

3. How does "the work" relate to "the hour?"[35] In contrast to "the hour," which looks forward to the glorification of the Son, does "the work" look backward to the Father already being glorified?[36] Is there a development, consistency, or significant end to the work?

4. What is the use of "completed" elsewhere in John, and what are the views on such a completion? What, if any, is the substantial difference between τελειόω (17:4, 19:28d) and τελέω (19:28c, 19:30)? How does John 17:4 relate to John 4:34 and 19:30?[37]

5. What is the relationship of "the work" (τὸ ἔργον) to "the works" (τὰ ἔργα) in John?[38]

6. How then should we read John 1:19–16:33, 17, and 18–20?[39]

I also find it important to address the aspectival functioning of the aorist verbs in John 17:4. That is, as aorists, both ἐδόξασα[40] and τελειώσας[41] are

---

only in 8:54, 11:4, and 17:5. There are eight total usages each in John 12 and John 17.

34. Although "Father" (πατήρ) does not appear in 17:4, Jesus addresses his prayer to the Father and speaks to the Father. Jesus specifically speaks of glorifying the Father (17:1; cf. 1:14; 11:40; 17:4).

35. The writer of the Gospel of John toggles between "my hour" (ἡ ὥρα μου, 2:4), "his hour" (ἡ ὥρα αὐτοῦ or αὐτοῦ ἡ ὥρα, 7:30; 8:20; 13:1), "the hour" (ἡ ὥρα, 12:23; 17:1), and "this hour" (ὥραν ταύτην, 12:27).

36. Compare "that the Son may glorify you" in 17:1 (ἵνα ὁ υἱὸς δοξάσῃ σέ) to "I have brought you glory" in 17:3 (ἐγώ σε ἐδόξασα).

37. There are similarities between John 4:34 (λέγει αὐτοῖς ὁ Ἰησοῦς, Ἐμὸν βρῶμά ἐστιν ἵνα ποιήσω τὸ θέλημα τοῦ πέμψαντός με καὶ τελειώσω αὐτοῦ τὸ ἔργον), 5:36 (ἐγὼ δὲ ἔχω τὴν μαρτυρίαν μείζω τοῦ Ἰωάννου· τὰ γὰρ ἔργα ἃ δέδωκέν μοι ὁ πατὴρ ἵνα τελειώσω αὐτά, αὐτὰ τὰ ἔργα ἃ ποιῶ μαρτυρεῖ περὶ ἐμοῦ ὅτι ὁ πατήρ με ἀπέσταλκεν), and 19:30 (ἐγώ σε ἐδόξασα ἐπὶ τῆς γῆς, τὸ ἔργον τελειώσας ὃ δέδωκάς μοι ἵνα ποιήσω).

38. In contrast to only two uses of "the work" in the singular (4:34 and 17:4), "works" appears in reference to the actions of Jesus (5:26, 5:30 [2x]; 7:3; 8:41; 9:3, 4; 10:25, 32, 37, 38; 14:10, 11, 12).

39. Examining a reading strategy for John is outside of the scope of this dissertation. However, the question of what the writer is doing is helpful in guiding me as I argue for my thesis in the chapters to follow.

40. Aor. act., ind., 1st pers., sg., from δοξάζω, *to glorify*.

41. Aor., act., part., nom., sg., from τελειόω, *to finish, complete, or perfect*.

perfective in their aspects based on their tense forms.⁴² But whether the verbs have an expression of a sense of time—i.e., completed action in the past, future, or combination of past action with future implications—depends upon other factors in the context of John 17:1–5.⁴³

THESIS

On John 17:4, Carson writes, "The difficult point of this verse is the uncertainty as to whether the work that Jesus has completed refers to everything he has done *up to this point*, or proleptically included his obedience unto death, the death that lies immediately ahead... Either interpretation can be made to 'fit' the passage."⁴⁴ I believe Carson adequately frames the issues at stake in the interpretation of John 17:4—a reflective view versus a proleptic view. However, I think that it is possible to make a strong case for only one interpretation of John 17:4 to "fit" this passage.

I will propose that the completed work of Christ in John 17:4 is *to reveal God the Father*. I will be proposing that Christ completes the work to reveal the Father in his earthly public and private ministries. It seems that John portrays the completion of the work in the editorial work of the prologue in John 1:1–18 and by means of narrative and discourse in John 1:19–12:20 and John 13:1—16:33.

I intend to demonstrate that the completed work of Christ to provide revelation of God the Father to the world publicly and to the disciples privately during his earthly ministry terminates at John 16:33. The "work" that Christ completes is perfective and does not have a proleptic aspect. I am proposing that the completion in John 17:4 (τελειώσας) refers to a different work than the completed work in John 19:30 (τετέλεσται). The work in John 17:4 concerns *revelation*, whereas

---

42. My use of "perfective" throughout this work, as a standard term of linguists, refers to the aspectual sense of a verb. I will use it to refer to the aspect value of the *aorist* (or aorist tense, or aorist tense-form) and *perfect* (or perfect tense, or perfect tense-form) in Greek. The *perfect tense-form* is not the same as the *perfective aspect*. *Perfect*, with respect to tense (or tense-form) concerns the primary form and conjugated forms of the verb. *Perfective* refers only to a verb's aspectual sense. I will discuss aspect and tense-form at length in chapter 4 of this work.

43. For more on the discussion of whether aorists and perfects carry any temporal sense, see Crellin, "The Semantics of the Perfect in the Greek of the New Testament," 430–57. Porter does not view the aorist and imperfect being restricted to past tense use. Porter, *Verbal Aspect in the Greek of the New Testament*, 211–38.

44. Carson. *John*, 556–57. Carson references Riedl, *Das Heilswerk Jesus nach Johannes*, 69–186.

the work in John 19:30 concerns *the final humiliation of Christ* in his passion ministry (e.g. John 18:1—19:30).

Carson is representative of a proleptic view when he writes,

> A contrast is drawn between the glory that Jesus by his work has brought to the Father on earth, and the glory he asks the Father to give him (*cf.* 13:31–32) in heaven. Once that is seen, it makes best sense if v. 4 includes *all* the work by which Jesus brings glory to his Father, and that includes his own death, resurrection and exaltation (*cf.* 4:34; 5:36; 19:30). So he is speaking proleptically.[45]

Carson recognizes that one's understanding of the verbal aspect of the aorists in 17:4 influences one's conclusions about a proleptic view. He notes,

> Part of the problem is introduced by the widespread tendency to translate certain Greek verbs rather rigidly by time-based English verbs, even though the differences among the "tenses" of Greek verbs are best understood to be based on distinctions in "verbal aspect," not time: *cf.* Porter. Thus "I *have brought you glory* (*edoxasa*, aorist tense)" is not necessarily past-referring. Rather, the author chooses to view the work that brings the Father glory as a complete whole, and therefore selects the aorist.[46]

John Lange also represents a proleptic position on 17:4. First he argues on the basis of viewing the aorists themselves as proleptic: "I glorified Thee on the earth [ἐγώσε ἐδόξασα ἐπὶ τῆς γῆς, τὸ ἔργων τελειώσας (rec. ἐτελείωσα). The aorists are proleptic and should not be rendered as perfects as in the E. V.—P. S.]"[47]

Lange continues, however, seemingly agreeing with a reflective position on Jesus's words. He says,

> And this is Christ's meaning; He says: I glorified Thee *on the earth*, and in elucidation of these words He adds: I have finished the work, etc. In His doctrine and life *He had manifested the Father* conformably to the grace and truth of the latter, chap.

---

45. Carson, *John*, 557.

46. Carson, *John*, 557n8. "Porter" is a reference to Stanley Porter, *Verbal Aspect in the Greek of the New Testament.*

47. Lange and Schaff, *A Commentary on the Holy Scriptures: John*, 515. Lange's commentary was translated from the German 3rd ed. into English by Schaff and published in 1869.

1:17. He could lay this work before the Father as finished and complete.[48]

Yet, following Augustine and Gerhard, and against Socinian exegesis, Lange concludes that the verse is proleptic by bringing the yet future passion narrative into consideration. Lange proposes,

> It is more decisive, however, that Christ here reckons His death as comprising one point in the *Father's* glorification of the *Son*. Hence it is doubtless in the more limited sense that He has been speaking of the work which the Father has commanded Him *to do*; in a sense similar to that of the words: I must work as long as it is day; the night cometh, *etc.*, chap. 9:4. Now, however, this work is brought to a conclusion; He makes His high-priestly offering of Himself and seals *that* with His Passion. The Passion comes under consideration as the conclusion of His obedient doing.[49]

Two recent works, one being an exploration of Christ's obedience and the other an exegetical handbook to the Fourth Gospel, both view John 17:4 as proleptic in its denotation. First, Murray Harris proposes that the verse speaks "proleptically," including Jesus's death in the "work" to which Jesus was called.[50] Second, Brandon Crowe, who looks at the purpose for Jesus's coming, writes, "Certainly we must read 17:4 in light of the finality of the completion in view at the cross in 19:30, but the emphasis on completion in 17:4 (*teliōsas*), along with the glory that Jesus has already brought to the Father (*edoxasa*), seems rather to indicate the full accomplishment of Jesus's work thus far."[51]

Francis Moloney takes a mediating position on 17:4, strongly seeing reflective thought in view, while leaving room for a proleptic aspect. For Moloney, "the task given him by the Father ... is now regarded as accomplished (17:4, τὸ ἔργον τελειώσας) ... The revelation of God is complete, and thus Jesus can ask that the Father enter his story in a final way."[52] The reference to the work as completed "revelation," rather than to the crucifixion, indicates a reflective position. Elsewhere, he also says, "In being the revelation of God, the Son brings to perfection the task given him by his Father (4:34; 17:4)," and "in 4:34, 5:36, and 17:4 Jesus' own

---

48. Lange and Schaff, *John*, 515 (italics mine).
49. Lange and Schaff, *John*, 516.
50. Harris, *Exegetical Guide to the Greek New Testament*, 286.
51. Crowe, *The Last Adam*, 123.
52. Moloney, *The Gospel of John*, 293–94.

words establish that he has been sent to bring to perfection the task given to him by his Father: to make God known."[53]

Yet Moloney also writes, "It is on the cross that Jesus makes known the glory of God in this moment of consummate loving (13:1; 17:4), and it is through the cross that he himself is glorified (11:4; 17:4)."[54] The proleptic-leaning comments, however, are not a major emphasis of Moloney's thesis.

In contrast to seeing a proleptic idea in John 17:4, Lindars writes, "There are two stages in [Jesus's] mission of revealing the glory of God. First, there is the whole of his work on earth, the work which thou gavest me to do. This has been accomplished. Now it must be followed by the second stage, the glorification of the Son of man, without which it remains incomplete and unconvincing."[55]

Similar to Lindars, I propose that by recognizing references to two different telic works in John 17:4 and John 19:30, one can develop a reading strategy for the Gospel of John. John 1:19—16:33 is the development of Christ's revelation of God the Father. Christ's prayer in John 17:1-26 transitions the reader from Christ's revelation of the Father to a new work not yet fully disclosed. Christ speaks of the second "work" throughout the Gospel in references such as the prophesying of the destruction of the temple (2:19, 21), laying down his life for his sheep (10:11, 15), being the Resurrection and the Life (11:25-26), washing the disciples' feet (13:8-10), and giving the parable of the woman in travail (16:20-22). Yet in John 17 the writer moves from an expectation of "the hour" to the arrival of "the hour." I will propose that "the hour" arrives upon the completion of the revelation work. This hour concerns the atoning work, which in John's narrative presentation begins at 18:1.

In proposing that the completed work of Christ stated in John 17:4 is the revelation of God the Father, I am also proposing that the theme of bringing glory to the Father supports the idea of perfective work in John 17:4. Moreover, the frequency of John's usage of terms for "Father" supports the idea of distinctive works in John 1:18—16:13 and 18:1—20:31,

---

53. Moloney, *Love in the Gospel of John*, 34 and 55.

54. Moloney, *Love in the Gospel of John*, 159.

55. Lindars, *The Gospel of John*, 520. Similarly, Hillary of Poitiers writes, "The Son reveals by works of power to the ignorance of the heathen and to the foolishness of the world, Him from Whom He is . . . The Father is glorified on earth because the work which He had commanded is finished. Hillary of Pointers, "On the Trinity (Book 4)."

as the frequency of references to the Father decrease dramatically once Christ has completed his role as Revealer.[56]

OVERVIEW OF JOHN 17

Prior to giving an overview of the remainder of this work, I offer the following overview of John 17. The overview will set forth a general understanding of the content of John 17 and its situation in the Fourth Gospel. I will include an amplified gloss of the immediate pericope, 17:1–5, without explanation, as the exegesis in the latter chapters will support the reading provided here.

Length, Theology, and Placement Factors

John 17 stands uniquely within the four Gospels as the longest pericope given to a prayer in the life of Jesus. In *length*, as the only full pericope given to prayer in the Fourth Gospel, it is reminiscent of the long, intercessory prayers on behalf of Israel given by Moses, David, Solomon, Nehemiah, and Daniel. Prior to this, the subject of prayer in the Fourth Gospel consists of (1) references to Jesus giving thanks before distributing the fish and loaves in the feeding of the 5000 (6:11, 23); (2) the blind man explaining that God does not listen to sinners (9:31); (3) Martha trusting God the Father to hear any petition Jesus makes, including one for the life of Lazarus (11:22); (4) Jesus giving thanks at the tomb of Lazarus (11:41–42); (5) of Jesus repeatedly admonishing the disciples to ask the Father for things in Jesus's name (14:13, 14; 15:16; 16:23, 24, 26); and (6) of Jesus informing the disciples of his intent ask the Father to send another Helper (14:16).[57] The totality of the six reference in the Farewell Discourse of John 14–16 is nearest to a discourse on prayer outside of John 17.

---

56. I will capitalize "Revealer," in order to be consistent with the usage of the term in Bultmann, *The Gospel of John*.

57. Consistent with the Synoptics' structure, John 18 records Jesus entering the garden (of Gethsemane) where he will be betrayed by Judas. However, unlike the Synoptic accounts, the writer of John does not record Jesus praying or exhorting the disciples to pray while in the garden. Thus, John 17 becomes the high point of prayer in the Fourth Gospel rather than Gethsemane possibly serving as such (cf. Matt 26:36–46; Mark 14:32–42; Luke 22:40–46).

Theologically, John 17 consists of a direct address to the Father, similar to the direct address in 11:41.[58] But this direct address is followed by a much lengthier discourse—the entirety which appears to be a true petition and not a witness-bearing petition as the one in 11:41-42.[59]

In terms of *placement* in the Fourth Gospel, John 17 brings to a close the public and private ministries of Jesus.[60] It does not simply bring the public ministry to a close; the full narrative of work prior to the suffering, death, and resurrection of Jesus comes to a close. John 18-21 will present new material, beginning with the betrayal of Christ by Judas, and completing a passion narrative very similar to the pattern in the Synoptics. John 17 stands between the movements of 1:19-16:33 and 18-21, acting as a pivot that transitions the story of the public and private ministries to the story of the passion. Where a reader of the first three Gospels would expect an immediate transition to a scene on the Mount of Olives and Gethsemane, as in Matt 26:35-36; Mark 14:31-32; and Luke 22:38-39, one gets a detailed prayer that occurs *prior to* the acts of prayer in Gethsemane. Instead of the prayer after the Upper Room discourse being a request for a path other than the cross and an embracing of the will of God, one hears of the glorifying of the Father and the Son and the sanctifying of the disciples. Therefore, it seems that as a pivot in the Fourth Gospel and interruption to the life-of-Christ-pattern in the Synoptics, John 17 would be a good candidate to provide a key to reading the Fourth Gospel—to understanding the uniting of its various themes, its literary structure, and its subject.

---

58. John 11:41 reads, ὁ δὲ Ἰησοῦς ἦρεν τοὺς ὀφθαλμοὺς ἄνω καὶ εἶπεν, whereas 17:1 reads Ἰησοῦς καὶ ἐπάρας τοὺς ὀφθαλμοὺς αὐτοῦ εἰς τὸν οὐρανὸν εἶπεν. The two verbs for the raising of the eyes are different, with John 17:1 using the intensified compound ἐπαίρω rather than αἴρω, and the location of the focus of the eyes differs, as 11:41 says "above" (ἄνω) and 17:2 says "to heaven" (εἰς τὸν οὐρανὸν). Louw-Nida distinguishes the two verbs, saying of ἐπαίρω, it is "(an idiom, literally 'to lift up the eyes') to direct one's attention to something by looking closely at—'to notice, to look,'" but of αἴρω, saying, "to lift up and carry (away)," (L&N, 206, 280). BDAG suggests the distinction is that ἐπαίρω means, "to cause to move upward, *lift up, hold up*," and αἴρω means, "to raise to a higher place or position, *lift up, take up, pick up*" (BDAG, 28, 357). The difference is slight, but it may be that in the Lazarus narrative, Jesus simply lifts his eyes in the direction of heaven, whereas in the prayer of John 17, Jesus intentionally, deliberately fixes his eyes into heaven from the earthly discourse to demonstrate a marked distinction between speaking to the disciples and speaking to the Father.

59. E.g. "I knew that you always hear me, but I said this *on account of the people standing around, that they may believe that you sent me.*"

60. It is common to subdivide the Fourth Gospel as the Public Ministry of Jesus (1:19-12:50) and the Private Ministry of Jesus (13-16).

Pericope Structure

There are three subunits of thought that allow one to discern the structure of John 17. John 17:1–5 focuses on the glorifying of the Father and the Son. Forms of the verb δοξάζω appear in 17:1 (2x), 4, and 5, and the noun δόξα appears in 17:5. The two verses in which δοξάζω and δόξα are absent are joined in the discussion of glory by the adverbial comparative conjunction καθώς ("since" or "just as") at the beginning of 17:2, and the δέ clause—αὕτη δέ ἐστιν ἡ αἰώνιος ζωὴ—of 17:3. Within verses 2–3, "eternal life" is a link between the two verses: ἵνα πᾶν ὃ δέδωκας αὐτῷ δώσῃ αὐτοῖς ζωὴν αἰώνιον (2); αὕτη δέ ἐστιν ἡ αἰώνιος ζωὴ (3).

John 17:6–19 is marked by a discussion of the followers of Christ—people *given* to Jesus from out of the world.[61] In addition to this designation, the English text of the ESV reflects a toggling back and forth of the people as "them" and "they" based upon the verbs (third person) and pronouns in 17:6–19: "They" (ἦσαν) . . . "them" (αὐτοὺς) . . . "they" (τετήρηκαν) (6); "they" (ἔγνωκαν) (7); "them" (αὐτοῖς) . . . "they" (αὐτοὶ) . . . "they" (ἐπίστευσαν) (8); "them" (αὐτῶν) . . . "they" (εἰσιν) (9); "them" (αὐτοῖς) (10); "they" (αὐτοὶ) . . . "them" (αὐτοὺς) . . . "they" (ὦσιν) (11); "them" (αὐτῶν) . . . "them" (αὐτοὺς) . . . "them" (*added for readability in English but not reflective of the Greek text*) . . . "them" (αὐτῶν) (12); "they" (ἔχωσιν) (13); "them" (αὐτοῖς) . . . "them" (αὐτούς) . . . "they" (εἰσὶν) (14); "them" (αὐτοὺς) . . . "them" (αὐτοὺς) (15); "they" (εἰσὶν) (16); "them" (αὐτοὺς) (17); "them" (αὐτοὺς) (18); "them" (αὐτῶν) . . . "they" (αὐτοὶ) (19).[62] In 17:10, this group is identified possessively—as belonging mutually to the Father and the Son: τὰ ἐμὰ . . . σά . . . τὰ σὰ ἐμά.

In 17:6–19, the writer emphasizes the coming/incarnation of Jesus, and the going/ascension of Jesus: "I came from you" (παρὰ σοῦ ἐξῆλθον, v. 8), "I am coming to you" (κἀγὼ πρὸς σὲ ἔρχομαι, v. 11), "I am coming to you" (πρὸς σὲ ἔρχομαι, v. 13), "as you sent me into the world" (ἐμὲ ἀπέστειλας εἰς τὸν κόσμον, v. 18). The ascent/descent terms in John provide a time framework for understanding the mission of Jesus with respect to the disciples' mysterious union and eschatological hope. Jesus

---

61. With reference to the followers of Christ, the writer identifies them by forms of δίδωμι three times in 17:6 (2x) and 17:9. But the people will be identified as the object of Jesus's ministry throughout 17:6–9: There are nine additional uses of δίδωμι in 17:6–19 (7, 8 [2x], 12, 14, 22 [2x]). Below I will identify "all to whom you have given him" simply as "the elect."

62. What I have translated as "them" in 17:19 is "their" in the ESV text. But it is reflective of the genitive αὐτῶν which is "of them."

seeks the keeping of the disciples in holiness in the world after his departure: "*Keep them* in your name . . . that they may be one" (τήρησον αὐτοὺς ἐν τῷ ὀνόματί σου, v. 11), "*I kept them* in your name" (ἐγὼ ἐτήρουν αὐτοὺς ἐν τῷ ὀνόματί σου, v. 12), "I have guarded them" (ἐφύλαξα, v. 12), "*keep them* from the evil one" (τηρήσῃς αὐτοὺς ἐκ τοῦ πονηροῦ, v. 15), *sanctify them* in truth (ἁγίασον αὐτοὺς ἐν τῇ ἀληθείᾳ, v. 17), "that they also may be sanctified in truth" (ἵνα ὦσιν καὶ αὐτοὶ ἡγιασμένοι ἐν ἀληθείᾳ, v. 18).

John 17:20–26 forms a different subsection with a petition for "those who will believe in me through their word." This new population is distinct from the disciples' in the care of Jesus during his earthly ministry, identified by "these" (τούτων) and "their" (αὐτῶν)—those who are being sanctified in the truth in 17:6–19.[63] The petition seeks the unity of the first followers of Christ with second and subsequent generations of follows who will arise as a result of the gospel proclamation of the first followers—"that they may all be one" (21; see also similar terms in 22, 23).[64] The first generation of followers includes those who will become the eleven Apostles who give proclamation of the word of God in Acts.[65]

The unity is mysterious in its union, not simply ecumenical, for three reasons: (1) *it is based in the unity shared by the Father and the Son*. The "just as" (καθώς) makes a comparison between the kind of unity the Father and the Son share mutually. That *experience* of ontological unity with the Father stands as the launching point for the prayer, for without that experience, there would be no intercession for the first generation believers and subsequent generations to share any unity.[66] (2) *It allows*

---

63. The αὐτῶν (gen., pl., mas.) in 17:19 is antecedent to the αὐτῶν (gen., pl., masc.) and the demonstrative pronoun, τούτων (gen., pl., masc.) in 17:20.

64. So notes Borchert, saying, "The thrust of Jesus' prayer is that disciples are to communicate the saving message to those who would come after them ('believe in me through their word'—*logos*). The good news was not intended to be held exclusively (*monon*, "alone") by the first disciples. It was to be shared with succeeding generations of disciples. The prayer therefore is also a mandate to mission and to making new disciples (cf. Matt 28:19). Borchert, *John 12–21*, 206. Similarly, Whitacre writes, "Jesus then prays for all who will become believers through the witness of the eleven, that they may share in the divine oneness (vv. 20–24)." Whitacre, *John*, 403.

65. "Eleven" means to indicate the loss of the "son of destruction," as Jesus says within this prayer (17:12). It does not intend to make comment on the later addition of the Apostle Paul, who is included within the prayer as a follower of Jesus, but is not a direct subject of or participant in the earthly ministry of Christ in the three years leading up to the crucifixion, resurrection, and ascension of Jesus.

66. Carson concludes the same: "This is not simply a 'unity of love.' It is a unity predicated on adherence to the revelation the Father mediated to the first disciples through his Son, the revelation they accepted (vv. 6, 8) and then passed on ('those who

the followers of Christ to participate in the unity shared between the Father and the Son. The second ἵνα clause in v. 21 indicates *purpose*; the purpose of gaining unity is that such unity provides a means to enter into the unity the Father and the Son share. Such unity is not visible or full, yet it is a present reality; the full unity awaits the result of the petition, "in order that they may be with me where I am" (v. 24).[67] (3) *This unity between generations of followers of Christ intends to portray the mysterious unity of the Father and the Son.* The third ἵνα clause in v. 21 also indicates purpose. The further intention of the unity is for those generations of believers to show the world that the Father did indeed send the Son into the world. That display occurs through the disciples achieving a unity that could only come through the revelation of the Son coming to the believers, their faith in this Son, and their reception of power to have the mysterious unity as evidenced in their practice before others.[68] Thus, the mysterious union of the generations of disciples, with one another and in the Father and Son, largely distinguishes the main thoughts of 17:20–26 from 17:6–19.

Structurally, therefore, John 17 has three units of thought which manifest themselves in three macro-requests of Jesus, the Son, as part of one large intercessory prayer:

---

will believe in me *through their message*', v. 20). It is analogous to the oneness Jesus enjoys with his Father, here fleshed out in the words *just as you are in me and I am in you*. The Father is actually in the Son, so much so that we can be told that it is the Father who is performing the Son's works (14:10); yet the Son is in the Father, not only in dependence upon and obedience to him, but his agent in creation (1:2–3) and his wholly concurring Son in the redemption and preservation of those the Father has given him (*e.g.* 6:37–40; 17:6, 19). The Father and the Son are distinguishable (the pre-incarnate Word is 'with' God, 1:1; the Son prays to his Father; the Father commissions and sends, while the Son obeys), yet they are one." Carson, *John*, 568.

67. That is, ἵνα ὅπου εἰμὶ ἐγὼ . . . ὦσιν μετ' ἐμοῦ.

68. Carson expresses similar sentiments when he writes, "As the display of genuine love amongst the believers attests that they are Jesus' disciples (13:34–35), so this display of unity is so compelling, so un-worldly, that their witness as to who Jesus is becomes explainable only if Jesus truly is the revealer whom the Father has sent. Although the unity envisaged in this chapter is not institutional, this purpose clause at the end of v. 21 shows beyond possibility of doubt that the unity is meant to be observable. It is not achieved by hunting enthusiastically for the lowest common theological denominator, but by common adherence to the apostolic gospel, by love that is joyfully self-sacrificing, by undaunted commitment to the shared goals of the mission with which Jesus' followers have been charged, by self-conscious dependence on God himself for life and fruitfulness. It is a unity necessarily present, at least *in nuce*, amongst genuine believers; it is a unity that must be brought to perfection (v. 23)" (Carson, *John*, 568).

THE COMPLETED EVENT THAT IS YET TO HAPPEN OR IS FINISHED   19

1. *Jesus's request for the Father to glorify the Son in the decreed hour* rests in the completed work of the Son in election, for the sake of the glory of the Father (17:1–5).

2. *Jesus's request for the Father to keep those elected in a sanctifying manner* seeks the unity of the believers, in reflection of the Trinity and the believers' joy, resting on both (1) the Son's completed work to reveal the words of God and (2) the elect's belief in the Son through the work and the words, in light of the reality of the evil of (1) the son of destruction, decreed to be lost; (2) the evil one; and (3) the world (17:6–19).

3. *Jesus's additional request for the Father to keep—in a sanctifying manner—the generations of believers who will come on the basis of the apostolic preaching of the gospel* seeks for them a unity reflective of the unity of the Father and Son, that Christ may be manifest in the world and that the believers may know the full love of God in his presence (17:20–26).

All three of these sections, while united by the separate macro-requests, are also unified by the revelation of the knowledge of God:

> "And this is eternal life, *that they know you*, the only true God, and Jesus Christ whom you have sent" (17:3).

> "*I have manifested your name* to the people whom you gave me out of the world. Yours they were, and you gave them to me, and they have kept your word" (17:6).[69]

> "Now *they know* that everything that you have given me *is from you*" (17:7).

> "For I have given them the words that you gave me, and they have received them and *have come to know* in truth *that I came from you*; and *they have believed that you sent me*" (17:8).

> "O righteous Father, even though the world does not know you, I know you, and *these know that you have sent me*" (17:25).

> "*I made known to them your name*, and I will continue to make it known, that the love with which you have loved me may be in them, and I in them" (17:26).[70]

---

69. Ἐφανέρωσά ("I have manifested") is aor., act., ind., 1st per., sg. from φανερόω: "I cause to become visible, *reveal, expose publicly*, or I cause to become known, *disclose, show, make known*" (BDAG, 1048). The aorist demonstrates completed action.

70. The term, ἐγνώρισα, is aor., act., ind., 1st per., sg. from γνωρίζω: "I make know, or I reveal" (BDAG, 203). The aorist demonstrates completed action.

The knowledge of God that Jesus revealed includes the revelation of God's name—which is to know God himself. As Andrew Lincoln notes, "In the ancient world the name stood for who the person was and what the person represented, that person's identity and reputation. Jesus has therefore made known who God is and what is involved in God's reputation."[71]

Structurally, therefore, one may conclude the following unifying idea derived from the three subunits:

> *Jesus's intercession for the elect* seeks the sanctification and unity of the believers on the basis of the faithful work of the Son to reveal the Father for the sake of the Father's glory, the manifestation of the Son in the world, and the believer's full knowledge of the Father and Son in the presence of God.

The unifying (or exegetical) idea for John 17:1–7 allows one two draw two conclusions on items significant to the analysis to follow in the coming chapters. First, the know/knowledge-related terms in the passage, with respect to the believers, concerns revelation of the Father that produces belief. A syllogism demonstrates this:

Major Premise: If the exegetical idea, reflective of the passage's terms and structure, concerns "on the basis of the faithful work of the Son to reveal the Father,"

Minor Premise: and "that they may know you, the one true God" is a component of that exegetical idea,

Conclusion: then "that they may know you" flows from the work of the Son to reveal the Father—it is salvific knowledge.

The knowing in John 17 leads to eternal life (v. 3). It awaits full knowledge in the very presence of the Father and the Son.

Similarly, a second syllogism shows the significance of the exegetical idea—the whole of John 17—for the understanding of the completed work in John 17:4:

Major Premise: If the exegetical idea, reflective of the passage's terms and structure, concerns "on the basis of the faithful work of the Son to reveal the Father,"

Minor Premise: and "I have completed the work you called me to do" is a component of that exegetical idea,

---

71. Lincoln, *The Gospel According to Saint John*, 435–36.

Conclusion: then "I have completed the work" concerns the faithful work of the Son to reveal the Father.

The Son does not do two works of revealing the Father and going to the cross. Instead, the only work mention in this passage is one of making the Father known to the ones Jesus has kept. The work of sanctification is separate from the work of revelation. However, the making known of God's name is completed in 17:6, 7, 8, 25, and 26.[72]

The significance of the exegetical idea—as made manifest by the structured pattern of the terms in 17:1–16—should not be understated or minimized. The weight of the discourse in John 17 centers around the manifestation of the name (or character or person) of God the Father (17:6, 26), also spoken of as the revelation—the making known of God the Father (17:3, 7, 8, 25)—to those given to Jesus by the Father. The stewardship of Jesus over the elect is one of giving salvific knowledge to the elect. The elect's response to the salvific knowledge is belief. Mysteriously, from all eternity, the belief works within the decree to those given to Jesus by the Father (17:2, 6, 9, 24).[73] Anticipating the future glorifying of Christ in crucifixion, resurrection, and ascension back to the Father, it is these given ones whom Jesus requests the Father to keep in a sanctifying way, in accordance with the Father's granting to Jesus in salvation those to whom Jesus makes known the Father.

Although Carson's full comments on John 17 support a proleptic view of 17:4, he does make a reference to 17:4 that seems to equate Jesus's making of God's name known with Jesus's work of bringing the Father glory on the earth. He writes,

> The revelation of God's name does not seem greatly different from the glorification of God on earth (v. 4) . . . God's "name" embodies his character; to reveal God's name is to make God's character known. It is hard not to detect the hint of a reference to Ex. 3:13–15 . . . Jesus' disclosure of the name of God is coincident with his "narration" of the invisible God (*cf.* notes on 1:18),

---

72. Ἐφανέρωσά (aorist, 17:6), ἔγνωκαν (perfect, 17:7), ἔγνωσαν and ἐπίστευσαν (both aorist, 17:8), ἔγνωσαν (aorist, 17:25), and ἐγνώρισα (aorist, 17:26) each are perfective in their verbal aspects based on their tense-forms.

73. The Fourth Gospel previously describes these same followers of Jesus as those *the Father* has given to come to Jesus (6:37), drawn to Jesus (6:44), provided hearing and learning to come to Jesus (6:45), and granted to come to Jesus (6:65).

in fulfillment of the biblical prophecy, "Therefore my people will know my name" (Is. 52:6).[74]

Hans Bietenhard equates the revelation of the name of the Father with "the supreme work of Christ," noting,

> The prayer of Jesus and God's answer do not have as their goal merely God's self-glorifying. God is addressed as Father, and He reveals Himself as Father, as the loving God (Jn. 3:16; 17:12, 26), by glorifying His name in the life and work of Jesus, and by glorifying it again in the death and resurrection of Jesus. The glorifying of God's name is affected by Christ's work, and to this again it belongs that Jesus should reveal God's name to men as that of the Father (Jn. 17:6; cf. v. 26 and 12:28). God's name is obscure to men; it is strange and general. But to those whom the Father has given Him Jesus makes this name manifest, certain and plain, so that it again acquires specific content: Father. In His Son, Jesus Christ, God is the Father and Reconciler of the world. A mark of the divine sonship of Jesus is His ability to make known this name of God to men. To be received ἐν τῷ ὀνόματι is to stand in the sphere of the love of the Father and the Son. This is to stand in the sphere of a force which unites the disciples in relationship with one another, Jn. 17:11, 12, 21. The declaration of the name finds its goal in the presence of the Father's love for the Son in those who believe in Him (Jn. 17:26), in the demonstration in them of its power to awaken life (1 Jn. 4:7), in the presence of the Son in them in the love of the Father. *From this standpoint the glorification and declaration of the Father's name are the supreme work of Christ. They characterize this work as the Father's work of revelation and salvation in the work of the Son. As the Church is grounded in Jesus' work of revelation, so it stands constantly under the promise that His work will be continued in it:* "And I have declared thy name, and will declare it (γνωρίσω)," Jn. 17:26.[75]

---

74. Carson, *John*, 558.

75. Bietenhard, "Ὄνομα, Ὀνομάζω, Ἐπονομάζω, Ψευδώνυμος," in *TDNT*, 5:272, italics mine.

Amplified Gloss of John 17:1–5 in Light of the Structured Exegetical Idea of John 17

Therefore, in view of the hour to reveal the Son of God as the Christ via his suffering, death, and resurrection, Jesus requests of the Father glory in the work of the cross and the resurrection. The death of Christ, though an ignoble death in human eyes, will be glorious because of the resurrection; the Father glorifies the Son through the resurrection. As human eyes view the resurrected Christ, he will be found most praiseworthy, as will be the Father who sent him and raised him up as foretold and promised.

The glory in the resurrection is necessary in order for Jesus to exercise decreed authority over all life—in order for him to grant eternal life to those given to him by the decree of the Father. Yet, mysteriously, the eternal life granted by the Father depends on the Son making known salvifically the Father as the only true God—which also is to make the Son known salvifically. The Son has completed the work of making the Father known through the words and works of the Son. Having completed that work on which the glory of the Son and Father depend, Jesus can ask for the final glory—via the ascension—the perfective, unlimited, visible, eternal, all-powerful display of the praiseworthiness of God—the beauty of God.

STRUCTURE OF STUDY TO FOLLOW

Chapter 2: The Tale of Two Readings

The second chapter demonstrates that the most widely held view of John 17:4 in Johannine scholarship is the proleptic view—that "I have completed the work" inclusively points forward to the cross as a completed event in the mind of Christ. I will demonstrate that there are views of John 17:4 that are reflective in nature, indicating that the completed work of Christ concerns a past work with reference to the time of Jesus speaking in John 17. Also, I will seek to show that some writers make proleptic conclusions by reasoning on the basis of different *motifs* within the Fourth Gospel, including the motifs of "glory" or glorification, the descent/ascent of Christ, and "the hour." Additionally, I will demonstrate that some proleptic readings rest on a false *exegetical* foundation—on an archaic view of the aorist as communicating a tense.

In this chapter, I endeavor to show that there is a social aspect to the continuance of the proleptic view. That is, many writers repeat a proleptic concept without giving exegetical or literary reasoning, other than repeating what previous writers have concluded. Augustine is one of the earliest writers to provide a proleptic reading of John 17:4.[76]

In contrast to the proleptic views of John 17:4, I will present reflective views of John 17:4. The various views understand the completed work in 17:4 as having a referent in the past—in the whole of John 1–16. The backward pointing referent might be unspecified, simply recognizing completion in a perfective aspect. The referent might be general in the sense of referring to the obedience of Jesus or Jesus's accomplishment of the will of God. Some who hold to a referential view of 17:4 combine it with a proleptic view—with multiple ways of expressing this—so as to see the full scope of Jesus's ministry as the focus of the verse. Still others see Jesus's "works" in view, often due to a conflation of "work" and "works" in their interpretation of John.[77]

Chapter 3: Making God Known Publicly and Privately

This chapter will provide a thematic discussion of "I have glorified you on the earth." I will divide the discussion into two parts: (1) I will explain uses of "glory" in the Fourth Gospel and argue that the "glory" of John 17:4 concerns Jesus's incarnational ministry, and (2) I will explain that "on the earth" concerns Jesus's public and private ministries in John 1:19–12:50 and 13–16.

---

76. "But how has He finished the work which was committed unto Him to do, when there still remains the trial of the passion wherein He especially furnished His martyrs with the example they were to follow, whereof, says the apostle Peter, 'Christ suffered for us, leaving us an example, that we should follow His steps:' 1 Peter 2:21, but just that He says He has finished, what He knew with perfect certainty that He would finish? Just as long before, in prophecy, He used words in the past tense, when what He said was to take place very many years afterwards: 'They pierced,' He says, 'my hands and my feet, they counted all my bones;' He says not, They will pierce, and, They will count. And in this very gospel He says, 'All things that I have heard of my Father, I have made known unto you;' to whom He afterward declares, 'I have yet many things to say unto you, but you cannot bear them now.' For He, who has predestined all that is to be by sure and unchangeable causes, has done whatever He is to do: as it was also declared of Him by the prophet, 'Who has made the things that are to be.'" Augustine, *The Gospel of John: Tractate 105*. Later in my work, I will examine Augustine's full, and very complex, commentary on John 17:4 and his broader use of Scripture to formulate a proleptic reading.

77. Von Wahlde, "Faith and Works in Jn 6.28–29."

In Chapter 3, I endeavor to show that John makes at least three uses of "glory" (δόξα) in his gospel account.[78] First, John uses δόξα to speak of the visible manifestation of God's power or attributes through Jesus's works (cf. John 1:14; 2:12; 11:4).[79] This use of δόξα reflects OT concepts in Exod 33:18–34:8; 40:35; Isa 6:17; Ezek 8:2; 10:18; 43:2; Hab 2:14. John 1:14 serves as a starting point for speaking of "glory" in John. I am seeking to show, therefore, that the entirety of John concerns the revelation of the glory of God in the flesh in the person of Jesus.

Second, the writer of John uses δόξα to speak of the exaltation of Christ in his suffering, atoning work, resurrection, and ascension (7:39; 12:16, 23; 13:32; 17:1, 28). Third, the Fourth Gospel uses δόξα to speak of the full manifestation of the beatific character of God in eternity shared by the Father and the Son (cf. 17:5).

Within the discussions, I will demonstrate that the phrase "on the earth" is not a Johannine equivalent of "kingdom of God." I will propose how the Gospel of John presents Jesus bringing glory to God the Father. I will seek to show that "glorified . . . on the earth" is a fulfillment of the OT idea of the Lord's glory being revealed to all on the earth (cf. Num 14:21; Ps 57:5, 11; 72:19; 108:5; Ezek 43:2; Isa 49:3, 55:5).

---

78. Others have explored the concept of "glory" in the Fourth Gospel: Bauckham, *The Gospel of Glory*; Bratcher, "What Does 'Glory' Mean in Relation to Jesus? Translating *doxa* and *doxazo* in John," 401–8; Caird, "The Glory of God in the Fourth Gospel, 265–77; Coleman, "Doxa and the Passion in the Fourth Gospel;" Cook, "The 'Glory' Motif in the Johannine Corpus," 291–97; Ellis, "An Investigation into the Meaning of [DOXA] in the Fourth Gospel;" Gentry, "'The Glory of God'—The Character of God's Being and Way in the World: Some Reflections on a Key Biblical Theology Theme," 149–61; Gregory, "The Glory of God as Driving Force for Missions;" Jin, "DOXA and Related Concepts in The Fourth Gospel: An Inquiry into the Manifestation of DOXA in Jesus' Cross;" Köstenberger, "The Glory of God in John's Gospel and Revelation," 108–27; Mahoney, "The Glory of God in St John's Gospel," 21–37; Matson, "The Glory of God: Echoes of Exodus in the Gospels," 1–5; Nielsen, "The Narrative Structures of Glory and Glorification in the Fourth Gospel," 343–66; Pamment, "The Meaning of *Doxa* in the Fourth Gospel," 12–16; P. E. Robertson, "Glory in the Fourth Gospel," 121–31; Van der Merwe, "The Glory-Motif in John 17:1–5: An Exercise in Biblical Semantics," 226–49; Wong, "The Doxa of Christ and His Followers in the Fourth Gospel." Van der Watt views John's use of δόξα as a double-entendre (Van der Watt, "Double Entendre in the Gospel According to John," 463–81).

79. Köstenberger calls this aspect of the revelation of Jesus's glory "many remarkable demonstrations of his identity," (Köstenberger, "The Glory of God in John's Gospel," 110).

Chapter 4: The Book with Two Completions

The goal of Chapter Four is to provide exegesis of ἐδόξασα and τελειώσας (John 17:4), and Τετέλεσται (John 19:30). The chapter will consider how the verbal aspect of the aorists of the verbs is perfective, explain the intent of the different verbal tense forms in John 17:4, and demonstrate how the greater context suggests a perfective verbal tense. In this chapter I will make a comparison of John 17:4 to John 4:34, 5:26, 19:28, and 19:30.[80] I will briefly examine the use of δοξάζω in the LXX.

Chapter 5: The Work of the Words and Works

Chapter Five will contrast and compare diverse views of "the work" in John in 17:4. I will seek to explain how "the work" (17:4b) relates to "glory on the earth" (17:4a), recognizing that the proposition of the first clause in 17:4 depends on the proposition of the second and third clauses.[81] I will show that the Father only is glorified by the Son via a specific, singular work.

I intend to demonstrate that "the work" differs from "works" in the Fourth Gospel, addressing proposals of the relationship between the two terms and concepts. Also, I intend to argue that John 19:30 is not saying, "'the work' of John 17 is finished," or "As I said before, 'the work is completed.'" Rather, the referent for John 19:30 is broader than "the work" of John 17:4.[82]

---

80. I am looking at whether the tense form of the aorist can be interpreted with any temporal sense on the basis of the context, as Crellin discusses (Crellin, "The Semantics of the Perfect," 430–54). Even so I recognize that Crellin and the writers in the aforementioned volume edited by Runge and Fresch hold to a different view of the functioning of verbal aspect than Campbell, Porter, and Carson, having critiques of Porter and Carson similar to those of Fanning. I will discuss how each view of verbal aspect effects the interpretation of John 17:4, and I will argue for a preferred view. See Campbell, *Advances in the Study of Greek*; Campbell, *Basics of Verbal Aspect in Biblical Greek*; Campbell, *Verbal Aspect, the Indicative Mood, and Narrative*; Campbell, *Verbal Aspect and Non-indicative Verbs*; Fanning, "Approaches to Verbal Aspect in New Testament Greek: Issues in Definition and Method," 46–62; Fanning, "Greek Presents, Imperfects, and Aorists in the Synoptic Gospels: Their Contribution to Narrative Structuring," 157–90; Fanning, "Greek Tenses in John's Apocalypse: Issues in Verbal Aspect, Discourse Analysis, and Diachronic Change," 328; Fanning, *Verbal Aspect in New Testament Greek*.

81. In the Greek text there are three clauses, as opposed to the two reflected in the English translations.

82. On Τετέλεσται, C. H. Dodd proposes, "We are almost certainly intended to

Chapter 6: The Absentee Father

The Sixth Chapter will examine the use of "Father" terms for God the Father in the Fourth Gospel. I will consider all uses of πατήρ in John's Gospel that are referring to God the Father. By displaying the frequency of usages of the terms before and after John 16:33, I will argue that John has completed the work of revealing the Father. I will conclude (1) that it is unnecessary for the writer of the Fourth Gospel to speak of the Father, now revealed, with the same frequency with which he spoke of him in 1:19—16:33 and (2) that the distribution of the use of terms referring to the Father supports two major divisions in the Gospel of John, those being 1:18—16:33 and 17:1—20:31.

A preliminary exploration of the use of πατήρ reveals that every chapter in 1:18-16:33 speaks of the Father directly except John 9.[83] It is evident that references to God as "Father" decrease significantly after John 17.[84] I will argue that the dramatic change in the use of πατήρ supports the thesis of the completed work as revelation. That is, the references to the Father disappear almost completely in John 18-20 because Jesus revealed the Father in 1:19—16:33.

LIMITATIONS

This document intends to be comprehensive in its examination of John 17:4. However, it is not my intention to exhaust the LXX's use of the terms under examination. I am not arguing, per se, that John 17:4 represents, in total, the fulfillment of an OT verse or set of verses. I will draw some conclusions regarding echoes in the OT, but only where necessary to support

---

understand this with reference to xvii.4 (τὸ ἔργον τελειώσας), it is therefore closely related to the Johannine theology." Dodd, *Interpretation*, 428. Dodd sees a connection between 17:4 and 19:30 that later he will term an "echo" (437). Yet the slight difference in the verbs for *completion* and *finish* in 17:4 and 19:30 lead Dodd to conclude, "In the prayer of ch. xvii the work is declared to be completed [τελειόω]—on the plane of pure spiritual activity, that is, since Christ then and there offers Himself in sacrifice; but it is completed [τελέω] as a concrete act on the plane of history only when the sacrifice is consummated in his death" (437–38).

83. John 9 does not use πατήρ. However, John speaks of the Father by the synonymous terms "God" (9:3, 16, 24, 29, 31 [3x], 33), and "him who sent me" (9:4).

84. Akala also recognizes the shift in the frequency of usage of Father terms in the Fourth Gospel, although she does not relate the reduction in usage to a completed work in John 1:19-16:33. Akala, *The Son-Father Relationship*.

the thesis on the completed work as revelation. The NT use of the OT is not the focus of this work.

Neither do I intend to explore the entirety or bulk of the current debate over verbal aspect theory. It is outside of the scope of this work to discuss cognitive-linguistic theories of "viewpoint," "mental space," and "conceptual blending."[85] Providing an examination of linguistic philosophies that support the various theories of verbal aspect would not strengthen my argument or conclusions.

Further, I do not find it necessary to explore synonymous terms for πατήρ when used to speak of God. I will not examine pronouns, verbal endings, or the use of θεός when referring to God the Father. The conclusions I am drawing are unaffected by looking at such pronouns, verbal endings, or θεός because these terms are used overwhelmingly within proximity to πατήρ when the writer of the Fourth Gospel uses πατήρ to speak of God. These terms have πατήρ as their antecedent noun, or, in the case of θεός, are evident as a referent to God the Father.

CONCLUSION

I will explain in the introduction that I prefer a reflective view rather than proleptic view of John 17:4 because it (1) better ties 17:4 to the meaning of the Gospel of John as a whole, which I will demonstrate in the last chapter of the dissertation; (2) resolves problems of "I have glorified" and "I have completed," both of which need to have forward-looking temporal senses in order to interpret their verbal aspects consistently; (3) resolves "on the earth" with respect to the public and private ministries of Christ as portrayed in the Fourth Gospel; (4) resolves the problem of an apparent double completion of Christ's work with the use of τελειώσας in 17:4 and Τετέλεσται in 19:30; and (5) keeps John from being read as over-realized eschatology with respect to the "now but not yet" Johannine perspective of the atonement.

---

85. For this discussion most recently, see Brookins, "A Tense Discussion," 147–68.

2

The Tale of Two Readings

VIEWS TOGGLING BETWEEN REFLECTIVE-REVELATORY and proleptic-anticipatory readings of John 17:4 have a long history in writings on the Fourth Gospel. There is a lack of uniform agreement on the sense of completion and on the nature of the work.[1] Yet much of the history of Johannine studies and preaching of the Gospel of John leans toward finding a proleptic idea within 17:4, even where reflective views also are expressed. As Beasley-Murray suggests, "Is this final 'work' included in the τελειώσας, 'the accomplishing,' of v 4 . . . ? From Chrysostom onward, most writers include the death with the works of the ministry as a unity, and it is difficult to avoid that conclusion."[2] Among writers in the modern era, Lincoln,[3] Paddison,[4] and Broachert,[5] well express the

---

1. I am reserving the full discussion on the sense of "completed" (τελειώσας) for chapter 4.

2. Beasley-Murray, *John*, 298.

3. Lincoln's proleptic perspective "views Jesus' death-as-glorification as having already been accomplished and is in line with his final words on the cross—'It is completed' (19:30)." Lincoln, *The Gospel According to Saint John*, 435.

4. Paddison's proleptic view suggests, "It is only on the cross, the hour which Jesus' entire life has been moving towards, the taking up of the command which he has followed through to the end (Jn 10:18; 15:10), and the cup which he consents to receive from the Father (Jn 18:11), that he can say 'it is finished' (Jn 19:30)." Paddison, "Engaging Scripture: Incarnation and the Gospel of John," 153.

5. Borchert, similar to Lincoln and Paddison, concludes that 17:4 is "both reflective of the past and serves as the basis for the prospect of the future in the petition of the next verse" because "Jesus anticipated the cross." Borchert, *John 12–21*, 191.

general sentiment of a proleptic interpretation, while Paterson expresses the tenor of a reflective position.[6]

The writer of John establishes that Jesus brought the Father glory during the tenure of his incarnational ministry on earth (1:14; 2:11; 7:18; 8:50, 54; 11:4, 40; 12:28, 41; 13:31, 32; 14:13; 15:8; 17:1, 24; 21:19).[7] All glory that Christ displays points to the Father via Christ's uniqueness as the Son (1:14). The glory of the Father manifests itself through Christ's works (2:11) and words (7:18).[8] The manifestation occurs regardless of whether those Christ encounters believe on him so as to see the glory (11:40) or reject him and fail to see the glory (5:44; 12:42–43).

A question of the mechanism or mechanisms of Jesus's revelation of the Father's glory sways the views between reflective and proleptic. Carson, as quoted earlier, leans toward a proleptic interpretation of John 17:4. In the fuller quote he explains the issues in view, writing,

> The difficult point of this verse is the uncertainty as to whether the work that Jesus has completed refers to everything he has done *up to this point*, or proleptically includes his obedience unto death, the death that lies immediately ahead . . . Either interpretation can be made to 'fit' the passage. Some have argued for the former by appealing to the contrast implicit in the words *And now* (v. 5), which introduce the glorification of Jesus (= his death/exaltation). This misses the mark. There is certainly a contrast between v. 4 and v. 5, but it is not between previous work that Jesus has completed and his cross-work that lies immediately ahead. Rather, a contrast is drawn between the glory that Jesus by his work has brought to the Father on earth, and the glory he asks the Father to give him (*cf.* 13:31–32) in heaven. Once that is seen, it makes best sense if v. 4 includes *all* the work

---

6. Paterson proposes that the verse is proleptic, referring to the entirety of Jesus's earthly ministry. Yet "this verse does have specific reference to the ways in which Jesus had already revealed more of the character of God through what he said and did . . . for each action and word revealed something more of the true character of Almighty God." Paterson, *Opening Up John's Gospel*, 139–40.

7. Köstenberger demonstrates that the concept of "glory" runs through both the "Book of Signs" (1–12) and the "Book of Glory" (13–21). Köstenberger, "The Glory of God in John's Gospel and Revelation," 108. For similar studies, see Caird, "The Glory of God in the Fourth Gospel," 265–77; and Cook, "The 'Glory' Motif in the Johannine Corpus," 291–97.

8. Commenting on 7:16–18, Köstenberger notes, "Thus it is not only Jesus' works (particularly his signs) but also his words (his teaching) that reveal God's glory, and rejection of Jesus' works *and* words reveals lack of a true desire to discern whether the source of Jesus' mission is God" (Köstenberger, "Glory," 112).

by which Jesus brings glory to his Father, and that includes his own death, resurrection and exaltation (*cf.* 4:34; 5:36; 19:30). So he is speaking proleptically (as in v. 12, 'While I was with them . . .'), oscillating with a more prosaic description of his place at this moment in the flow of redemptive history (*e.g.* v. 11, 'I am coming to you . . .').[9]

In agreement with Carson, I see many attempts by scholars to make both reflective and proleptic views "fit" John 17:4, even though the two views are mutually exclusive when referring to one specific "work."[10]

Investigative in nature, this chapter intends to collect a survey of various reflective and proleptic views of John 17:4 throughout history. I will consider major works in history and several works written since 1900. I will analyze each author's means for establishing his view of the passage. Then, I will synthesize the views, drawing conclusions about the categories of views and the means by which they are achieved.

I propose that authors derive proleptic views historically on the basis of approaching John 17:4 through the lenses of Biblical Theology and/or Systematic Theology rather than Exegetical Theology—an exegesis of the details of the verse itself, the immediate context of John 17, and the details of the Gospel of John. I propose, too, that a few exceptions to a primarily proleptic reading of John 17:4 will emerge in the post-Reformation periods of history. I further propose that the views will reveal that those who attempt Exegetical Theology and an examination of the verbs in 17:4 find means other than exegesis to propose a proleptic reading.

---

9. Carson, *John*, 556–57. Here I refer to Carson to establish the concerns of this chapter. I will interact with Carson's proleptic understanding below.

10. The views are mutually exclusive if someone reading the verse gives the aorist verbs ἐδόξασα and τελειώσας one consistent sense, whether that means that both speak perfectively only, both speak proleptically only, or one speaks in one sense and the other speaks in a different sense. I am using "sense" to capture tense-form and aspect under one idea until the discussion of verbal aspect in chapter 4 below. In assessing the variously expressed views of John 17:4, I consistently observe writers wishing to give "completed" both perfective and proleptic senses in order to establish their proleptic or reflective-proleptic positions. Also, I find little consideration given to the possible need to give the two aorist verbs—if not also the third (ποιήσω)—consistent senses. If, however, one consistently interprets τελειώσας with only one sense rather than as a verb containing two senses at once, the proleptic and reflective *readings* become mutually exclusive. Yet one can retain the idea that John has two works in mind in the whole of the Gospel. In chapter 3 (below), I will make comments on the difference in John's Gospel between "the work" (τὸ ἔργον, 4:34 and 17:4) and "works" (ἔργα, 5:20, 36; 7:3; 9:3, 4; 10:25, 32, 37, 38; 14:10, 11, 12; 15:24) with respect to Christ.

I have divided the analysis according to Patristic, Medieval and Reformation, 19th century, and 20th and 21st century commentary writers. The divisions allow me to consider major contributors to the study of the Gospel of John within each era, while overlooking contributions of smaller works. I combine the Medieval and Reformation periods because few authors wrote commentaries on John during the Medieval period, and of the commentaries written during the Reformation period (and 18th century) few are helpful to this study.[11]

I limit the study to commentaries on John's Gospel because the commentary writers are considering John 17:4 within the whole of their analysis and understanding of the Fourth Gospel. As a whole, commentaries, especially those since the nineteenth century, consider all things specialized studies would consider, including studies of various themes related to the terms and concepts within John 17:4. Also, later commentaries attempt exegetically based discussions of the verse, to which I must give interaction within the scope or my argument. I will examine specialized studies later in this work. Where I have made an exception in this chapter, I have indicated such.

PATRISTIC ERA: CHRYSOSTOM, AUGUSTINE, CYRIL

During the period of the early church, Origen, Chrysostom, Augustine, and Cyril were major commentators on John. Origen does not comment on John 17:4.[12]

---

11. I am aware of commentaries by Nonnus of Nisibis and Theodore of Mopsuestia in the Eastern Christian Tradition. However, neither of them added comments that would contribute to this study. See Nonnus of Nisibis, *Commentary on the Gospel of Saint John*, and Theodore of Mopsuestia, *Commentary on the Gospel of John*. I also am aware of the commentary on the Gospels by Hildegard of Bingen, but she does not make any commentary on John 17. See Hildegard of Bingen, *Homilies on the Gospels*. Nicholas of Gorran (1232–1295) has a commentary of which the British Library, the national library of the United Kingdom, seems to hold the only extant copy. See "Nicholas of Gorran's Commentary on John."

12. Although Origen contributed a commentary on John prior to Augustine, I skip Origen in my investigation because he does not make comments on John 17:4, but only on verses 1, 3, 20, 21, and 24. See also, Milewski, "Nos Locus Dei Sumus," 14.

Chrysostom (c. 349–407)

Chrysostom's *Homilies on the Gospel of John* constitutes one of the earlier running commentaries on John. Although they are sermons and not exegetical commentary, the homilies still offer tremendous insight into Chrysostom's treatment of John's theology. Chrysostom particularly is interested in practical application, not the detailed explanation of every verse.[13] So his comments on John 17 reflect a concern with Christian living as much as critical thinking on the intercessory prayer.

For Chrysostom, the work of Christ which glorifies the Father is a proleptic work done in "the service of men." The work is completed in the senses of being "but the beginning" and "not yet beginning," which appear to be both reflective and anticipatory:

> "I have glorified Thee on the earth." Well said He, "on the earth"; for in heaven He had been already glorified, having His own natural glory, and being worshiped by the Angels. Christ then speaketh not of that glory which is bound up with His Essence, (for that glory, though none glorify Him, He ever possesseth in its fullness,) but of that which cometh from the service of men. And so the, "Glorify Me," is of this kind; and that thou mayest understand that He speaketh of this manner of glory, hear what follows. "I have finished the work which Thou gavest Me that I should do it." And yet the action was still but beginning, or rather was not yet beginning. How then said He, "I have finished"? Either He meaneth, that "I have done all My part;" or He speaketh of the future, as having already come to pass.[14]

If, "but the beginning," says Chrysostom, then Christ means, "I have done all my part" (e.g., reflective). This would render a completely perfective statement in 17:4, referencing Christ gaining glory in his ministry in the present in general, as Chrysostom does not specify the features of the completion. If, "not yet the beginning," then Christ's words "speak of the future, as having already come to pass" (e.g., proleptic). It is, "not yet

---

13. "Chrysostom's preaching, however, does not automatically make an easy fit with John's Gospel. John the evangelist was universally revered for conveying the deepest spiritual truths of the four Gospels; whereas, John the Golden Mouth was a teacher who anticipated immediate, practical applications for his sermons," and "Chrysostom does not preoccupy himself with every detail of John 17 in the three sermons focused on that chapter" (Milewski, "Nos Locus Dei Sumus," 18, 19).

14. Chrysostom, "Homilies," 297.

beginning," for Christ is not experiencing the cross itself at the moment of the words. Yet he speaks as if the work of the cross is completed.

However, Chrysostom does not have a straightforward proleptic view. In contrast to the potential reflective and proleptic views expressed, he proposes a third view of his own, which one may "most of all" say is the correct reading. Chrysostom continues by saying,

> Or, which one may say most of all, that all was already affected, because the root of blessings had been laid, which fruits would certainly and necessarily follow, and from His being present at and assisting in those things which should take place after these. On this account He saith again in a condescending way, "Which Thou gavest Me." For had He indeed waited to hear and learn, this would have fallen far short of His glory. For that He came to this of His own will, is clear from many passages. As when Paul saith, that "He so loved us, as to give Himself for us" (Eph. 5:2); and, "He emptied Himself, and took upon Him the form of a servant" (Phil. 2:7); and, "As the Father hath loved Me, so have I loved you." (c. 15:9.)[15]

"All" in the earthly ministry is "effected" in a seed-germinating sense. The seed of the work of Christ in the atonement has been laid "in the service of men." The yield of the fruits would "certainly and necessarily follow" as the goal of the service. The yield from the seed is possible because Christ is "present at and assisting" the earthy work from service to atonement: "For that He came to this [his death] of his own will."

The proleptic event exists as seamless growth of the reflective acts. It is not enough for Chrysostom to leave the work as "the service of men," for the service is yielding fruit; but the yield does not arise from the analysis of the word of completion. Chrysostom offers a proleptic reading—proleptic in a seed-germinating sense. His proleptic view does not come as an addition or in opposition to a reflective view, but neither is it straightforwardly anticipatory of the cross. It is a prolepsis organically growing from the reflective work.

Chrysostom's proleptic and reflective views are separate, complementary options for reading 17:4 legitimately. Later works on the Fourth Gospel do not show such uncertainty in perspectives, even as much as Chrysostom's proleptic and reflective views do not demonstrate the proleptic concerns of later writers.

15. Chrysostom, "Homilies," 29.

Augustine of Hippo (354–430)

On Augustine's view,[16] it is important to see that he thinks the reflective work is revelatory:

> In this way, therefore, the Son glorifies You, that He makes You known to all whom You have given Him. Accordingly, if the knowledge of God is eternal life, we are making the greater advances to life, in proportion as we are enlarging our growth in such a knowledge. And we shall not die in the life eternal; for then, when there shall be no death, the knowledge of God shall be perfected. Then will be effected the full effulgence of God, because then the completed glory, as expressed in Greek by δόξα. For from it we have the word δόξασον, that is used here, and which some Latins have interpreted by clarifica (make effulgent), and some by glorifica (glorify). But by the ancients, glory, from which men are styled glorious, is thus defined: Glory is the widely-spread fame of any one accompanied with praise.[17]

In the above comments, Augustine reasons from John 17:3 that the Son glorifies God by making him known. In effect, Augustine supplies a logical connection between 17:3 and 17:4, as if to say, "Since eternal life is to know God [the Father] and his Son, I therefore have glorified you, for I have made you known." It is from this point that Augustine then reasons

---

16. Prior to Augustine, Theodore, Bishop of Mopsuestia (AD 350–428), wrote a commentary on the Gospel of John. However, in the Ancient Christian Texts edition of Theodore's commentary on John, only one reference to 17:4 appears in the work, and it is within the commentary on 17:3: "'I have accomplished what I was supposed to do,' he says. 'I have revealed your glory to everyone on the face of the earth and have perfectly fulfilled the task given to me for the salvation of all.'" Conti and Elowsky, eds. *Commentary on the Gospel of John*, 143. Milewski understands Theodore to see John 17:4 among passages which "underscore the sense of God's sovereignty at work in history . . . difficult passages where Jesus speaks of future events as already accomplished (vv. 4, 6, 7, 8, 19, 22, and 23)" (Milewski, "Nos Locus Dei Sumus," 35). Despite the brevity of Chrysostom's commentary on 17:4, Milewski concludes that "Theodore interprets [such verses] as prophetic utterances augmenting the sense of divine authority" (Milewski, "Nos Locus Dei Sumus," 36). One can discern a reflective concept in the words, "revealed your glory to everyone on the face of the earth." One also senses a possible proleptic concept in the words, "for the salvation of all." Yet Theodore's commentary is of great brevity and I cannot draw a solid conclusion on Theodore's view, nor do I think Milewski has grounds for including the verse among Chrysostom's examples of "prophetic utterances." Because of the shortness of Chrysostom's comments, I do not include him in my historical investigation. Also, it is worth noting that the Scripture Index of the Ancient Christian Texts edition does not give any references for John 17:4, although the above reference does appear in the work.

17. Augustine, *The Gospel of John: Tractate* 105.

first that the work of sanctification includes increasing in the knowledge of God and *second* that eternal life excludes death permanently because the increase of the knowledge of God in sanctification gives way to the perfection of the knowledge of God in full glorification. For Augustine, a reflective reading of the work—the work that glorifies the Father—contributes to his theology that views knowing God as the work of justification, sanctification, and glorification.

Augustine continues his thought by recognizing that the glorification of God [the Father] will take place in his "house" in the praises of his house dwellers forever—that is, "without end." In this eschatological period, the believer will experience the full knowledge of God—which is to experience glorification to the fullest, what Augustine also terms "the complete effulgence." This is a concept of glorification that looks for fulfillment in the future. Augustine comments,

> But if a man is praised when the fame regarding him is believed, how will God be praised when He Himself shall be seen? Hence it is said in Scripture, Blessed are they that dwell in Your house; they will be praising You for ever and ever. There will God's praise continue without end, where there shall be the full knowledge of God; and because the full knowledge, therefore also the complete effulgence or glorification.[18]

To this concept, Augustine immediately adds an earthly, present aspect to the glorification of God: "God first of all is glorified here." The means by which God's glorification takes place in the present world is through the revelatory acts of personal witness and "through the faith of believers."

> But God is first of all glorified here, while He is being made known to men by word of mouth, and preached through the faith of believers. Wherefore, He says, I have glorified You on the earth: I have finished the work which You gave me to do. He does not say, You ordered; but, You gave: where the evident grace of it is commended to notice. For what has the human nature even in the Only-begotten, that it has not received? Did it not receive this, that it should do no evil, but all good things, when it was assumed into the unity of His person by the Word, by whom all things were made?[19]

---

18. Augustine, *The Gospel of John: Tractate 105*.
19. Augustine, *The Gospel of John: Tractate 105*.

Augustine recognizes the problem caused by Christ claiming a completed work when the work on the cross is yet future: *"But how has He finished the work which was committed unto Him to do, when there still remains the trial of the passion wherein He especially furnished His martyrs with the example they were to follow . . . ?"*[20] He immediately will resolve the apparent dilemma by appealing to various workings of prophetic revelation in four passages: 1 Pet 2:21[-24]; Ps 22:16; and John 15:15; and 16:12, saying,

> Whereof, says the apostle Peter, Christ suffered for us, leaving us an example, that we should follow His steps: 1 Peter 2:21 but just that He says He has finished, what He knew with perfect certainty that He would finish? Just as long before, in prophecy, He used words in the past tense, when what He said was to take place very many years afterwards: They pierced, He says, my hands and my feet, they counted all my bones; He says not, They will pierce, and, They will count. And in this very Gospel He says, All things that I have heard of my Father, I have made known unto you; to whom He afterward declares, I have yet many things to say unto you, but you cannot bear them now. For He, who has predestinated all that is to be by sure and unchangeable causes, has done whatever He is to do: as it was also declared of Him by the prophet, Who has made the things that are to be.[21]

First, Augustine proposes that the need for Christ to set an example of suffering for persecuted believers, as revealed in 1 Pet 2:21–24, should influence the interpretation of the words in John 17:4. One only can say the work is completed if Christ has established the model witness of suffering that Peter describes.[22] That suffering includes the substitutionary work of bearing the sins of the elect in his body while on the cross.[23] Yet Augustine also holds to a proleptic idea of the work because of an *a*

---

20. Augustine, *The Gospel of John: Tractate 105*.
21. Augustine, *The Gospel of John: Tractate 105*.
22. In 1 Pet 2:21, ἔπαθεν ὑπὲρ ὑμῶν ("suffered for you") will real itself to be a reference that includes the work of Christ on the cross—τὰς ἁμαρτίας ἡμῶν . . . ἀνήνεγκεν ("bore our sins")—as the two parallel ἵνα clauses in 2:21 and 2:24 also indicate: "because Christ also suffered for you, leaving you an example, so that (ἵνα) you might follow in his steps," and, "He himself bore our sins in his body on the tree, that (ἵνα) we might die to sin and live to righteousness."
23. In the phrase, ἀνήνεγκεν . . . ἐπὶ τὸ ξύλον ("bore . . . on a tree"), "tree" refers to the cross. The term "tree" invokes the idea of the work of Christ on the cross as the means by which the curse of sin has been removed, with reference to Deut 21:23 (cf. Gal 3:13).

priori assumption that the work includes the passion. Augustine does not make any attempt to demonstrate the reason he finds the glorifying act to include the passion. He alone or only twice appeals to the work of God in prophecy.

Second, Augustine references the words of David in Ps 22:16. In doing so, he places the prophetic words of David in the mouth of Christ at the time they were spoken by David. Thus, a means by which Augustine establishes a proleptic reading is to see continuity between Christ speaking prophetically in the mouth of the tenth century BCE prophetic speaker and Christ seemingly speaking of the passion yet to come in John 17. In both cases, Christ must be present to speak effectively where he is not present physically. For the one, he must be present effectively ten centuries prior to his incarnation. For the other, he must be present effectively a day before his actual crucifixion.

Third, Augustine makes reference to words of Christ in the Fourth Gospel that at first seem to cause an apparent contradiction for Augustine. In John 15:15, Christ has taken all things heard from his Father and revealed them, whereas in 16:12, Christ still has "many" words to give. He resolves the apparent contradiction by recognizing that "all things" up to a point in time does not preclude further knowledge from being shared.

For Augustine, the prophetic workings of the four passages that support his proleptic view of John 17:4 are consistent with the freedom of God in his eternal decree. As God must bring to pass all that he has predestined, so the prophet speaks of them as completed. John 17:4, referencing the sovereign commissioning of Christ by God—"which you called me to do"—must therefore be completed. Christ is able to speak of the completion of the work on the cross before the event because his speech has the same prophetic-proleptic character as other parts of scripture (as already evidenced in John 15:15 when compared to 16:12).

Augustine is asking for the means or mechanism by which Christ could make a proleptic statement.[24] Augustine will conclude that Christ intends to speak in an *anticipatory* manner, and that such is based on the *predestination* work of the Father, seeing the term "given" as *decree* rather

---

24. Downing makes a statement of Augustine's question when he writes, "The glorifying of the Father by the Son is a work ever going on. He speaks of having *finished* the work, though the offering of Himself on the cross was still to come; since, as St. Augustine expresses it, 'He said that He had finished that which He knew most certainly He should finish.'" Downing, *Short Notes on St. John's Gospel*, 171.

than *simple stewardship of a commission*. To make his case takes multiple points of reasoning.

First, Augustine demonstrates that the goal of the Son in making a request to be glorified by the Father is for the Son to bring glory to the Father:

> In a way similar, also, to this, He proceeds to say: And now, O Father, glorify me with Your own self with the glory which I had with You before the world was. For He had said above, Father, the hour has come; glorify Your Son, that Your Son may glorify You: in which arrangement of the words He had shown that the Father was first to be glorified by the Son, in order that the Son might glorify the Father.[25]

The glorification of the Son is penultimate in the work of Christ on the earth; the glorification of the Father is ultimate. The request, "that the Son may glorify you," keeps the revelation of the Father in focus as the ministry of the Son: "glorify your Son."

Second, on the basis of the ultimate and penultimate goals of the glorification requests, Augustine reasons that if both goals are yet future, then one should understand the statement, "I have brought you glory," to have a future sense, for this is the sequence in which Jesus speaks:

> But now He said, I have glorified You on the earth: I have finished the work which You gave me to do; and now glorify Thou me; as if He Himself had been the first to glorify the Father, by whom He then demands to be glorified. We are therefore to understand that He used both words above in accordance with that which was future, and in the order in which they were future, Glorify Your Son, that Your Son may glorify You: but that He now used the word in the past tense of that which was still future, when He said, I have glorified You on the earth: I have finished the work which You gave me to do. And then, when He said, And now, O Father, glorify Thou me with Your own self, as if He were afterwards to be glorified by the Father, whom He Himself had first glorified; what did He intimate but that, when He said above, I have glorified You on the earth, He had so spoken as if He had done what He was still to do; but that here He demanded of the Father to do that whereby the Son should yet do so; in other words, that the Father should glorify the Son,

---

25. Augustine, *The Gospel of John: Tractate 105*.

> by means of which glorification of the Son, the Son also was yet to glorify the Father?[26]

Since the Son intends to glorify the Father (17:1), when he speaks of having brought the Father glory (17:4), he speaks of the future glorification. That glorification itself, though spoken of in the past tense seemingly, rests on the work of the Father to glorify the Son. Augustine does not consider that the writer might use "glorify" in different senses or speak of different aspects of glory.

Third, Augustine suggests putting the aorist of *doxazo* in the future tense: "I will glorify you on the earth. I will finish the work which you have given me to do." For Augustine, the changing of the tense of the verb removes any apparent obscurity in 17:4 and makes its meaning consistent with, or "as plain as," 17:1. That is, "I have glorified you" and "Glorify your Son, that Your Son may glorify you" will share the same sense. Augustine determines,

> In fine, if, in connection with that which was still future, we put the verb also in the future tense, where He has used the past in place of the future tense, there will remain no obscurity in the sentence: as if He had said, I will glorify You on the earth: I will finish the work which You have given me to do; and now, O Father, glorify Thou me with Your own self. In this way it is as plain as when He says, Glorify Your Son, that Your Son may glorify You.[27]

Augustine's proleptic, anticipatory view, therefore requires an emendation to any past-tense perspective. Instead of asking why the writer of John did not use a simple future tense to express the future, as he does elsewhere in the gospel account, Augustine seems to assume that the only means of finding congruency between the glorification statements is to make a text speak in a tense not evident in its form, and justify why that form must have a different sense.

---

26. Augustine, *The Gospel of John: Tractate 105*.

27. Augustine, *The Gospel of John: Tractate 105*. Milewski, reading, "there will remain no obscurity in the sentence" (*nulla sententiae remanebit obscuritas*) in *Tractate 105*, indicates, "Augustine allows that in some cases, as in v. 4, one may legitimately substitute past tenses with future tenses and find no difference of meaning" ("Nos Locus Dei Sumus," 136). However, it does not appear that Augustine is equating the meaning as much as he is saying that rendering the verse in the future tense will not discolor what was meant by the use of the past tense.

Fourth, Augustine will appeal to the theological idea of predestination, so that what he concludes with respect to a reflective idea may speak in finality of a proleptic idea. Again, recognizing that the penultimate and ultimate acts of glorification are mutually dependent upon one another, he understands them to have a logical order that influences the interpretation of the passage—"He showed them assuredly the manner of both glorifications."[28] Yet without concession or explanation, Augustine capitulates on this point when he intimates that glorifying the Father on the earth—which previously he indicates is both future and in full agreement with the sense of the request of the future glorification of the Father and Son—concerns Christ's revelation of God the Father to the nations: "For He Himself glorified the Father on earth by preaching Him to the nations."[29]

In order to avoid what now could draw an accusation of doublespeak, incongruence, or contradiction in his reasoning, he will again appeal to the Father's role in glorifying the Son in the verses preceding 17:4, so that 17:1 always determines the interpretation of 17:3 for Augustine: "The Father glorified Him with His own self in setting Him at His own right hand." Augustine further proposes,

> But on that very account, when He says afterward in reference to the glorifying of the Father, I have glorified You, He preferred putting the verb in the past tense, in order to show that it was already done in the act of predestination, and what was with perfect certainty yet to take place was to be accounted as already done; namely, that the Son, having been glorified by the Father with the Father, would also glorify the Father on the earth.[30]

Since the act of exaltation to the right hand is future, in the interdependent relationships of "glorify the Son," "that the Son may glorify you," and

---

28. Augustine, *The Gospel of John: Tractate 105*.

29. Augustine, *The Gospel of John: Tractate 105*. In context, the statements read, "And this is indeed the whole sentence, save that here we are told also the manner of that same glorification, which there was left unnoticed; as if the former were explained by the latter to those whose hearts it was able to stir, how it was that the Father should glorify the Son, and most of all how the Son also should glorify the Father. For in saying that the Father was glorified by Himself on the earth, but He Himself by the Father with the Father's very self, He showed them assuredly the manner of both glorifications. *For He Himself glorified the Father on earth by preaching Him to the nations; but the Father glorified Him with His own self in setting Him at His own right hand*" (italics mine).

30. Augustine, *The Gospel of John: Tractate 105*.

"I have glorified you on the earth," all three symbiotic actions must be future. However, this further reasoning requires additional explanation for the "verb in the past tense," for its semantic form is past even though Augustine is convinced it must be future. Therefore, Augustine relates the past *form* to predestination, while relating the future *sense* to the cross. In *the eternal decree*, the work is completed—"In the act of predestination . . . [the work] was to be accounted as already done." In *experience*, the work is yet future—"what was with perfect certainty yet to take place." So then rather than having brought glory to the Father in previous actions, and rather than the glorification of the Son awaiting the Ascension of Christ to the Father, Augustine comes to the proleptic conclusion, "the Son . . . *would* also glorify the Father on the earth."

In summary, Augustine holds to a proleptic view of John 17:4 that encompasses a reflective view. The reflective view stems from seeing "the work" as Christ making God known, and that knowledge of God is increasing from justification through sanctification until glorification because only then will the full knowledge of God be revealed to the believer. The future glorification does not hold at bay Christ's present glorification of the Father, for the personal proclamation of God and subsequent faith in the gospel of God express on earth what will be expressed in heaven. So Augustine initially makes his proleptic aspect concern heaven and not the cross of Christ. However, it paves the way for him to develop a reflective view mixed with a proleptic view that sees the cross as part of the work.

The proleptic work posits the atonement work *a priori* in order to include the example of suffering he set for believers—without which "the work" could not be said to be complete. The proleptic idea of the work of 17:4 has precedent in prophetic texts on the atonement. Augustine will make his proleptic view consistent with the eternal decree of God and the intent of the Father to glorify the Son.

Thus, for Augustine, a reflective reading of the work that glorifies the Father contributes to his theology that views knowing God as the work of justification, sanctification, and glorification. He sees a future glory as God's people dwell in his eternal house, praising him forever. Yet Augustine also sees God glorified on the present earth in the preaching of the gospel to the nations. His view stands without contradictions by separating the function of the *form* of the verb "glorified" from the function of the *sense* of the verb.

Cyril of Alexandria (376–444)

In reading Cyril, it is important to recognize that his approach is not an attempt at historical-critical exegesis. Rather, as a Patristic exegete, in any given passage, he is "interpreting a given text in light of the overall sweep of God's plan of salvation."[31] Also, prior to comments on John 17:4, Cyril makes an atonement reading of John 4:34: "'My food is to do the will of him who sent me and to complete his work.' Would it not, then, be clear from this that he considers it a joy and a delight to do the Father's will that is, to return to salvation those who had fallen into destruction? There is no doubt."[32]

Similarly, Cyril previously writes, "The life of all, then, is the fruit of the mercy of God the Father, carried out, that is, by Christ. That is why he himself said somewhere, addressing God the Father, 'I glorified you on earth by finishing the work that you gave me to do.' The Only Begotten was entrusted, as it were, by the Father with the salvation of us all."[33] A proleptic understanding is *a priori* for Cyril. However, again, he is not analyzing the passage in terms of the whole of John 17, the Farewell Discourse, and related historical background information. He is placing the exegesis in the context of a sweeping view of redemptive history.

Cyril promotes Christ's own desire to save the world as reason for the incarnation into an earthly ministry. Cyril writes,

> What work, then, has He fulfilled, whereby He says that He glorified the Father? For while He was the true God He became Man, by the approval and will of the Father, through His desire to save the whole world, and raise up anew the fallen race on the earth to endless life and the true knowledge of God. And this was in very truth accomplished by the Divine power and might of Christ, who made death powerless, upset the dominion of the devil, destroyed sin, and showed incomparable love towards us, by remitting the charges against us all, and giving light to those astray, who now know the One true God.[34]

Serving on the earth, Christ participates in many acts necessary to "raise up anew the fallen race," including destroying of death, ruling to

---

31. Cyril of Alexandria, *Commentary on John*, xxii.
32. Cyril of Alexandria, *Commentary on John*, 229.
33. Cyril of Alexandria, *Commentary on John*, 225.
34. Cyril of Alexandria, *Commentary on John*.

dismantle the reign of the devil, removing sin and canceling the record of debt against us, and providing revelation of the gospel to closed eyes.

Occasionally, Cyril will use revelatory terms to describe the work of Christ. He does not use them to establish "the work" as reflective or as in contrast to a proleptic work. Instead, the terms are speaking of the work of Christ to rescue those in need of salvation by "giving light to those astray, who now *know* the One true God."[35] They are revelatory, but as a seamless piece of the proclamation of the gospel through Christ to those lacking salvation. Cyril makes similar comments in the subsequent commentary:

> Christ, then, having accomplished this by His own power, the Father was glorified by all—I mean all those in the world who knew His wisdom, and power, and the mercy and love towards mankind, which is in Him. For He has shone forth and manifested Himself in the Son, Who is, as it were, the Likeness and Express Image of His Person; and by its fruit the tree is known, according to the Scripture.[36]

The Father's manifestation of "Himself in the Son" is the occasion for the Father to be glorified by all. That is, as the fruit of a tree points to the type of tree, so the Son, as begotten of the Father, points to the type of God the Father is, manifesting the Father's "wisdom . . . power . . . mercy and love toward mankind."

Yet, revelatory pointing remains only a small aspect of Cyril's full position. He continues with a broadly proleptic idea of the completed works, noting, "When the works were fulfilled, and the wonderful scheme of our redemption brought to its fitting conclusion, He returns to His own glory, and assumes His ancient honor."[37] The fulfillment of the earthly works, to which "the work" also refers for Cyril, concludes the work of redemption in the ministry of Christ. On that basis, Christ makes a request to receive his pre-incarnate glory. Thus, Cyril's ideas are proleptic, mingled with reflective strands, with "the work" being the atoning work of Christ, including the defeat of the devil.

---

35. Cyril of Alexandria, *Commentary on John*.
36. Cyril of Alexandria, *Commentary on John*.
37. Cyril of Alexandria, *Commentary on John*.

MEDIEVAL AND REFORMATION: BONAVENTURE, AQUINAS, AND LUTHER

Within the Medieval and Reformation periods, I will consider three representative commentaries by St. Bonaventure, St. Thomas Aquinas, and Martin Luther. In the footnotes, I will interact with Calvin, due to the volume of his contribution to Protestant Theology and whole-book commentaries and not due to any chiefly important or unique contribution to writings on the Gospel of John.

St. Bonaventure (1221–1274)

On John 4:34, Bonaventure determines, "The will of God is our salvation."[38] The fulfillment of the work of redemption is the goal of the will of God, which Bonaventure concludes by an appeal to John 6:40: "For this is the will of my Father, that everyone who looks on the Son and believes in him should have eternal life, and I will raise him up on the last day." The work, therefore, is conversion. Bonaventure finds support in John 6:29.

Bonaventure will complement his comments on 4:34 with small comments at 17:4. Referring to the completed work, he says, "He has accomplished it because he was obedient till death."[39] Bonaventure draws support for his interpretation of 17:4 from the perfection of Christ in his baptism of suffering in Luke 12:50 and the accomplishment of the perfection of believers' salvation through suffering (on the cross) in Heb 2:10. Bonaventure alone considers the work in 17:4 to refer to God's will for Christ to redeem fallen people through his suffering and crucifixion and in no way hints at any reflective concepts with the verse.

Thomas Aquinas (1225–1274)

A contemporary of Bonaventure, Aquinas's understanding of John 17:4, like Augustine's, closely relates to his understanding of "glory," "glorify," and "glorified" in John 17:1–5. He finds three distinct aspects of glorification in John 17:4.[40] The first aspect involves the revelatory and reflec-

---

38. St. Bonaventure, *Commentary on the Gospel of John*, 249.
39. St. Bonaventure, *Commentary on the Gospel of John*, 249.
40. Aquinas, *Commentary on John*, 17.1.2181. Aquinas, in parallel, distinguishes

tive work of "teaching," stated generally by Aquinas, without a specific subject. For he says, "[Christ] states that he merited to be heard for two reasons. First, because of his teaching, when he says, I glorified you on earth, that is, in the minds of men, by manifesting you in my teaching: 'Glorify the Lord in teaching' [Is 24:15]." All of Jesus's teaching and each of his teachings brought glory to God, making him known. This glorification was "in the *minds* of men by manifesting [the Father]." Aquinas finds a background for Jesus' teaching-as-glorification in Isa 24:15.[41]

The second aspect also is reflective, although not revelatory: "Secondly, I glorified you by my obedience; thus he said, I . . . having accomplished the work. He uses the past tense in place of the future: I glorified for 'I will glorify,' and accomplished in place of 'I will accomplish.'"[42] In his "obedience," Christ is doing the work his Father sent him to do. Having been obedient without fail, the work of obedience is completed in one sense. With these conclusions, Aquinas seems to be following the narrative of the Fourth Gospel and the gospel story as a whole (cf. John 5:19, 30; 6:38; 14:31; 15:10; cf. Matt 6:10; 26:39, 42).

The third aspect follows Augustine in seeing a verb as having enough fluidity to speak reflectively and forwardly at the very same time. In order to do this, Aquinas gives future aspects to the aorist verbs. He proposes, "[Christ] does this because these things had already begun, and also because the hour of his passion, when his work would be accomplished, was very near."[43] Aquinas finds support for his understanding of the double sense of the verbs in the arrival of the in the Johannine "hour" (12:33; 13:1; 17:4). He assumes that "the work" includes the cross on the basis of the proximity of the intercessory statement chronologically, e.g., "very near."

Aquinas's explanation of the work in John 17:4 complements his earlier comments on 4:34. Aquinas reasons,

---

three aspects of Christ's request to be glorified by the Father: (1) in the passion, as fulfilled in the subsequent miracles at the time of the death of Christ; (2) in the resurrection; and (3) in "the knowledge of all people."

41. In John 17:4, Aquinas seemingly sees Christ fulfilling Isa 24:15 by bringing glory to the Father by means of teaching. The translation "in teaching" in Isa 24:15 follows the Vulgate's "in doctrinis": "propter hoc *in doctrinis* glorificate Dominum in insulis maris nomen Domini Dei Israhel." Yet, the LXX has ἐν ταῖς νήσοις ("in the islands"), and the MT has בָּאֻרִים ("in the lights"), meaning "in the east"—the region of light. The Vulgate reading does not derive from the LXX or the MT. Therefore, one lacks a basis for seeing a fulfillment of Isa 24:15 in John 17:4 even if one sees the work as revelatory.

42. Aquinas, *Commentary on John*, 17.1.2190.

43. Aquinas, *Commentary on John*, 17.1.2190.

> It is perfectly reasonable for Christ to say, My food is to do the will of him who sent me, to accomplish his work. For as bodily food sustains a man and brings him to perfection, the spiritual food of the soul and of the rational creature is that by which he is sustained and perfected; and this consists in being joined to his end and following a higher rule. David, understanding this, said: "For me, to adhere to God is good" (Ps 72:28). Accordingly, Christ, as man, fittingly says that his food is to do the will of God, to accomplish his work.[44]

By using an analogy related to eating food and finding an analogous example in the life of David, Aquinas postulates that Christ experiences sustenance of soul and perfection in righteousness in his humanity by accomplishing "the work." That is, Christ does more than bring a work to perfection by completing it. *He himself is perfected by the work*. What he completes is not simply for others; Christ also is completing something upon himself.

In the analogy, "spiritual food" does for the soul what eating physical food does for the body. As man eats, he finds nourishment for tasks and comes to a place of bodily perfection—full strength—for all tasks in life. In the same way, as the inner man "eats" of spiritual things, he is sustained in the work he does for the Lord and comes toward a place of glorification. Seemingly, Christ, "as a man," whose spiritual food for his soul is to do the will of God, is brought to a place of glorification by accomplishing the work.

Aquinas reads Christ's use of "food" analogously rather than metaphorically. It is Christ who compares physical food to spiritual food as tools of sustenance and perfection. However, Christ uses "food" metaphorically to speak of his priority, as indicated by comparison of the immediate references, "yet four months and then comes harvest" (4:35), "the fields are white for harvest" (4:35), and the time marker, "already" (4:36). It is only by making the figurative use of "food" mean "sustenance" and "perfection" that Aquinas can depict Christ being perfected by the work even as he is the perfector of the work. Yet in doing so, Aquinas overlooks a theme developing in John in which there is an announcement of the perfect work as a priority of ministry in 4:43 and then a completion of that work by the episode of John 17. It would seem that Aquinas has opportunity to lay the foundation to develop a reflective and

---

44. Aquinas, *Commentary on John*, 4.4.640.

revelatory view of John 17:4, but his misreading of the figurative use of "food" miscolors his understanding of "[the Father's] work."

However, Aquinas continues commenting on 4:34 by providing options for equating or distinguishing between "to do the will of God" and "accomplish his work," stating, "These two expressions can be understood as meaning the same thing, in the sense that the second is explaining the first. Or, they can be understood in different ways."[45] So, *first*, Aquinas will understand (1) 4:34 to exhibit two different works at hand—one revelatory and the other passion-related, even though he understands 17:4 to speak of a passion-related work and (2) "the work" to be perfective in man:

> If we understand them as meaning the same, the sense is this: My food is, i.e., in this is my strength and nourishment, to do the will of him who sent me; according to, "My God, I desired to do your will, and your law is in my heart" (Ps 39:9), and, "I came down from heaven not to do my own will, but the will of him who sent me" (below 6:38). But because "to do the will" (*facere voluntatem*) of another can be understood in two ways—one, by making him will it, and second, by fulfilling what I know he wills—therefore, explaining what it means to do the will of him who sent him, the Lord says, to accomplish his work, that is, that I might complete the work I know he wants: "I must do the works of him who sent me while it is day" (below 9:4).[46]

Aquinas reads "the will" and "the work" both as sustenance, equating the two ideas, by relating 4:34 to statements of (1) Christ's desire to obey the law of God (prophetically spoken in the mouth of David in Ps 39:9) and (2) Christ's purpose in his mission in the incarnation (spoken in John 6:38). To this theological correlating, he adds two options for understanding "to do the will," the former, which is to see the Father decreeing the accomplishment of his work through Christ, and the latter, which is to see Christ fulfilling what the Father, apart from the person of Christ, has decreed Christ to do. Opting for the latter understanding, Aquinas concludes that Jesus explains "to do the will of him who sent me" as "to accomplish his work" on the basis that John 9:4 supports the correlating of John 4:34 to 6:38 and Ps 39:9, even though 9:4 speaks of doing "works" rather than of "the work." Aquinas does not yet draw any conclusions as to whether equating the two works results in a reflective or proleptic view of the work.

45. Aquinas, *Commentary on John*, 4.4.640.
46. Aquinas, *Commentary on John*, 4.4.640.

Second, Aquinas explains the ramifications of the "work" of 4:34 if it differs from "to do the will of him who sent me." He proposes,

> If these two expressions are understood as different, then we should point out that Christ did two things in this world. First, he taught the truth, in inviting and calling us to the faith; and by this he fulfilled the will of the Father: "This is the will of my Father, who sent me: that everyone who sees the Son and believes in him should have eternal life" (below 6:40). Secondly, he accomplished the truth by opening in us, by his passion, the gate of life, and by giving us the power to arrive at complete truth: "I have accomplished the work which you gave me to do" (below 17:4). Thus he is saying: My food is to do the will of him who sent me, by calling men to the faith, to accomplish his work, by leading them to what is perfect.[47]

For Aquinas, John 4:34 contains two different works on the basis of the distinction of two separate, not equivalent ideas. Both ideas are related to "the truth" in keeping with the Johannine idea of truth coming in a unique way in the incarnation (1:14, 17; 5:33; 8:32, 40, 44, 45; 14:6; 18:37). As truth, both ideas are revelatory.

The first work is Christ's teaching of the truth, which arises again in 17:4 where Aquinas sees a fulfillment of Isa 24:15. In this work, "the truth" is the gospel, for it consists of "inviting and calling us to the faith." This truth issues a general calling to all in the gospel's inherent general *invitation*, which elsewhere Scripture expresses as "many are called" (Matt 22:14, cf. Rom 1:16–17). Likewise, this truth issues a special *calling* that brings some to faith, which elsewhere Scripture expresses as "few are chosen" (Matt 22:14). Both the general and specific acts seek a response from the hearer "that brings some to faith"—that results in "eternal life." Therefore, both the invitation and calling are revelatory, in revealing the truth of the gospel in general to all and in awakening faith in others. Thus, Aquinas's "teaching of the truth" is revelatory, making this first work *reflective*. Drawing upon John 6:30, he equates this work with "the will of [Jesus's] Father."

The second work entails both (1) the accomplishment of the truth in believers to "open the gate of life" and (2) the provision of power to aid the believer in coming to the full truth of Christ. This work is not revelatory, but atoning, for it is "by his passion." Thus, the second work—"to accomplish his work"—is proleptic, for the narrative still is in the early

47. Aquinas, *Commentary on John*, 4.4.641.

years of the Fourth Gospel's portrayal of the Public Ministry of Christ (1:19–12:31), looking forward to the work of Christ on the cross several chapters in the future. Apparently recognizing the literary similarities between 4:34 and 17:4, Aquinas invokes 17:4 to support his conclusion. In doing so, he infers that John 17:4 has a proleptic aspect.

Similar to his analysis of 17:4, in 4:30 Aquinas sees both reflective and proleptic aspects. The reflective aspect is in calling men through the truth to faith, which is "to do the will of him who sent [Jesus]." The proleptic aspect is in the leading believers to "what is perfect" (e.g., Christ in his fullness), which is to accomplish [the Father's] work."

Aquinas elaborates on his understanding of the proleptic work, referring to things beneficial to humankind as inclusive within the work. On the one hand, following Origen, the "great and first commandment" (Matt 22:38) and the "second" (Matt 22:39) frame his interpretation of "the work." "The work" of Christ on earth, in this elaboration, falls within "good works" of any man.[48] Therefore the objective of Christ's work, as a good work, must have the love of God and love of neighbor as ends.

As relates to his view of seeing two statements within John 4:34, Aquinas directs the Great Commandment toward "to do the will of him who sent me," and he directs the Second Commandment toward "to accomplish his work." He takes liberty to broaden or reshape the commandments' concepts of "love" so that toward God "love" becomes "honor," and toward neighbor "love" becomes that which is for "the benefit and perfection of man." Aquinas comments,

> "The work" are things benefiting man—perfecting man. Another interpretation, given by Origen, is that every man who does good works should direct his intention to two things: the honor of God and the good of his neighbor: for as it is said: "The end of the commandment is love" (1 Tim 1:5), and this love embraces both God and our neighbor. And so, when we do something for God's sake, the end of the commandment is God; but when it is for our neighbor's good, the end of the commandment is our neighbor. With this in mind, Christ is saying, My food is to do the will of him who sent me, God, i.e., to direct and regulate my intention to those matters that concern the honor of God, to accomplish his work, i.e., to do things for the benefit and perfection of man.[49]

---

48. Aquinas's discussion of "every man who does good works" concerns those seeking to love God and neighbor—e.g. believers.

49. Aquinas, *Commentary on John*, 4.4.642.

So Aquinas again is able to draw man's completion of spiritual righteousness into his view of the completed work of Christ in John 4:34. This requires a proleptic reading of "the work" in John 4:34.

Aquinas further supports the proleptic reading of 4:34 though some theological anthropology musings that reply to the view of Origen:

> I answer that among lower creatures, man is the special work of God, who made him to his own image and likeness (Gn 1:26). And in the beginning God made this a perfect work, because as we read in Ecclesiastes (7:30): "God made man upright." But later, man lost this perfection by sin, and abandoned what was right. And so, this work of the Lord needed to be repaired in order to become right again; and this was accomplished by Christ, for "Just as by the disobedience of one man, many were made sinners, so by the obedience of one man, many will be made just" (Rom 5:19). Thus, Christ says, to accomplish his work, i.e., to bring man back to what is perfect.[50]

In tracing the story of man's journey from perfection in creation to imperfection in the fall to reclamation of perfection in Christ, Christ completes the work of God by bringing man back to a state of original perfection. Later, this reading will coincide with Aquinas's proleptic reading of John 17:4.

In summary, Aquinas's view is proleptic and revelatory. It is based on nearness of the prayer in John 17 to the passion narrative events rather than on anticipation of completeness of the atoning work by Christ. The slight conceptual difference between *nearness* and anticipation is significant, for Aquinas's primary reasoning is not based on Christ's knowledge of the future or Christ's commitment to the decree of God, but chronology of events.[51] The proleptic reasoning from chronology accords with his proleptic reading of "the work" as Christ bringing man to perfection—the latter reading implying that the work includes Christ's death and resurrection.[52]

---

50. Aquinas, *Commentary on John*, 4.4.642.

51. Poole similarly proposes a proleptic reading based on chronological proximity of the events when he writes, "But how could Christ say this, who had not yet died for the sins of men, which was the principal piece of his work? *Answ*. It was so nigh, that he speaks of it as already done: so, ver. 11, he saith, *I am no more in the world*, because he was to be so little a time in the world. Again, he speaks of what he was fully resolved to do, as if it were already done." Poole, *Annotations upon the Holy Bible*, 368.

52. Gill (1697–1771) holds a mixed reflective-proleptic view that seems to draw from Aquinas' language. Gill, *An Exposition of the Gospel According to John*, 510–11.

Martin Luther (1528)

In his sermons on John 17, Luther proclaims,

> For if the glory and knowledge of God could have been revealed through the Law, then Christ would not have had to come preach, suffer, and die in order to glorify the Father. This should also serve to teach us how to seek and apprehend God aright, how to deal with him. For "to glorify the Father" (as we have said) is nothing else than that we acknowledge him and know who he is, what his intentions are, and how we stand with him. No man can arrive at such knowledge except through Christ. For he has willed to reveal himself and to make his heart and will visible nowhere else, but only in and through him. Now in Christ we see nothing but pure, heartfelt, unfathomable love and grace, but outside of him nothing but wrath and displeasure.[53]

Evident in this sermon is Luther's revelatory understanding of the work of Christ in 17:4. Both "glory" and "knowledge" of God—which Luther separates rather than equates—are revealed through Christ rather than the Law (cf. John 1:17). That knowledge is available through Christ alone. What is "heartfelt" and "unfathomable" of God's perfections, one can see through Christ, the revelator.

What then follows is an explanation of the glory of Christ within the context of the three types of glorification in John 17: "Glorify the son" and "glorify me" (17:1, 5), "that I may glorify you" (17:1), and "I have brought you glory" (17:4). Luther declares, "The Lord Christ, when he came to earth, glorified the Father by praising, magnifying, and honoring him, as we see throughout the Gospel that he continually preaches and extols how he was sent by the Father, directing and attributing to the Father above all His words and works, all his life, deeds, possessions, and power."[54] Thus, Luther equates glorification with the attribution of all of the words and works of Christ to the Father. Taking place "when he came to earth," the words and works of Christ have reference to the mode of Christ's service prior to his high priestly prayer. Here, Luther makes no hint of the inclusion of the work of the cross within the scope of Christ's glorification of the Father.

---

53. Brown, ed. *Luther's Works: American Edition vol. 69. Sermons on the Gospel of St. John Chapters 17—20*, 27.

54. Brown, *Luther's Works*, 45.

However, Luther, uniquely, quickly turns Christ's completed glorification into experiences of the full scope of Christ's ministry on the earth, including his humiliation. The persecution of Christ comes as a result of his preaching, performing miracles, and living an obedient life. Luther proclaims,

> "This work and glorification have now been carried out," he wants to say, "therefore glorify me now again." This sounds as though he were saying again what he said above. "If I am to exalt your glory, honor, and praise, then I must come into darkness and shame." For because he did the Father's will, preaching and performing miracles and leading a life pleasing to God, the world became hostile to him and could not endure him. For [the Father's] sake, therefore, he had to be darkened and oppressed and be condemned to a most shameful death. Thus, he completed the work that was given him to do.[55]

The inclusion of Christ's sufferings—which, beyond the Jews' national rejection of him by the time of the narrative of John 12 (cf. John 1:9–10), refer to his physical sufferings and atoning work—means Luther sees Christ looking forward to what occurs in John 18–19. Even though more explicit proleptic terms are absent, the anticipation concept is inherent within the inclusion of the future sufferings.

Luther's interpretation of John 17:4 is highly revelatory and reflective, but also proleptic. The glorification "carried out" includes the "shameful death." Later in this sermon, Luther speaks with great clarity on this view of the completed work, declaring, "This is what he calls the work that the Father gave him to complete—to take upon himself all shame and disgrace, suffering and death, to the glory of the Father. And this is all for our sake, that we might be redeemed and have eternal life, as was explained sufficiently above."[56]

NINETEENTH CENTURY

I will survey a handful of nineteenth century commentaries representative of Johannine scholarship of the period as a whole. Except for Lightfoot's work, I will consider them in the order they were published: Simeon (1833), Tholuck (1836), Downing (1861), J. John Owen (1861),

---

55. Brown, *Luther's Works*, 45.
56. Brown, *Luther's Works*, 46.

Hengstenberg (1865), Govet (1881), Hovey (1885), Whitelaw (1888), Kelly (1898), and B. F. Westcott (1896). Although there is little variance in view from those of the Medieval and Reformation periods, the manifestation of consistent thought and approach to the verse is important for seeing trends toward one or more views.

Charles Simeon (1833)

Simeon begins by reviewing the life, doctrine, and miracles of Christ—all of which are contained in the reference to glorifying God on earth. These acts are wholly revelatory, in that they are (1) both for the "*executing* of his will" and "the *promotion* of his glory," (2) "when he *testified* of himself" as one "*bearing* a commission from the Father," and (3) "by his own power" yet "always ascribed . . . to the Father."

> The Lord Jesus, in his Mediatorial capacity, was a servant, sent by God to execute an appointed work: and, having executed it, he here appeals to God, 1. That "he had glorified God on earth"—[This, in fact, had been the one end for which he had lived. He had glorified his Father *in his life*; every hour of which had been devoted to the executing of his will, and to the promotion of his glory. He had glorified him especially *in his doctrine*. Never once had he sought his own glory, but, on all occasions, the glory of Him who sent him: and when he testified of himself, it was only as the person bearing a commission from the Father, and as sent by him to open for men *a way* of access to him as a reconciled God. He had glorified him no less *by his miracles*: for though he wrought them by his own power, yet he always ascribed them to his Father.[57]

Explicitly, of the miracles Simeon concludes Christ "constrained the beholders to acknowledge the Father" in their concurrent "exercises of omnipotence." He proposes,

> Thus he had constrained the beholders to acknowledge the Father in them. But, above all, he had in *purpose*, though not in act, glorified his Father *in his death*: for in death he not only displayed the power of the Father, who upheld him under all his trials, but reflected honour on all the perfections of the Deity; causing them all to shine forth in united and harmonious splendour, and every attribute to appear more glorious than it

---

57. Simeon, *Horae Homileticae: John XIII to Acts*, 116–17.

could possibly have done in any other way. Hence, on the near approach of this great event, the Lord Jesus said, "Now is the Son of man glorified, and God is glorified in him. If God be glorified in him, God shall also glorify him in himself, and shall straightway glorify him."][58]

Even in speaking of glorifying the Father in his death, while separating purpose from act, Simeon offers a view of the work that is revelatory: "He . . . displayed the power of the Father . . . reflected honor on all the perfection of the Deity, causing them to shine."[59]

Simeon draws from themes within the Fourth Gospel in order to develop a three-fold understanding of the nature of the work Christ completed:

> That "he had finished the work which God had given him to do"—[This was a work which none but an incarnate God could ever have affected. For, first of all, *he was to expiate the sins of a ruined world.* This was to be done by offering himself a sacrifice for sin. And though this was not *literally* fulfilled in all its extent, till he died upon the cross, yet, in mind *and intention*, it was already done; and there were but a few hours to elapse before the mighty debt would be discharged, even to the uttermost farthing: so that justice itself would have nothing further to require of those who should plead the payment made by Him, as their Surety.[60]

To "expiate the sins of a ruined world," draws from ideas manifested early in the gospel account (cf. John 1:29, 36; 6:33, 51; 10:17-18; 11:50, 51). Jesus is the lamb whose blood will make atonement for the people. The

---

58. Simeon, *Horae Homileticae: John XIII to Acts*, 116-17.

59. Earlier, yet similarly, John Calvin proposed a view that is both reflective and prophetic: "*I have glorified thee.* His reason for saying this is, that God had been made known to the world both by the doctrine of Christ, and by his miracles; and the *glory* of God is, when we know what he is. When he adds, *I have finished the work which thou gavest me to do*, he means that he has completed the whole course of his calling; for the full time was come when he ought to be received into the heavenly *glory*. Nor does he speak only of the office of teaching, but includes also the other parts of his ministry; for, though the chief part of it still remained to be accomplished, namely, the sacrifice of death, by which he was to take away the iniquities of us all, yet, as the hour of his death was already at hand, he speaks as if he had already endured it." Calvin and Pringle, *Commentary on the Gospel According to John*, 168. Both Calvin and Simeon demonstrate that reflective views on John 17:4 that are revelatory may yet also be proleptic. Some such proleptic views focus on obedience as the ultimate end, while others view Christ's obedience as penultimate to revelation.

60. Simeon, *John XIII to Acts*, 116-18.

work includes Christ's death "payment" to fulfill the just demands of the law of God (cf. Matt 5:17–18; Rom 8:3–4; 10:4; Gal 3:23–25; Eph 2:15). By his work, Christ acts as the surety guaranteeing salvation for his own (cf. Rom 6:10; Eph 1:7; Titus 2:14; Heb 7:22).

Even with these themes, he separates what is "literally fulfilled" prior to the cross from those "in mind and intention . . . already done." Specifically, Simeon distinguishes the literal (historically preceding) from the intent to do (yet future) with reference to the expiation of sins of the world. But a pattern emerges in his comments in which he recognizes the experience of a "trust in him" and the future "circumstances of trial" in fulfillment of the law of God. This pattern portrays both the kingdom of inaugurated messianic expression "not in . . . carnal ordinances" and the kingdom in final form of "righteousness, peace, and joy in the Holy Ghost." Simeon continues,

> Next, he was *perfectly to fulfil the law of God;* so that all who should trust in him might have a perfect righteousness made over to them for their justification before God. And this also he did: for, though he was in circumstances of trial which far exceeded any that ever were sustained by mortal man, he never, either in word or thought, transgressed any one command: and all, not excepting even his bitterest enemies, were constrained to acknowledge that they could find no fault in him. Further, he was to *introduce and establish a new dispensation.* And this, too, he did; fulfilling and abrogating every part of the Mosaic Law; and erecting "a kingdom, which consisted not in meats and drinks and carnal ordinances, but in righteousness and peace, and joy in the Holy Ghost."[61]

To "perfectly fulfill the law of God" references the impeccable nature of Christ (cf. John 8:46; 18:23, 38, 19:4, 6). Although John is not explicit in stating the death of Christ fulfilled the righteous requirement of the law, he dies as according to the law (19:7) as one in whom there is no fault (19:6). In contrast, to "introduce and establish a new dispensation," in terms of "fulfilling and abrogating the Mosaic Law" is an idea evident in the prologue of John: "The law came through Moses; [but] grace and truth came through Jesus Christ" (1:17). Elsewhere, John portrays Christ as Lord of the Sabbath—one who rightly interprets the Sabbath law while working on the Sabbath (5:16, 18; 7:22, 23–24; 9:14, 16).

---

61. Simeon, *John XIII to Acts*, 117–18.

Simeon, therefore, finds the "mediatorial . . . appointed work" to have been "executed" (completed) in full, concluding, "In a word, there was not any one part of his mediatorial work, so far as it could be completed at this time, that had not been accomplished: so that our Lord's appeal, in relation to it all, was just and true.]"[62] There is nothing of the mediatorial work of Christ "that had not been accomplished." Yet even in his concluding summary, Simeon carefully maintains his distinction between what is fulfilled in the past (literally) and what remains to be filled in actuality (intention), as he speaks of parts completed "so far as it could be completed at this time"—at the time of Christ's intercessory prayer. Simeon's conclusion is reflective mixed with proleptic ideas but separating proleptic intension from the proleptic act.

August Tholuck (1836)

The language Tholuck uses manifests both reflective and proleptic-anticipatory views. Jesus's work of glorifying the Father makes the offer of eternal life wide among people, such that, "To glorify the Father is to spread abroad that eternal life among men."[63] The idea carries an unwritten but intrinsic idea of Christ's proclamation of himself as the means of salvation—the way to God. This involves revelation, even though the specific referent of the revelation is "eternal life" and not the Father. However, the close connection of 17:4 to 17:3 supports the idea that eternal life and revelation of the Father are intertwined concepts, with knowledge of the Son and the Father being both the means and content of eternal life. Tholuck suggests this by saying, "For the more the archetype in which man was created is rendered conspicuous among men, the more is God himself glorified in the world." Christ, the "archetype" of man, "is rendered conspicuous among men" by the work of Christ.[64] This is the spreading abroad of eternal life of the earlier statement.

Yet it is not sufficient for Tholuck to suggest a revelatory idea as the work of Christ. Tholuck weaves in the idea of Christ's obedience within the work, along with an anticipation of completion of redemption as the means by which the Father is glorified on the earth—"among humanity."

---

62. Simeon, *John XIII to Acts*, 118.
63. Tholuck, *A Commentary on the Gospel of St. John*, 388–89.
64. Tholuck, *A Commentary on the Gospel of St. John*, 388–89.

> The fountainpoint of the archetypal life was given in the manifestation of the sinless Redeemer as man, and with the setting forth of the most perfect obedience in humanity, Rom. 5:19; Heb. 5:8. Phil. 2:8. This work the Redeemer had completed—for he anticipated the last τετέλεσται, it is finished! 19:30. God was glorified in humanity; and from this point of commencement he should be still more and more glorified forever.[65]

Tholuck, therefore, leans toward a reflective-revelatory interpretation of 17:4, but makes the verse proleptic-anticipatory in light of John 19:30.

Henry Downing (1861)

Two things are unique in Henry Downing's postulations. First, Downing sees the work of glorification as the work in view: "Christ had glorified the Father on earth by bringing 'grace and truth;' (see ch. 1:17). The glorifying of the Father by the Son is a work ever going on."[66] This work is both ongoing—"ever going on"—and static in a reflective sense in that it brought "grace and truth" (cf. 1:17). The static portion of the work is also a proleptic act in that "the offering . . . was still to come."

Second, Downing supports his proleptic understanding only by means of an appeal to Augustine's view. This is evident in Downing's larger comments on the verse: "[Christ] speaks of having *finished* the work, though the offering of Himself on the cross was still to come; since, as St. Augustine expresses it, 'He said that He had finished that which He knew most certainly He should finish.'"[67] Downing offers a reading that

---

65. Tholuck, *A Commentary on the Gospel of St. John*, 388–89.
66. Downing, *Short Notes on St. John's Gospel*, 171.
67. Downing, *Short Notes on St. John's Gospel*, 171. It is important to recognize that Downing makes a statement of what Augustine poses as a question. Again, Downing writes, "as St. Augustine expresses it, 'He said that He had finished that which He knew most certainly He should finish.'" Augustine does express a proleptic understanding but is yet posing it as a question to understand at the point at which he states the above words. His longer statement asks, "But how has He finished the work which was committed unto Him to do, when there still remains the trial of the passion wherein He especially furnished His martyrs with the example they were to follow, whereof, says the apostle Peter, Christ suffered for us, leaving us an example, that we should follow His steps: 1 Peter 2:21 but just that He says He has finished, what He knew with perfect certainty that He would finish?" (Augustine, *Gospel of John: Tractate 105*.) As I will discuss below, Augustine is asking for the means or mechanism by which Christ could make a proleptic statement.

is proleptic, but certain rather than anticipatory, and expressly Augustinian in its reasoning.

John J. Owen (1861)

Owen develops a proleptic, anticipatory view of 17:4, based on the necessity of the passion to be part of the completed work. His thoughts come in contrast to his interaction with the reflective view of Winer's Greek Grammar. Owen intimates,

> In this and the verse following, our Lord refers specifically to the three great periods of his preëxistent glory with the Father (v. 5 end); of his condition of humiliation on earth (*I have glorified thee on the earth*); and of his future exaltation at the right hand of God (*and now glorify thou me*, &c). *I have glorified—I have finished;* literally, *I glorified—I finished*, which Winer refers to our Lord's past acts, viewed as filling only one point of time past, as simply a past event.[68]

By speaking of "I have brought your glory on the earth" as "his condition of *humiliation*," Owen draws in the cross of Christ via systematic theology, yet apart from exegesis of the pericope. Specifically, "humiliation" makes reference to the Westminster Larger Catechism (1648), Question 46, and the Westminster Shorter Catechism (1648), Question 27:

Q. 46.	What was the estate of Christ's *humiliation*?
A.	The estate of Christ's *humiliation* was that low condition, wherein he for our sakes, emptying himself of his glory, took upon him the form of a servant, in his conception and birth, life, death, and after his death, until his resurrection.[69]
Q. 27.	Wherein did Christ's *humiliation* consist?

---

68. Owen, *A Commentary, Critical, Expository, and Practical, on the Gospel of John*, 410–11. The "Winer" reference is to G. B. Winer, *A Treatise on the Grammar of New Testament Greek Regarded as A Sure Basis for the New Testament Exegesis*, 345. Winer's grammar originally appeared in 1822. Winer writes, "There is no passage in which it can be certainly proved that the aorist stands for the perfect... More specious examples of this interchange would perhaps be ... Jo. Xvii. 4 ... But in all these instances the action is merely represented as having occurred, as filling a point in past time, as simply and absolutely past" (344–45).

69. The Orthodox Presbyterian Church, *Larger Catechism*. Henceforth *WLC*.

> A.   Christ's *humiliation* consisted in his being born, and that in a low condition, made under the law, undergoing the miseries of this life, the wrath of God, and the cursed death of the cross; in being buried, and continuing under the power of death for a time.[70]

The catechisms develop theological propositions of Christ's "humiliation" on the basis of collecting what Scripture teaches on Christ's incarnation and earthly life. Especially important to the systematized view of the confessions is Phil 2:6–8, which uses the terms "*humbled* himself," the verbal basis for "humiliation."

Even if the primary referent is, "He humbled himself" (Phil 2:7, KJV), rather than the confessions, Owen draws his conclusion via systematic theology rather than exegetical theology, for he imposes, "and became obedient unto death, even the death of the cross," onto, "I have brought you glory on the earth." While the incarnation of Christ is assumed by John's readers by this point in the narrative,[71] the act of the incarnation is not the focus of John 17.

Owen will say, "[Christ] takes full possession of the joy which was set before him," making a reference to Heb 12:2: "Looking unto Jesus the author and finisher of *our* faith; who for the joy that was set before him endured the cross, despising the shame, and is set down at the right hand of the throne of God."[72] For Owen, the entirety of the prayer itself is anticipatory. Owen states,

> *I glorified* in my whole past life, &c. But it is preferable to take the tense in a *proleptic* sense, inasmuch as *our Lord could not say that he had finished his work*, until after his suffering and death on the cross. This whole prayer is anticipatory of his heavenly mediation. Wrapt in divine ecstasy, he takes full possession of the joy which was set before him, and speaks of his work as already finished. This manifests his unshaken purpose to undergo the bodily and mental sufferings, which in the garden and upon the cross awaited him.

---

70. The Orthodox Presbyterian Church, *Shorter Catechism*. Henceforth *WSC*. I suggest that Owen evidences use of the catechism is his language below when he speaks of "the death of the cross," although he will earlier speak of "death on the cross." Previous Christian creeds, catechisms, and confessions do not use the specific language of "humiliation."

71. E.g., John 1:14; 3:13, 17; 6:33, 38, 42, 50, 51, 62; 10:10, 36.

72. *The Holy Bible: Authorized King James Version*.

Owen is doing Biblical Theology. He is seeing John 17:4 as part of a larger theology of verses related to Christ's anticipation of the work of atonement on the cross, but without justification within John 17. However, the appeal to Heb 12:2 does not clarify John's use of "I have brought you glory on the earth," as Owen assumes. By superimposing Heb 12:2 on John 17:4, Owen overlays the sufferings of Christ onto 17:4.

Owen bases his proleptic view on two additional assumptions. The first is that the whole of John 17, as a genre, "anticipates"—that is, that *prolepsis* characterizes this chapter.

> The reference then in *I have glorified thee*, is not *only* to the days of his ministry, which were now ended, but to his obedience to the death of the cross, which in the proleptic style of this prayer is regarded as already past, although in reality yet to be undergone. This reference both to his ministerial life and his passion, is repeated in the next clause *I have finished;* (literally, *finished, brought to a full close*) *the work*, which serves also to explain in what sense he had glorified God on earth. The word *work*, is here employed generically for the whole work of his ministry, including, as has been remarked, also his death on the cross, and its attendant sufferings. *Which thou gavest me to do.*

In order to establish the entirety of the prayer of John 17 as stylistically "proleptic," Owen overlays an extrinsic idea on the passage. The passage is at best *prophetic*, for there are requests for things spoken by Christ which the Father must fulfill. Yet they are *requests*, or petitions, which by their nature await for God to fulfill them in the unspecified future—unspecified with respect to the human requestor, although known from eternity by God the time and means that he will fulfill the request. The requests do not take on an additional sense of lacking fulfillment, for they are not predictions; they are supplications, which are not looking for the completion of words of promise, but the answering of words of dependency.

Jesus awaits personal glorification in the resurrection, ascension, and return to the presence of the Father in heaven (John 17:1–5). In the Johannine narrative, mysteriously and powerfully, the Father will raise Christ from the dead even as Christ takes up his life from the dead (John 2:19; 5:21; 10:17, 18; 11:25; 12:28). Many passages in the NT affirm the working of the Father and Spirit to raise Christ from the dead.[73]

---

73. Acts 2:24, 32; 3:15, 26; 4:10; 5:30; 10:40; 13:30, 33, 34, 37; Rom 1:4; 4:24; 6:4; 8:11; 10:9; 1 Cor 6:14; Gal 1:1; Col 2:12.

Jesus, too, requests the Father to keep and sanctify the present disciples while they continue in the present world (John 17:11–19). Jesus is not anticipating but asking for the Father to do a work which he is free to complete or not.[74]

Similarly, Jesus states a desire for the second generation of disciples and the following generations (John 17:20–26); in 17:24, θέλω expresses a wish.[75] A wish does not anticipate the glorification of the believer in Christ's presence. Later, Paul will speak of believers' glorification in a proleptic sense (Rom 8:30).

Second, depicting Jesus as "wrapped in ecstasy" draws in concepts related to the work of seers and prophets in the scriptures (Num 24:1–2; 1 Sam 19:20, 23; 2 Chron 15:1; 20:14, 20; Acts 7:55; Rev 1:10). Jesus speaks as a seer.

The lack of a reference to the working of the Spirit within the prophet—as the indicator of ecstatic vision in John 17:1—does not seem to factor into Owen's reasoning. The writer of the Fourth Gospel frames the mediation of John 17 as simple prayer in which Christ is looking toward heaven with his words rather than capturing a vision from heaven. Therefore, there is no need for Owen to conclude that a unique working of the Spirit provides an ecstatic utterance by which Jesus is justified in speaking with proleptic intent. In the Gospels, the one possible ecstatic

---

74. By indicating the freedom of the Father to respond to Jesus's request with affirmation or inactivity, I am speaking of the nature of God with respect to prayer in general: *prayer does not force the hand of God to act even though one is fully assured of the goodness, power, and knowledge of God to act*. In the prayer of Jesus, because Jesus always is doing the Father's will, the prayer only would be in accordance with the will of the Father—the very working of the Father's words in Christ (John 5:19, 30; 6:36; 8:28; 12:49, 50; 14:30; cf. Heb 10:7, 9, 10). Therefore, although God is free, it is certain that he will answer the prayer of Jesus, for Jesus is asking the Father to do what the Father wills to do. However, this still remains different from the fulfillment of prophetic words from God, for words of prophesy are promissory, and the Lord is binding himself to act. There is not freedom of God to refrain from fulfilling what he has promised (cf. Num 23:19; 1 Sam 15:29; Titus 1:2; Heb 6:17, 18). God exercised his freedom in the giving of the promise.

75. The *TDNT* entry over-expresses the intent of in 17:24: "John testifies with solemn emphasis that this almighty θέλειν of the Son expresses itself with reference to the disciples as a declaration of His will in prayer which irresistibly makes His own participants in His glory (17:24)" (Gottlob Schrenk, "Θέλω, Θέλημα, Θέλησις," in *TDNT*, 3:48). The present, active, indicative use of θέλω expresses what one *wishes*, as in John 21:18: "another . . . will carry you where you do not *wish*." It is not the determinant will that Peter's persecutor overrides, but the desire for something other than death on a cross. This seems to be the intent of θέλω followed by ἵνα, as in Matt 7:12; Mark 6:25; 9:30; 10:35; Luke 6:31 (BDAG, 447).

expression of Jesus in Luke 10:21 occurs long before the events of Luke's Passion Week narrative.

Yet overlooking the absence of ecstatic vision in 17:4, Owen then concludes that the "work" is self-evident within his argument. He continues, "In the very midst of utterances which he could only make, as the coequal with the Father and possessed of supreme divinity, our Lord makes constant reference also to his official subordination, as one sent of the Father (vs. 3, 8, 18, 21, 23, 25), and as having a definite service given him to execute."[76]

Building upon the idea of anticipation-genre and ecstatic-intercession, Owen then assumes the nature of the "work" as proleptic. Before giving discussion to the work itself, three times he makes the assessment of proleptic: (1) "Our Lord could not say that he had finished his work, until after his suffering and death on the cross," (2) "speaks of his work as already finished," and (3) "the reference then in *I have glorified thee*, is . . . to his obedience to the death of the cross, which in the proleptic style of this prayer is regarded as already past, although in reality yet to be undergone." Therefore, when Owen concludes, "The word *work*, is here employed generically for the whole work of his ministry, including, as has been remarked, also his death on the cross, and its attendant sufferings," he is begging the question, as do other commenters on this verse. He identifies the passage as reflective but adds a proleptic reading without any textual basis.

E. W. Hengstenberg (1865)

Although brief in its commentary, Hengstenberg's view is unique, seeing in John 17:4 a proleptic expression, but recognizing an actual lack of completion until 19:30. For Hengstenberg writes, "When the Lord says, 'I have finished the work,' He anticipates what still remained of it, which was to be accomplished in the next approaching hours. It was not really fulfilled until the Lord could say, 'It is finished.'"[77] Hengstenberg indicates that the writer of the Fourth Gospel portrays Jesus as anticipating the work ahead, but in no sense is the work completed. The work is not completed until later, removing a real sense of completion from view.

---

76. Owen, *Gospel of John*, 410–11.
77. Hengstenberg, *Commentary on the Gospel of St John*, 315.

Robert Govett (1881)

Govett promotes both reflective and proleptic interpretations based on theological ideas he associates with specific parts of the prayer. He frontloads "the work of redemption" onto the exposition. As a result, his analysis will yield a proleptic idea with certainty rather than anticipation. The proleptic idea is mixed with reflective "doctrine" and "acts," based on narrowing "glory" to "glory in redemption." Govett notes,

> The first sentiment was—'Glorify Thy Son, that *I may* glorify Thee, O Father!' This is—'Glorify me, for *I have* glorified Thee.' God is glorified by creation; how much more by the work of redemption, wrought at such charges to Himself, and to His Son! *How* had Jesus glorified Him? (1) By *doctrine*—by His declaring the new name of the Father. (2) By *acts*—His life of benevolence and humiliation, and His miracles of mercy.[78]

Govett's idea of "the work" is reflective with respect to both Christ's revelation of the Father and Christ's obedience. "I have glorified Thee on the earth; the work which Thou gavest me to do, I have fulfilled," Govett reinterprets.

In Govett's logic, Jesus's obedience on earth within the plan of redemption demands glorification:

> There was a work of obedience and death, to be done on earth by the Mediator, as Son of God and Son of Man; necessary to the Father's glory in redemption, and to man's salvation. *That* the Saviour presents to the Father, as now accomplished; it being certain, at this latter stage, that He would not draw back from the completion of it in His sufferings unto death. Must not the Father, then, in requital for obedience so glorious, exalt Him, as never one before?[79]

Because Christ's perfect obedience and atoning death are necessary to both glorify the Father and provide eternal salvation for man, Christ will complete the work with certainty. Govett assumes the work is one of redemption rather than revelation, as do many of his predecessors and contemporaries. Once he establishes this assumption, then completion of the work is certain, as is post-cross glorification. In the mind of Govett, the request for glory comes in response to the sure fulfillment of the work

---

78. Govett, *Exposition of the Gospel of St. John*, 283.
79. Govett, *Exposition of the Gospel of St. John*, 283.

of redemption. As he later writes, "Jesus here says—'What was necessary to be done by Me as man on earth, and what could be done here below, I have effected.'"[80] His conclusions are proleptic-anticipatory, nuanced with the glorification of the Father leading the idea.

Alvah Hovey (1881)

At the outset of his comments, Hovey assumes a proleptic understanding of 17:4. However, it soon becomes clear that while his view is anticipatory of the cross, it is also mixed with reflective ideas:

> Jesus places himself, in thought, at the end of his earthly ministry, including his voluntary sacrificial death, and looks back upon it as a completed service. In and by it he has already revealed the character of the Father, thus glorifying him in the only possible way. Looking at his work on earth as virtually accomplished, he perceives in it no defect, as the next clause expressly affirms.[81]

Hovey perceives of a virtual accomplishment that denotes a certain fulfillment of the work of redemption on the cross. This virtual accomplishment does not exclude reflective ideas from 17:4. The earthly ministry also reveals the character of the Father. However, as the earthly ministry includes the passion of Christ, one should not think Hovey's revelatory view is a reference to the works in John 1–16 only.

Significantly, Hovey will make text-critical remarks with specific reference to the aorist of "having accomplished."

> *I have finished the work*, etc. Here, too, the form of the Revised Version is more exact, viz.: *having accomplished the work which thou hast given me to do*. The participle *having accomplished*, etc. (Substituting the aorist participle for the personal verb, with Lach., Tisch., Treg., West. & Hort, Anglo-Am. Revisers, after ℵ A B C L Π, 1, 33, etc.), states the way in which he had glorified the Father—*i. e.*, by completing the work committed to him. *Having accomplished* expresses more precisely the force of the Greek term than *having finished*, for the term (τελειώσας) means to make perfect, complete, to bring to a true end, rather than

---

80. Govett, *Exposition of the Gospel of St. John*, 283.
81. Hovey, *Commentary on the Gospel of John*, 337.

simply to finish, to bring to an end. (Comp. 4:34; 5:36; 17:23; 1 John 2:5; 4:12, 17; Heb. 2:10; 5:9; 7:28.)[82]

Hovey argues that the English translation in the Revised Version (1885) "having accomplished," which has the perfective sense, is more precise in expressing the force of the Greek aorist participle than the KJV's "having finished." While this is not his point, inherent in his argument is the precision of the force: it is a perfective, completed sense, as Hovey says, "to make perfect, complete, to bring to a *true* end, rather than simply to finish, to bring to an end."

For support Hovey appeals to Weiss, who depicts a proleptically speaking Jesus, seeing the accomplishment in his earthly ministry without preventing him from looking to future accomplishment on the cross. Hovey observes,

> Weiss remarks: "*Having accomplished*; because Jesus stands at the goal of his earthly course; he has accomplished his life-work, in so far as it could be accomplished in the calling of his earthly life, but this does not prevent its being still further accomplished in his death, though we must not here include that further accomplishment."[83]

Hovey quotes Weiss, who, speaking against a proleptic reading that includes Christ's work on the cross, indicates "we must not include that further accomplishment." Instead, the accomplished work refers to things accomplished in Jesus's public and private ministries prior to John 17.[84]

Hovey finds the exegesis limiting the text to a reflective view. But he still proposes a proleptic view without any stated reasoning.[85]

---

82. Hovey, *Commentary on the Gospel of John*, 337.

83. Hovey, *Commentary on the Gospel of John*, 337.

84. "The expression used by Jesus might, very naturally, refer to his work in preaching the gospel of the kingdom, in gaining disciples from the people, and in training a select company of these by special instruction to carry forward his work after his return to glory" (Hovey, *Commentary on the Gospel of John*, 337).

85. The most Hovey adds is, "But the analogy of certain passages already considered, leads rather to the view stated above, that he anticipates the moment of his death, and looks back upon his work as brought to a perfect end by that propitiatory sacrifice" (Hovey, *Commentary on the Gospel of John*, 337).

Thomas Whitelaw (1888)

Whitelaw recognizes the work to be "a retrospect," that is, reflective. Tying in 17:6, the work has *specific* identification as "the manifestation of the Father's name."

> *I glorified Thee upon the earth.* A retrospect upon His world-historical life (now approaching its termination) which in its essential character had been a glorification of the Father. *Having accomplished the work which Thou hast given Me to do.* That work, specified (ver. 6) as the manifestation of the Father's name, must not be restricted *to the promulgation of gospel truth, or the exemplification in actual life of the Father's character, but interpreted as embracing the sacrificial death upon the cross, its culminating act.*[86]

Without reason, Whitelaw speaks against a view that is exclusively reflective even though he denotes the accomplished work as "specified." Both Christ's preaching of the gospel and the revelation of the Person of the Father (e.g., "character") are too restrictive to explain "that work, specified." Apparently, they are legitimate, viable options for "the work," singularly—either the preaching of the gospel or the modeling of the Father is "the work"—or collectively, in which the preaching combined with the modeling comprise the one work.

Instead, Whitelaw goes beyond what is specific to an addition. Important in his method of reasoning is his explicit use of "interpreted." One must wonder what theory of reading allows for a term that is narrow and exclusive in one sense to be read as a broader and encompassing term in another sense in the same use and context. With that very hermeneutic, Whitelaw concludes that Christ's atoning work on the cross is "the culminating act" of the work; this is the "embracing" of Christ's sacrifice as the telic work of "the manifestation of the Father's name." Whitelaw sees the supreme act of the gospel within his reflective view, not simply the proclamation of the supreme act. His view of 17:4 is reflective and revelatory, but also proleptic-revelatory.

---

86. Whitelaw, *The Gospel of St. John*, 351.

William Kelly (1898)

In a comparison of John 13:31–32 to John 17:1–5, Kelly juxtaposes Christ's glorifying of "God," the judge of all sin, against Christ's glorifying of "His Father." The earlier context of glorification concerns the eschatological wrath of God, the "unsparing judgment . . . that final dealing."[87] Kelly indicates, "The language here is more of sustained relationship than in chapter 13:31, 32, where it is a question of glorifying *God*, before Whom sin comes into unsparing judgment. Here it is glorifying His Father, and so there is no special contemplation of that final dealing where all that God is and feels came out against evil imputatively laid on the head of the Son of man."[88]

For Kelly, John 17:1–5, the words of Christ reflect the earthly ministry of Christ:

> *Here the entire path of Christ on earth in giving Himself up to obey and please His Father is summed up.* Therefore it was the more needful to specify its completion, "having finished the work which thou hast given me to do." *He speaks not more as the faithful servant than as the conscious Son of God Who sees all completed to the Father's glory*, Who had given Him the work that He should do it Who alone could.[89]

The summing up of "the entire path" envelops the full ministry of John 1:19–16:33, enfolding the words and works of Christ, all proclamation and signs, both public and private. Although Kelly's view of the completion of the work is not necessarily *revelatory*, it is *reflective*. Nevertheless, because it concerns that which is "on earth," proleptic strands of thought are within the scope of the completed work, even though they are not the emphasis of the thought.

Kelly's view rests on separating two functions and intra-relationships within the Godhead. First, as mentioned above, Kelly proposes that Christ purposes to bring glory to God the Judge (John 13:31–32) separately from his purpose to bring glory to God as his Father (17:1–5). Initially, this allows him to keep acts of atonement and/or propitiation—any acts of "evil *imputatively* laid on the head of the Son of Man"—from annexing themselves to the completed work in 17:4. He excludes, at least temporarily, a

---

87. Kelly, *An Exposition of the Gospel of John*, 351.
88. Kelly, *An Exposition of the Gospel of John*, 351.
89. Kelly, *An Exposition of the Gospel of John*, 351.

developed proleptic reading by making a distinction in the functions of God the Father as final "Judge," and God the Father as "Father."[90]

Second, Kelly proposes a distinction in Christ's role as the Servant and his role as the Son of God.[91] The Son intends to "obey and please His Father." The son speaks not as a servant [sent?], but as the Divine Son who alone could do all things commissioned to him by his Father. In this "alone" sense, the completed work appears to be a reference to Christ's work on the cross.

Kelly's position dichotomizes and oversimplifies the unity within Christ's person and works. In the Fourth Gospel, the Son intends to honor the Father as the judge who has given the stewardship of judgment to the Son (John 5:22-24, 27; 9:39). As a Son of "the Father" (13:1, 3), he serves the disciples. As a Son, Jesus serves Mary, Martha, and Lazarus (11:27), and as Son he serves by dying on the cross as a substitute (19:7). The Gospel of John does not present Jesus with disparate wills, or the Father with separated functions. Kelly's view divides the will of Christ and the functioning of God the Father unnecessarily in order to interject proleptic ideas into otherwise reflective conclusions.

B. F. Westcott (1896)

Westcott speaks of the completed work in perfective terms. The work is the "historical mission" with reference to the time of Christ's prayers, and it sits as "ended" with respect to its charge. He writes, "The historical mission of Christ is now regarded as ended; the earthly work is accomplished. By a life of absolute obedience and love Christ had revealed—and therefore glorified—the Father."[92] Without referencing directly John

90. "Father," when speaking of the Trinity and the triune relationships within the Godhead, can refer to the *position* of the first person of the Trinity in contrast to the positions of "the Son" and "the Spirit," (e.g., "the Father," 5:21, 22; 14:8 [2x], 10, 11 [2x]), or the *familial relationship* of the first person of the Trinity with the Son (e.g., "my Father," 2:16; 5:17, cf. 5:18; 14:2, 7).

91. Kelly speaks of Christ as "the faithful servant," rather than as a servant in general. This seems to speak of Christ in his role as the Isaianic Servant, or at least of a special "Servant" ministry within the Fourth Gospel. For earlier, speaking of Christ, Kelly says, "To the Father He turns as ever . . . always the Sent One and Servant in divine love" (Kelly, *An Exposition of the Gospel of John*, 348). Also, later he will say of an aspect of Christ's sufferings, "It was the positive side of what the Lord undertook with His own here below . . . as the righteous One, the Servant and Man, and as such Son of God" (352-53).

92. Westcott. *The Gospel According to St. John*, 240.

4:34, Westcott draws an obedience concept from that verse into his interpretation of 17:4. He also grabs the Fourth Gospel's thematic idea of the love of Christ and infuses it into his understanding of 17:4.[93] Fully obediently and completely lovingly, Christ revealed the Father. This, for Westcott, is the means by which Christ glorified the Father in ending the work that intended to bring glory to the Father. This work is "accomplished" as a historical assignment.

Later Westcott will propose a proleptic reading with little commentary, noting, "Here the work is contemplated in its unity, as accomplished, and there in its manifold parts, as still to be done."[94] The untied "work," being of "manifold parts," may be contemplated as something yet future. Westcott does not explain how the singular work, accomplished, divides itself such that an aspect of it remains unfulfilled. One only sees that he adds a proleptic understanding to the reflective words through some unknown means of dividing what appears to be of many folds.

TWENTIETH AND TWENTY-FIRST CENTURIES

The commentaries written within the twentieth and twenty-first centuries provide little deviation from the majority proleptic views of the past. For the most part, neither do they contribute to strong exegetical bases for their proleptic views, with Carson being a notable exception. Of the Johannine commentary writers for this period, I will include Eckman (1908), Spence-Jones (1909), Dodd (1953), Lenski (1961), Tasker (1960), Godet (1969), Morris (1971, 1995), Lindars (1972), Carson (1991), Ridderbos (1997), Whitacre (1999), and Köstenberger (various dates).[95]

As evident in the exploration of writers within the prior centuries, some notable writers and works will not appear because they add little to nothing to advance a discussion of proleptic and reflective thoughts on John 17:4, or they have no comment at all.[96] However, I will interact briefly with the views of Bultmann and Beasley-Murray within the footnotes.

---

93. On the love of Christ in John, see 11:3, 36; 13:1, 34; 14:21; 15:9, 10, 12, 13; 17:26; 19:26; 20:2; 21:7, 20.

94. Westcott, *St. John*, 240.

95. Dodd did not produce a commentary on John. However, I will consider his contribution because of his seminal works on the interpretation of the Gospel of John, *Historical Tradition in the Fourth Gospel*, and *The Interpretation of the Fourth Gospel*.

96. Among the most recent modern commentaries not considered is Moloney, *The Gospel of John*, although he comes to a reflective view, for his comments are very brief:

George P. Eckman (1908)

Eckman manifests clearly a proleptic interpretation in which Christ "anticipates" the atoning work yet to come in John 19. Yet both the mission and "task" of Christ's earthly ministry also are reflective, for Jesus glorifies the Father by making God the Father "intelligible." Eckman makes reference to the finished work of Christ in John 19:30 but does not demonstrate that anything other than a lexical connection exists. Making no comment on the uniqueness of the fulfillment of the completion concept in 19:30, Eckman intends for the reader to make a comparison between 17:4 and 19:30. Eckman comments, "Having anticipated the completion of His work, the Son asks for that glorification which evidences the

---

"The revelation of God in and through the words and action of Jesus is complete (v. 5b), and thus Jesus can ask the Father to glorify him (*nun doxason me*)" (461). Also Michaels takes a revelatory view in brief comments, without an exegetical argument: "What exactly was 'the work' he was given to do, and that he has in fact 'completed' it? At this point in the narrative, it cannot be the work of dying on the cross . . . Rather it is the work of revealing the Father's name (that is, the Father himself) in the world (*The Gospel of John*, 862). So too Klink draws what seem to be perfective conclusions—"just as the Son completed perfectly what the Father asked of him." But the comments are so brief and unspecified that when he also says, "the Son left the glory of God to complete his mission 'on the earth' and then will depart and return to his Father the glory of God," it is indeterminate whether the conclusions are reflective or proleptic. See Klink, *John*, 714–15). Keener notes that Minear views the hour of glorification "both proleptically and retrospectively," saying further only, "in the cross, [Jesus] finished the work the Father called him to do (cf. 4:34; 19:30), though his followers still need to be 'completed' or perfected in unity (17:23)." Keener, *The Gospel of John: A Commentary*, 2: 1050, 1055. The Minear reference is to Minear, "The Audience of the Fourth Evangelist," 343. Barrett does reason exegetically, but his comments are extremely brief, unspecified, and speculative: "The Son will glorify the Father by giving life to men; here the meaning of glorification is brought out by the next clause—τὸ ἔργον τελειώσας. The participle should be translated 'by finishing the work . . . '. The Son glorifies the Father by his complete obedience and faithful fulfillment of his task. τελειώσας looks back upon the completed life of Jesus, and probably upon his death too (cf. 19:30 τετέλεσται)." Barrett, *The Gospel According to St. John*, 420. Even briefer are the revelatory and proleptic comments of Beutler that come without explanation: "He has finished his work. It is this moment Jesus is anticipating in his prayer." Beutler, *A Commentary of the Gospel of John*, 431. Kruse has a simple revelatory view that "[culminates] in giving himself on the cross," but is *indeterminate* with respect to being proleptic or reflexive, for Kruse conflates references to "the work" with "works" when referring to "the work God gave him to do (cf. 4:34; 5:36; 9:3–4)." Kruse, *John*, 395. Beasley-Murray rightly asks, "Is this final 'work' included in the τελειώσας, 'the accomplishing of v 4?" While exploring the views of others, he never posits a conclusion. Instead, he gives his attention to the circumstances of the writing of the prayer from the post-Pentecostal period and of Jesus's speaking of the prayer "in the hour" (Beasley-Murray, *John*, 297). Thus Beasley-Murray's comments also do not contribute to the current analysis.

fulfillment of His mission (4, 5). He has finished the task assigned to His earthly career (compare 19:30), and has thus glorified, or made intelligible, the Father who sent Him."[97]

Eckman will equate Christ's glorification of the Father with eternal life. This is the meaning of "eternal life" in John 17:3. Eckman, explains:

> The definition of eternal life (3) is here given. It ignores time relations, expresses its qualitative character, and shows that it is attainable in this present world. (3:36; 5:24.) Eternal life so described does not consist in a complete but a growing knowledge of the true God, in contrast with the superstitious veneration of the heathen for fictitious gods. (1 Cor. 8:5-6.) But this knowledge involves also the recognition of Jesus as the Christ whom the Father has sent. This aspect of the truth was particularly necessary for the Jews as well as for the Gentiles. (1:18; 14:6.)[98]

In Eckman's Fourth Gospel missiology, the heathen come out of their superstitious religions unto eternal life as they are introduced to "a growing knowledge of the true God" instead of worship of false gods. The summation of "intelligible" is knowledge that "involves also the recognition of Jesus as the Christ."

Eckman's position is revelatory, in one sense, in spite of the anticipatory element that is tied to the glorification Jesus seeks. Eckman further writes,

> No one can know the Father without the Son, nor have eternal life apart from Him whom God sent to reveal and bestow it. This definition of eternal life illustrates the fact that this prayer was intended in large part for the instruction of those who heard it. Their conception of eternal life would be corrected by these wonderful words . . . The distinct personality of the Son, His pre-existence in the form of God (Phil. 2:6), His restoration in His perfected humanity (Heb. 2:9-11) to the heavenly glory He had formerly experienced, are all expressed in these two verses.[99]

Therefore, his anticipatory view is assumed without argument. He seems to hold to more of a revelatory and reflective view, for the means by which Christ "glorified" the Father in the past is to make him "intelligible."

---

97. Eckman, *Studies in the Gospel of John*, 183.
98. Eckman, *Studies in the Gospel of John*, 182-83.
99. Eckman, *Studies in the Gospel of John*, 182-83.

H. D. M. Spence-Jones (1909)

In one of the earliest twentieth century commentaries on John, Spence-Jones leans toward a reflective view of John 17:4. He understands the verse to be a reference to the whole earthly ministry of Christ as a revelatory work, writing,

> [Jesus] continues the prayer which he is offering for himself: *I glorified thee on the earth, having finished the work which thou hast given me to do* . . . Many expositors urge a proleptical or anticipatory assertion of the completion of his earthly work, as though the Passion were already over, and he were now uttering the *consummatum est* of the cross. *This is, however, included in the next clause.* The night has come when the earthly ministry is at an end. The Jesus Christ, whom the Father has sent, has completed his task. The whole work of the earthly manifestation of the Word was at an end. Suffering remains, the issues of the conflict with evil have to be encountered; but the die is cast—the thing is done. The godly life, as well as *the atoning death, are correlative parts* of the merits and work of Christ, and have glorified the Father.[100]

Differently than others, Spence-Jones appears cautious about viewing the object of, "I have completed" in 17:4 as the subject of the "It is finished" statement which Jesus cries on the cross in 19:30. Rather than being anticipatory, the writer of John includes the "consummatum est" in the "and now, Father, glorify me in your presence" of 17:5, e.g., "the next clause." In contrast, 17:4, being part of the Passover night events, brings to a close Christ's earthly ministry.[101]

Also differently, Spence-Jones limits the revelatory aspect to the person of the Word, without reference to the Father. The glorifying work is for Christ to reveal himself. So while reflective in nature, these comments do not suggest that "the work" in view concerns the revelation of the Father.

---

100. Spence-Jones, ed., *St. John*, 343. Correctly, *Spence-Jones* is the final editor of the multi-authored commentary on the Fourth Gospel bearing Spence-Jones' name. The final work gives no indication of what each author contributed to the commentary. Also, the commentary is sometimes identified as a work edited by "Spence" rather than "Spence-Jones." In 1904, Spence took up as his surname his wife's maiden name, "Jones." Various literature refers to him by either surname.

101. In keeping with the storyline of John, Spence-Jones' comments seem best to be understood as a reference to the public and private ministries of Christ, and the passion or John's epilogue.

C. H. Dodd (1953)

Dodd proposes a mixed proleptic-reflective reading of 17:4. Reasoning from John 4:35, in one sense Christ will "[bring] His work to completion—ἵνα ... τελειώσω αὐτοῦ τὸ ἔργον. That the word τελειόω is intended to carry full weight is shown by its recurrence in xvii. 4 . . ."[102] Dodd further indicates, "[Jesus'] mission is, not only to teach or to 'announce,' but to complete the work of man's salvation . . . in a word, to open to mankind a truly spiritual or divine life."[103] With the words, τὸ ἔργον τελειώσας, Christ "reports his full discharge" of his commission, as recited in 17:1–5.[104] This completed discharge would be proleptic, placing the completion of the work of the cross within the words of 17:4.

Later, commenting on the use of Τετέλεσται at the death of Jesus in John 19:30, Dodd discusses the difference between τελέω (19:30) and τελειόω (17:4):

> In recording the death of Jesus, the evangelist gives as his last word the pregnant Τετέλεσται. The verb τελεῖν sometimes has the meaning 'bring to an end;' but its dominant meaning in all periods of Greek is 'fulfill,' 'accomplish,' 'perform,' 'bring to completion.' It thus approximates in meaning to τελειοῦν, and I have suggested that it is intended to echo xvii. 4, which uses the latter verb of the 'completion' of Christ's earthly task. But τελεῖν has a special sense which may have dictated its use here. It is used of the due performance of religious rites, such as sacrifices or initiations . . . So here his death is declared to be the completion of the sacrifice, regarded as the means of man's regeneration, or initiation into eternal life. In xvii. 4, τελειοῦν is used of the completion of Christ's task, which is defined as the disclosure of the 'name' of God (6) and the deliverance of his ῥήματα (7) to men (which, as we know, are the vehicle of πνεῦμα and the media of eternal life [iii. 34, vi. 64, 68]).[105]

According to Dodd, therefore, the distinction between τελέω and τελειόω is that the former has a unique sense of "completion of the [cultic] sacrifice" in 19:30, and the latter concerns the "completion of Christ's task . . . disclosure of the name of God." While the completed work also involves

---

102. Dodd, *Interpretation*, 316.
103. Dodd, *Interpretation*, 316.
104. Dodd, *Interpretation*, 417.
105. Dodd, *Interpretation*, 437. For similar comments, see Dodd, *Historical Tradition*, 124.

the proclamation of his word, the work is not the work of salvation itself, but only the vehicle and medium for gaining eternal life. This distinction is important, for it proposes that "the work" in 17:4 is a means to a greater end; the disclosure of the name of God is a vehicle for the giving of the Spirit and life, but is not equated with such things.

Nevertheless, like many other scholars, Dodd creates a means of investing 17:4 with a proleptic idea by following the Johannine usage of τελειόω (τελειοῦν) in 4:34 and 5:36, and relating these verses to the sum total of the mission of Christ in the incarnation. Yet his proleptic terms about the accomplishment of Christ read in accord with reflective and revelatory ideas rather than a predominantly or purely proleptic idea:

> We may recall some earlier passages which use the same verb of Christ. In iv. 34 we learn that his βρῶμά (that by which he lives on earth) is ἵνα ποιήσω τὸ θέλημα τοῦ πέμψαντός με καὶ τελειώσω τὸ ἔργον αὐτοῦ. Again in v. 36, among the primary evidences of Christ's plenary commission are τὰ ἔργα ἃ δέδωκέν μοι ὁ πατὴρ ἵνα τελειώσω αὐτά, αὐτὰ τὰ ἔργα ἃ ποιῶ. Thus it appears that the very existence of the incarnate Word on earth is bound up with the accomplishment (τελείωσις) of the work of man's salvation according to the will of God. In the prayer of ch. xvii the work is declared to be completed (τελειοῦν)—on the plane of pure spiritual activity, that is, since Christ then and there offers himself in sacrifice; but it is completed (τελεῖν) as a concrete act on the plane of history only when the sacrifice is consummated in his death.[106]

The "accomplishment of the work of man's salvation," to which Dodd refers in 19:30, already is completed in 17:4. However, Dodd's sacrificial reading of τελειώσας allows him to label "the work" as a spiritual act in 17:4. This, though accomplished, is different from the final "concrete act on the plane of history" in 19:30. Dodd distinguishes the spiritual offering (17:4) from the "concrete" and the "plane of history." This suggests that, for Dodd, the work in 17:4—if the offertory, atoning work that is inclusive of the entirety of the earthly ministry is ethereal at the time

---

106. Dodd, *Interpretation*, 437–38. The 1963 edition prints 4:34 as ἵνα ποιήσω τὸ θέλημα τοῦ πέμψαντός με καὶ τελειώσω τὸ ἔργον αὐτοῦ, although the Greek text reads ἵνα ποιήσω τὸ θέλημα τοῦ πέμψαντός με καὶ τελειώσω αὐτοῦ τὸ ἔργον. Similarly, the 1963 edition prints 5:36 as τὰ ἔργα ἃ δέδωκέν μοι ὁ πατὴρ ἵνα τελειώσω αὐτά, αὐτὰ τὰ ἔργα ἃ ποιῶ, although the Greek reads τὰ γὰρ ἔργα ἃ δέδωκέν μοι ὁ πατὴρ ἵνα τελειώσω αὐτά, αὐτὰ τὰ ἔργα ἃ ποιῶ. There are no variant readings that agree with Dodd on either verse.

Christ speaks 17:4—does not rest on the plane of history, but on a plane not yet chronologically existing.

This does not imply that Dodd proposes a reflective or revelatory reading on John 17:4. Yet it does recognize that Dodd concludes that two very dissimilar types of "work" are in view in 17:4 and 19:30. Therefore, while Dodd proposes a mixed proleptic-reflective view, infusing the intercessory prayer of John 17 with the idea of religious sacrifice, he produces a reading that is not proleptic in any true sense. But it continues to open the possibility that one should not equate "the work" in 4:34, 5:36, and 17:4 with "the work" in 19:30, and that the distinction between τελειόω and τελέω intends to indicate this idea.[107]

R. C. H. Lenski (1961)

Lenski equates "glorified his Father" with the revelatory work of Christ and with the atonement. In his interpretation, the aorist of "completed" sufficiently states the fact of the revelation in the past and of the "plan and work of salvation" that is yet future. Lenski proposes, "Jesus glorified his Father on earth, revealing the Father with his divine attributes and with his blessed plan and work of salvation for men to see and to worship with adoration. The aorist states the great fact. This, Jesus says, he did by bringing to an end by completing the work the Father gave him to do."[108] This is a different understanding than that of other writers who see the aorist as perfective and thus reflective but wish to include a proleptic understanding in spite of perfective conclusions. Lenski sees fluidity, lexical ambiguity, or equivocalness in the aorist in a way that is not known for a singular term.

---

107. In clarification of and fairness toward the above comments on Dodd's thought, Dodd most certainly places great emphasis on the proleptic aspects of his interpretation of 17:4 (with 4:34 and 19:30). Elsewhere he writes, "Christ glorifies the Father by completing his work (xvii. 4), and the work is completed in his passion and death (xix. 30), for the ἐντολή of the Father, which the Son obeys, is to lay down his life (x. 17–18). This is the θέλημα of the Father which the Son seeks (v. 30), which he came to do (vi. 38), and which, while he is on earth, is his βρῶμά (iv. 34). It is thus that the sacrificial death of Christ (his self-dedication, xvii. 19), is his glory, because in it (his full acceptance of the Father's θέλημα) the Father is glorified. Thus, in the context of Johannine thought, there is no substantial difference between θέλημά [μου ἀλλά] τὸ σὸν γινέσθω [Luke 22:42] and δόξασόν σου τὸ ὄνομα [John 12:28]" (Dodd, *Historical Tradition*, 69n2).

108. Lenski, *Interpretation*, 1123–24. But Jesus is not now laying down his life. He is praying prior to the arrest. Lenski's view forces the atonement upon "work" to make it factual rather than anticipatory.

Lenski supports his view by identifying "the work" as "the mission of Jesus on earth." This allows him to expand the work into two parts—the benefit of redemption to people and the purpose of God to receive glory. Lenski further proposes,

> This "work" is the mission of Jesus on earth. While it is entirely for the benefit of men, namely for their redemption, it involved a higher purpose, the glorification of God. The world shines with the radiance of him who sent his Son to redeem us and to draw us to himself. Jesus says that he has brought this work to its completion. Its crowning point is his atoning death.[109]

As the "world shines with the radiance" of God through Christ, God receives glory. Thus, it seems that Lenski reasons that as the mission's two-fold work is redemptive and revelatory, the aorist of "completion" also is redemptive and revelatory. Jesus brings to completion the revelatory aspect, while the "crowning point" is in the future.

Lenski's understanding of the aorist of "completed" and of the mission of Jesus creates a situation in which he must justify seeing the future work as something accomplished:

> He can speak of this as being already a fact, for at this very moment he is laying down his life in compliance with his Father's behest (10:18). Note how the verb "to give" again appears: "which thou hast given to me," a gift that stands as such (perfect tense). The entire redemptive mission is viewed and is executed by Jesus, not as a burden, but as a loving gift to him on the part of the Father.[110]

What then is completed is the "entire redemptive mission." Attempting to be consistent in his verb use, he finds a perfective aspect only in the perfect of δέδωκάς ("gave").

Despite the intercessory work taking place in John 17, Lenski writes, "at this very moment he is laying down his life in compliance with his Father's behest (10:18)." This is disingenuous on the part of Lenski, for Jesus is praying, not laying down his life. The doublespeak seems to manifest an unwillingness for Lenski to admit that a reflective view is the best explanation of the verse. Therefore, his comments yield a view that is proleptic, reflective, and revelatory by especially appealing to a unique understanding of the use of the aorist tense.

---

109. Lenski, *Interpretation*, 1124.
110. Lenski, *Interpretation*, 1124.

R. V. G. Tasker (1960, reissued 1983), Frederick Louis Godet (1969), Leon Morris (1971, rev. ed. 1995)

Within twenty years of Dodd's study, three commentators present reflective-revelatory views of John 17:4. First, Tasker, penning only one sentence on the concept of the completed works, asserts, "[Christ] will have passed on to the disciples, who have been given him by the Father the fullness of divine truth."[111] The "passing on" of "divine truth" indicates that the work of Christ is to make the Father's identity know to the disciples. In "fullness" Christ has made the Father known, thus bringing his revelatory work to completion.[112] Like many before him who held to a proleptic view, Tasker does not give reasoning.

Second, Godet, proposes, "He has caused his holy and good character to shine in the hearts of men . . . The duty of every hour has been perfectly fulfilled. There has been in this same human life which he has now behind him, not only no spot, but no deficiency with reference to the task of making the divine perfection shine forth resplendently."[113] Godet's explanation concerns the character of Christ being known to people as his incarnational duty from God the Father. "Perfectly fulfilled" (or *perfectively*), this work is completed. This is an earthly work of the common "human life," but it is behind Christ chronologically, with respect to his statement in John 17:4, and not still before him; it is a past work, not one that is yet future. The task was completed with perfection and with "no deficiency"—with absence of misstep, disobedience, or sin.

Twice mentioned in terms of *shining*—"shine in the hearts of men" and "shine forth resplendently"—it is a *revealed* divinity. Seemingly for Godet, this is the divinity of both Christ and the Father, or of the Father through Christ, for it is "*his* holy and good character" that is manifest.

Third, although preeminently reflective in his viewpoint, Morris makes one of the most robust readings of Christ's work, filling the concept with various themes from the Gospel of John and the Old Testament. On John 4:34, the work of the "food" of Christ expresses what is "eloquent of a sense of mission and devotion." But Morris will complement this thought

---

111. Tasker, *The Gospel According to John*, 189.

112. Kruse, whose work replaces Tasker's in the Tyndale New Testament Commentary series, is inclusive of proleptic ideas with his revelatory thought: "This work, which involved revealing the Father through his life and ministry, and culminated in giving himself on the cross, glorified the Father by revealing his character to the world." Kruse, *John*, 340.

113. Godet, *Commentary on the Gospel of John*, 2:329.

immediately, saying, "There is a sense in which each stage of his work may be regarded as perfect and complete. And there is a deeper sense in which nothing is complete without the cross." The devotion speaks to the costliness of Christ's work that is finished in 19:30.[114]

Initially, Morris floats proleptic concepts with room for a reflective, perfect sense of understanding the work. There is a completed aspect, and there is some means by which there is a dimension or second level of understanding of the same words in which "work" and the "works" refer to the crucifixion. At 4:34, it is yet too early to come to a conclusion about the completed work, for here Jesus still seeks obedience to the will of the Father, of "him who sent me." Only at 17:4 can one begin to examine what is completed.

Morris sees a close relationship between the "work" of Christ (ἔργον, 4:34, 17:4; cf. 8:41) and the "works" of Christ (ἔργα, 5:20, 36 [2x]; 7:3; 9:4; 10:25, 32, 37, 38; 14:10, 11, 12; 15:24) in the Fourth Gospel.[115] Nevertheless, commenting on the completed work in greater volume, Morris suggests, "ἔργον here stands for his complete life's work . . . It is plain that Jesus regards his characteristic works as originating with the Father . . . now these works have a function in *teaching* people. They have value as *revelation* . . . Clearly the works, like the signs, have a *revelatory* function . . . Because they originate in God they have a *revelatory* function."[116] The work of Christ completed makes the Father known to the people Christ came to serve.

Morris's tying together "work" and "works" creates space for him to relate the work and works of Christ in John's gospel to the works of God in the Old Testament. In particular view are the works in creation (Gen 2:2–3; Ps 8:3; 104:24) and redemption from Egypt (Ps 44:1; 95:9, etc.).[117] It is in his use of ἔργον, according to Morris, that John indicates continuity between the earthly work of Christ and the work of God in the Old

---

114. Morris, *The Gospel According to John*, 245.

115. It does not appear to be Morris's intent to separate the singular usage from the plural, for he also writes, "John's characteristic use of ἔργον is for the works of Jesus . . . the word may be used in the singular, for an individual act or for the sum total of his earthly life, or the plural may be used of many individual deeds" (*According to John*, 611). In close proximity to these comments, Morris categorizes the "works" of 14:10 with the "work" of 4:34, writing, "'It is the Father, living in me, who is doing his works' (14:10) . . . Thus he can say it is his very meat to accomplish the Father's work (4:34)" (611–12).

116. Morris, *The Gospel According to John*, 612 (italics mine).

117. Morris, *The Gospel According to John*, 613.

Testament.[118] For Morris, there is a symbiotic unity of being and action among the Godhead.[119]

Barnabas Lindars (1972, reissued 1982, 1995)

In his comments on John 4:34, Lindars postures, without explanation, that the cross is in view in 17:4.[120] "The work" in 4:34 concerns "the whole purpose for which [Jesus] has been sent, his mission."[121] This whole purpose only finds completion "in his passion (17:4; 19:30)."[122] Yet in direct

---

118. Morris, *The Gospel According to John*, 613.

119. Morris, *The Gospel According to John*, 613. Later Morris posits on 19:30, "Jesus's work was finished. He came to do God's work, and this meant dying on the cross for the world's salvation. The mighty work of redemption has now reached its consummation," (720n77). It is difficult to discern if "God's work" refers to "the work" in 17:4, or if it is broader, speaking of the entirety of the work of redemption.

120. It would seem appropriate to enter Bultmann's position before Lindars, as Bultmann is the preeminent contributor to Johannine studies between Dodd (1963, 1968) and Carson (1991). However, I will not give fuller consideration to Bultmann's contribution for two reasons: (1) Bultmann makes little direct comment on the work at 4:34 or 17:4, for the concerns of his work relate more to myth and history, as well as the eschatology of the Fourth Gospel; and (2) it is well-known, and obvious within Bultmann's commentary, he understands John to portray Jesus as the "Revealer" as the major Christological concept in John's gospel. From the outset of his commentary, on John 1:1–2, Bultmann speaks of Jesus as, "The figure of the Logos, as Creator and Revealer." Bultmann, *The Gospel of John*, 31. Therefore, it would seem to be a foregone conclusion that Bultmann's view would be reflective and revelatory, at minimum. However, on 19:30, Bultmann comments, "The work of Jesus is completed; he has carried out that which his Father had commanded him (10:18; 15:10; 14:31). After he received the drink of vinegar he says, '*It is accomplished!*' (v. 30); he bows his head and dies. The ἐγώ σε ἐδόξασα ἐπὶ τῆς γῆς τὸ ἔργον τελειώσας ὃ δέδωκάς μοι ἵνα ποιήσω (17:4), which in the prayer had been uttered *sub specie* of the completion of the work, has now come to a historical reality" (e.g., a proleptic understanding, 674–75). Moloney disagrees with a Bultmannian interpretation, writing, "Jesus looks both backward and forward. The often-repeated claim that the prayer is written *sub specie aeternitatis* . . . is inaccurate, as it detaches the interpretation of the prayer from its present literary setting." Moloney, *The Gospel of John*, 464. On the latter point, I think Bultmann's followers should be cautious in seeing Bultmann interpreting John 17:4 as *sub specie aeternitatis* rather than simply as *sub specie*. While the former, since Spinoza, has come to mean. "from the perspective of the eternal," the latter means "under the form of." Bultmann may be discussing form at 17:4, even though he is fond of discussing the Johannine narrative as highly eschatological. In literature, it is unusual to see "sub specie" as an abbreviation for the saying, "sub specie aeternitatis."

121. Lindars, *The Gospel of John*, 194.

122. Lindars, *The Gospel of John*, 194. Beasley-Murray's comments on 4:34 are very similar: "The entire ministry of Jesus is represented by the Evangelist as obedience in action, which leads him finally to the surrender of himself in death (cf. 17:4)"

comments on 17:4 he offers a reflective and revelatory reading of the work, finding a two-stage revelatory work with respect to the glory of God. The "whole of his work on earth," the first stage, has been accomplished. So on the basis of the requests in 17:1–5, Lindars concludes of the first work that "it must be followed by the second stage, the glorification of the Son of man, without which it remains incomplete and unconvincing."[123]

Lindars raises the issues of completing and convincing within Jesus' work because glorification "is at once the completion of his mission and the vindication of his obedience even to death."[124] It is appropriate to conclude, then, that Lindars allows for one to read 17:4 as speaking of Jesus's actions that reveal the person of the Father and as including Jesus's work on the cross and in the resurrection. The greater purpose of Jesus's mission as the redemptive action envelops "the work."[125]

D. A. Carson (1991)

As manifested briefly in my comments opening this chapter, Carson supposes a proleptic reading of 17:4. He takes issue with those who propose a reflective reading on the basis of using "And now" as a time boundary between a previous work that brought glory to the Father and any work or works to come to bring glory to the Father.[126]

> This misses the mark. There is certainly a contrast between v. 4 and v. 5, but it is not between previous work that Jesus has completed and his cross-work that lies immediately ahead. Rather, a contrast is drawn between the glory that Jesus by his work has brought to the Father on earth, and the glory he asks the Father to give him (*cf.* 13:31–32) in heaven. Once that is seen, it makes best sense if v. 4 includes *all* the work by which Jesus brings

---

(Beasley-Murray, *John*, 63).

123. Lindars, *Gospel of John*, 520.

124. Lindars, *Gospel of John*, 518. Lindars comments later, "Jesus does not simply pray for vindication as the Son of Man, but for the completion of a process . . . the descent and return of the Revealer from the heavenly realm" (520).

125. Beasley-Murray disagrees with Lindars' distinctions between the work and glorification. He notes, "From Chrysostom onward most writers have included the death within the works of the ministry as a unity, and it is difficult to avoid that conclusion," (Beasley-Murray, *John*, 297).

126. Based on his comments, I cannot discern whether Carson takes issue with other reflective/reflective-revelatory proposals, for he directs his criticism only at the one means of developing a reflective view.

glory to his Father, and that includes his own death, resurrection and exaltation (*cf.* 4:34; 5:36; 19:30). So he is speaking proleptically (as in v. 12, 'While I was with them . . . '), oscillating with a more prosaic description of his place at this moment in the flow of redemptive history (*e.g.* v. 11, 'I am coming to you . . .').[127]

Carson is right to see a difference between a statement of past glorification in 17:4 and a request for future glorification in 17:5. Yet the clarification of what is in contrast does not negate the time marker of "And now." But it seems that Carson builds his "best sense" argument on an apparent parallel between glorification by the works of Christ and the glory that the Father will give to Christ. That is, as the Son will receive the full glory of the Father, all he did in his incarnation must be included in the means by which Christ glorified the Father. This amounts to an unequal comparison and an illogically developed conclusion. The *reception* of full glory in the future does not demand *execution* of the entirety of the earthly ministry's works of redemption. Neither does reception of full glory in the future require that glory in the past—prior to "And now"—be replete with all of the works of Christ. A syllogism representing Carson's argument demonstrates that the conclusion does not flow from the premises:

Major Premise: John 17:4 and 17:5 draw a contrast between the glory that Jesus brought to the Father on earth by his work and the glory he asks the Father to give him in heaven;

Minor Premise: John 17:4 speaks of the completion of "the work;"

Conclusion: John 17:4 includes *all* the work by which Jesus brings glory to his Father, and that includes his own death, resurrection, and exaltation.

Based on Carson's argument, instead of Carson's proleptic conclusion, one could conclude that the completed work in John 17:4, as the instrument of the glory Jesus brought the Father on earth, stands in contrast to the glory he asks the Father to give him—the very thing Carson criticizes in the views of others.

Thus, Carson draws a proleptic understanding—to the exclusion of a reflecting reading—on the basis of infusing implications of the request for future glory into the stated completed work. Yet minimizing the boundary established by "And now" and making implicit ideas of the

---

127. Carson, *John*, 557.

death, resurrection, and exaltation within "the work" cannot be explained by prosaic writing on the part of the author of the Fourth Gospel.

Herman Ridderbos (1997)

Similar to Lindars, Ridderbos understands that "It is that mission, that is, the authority given to Jesus by God and the gift of God comprehended in it, that determines his entire existence."[128] When Jesus speaks in 4:34 and 17:4 of "the work," which Ridderbos equates to "the works" throughout the Fourth Gospel, Ridderbos views a summation of Jesus's entire mission—both the words and deed.[129] Specifically, in 17:4, Jesus has "attained the full goal of the mandate (the 'work')," given to him by the Father.[130] That mandate is to grant eternal life through knowledge of the Father and Son in truth.[131] Ridderbos comes to proleptic ideas on the basis of the missional mandate of Jesus.

Rodney Whitacre (1999)

My analysis of Whitacre's position begins with his comments on John 4:34. Whitacre sees stages to Christ's completed work, equating it with the will of God, the obedience of Christ, and fulfillment of the calling of Israel. Initially, Whitacre mentions the disciples' failure to identify Jesus as the embodied "revelation of the Father." Yet he does not connect this revelation to any type of reflective view of the work, but only mentions this revelation within the disciples' failure to grasp the metaphoric statement about Jesus's food in 4:32:

> The section begins with the disciples' encouraging Jesus to eat something (v. 31). This expression of loving concern is met by an obscure response from Jesus: *I have food to eat that you know nothing about* (v. 32). His disciples are still very ignorant of who he really is and what he is really about. They have yet to see him as the revelation of the Father. Accordingly, the disciples do not

---

128. Ridderbos, *The Gospel According to John*, 168.
129. Ridderbos, *The Gospel According to John*, 168.
130. Ridderbos, *The Gospel According to John*, 549.
131. Ridderbos, *The Gospel According to John*, 549.

get Jesus' point and so have more unasked questions, such as wondering if someone has brought him food (v. 33).[132]

However, it is in the explanation of the statement in 4:32 that Whitacre sees Jesus equate his food with the will of God and the completion of God's work. Jesus fulfills the full obedience to the word of God that God started in, and expected of, the people of Israel:

> *My food . . . is to do the will of him who sent me and to finish his work* (v. 34). This saying calls attention to what is significant about his encounter with the Samaritan woman and indeed about all of his activity: he does God's will *and finishes God's work*. Jesus is the true Son of God, living out the obedience that was expected of the people of Israel, who were not to "live on bread alone but on every word that comes from the mouth of the LORD" (Deut. 8:3). Jesus is thus not only God's presence on earth but also the model of discipleship. Doing the will of God is Jesus' food and is such for his followers also.[133]

Whitacre makes modern discipleship the focus of his comments on Jesus's food. However, it is important to see that his understanding of the words of 4:34 as a fulfillment of Israel's mission negates a proleptic reading of the verse and the work, for the atoning work of the cross is a unique work given to the Son and not to Israel.[134] Christ might fulfill obedience to the Mosaic Law of God in a way that Israel failed to do (cf. Matt 4:4–10; Luke 4:7–12). But the accomplishment on the cross and in the resurrection were Christ's alone to do. If the work in 4:34 is a fulfillment where Israel failed, the cross and resurrection should be removed from Whitacre's consideration.

Yet Whitacre broadens Israel's mission to that of being "a source of God's salvation for the whole world."[135] If by "source" Whitacre intends revelation, in the sense of Isa 42:9 and 46:9, then Jesus fulfills that role as "the light of the word" (John 1:4, 5, 9; 8:12; 9:5). Whereas Israel was

---

132. Whitacre, *John*, 109–10.

133. Whitacre, *John*, 109–10.

134. In the Fourth Gospel, the uniqueness of the Son's work is evident in his "I am" statements, three of which are most exclusive: (1) Jesus is the Bread of Life to whom "no one" can come . . . unless the Father who sent [Jesus] draws him" (6:44); (2) Jesus is the Door that offers salvation in contrast to "*all* who came before him" (10:8–9); and (3) Jesus is the only way to the Father such that "no one" enters the Father's presence apart from him (14:6).

135. Whitacre, *John*, 407.

intended by God to be a mediatorial light pointing to the God who offers salvation, Jesus is the "light of life" in whom salvation is found. Jesus provides revelation that leads to life; thus he has fulfilled what Israel failed. Whitacre writes,

> Of special significance is his claim to *finish his* [God's] *work* (4:34). The Father has begun a project, and now Jesus is bringing it to its perfect completion (*teleiōsō autou to ergon*). Israel was to be a source of God's salvation for the whole world, and this is now coming to fulfillment, beginning with the Samaritans. Its extension to the rest of the world is represented later by the Greeks who come to Jesus, thereby indicating that the hour had come for him to be lifted up and draw all people to himself (12:20–23, 32).

Whitacre does not make a reference to 4:34 in his comments on 17:4. His latter discussion appears to take a perfective reading of the completion the work for two reasons. First, he will speak of the work as "*already* accomplished in [Jesus's] ministry."[136] Second, he takes issue with the NIV translation that makes the progressive reading "finishing" rather than offering a reading that would show that the work has been completed.[137] For Whitacre, "the works revealed the character of [the Father]" and "the words and deeds of Jesus revealed the Father's glory."[138]

Andreas Köstenberger (Various Dates)

In many of his works, Köstenberger assumes a proleptic reading of John 17:4. He reveals his view while explaining "Jesus's mission was fulfilled in his 'lifting up' on the cross,"[139] and in saying, "Jesus's work of salvation is

---

136. Whitacre, *John*, 407.

137. "The NIV translation is grammatically possible, but it misses the eternal, confident perspective evident in Jesus's statement that his work is already over" (Whitacre, *John*, 405–7). Although Whitacre was referring to the phrase "by completing the work" in the 1984 edition of the NIV, the 2011 edition retains the progressive sense with "by finishing the work."

138. Whitacre, *John*, 405–7. One should not understand Whitacre to equate "works" in John's Gospel with "the work," for here he speaks generally. Neither can one conclude assuredly that Whitacre equates "the work" with a combination of the "works" and "words." Yet, since the concern of the work is "the glorification of the Father," it seems that "the work" for Whitacre is the revelation of the Father through Christ's works—his words and deeds.

139. Köstenberger, *The Missions of Jesus*, 114.

everywhere presented in the Fourth Gospel as completed (cf., e.g., 17:4; 19:30)."[140] For Köstenberger, "the completion of the 'work' given to him by the Father (17:4) . . . incudes revealing the Father's 'name' to the disciples (17:6) and dedicating himself as a sacrifice (17:19).[141]

Elsewhere, Köstenberger speaks more explicitly about 17:4 in relationship to the cross of Christ: "The author's affirmation, 'We have seen his glory' (John 1:14), turns out to encompass the signs . . . as well as the cross (12:23, 28; 17:2, 4–5) in the remainder of the Johannine narrative."[142] For Köstenberger, 17:4 "anticipates 19:30."[143] Moreover, the resurrection is implicit in the statement about the completed work.[144]

All such proleptic conclusions are based on Köstenberger's understanding of the nature of Jesus's mission in the Gospel of John.[145] In some sense, the mission of Jesus in redemption seems to complete the work God began in the creation and continues to sustain.[146]

CONCLUSION

The most widely held view of John 17:4 in Johannine scholarship is the proleptic view—that "I have completed the work" is inclusive of pointing forward to the cross as a completed event in the mind of Christ. Occasionally, such a view is exclusively proleptic; at other times it is a mixed proleptic of various stripes and forms. The predominant view is a mix of proleptic with reflective, with more views placing greater weight on the proleptic aspect rather than the reflective aspect. The proleptic-reflective position holds in view both the earthly ministry prior to John 17 and the final atoning work in John 19.

---

140. Köstenberger, *The Missions of Jesus*, 190.

141. Köstenberger and Swain, *Father, Son, and Spirit*, 168.

142. Köstenberger, *A Theology of John's Gospel and Letters*, 49.

143. Köstenberger, *A Theology of John's Gospel and Letters*, 247. Prior to this, Köstenberger intimates, "This Jesus is to stay in anticipation of his victory over the world and its ruler at the cross, which will mark the 'Mission accomplished!' of the obedient Son sent from the Father (16:33; cf. 17:4; 19:30)" (246).

144. Köstenberger, *A Theology of John's Gospel and Letters*, 531.

145. This largely is the discussion of Köstenberger, *The Missions of Jesus*, 141–98. Of note, Köstenberger specifies that the ascending and descending terminology associated with the cross and resurrection "may be included in the 'work' of the obedient Sent One (cf. 4:34; 17:4)" (130).

146. Köstenberger, *John*, 161.

The basis and/or reasoning for such proleptic and mixed-proleptic interpretations of John 17:4 vary between an influence of Systematic Theology (ST), Biblical Theology (BT), Exegetical Theology (mildly; ET), or Historical Theology (HT). In terms of ST, one might come to proleptic reading by (1) simply assuming John's Gospel (or 17:4) is anticipatory, (2) appealing to the decree of God (Augustine) or the purpose of the incarnation (Cyril, Lindars, Ridderbos, Köstenberger), (3) including the sufferings of Christ within the glorification of the Father (Luther), (4) separating proleptic intentions from acts (Simeon) or separating reflective doctrine and acts (Govett), (5) appealing to a historical catechism (Owen), (6) dividing the will(s) of Christ or the functioning of the Father (Govett), (7) separating functions and intra-relationships within the Godhead (Kelly), or (8) finding symbiotic unity among the members of the Godhead (Morris).

As evident above, some writers rely on BT to come to proleptic conclusions. Augustine—whose view is comprehensive enough to have BT and ST bases—appeals to OT prophetic texts and their nature of speaking about future events as certain. Aquinas finds an echo of Isa 24:15 in John 17:4 in order to justify his reflective reading of the completed work. Owen refers to Heb 12:2, overlaying Christ's sufferings on John 17:4.

In terms of ET—working with the text of John only or John 17 only—Bonaventure draws on John 6:40 in order to reason about proleptic concepts in 17:4. Luther will follow the glory theme in John 17 and build a proleptic idea on this basis. Tholuck will appeal to John 19:30 to support his view of 17:4. Owen identifies John 17 as an anticipatory genre and reasons from the whole of the genre to the verse. Hovey and Lenski appeal to the use of the aorist in the verse. Carson utilizes the close proximity of the requests in John 17:1–5 to make a context for understanding the statement in 17:4 to be joined to 17:5 (and 17:1–5). Finally, in terms of HT, Aquinas and Downing appeal to Augustine as they draw their own conclusions.

Largely, writers draw proleptic conclusions on bases other than a historical-grammatical investigation of John 17:4.[147] In the coming chapter, I will begin such an investigation by exploring the glorification of the Father in the Fourth Gospel, to which 17:4 refers.

---

147. Writers holding to reflective views, whether exclusively and in combination with a proleptic view, largely do so on the basis of seeing a perfective idea in "I have completed."

Table 1. Summary of Primary-Proleptic Views

Summary of Primary-Proleptic Views				
Writer	Anticipatory (Y/N)	Certainly Completed (Y/N)	Reflective also, or Revelatory (Y/N)	Unique Features
Chrysostom	N	N	Y	Proleptic organically growing from reflective work
Augustine	Y	Y	Y	Proleptic concerns heaven and not the cross; separates the function of the form of "glorified" from the sense of the verb
Cyril of Alexandria	Y	N	N	Includes the defeat of the devil
St. Bonaventure	Y	Y	N	The work is conversion.
Thomas Aquinas	N	N	Y	Proleptic on the basis of the chronology of events—the nearness of John 17 to the passion narrative
Martin Luther	Y	N	Y	Proleptic means to take upon himself all shame, disgrace, suffering and death, to the glory of the Father
Henry Downing	N	Y	Y	Reasoning claims to follow Augustine expressly
John J. Owen	Y	N	Y	Proleptic flows from genre of John 17 as anticipatory in nature and as an ecstatic-intercession
E. W. Hengstenberg	Y	N	N	The proleptic in no sense is completed until John 19:30
Robert Govett	Y	Y	N	The work is redemption and not revelation
Barnabas Lindars	Y	N/A	N/A	N/A
D. A. Carson	Y	Y	N	Considers implications of request for future glory to construct view
Herman Ridderbos	Y	N/A	Y	Equates "the work" and "the works," and sees Jesus's entire missional mandate in the proleptic
Andreas Köstenberger	Y	Y	N	The missional nature of Jesus' work in Fourth Gospel shapes proleptic

Table 2. Summary of Primary-Reflective Views

Writer	Revelatory (Y/N)	Certainly Completed (Y/N)	Proleptic Also (Y/N)	Unique Features
Charles Simeon	N	Y	Y	What is completed is the mediatorial work of Christ (unspecified); proleptic intention is separated from the proleptic act
August Tholuck	Y	Y	Y	John 19:30 influences including proleptic-anticipatory view
Alvah Hovey	Y	Y	Y	Exegesis limits text to reflective, but still proposes proleptic view without reasoning
Thomas Whitelaw	Y	Y	Y	The completion of the atonement is within the reflective work.
William Kelly	Y	Y	Y	Divides both the will of Christ and God the Father's functioning in order to include proleptic view
B. F. Westcott	Y	N	Y	Divides the singular accomplished work to gain proleptic idea
George P. Eckman	Y	Y	Y	Christ intends to make "intelligible" the Father
H. D. M. Spence-Jones	Y	NA	NA	Limits revelatory aspect to person of the Word, without referencing the Father
C. H. Dodd	Y	Y	Y	Claims proleptic within reflective but fails to argue such; genre of John 17 is religious sacrifice
R. C. H. Lenski	Y	Y	Y	Mission is revelatory and redemptive; makes unique appeal to sense of aorist
R. V. G. Tasker	Y	Y	N	No reasoning given for revelatory inclusion

Frederick Louis Godet	N	Y	N	Completed with perfection, with "no deficiency"—with absence of misstep, disobedience, or sin.
Leon Morris	Y	Y	N	Revelatory function flows from the origin of the work in God
Rodney Whitacre	Y	Y	N	Does not see reflective nature of the work (although view amounts to such)

3

Making God Known Publicly and Privately

INTRODUCTION

G. B. Caird's study of δόξα and δοξάζω in the Gospel of John provide a starting point of discerning the issue of concern in this chapter.[1] Questioning what Jesus means in John 13:31 when he says that God is glorified, Caird writes,

> If we ask what John means when he says that the Son of Man is glorified and God is glorified in him, one proper and accurate answer is that he means the Cross. The "now" of this verse is the hour of Jesus's death, and John can use the aorist tense because, with the departure of Judas, all the actors in the drama, and Jesus in particular, are committed to their courses of action, which make the Crucifixion virtually accomplished. Most commentators provide some sort of elaboration of this aspect of the verse's meaning: the glorifying of God in the Cross is the accomplishment of his saving purpose of love for the world through the obedient surrender of Jesus, the process by which believers are brought into unity with the Son and therefore also with the Father. But no amount of elaboration can alter the fact that they are pointing to the referent of the word "glorify" without telling us anything about its sense. They are telling us (correctly) that

1. Caird, "The Glory of God in the Fourth Gospel," 265–77.

John uses the verb δοξάζεσθα to denote the Cross but not what John wishes to say about the Cross by the use of this verb.[2]

When Caird recognizes that the "sense" of "glorify" remains unstated for many commentators, he seems to be speaking of the significance of glorify to John's theology of the atoning work of Christ. For, writes Caird, "what John wishes to say *about* the Cross by use of this verb" is what is lacking. Caird's *a priori* assumption that the proleptic reading of 13:31 is "accurate" notwithstanding, he is correct in what he attempts to analyze with respect to commentators' communication of the meaning of δόξα: *Commentators often do not distinguish any significant variation in the senses of glorification terms in the Fourth Gospel, except a distinction between that of the cross and that of the Ascension (which is the glory of Christ's pre-incarnate existence).* As Caird rephrases, we are asking, "What sense does the word 'glorify' bear in this context; what semantic contribution does it make to the sentence."[3] Or in this work, what are the ways 'glory' and 'glorified' are used in John, and how do such usages contribute to one's understanding of 'glorified' in John 17:4?

In the first part of this chapter, I will consider the significance of *glory*—the glory of God—in the OT and in earlier passages in John. I will not examine every use of δοξάζω and δόξα in the LXX. Instead, I will demonstrate that the LXX does use δόξα in a revelatory sense. I will argue that John draws upon the OT sense of δόξα in the Fourth Gospel when writing of δοξάζω and δόξα.

In the latter part of the chapter, I will explore the use of ἐπὶ τῆς γῆς and its connection to the glorifying work of Christ. I will consider the OT background of ἐπὶ τῆς γῆς and its influence on the use in the Fourth Gospel.

This chapter will begin advancing a case for a reflective reading of the completed work of Christ in John 17:4 within its local context of John 17. In this chapter I will not discuss the verbal aspect of ἐδόξασα. It is not yet necessary to explain the verbal aspect in order to make a case for a reflective view of John 17:4, for few commentators see a proleptic-only view of 17:4.

In this chapter I will not explore the theories of semantic change of words, for that is outside the scope of this work. Limited too will be my exploration of the history of the semantic change of δόξα from the

---

2. Caird, "The Glory of God in the Fourth Gospel," 266.
3. Caird, "The Glory of God in the Fourth Gospel," 266.

classical Greek usage to the LXX and NT usage. Nor will I give extended discussion to the variant reading in 13:31–32, for both the Fourth Gospel and the textual criticism literature well account for the adopted reading, and the variant reading does not necessitate any change in my argument.

BACKGROUND OF ΔΟΞΑ IN LXX AND THE SEMANTIC TRANSFER FROM CLASSICAL GREEK

Both δόξα and δοξάζω derive from δοκέω ("to think" or "to seem"). In Classical Greek, δοκέω carried the meaning, "opinion, viewpoint, judgment," a vastly different idea than the later NT use of the terms.[4] In the passive verbal sense, it could indicate "reputation," or "fame," "honor," and "glory."[5] The origin of the verb stems from the noun: "Presumably because of the distinctive senses of δόξα, a new [verb] was derived from it, namely δοξάζω, even though δοκέω was already available."[6] Of the over 400 uses of δόξα in the LXX, nowhere is found the meaning "opinion." The LXX uses "δόξα" to render the Hebrew, כָּבוֹד.[7]

Sometimes כָּבוֹד could refer to inward character, such as the reputation or honor of a person.[8] For example, Joseph, once he reveals himself to be exalted above his brothers, desires for his brothers to communicate knowledge of his אֶת־כָּל־כְּבוֹדִי to his father Jacob (Gen 45:13).[9] At other times כָּבוֹד refers to external character, like "splendor."[10] In Isa 35:2, "the glory of Lebanon" stands in contrast to "the majesty of Carmel and Sharon." In an identical manner, in the rest of the verse, the "glory of the Lord" stands in parallel to "the majesty of our God:"[11]

---

4. Silva, "δόξα," in *NIDNTTE*, 1:761. For an extended discussion on the meaning of δοκέω, including emphasis on the concept relating to "to seem," and "to be held or considered or thought, appear, emerge," see the entry for "δοκέω" in Montanari, *The Brill Dictionary of Ancient Greek*, α–κ, 545.

5. Silva, "δόξα," 761–62.

6. Silva, "δόξα," 761–62.

7. Silva, "δόξα," 761–62. In the LXX, δόξα also renders the MT's תִּפְאֶרֶת (pride, beauty, ornament, glory, splendor, radiance, fame, honor, pride), הָדָר (majesty, splendor, adornment), and הוֹד (weight, power, splendor, or majesty).

8. Silva, "δόξα," 763.

9. The LXX has πᾶσαν τὴν δόξαν.

10. Silva, "δόξα," 763.

11. The LXX reads, καὶ ἐξανθήσει καὶ ἀγαλλιάσεται τὰ ἔρημα τοῦ Ιορδάνου, καὶ ἡ δόξα τοῦ Λιβάνου ἐδόθη αὐτῇ καὶ ἡ τιμὴ τοῦ Καρμήλου, καὶ ὁ λαός μου ὄψεται τὴν δόξαν κυρίου καὶ τὸ ὕψος τοῦ θεοῦ.

פָּרֹחַ תִּפְרַח וְתָגֵל אַף גִּילַת וְרַנֵּן כְּבוֹד
הַלְּבָנוֹן נִתַּן־לָהּ הֲדַר הַכַּרְמֶל וְהַשָּׁרוֹן
הֵמָּה יִרְאוּ כְבוֹד־יְהוָה הֲדַר אֱלֹהֵינוּ

It shall blossom abundantly
and rejoice with joy and singing.
The glory of Lebanon shall be given to it,
the majesty of Carmel and Sharon.
They shall see the glory of the Lord,
the majesty of our God.

Similarly, Kittel notes, "the כָּבוֹד of Moab (Is. 16:14) or of Kedar (Is. 21:16) is more than its material strength; it is its prestige among the nations, i.e., that which gives it standing and importance."[12] In both of these examples, δόξα translates כָּבוֹד, picking up the sense of the Hebrew: ἡ δόξα Μωαβ (Isa 16:14) and ἡ δόξα τῶν υἱῶν Κηδαρ (Isa 21:16).

Although כָּבוֹד does refer to character and honor, it also refers to a visible display—of *revelation*. Three well known episodes in the OT demonstrate this usage. First, in Exod 33, when Moses asks the Lord to make his *glory* (Heb. אֶת־כְּבֹדֶךָ) known to him, he uses הַרְאֵנִי in a request to see something visible.[13] The LXX of Exod 33:18 reflects the verb for a visible display in both the Swete[14] and Rahlfs[15] traditions. Similarly, in Exod 33:22–23, the כְּבֹדִי passing by requires the Lord to say to Moses, "and I will cover you" (Heb. וְשַׂכֹּתִי) so that the Lord's face "shall not be *seen*" (Heb. לֹא יֵרָאוּ).[16]

---

12. Kittel, "Δοκέω, Δόξα, Δοξάζω, Συνδοξάζω, Ἔνδοξος, Ἐνδοξάζω, Παράδοξος," in *TDNT*, 2:238.

13. BDB, 908.

14. The Swete edition has καὶ λέγει Ἐμφάνισόν μοι σεαυτόν. καὶ εἶπεν Ἐγὼ παρελεύσομαι πρότερός σου τῇ δόξῃ μου . . . (Swete, *The Old Testament in Greek*), Exod 33:18–19. The Brenton translation agrees with the Swete tradition: Καὶ λέγει, ἐμφάνισόν μοι σεαυτόν. Καὶ εἶπεν, ἐγὼ παρελεύσομαι πρότερός σου τῇ δόξῃ μου (Brenton, *The Septuagint Version*, Exod 33:18–19. *A New English Translation of the Septuagint* also reflects the concept of display: And he says, "Show me your glory!" *A New English Translation of the Septuagint*, http://ccat.sas.upenn.edu/nets/ edition/02-exod-nets.pdf (henceforth *NETS*).

15. The Rahlfs edition has καὶ λέγει Δεῖξόν μοι τὴν σεαυτοῦ δόξαν. Rahlfs, *Septuaginta: With Morphology*, electronic ed., Exod 33:18.

16. In the LXX, despite a change in the placement of the pronominal, "my," and verb tense of "passes by" (παρέλθῃ μου ἡ δόξα [Swete, Rahlfs] vs. παρελθῃνῇ ἡ δόξα μου [Brenton]), the Swete and Rahlfs traditions, and the Brenton translation, are in agreement on the visible display of the glory of God communicated by כְּבֹדִי: ἡ δόξα . . . σκεπάσω . . . μου οὐκ ὀφθήσεταί σοι. The *NETS* reflects the inability of the Lord's face to be seen: "And I will take my hand away, and then you shall see my hind parts, but my face will not appear to you." *NETS*.

Second, in 2 Chr 5:13-14, when the Lord descends upon Solomon's temple at the dedication ceremony, "the house, the house of the Lord, was filled with a cloud" (Heb. וְהַבַּיִת מָלֵא עָנָן בֵּית יְהוָה). The cloud is visible enough in its presence to crowd out the priests from their places of service within the temple. The later description of the Lord's cloud-like appearance and the reason for the priest's exodus from the temple is, "for the glory of the Lord filled the house of God" (Heb. כִּי־מָלֵא כְבוֹד־יְהוָה אֶת־בֵּית הָאֱלֹהִים). What is visible in the form of a cloud in 5:13 is the כְּבוֹד־יְהוָה.[17]

Third, in Num 16:42,[18] when the Lord appears in a cloud that covers the tent of meeting, the writer says of the event, "The glory of the Lord *appeared*" (וַיֵּרָא כְּבוֹד יְהוָה). The *nif'al* of ראה has the sense of, "to become visible."[19]

In the LXX, in each of the above examples, a form of δόξα renders the כָּבוֹד term of the MT. God's honor, glory, and power are the primary expressions of δόξα in the LXX. The idea of visibility (or revelation) is inherent in the LXX term.[20] Some, such as Cook, drawing from the idea of weightiness within כָּבוֹד and the idea of visibility carried over into δόξα, understand that *revelation of character* is in view when δόξα refers to God. Cook notes,

> In the LXX *doxa* is the translation of *kābôd*. The Hebrew term refers to that which is weighty or impressive and may be used of man or God . . . When used of God it seems to refer to the impact made on man from God's self-manifestation . . . The LXX, then, becomes a significant background influence on the NT in the use of *doxa* to refer to the visible brightness or splendor

---

17. In the LXX, there is agreement in the manuscript on καὶ ὁ οἶκος ἐνεπλήσθη νεφέλης δόξης Κυρίου for the clause in 5:13, and only a slight variation in the verb, ἐμπίπλημι—ἐνέπλησεν (Swete, Rahlfs) vs. ἐνέπλησε (Brenton)—on 5:14 for the latter clause in discussion: ὅτι ἐνέπλησεν δόξα κυρίου τὸν οἶκον τοῦ θεοῦ. The LXX editors interpret the "cloud" as "the cloud of the glory of the Lord," seemingly doing so on the basis of the parallel thought in the Hebrew—that the cloud is a visible manifestation of glory of the Lord. The *NETS* has, "the Lord's glory had filled the house" (2 Chr 5:14).

18. MT (BHS) and LXX (Rahlfs) Num 17:7; LXX (Swete, Brenton, *NETS*) Num 16:42.

19. *HALOT* 1160. When used of God, BDB notes it can mean "appear" (908). The LXX of the Brenton, Rahlfs, and Swete traditions reflect the same sense with ὤφθη ἡ δόξα κυρίου. The *NETS* translates the last clause as, "the cloud covered it, and the glory of the Lord *appeared*" (Num 16:42), *NETS*.

20. "It does not refer to God in his essential nature, but to luminous manifestation of his person, his glorious revelation of himself. Characteristically, the word is linked to vbs. of seeing and appearing (Exod 16:7, 10; 33:18; Deut 5:34; Isa 40:5; 60:1)" (Silva, "δόξα," 763).

issuing from God's presence or to the honor and glory that come to him through the manifestation of his character.[21]

God's honor, glory, and power are the primary expressions of δόξα in the LXX. As Silva writes, "It does not refer to God in his essential nature, but to luminous manifestation of his person, his glorious revelation of himself. Characteristically, the word is linked to vbs. of seeing and appearing (Exod 16:7, 10; 33:18; Deut 5:34; Isa 40:5; 60:1)."[22] The classical concept of "opinion" no longer is evident within δόξα.[23] The reasons the LXX translators used δόξα for כָּבוֹד are unknown. However, "once the connection between the two terms had been made, the meaning of δόξα was expanded so as to correspond more closely with כָּבוֹד—a typical semantic borrowing."[24] Thus δόξα becomes a term for the revelation of the *unseeable* God.[25]

---

21. Cook, "The 'Glory' Motif in the Johannine Corpus," 292. It is evident that Cook develops his thought from Kittel's: "If in relation to man כָּבוֹד denotes that which makes him impressive and demands recognition, whether in terms of material possessions or striking *gravitas*, in relation to God it implies that which makes God impressive to man, the force of His self-manifestation. As everywhere attested in the OT, God is intrinsically invisible. Nevertheless, when He reveals Himself, or declares Himself, e.g., in meteorological phenomena, one may rightly speak of the כְּבוֹד יְהוָה, of a manifestation which makes on man a highly significant impression. The more seriously religious reflection took the idea of Yahweh's invisibility and transcendence, the more this expression for the impressive element in God became an important technical term in OT theology." Kittel, "Δοκέω, Δόξα, Δοξάζω, Συνδοξάζω, Ἔνδοξος, Ἐνδοξάζω, Παράδοξος," in *TDNT*, 2:238-39.

22. Silva, "δόξα," 763.

23. "In the LXX, as in the NT, we have a very different usage from that which prevailed in the Greek world. The word δόξα is very widely used, some 280 times in the canonical books and some 445 altogether. There are 25 different Hebrew equivalents, although some of these are very rare. On some 180 occasions the Hebrew word is כָּבוֹד, and this is the true and dominant equivalent of the LXX δόξα, the others either having the same, or much the same, meaning as כָּבוֹד. The LXX word receives its distinctive force from the fact that it is used for כָּבוֹד. We find in it the meanings of כָּבוֹד, and we do not find in the LXX term the meanings of the Greek δόξα. It has become identical with כָּבוֹד . . . In sum, about half of the occurrences in the LXX are renderings of a derivative of כבד. The possible meanings are exactly the same as those of the OT word" (Kittel, "Δοκέω, Δόξα," 242).

24. Silva, "δόξα," 763. Silva also suggests that the LXX probably builds on the use of the passive voice in the Hellenistic period "with the meaning, 'to be held in honor, have renown'" (763).

25. "In the LXX and therefore in the Bible generally *doxa* acquires its distinctive sense as a term for this divine nature or essence either in its invisible or its perceptible form" (Kittel, "Δοκέω, Δόξα," 244, cited in Cook, "Glory Motif," 292).

DEVELOPMENT OF ΔΟΞΑ IN JOHN VIA DEVELOPMENT IN THE NT

Use of Δόξα in the NT as a Carryover from the OT

It would appear that the writer of the Fourth Gospel uses the idea of δόξα in the LXX for his concept of δόξα in reference to God.[26] This use is consistent with the uses of the synoptic evangelists. For example, δόξα is used in the sense of "splendor" in Matt 4:8 (par. Luke 4:6), and Matt 6:29 (par. Luke 12:27). In Matt 4:8, with reference to the kingdoms of the world, the devil "showed [Jesus] all their glory" (δείκνυσιν αὐτῷ πάσας τὰς ... τὴν δόξαν αὐτῶν).[27] In Matt 6:29, Jesus speaking of Solomon, says, "even Solomon in all of his glory was not arrayed like one of these" (ὅτι οὐδὲ Σολομὼν ἐν πάσῃ τῇ δόξῃ αὐτοῦ περιεβάλετο).[28]

As another example, in Luke 9:32, the disciples "see" the δόξα of Christ in the transfiguration account: εἶδον τὴν δόξαν αὐτοῦ.[29] The writer

---

26. In the NT, δόξα occurs over 160x in noun form, including 15x in the Gospel of John. In the NT δοξάζω occurs nearly 60x and 23x of those appearances are in the Gospel of John. Seemingly, the NT use of δόξα and δοξάζω derive from the LXX "and the underlying Heb. terms" (Silva, "δόξα," 764). Caird suggests, "Now when a Hebrew word is regularly rendered by a Greek one with which it is not wholly synonymous, one of two things may happen: either the Greek sense will prevail, and the translated sentence will convey a different meaning from that of the original; or the Hebrew sense will prevail and set up a process of semantic change in the meaning of the Greek word. So complete was the semantic change which overtook δόξα and because of their use in the LXX, that they simply assumed all the meanings and association of the Hebrew words that they had been used to translate. It is therefore to the LXX that we must go to discover the sense they bear in the Fourth Gospel" (Caird, "The Glory of God," 268). I agree with Caird that John's Gospel seems to pick up the sense of δόξα carried by the LXX. Yet, in fairness, I would suggest that one must consider that it is possible (although not probable) that the writer of the Fourth Gospel could be using δόξα in a sense different than that of the LXX, just as the LXX uses it in a sense different than Classical Greek. I will labor to demonstrate that the LXX and Fourth Gospel senses are the same.

27. The verb δείκνυσιν is pres., act., ind., 3rd., sg. of δείκνυμι, meaning "'to show' in the sense of 'to point to something' and thus to draw attention to it." Heinrich Schlier, "Δείκνυμι, Ἀναδείκνυμι, Ἀνάδειξις, Δειγματίζω, Παραδειγματίζω, Ὑπόδειγμα," in *TDNT*, 2:25.

28. The verb περιεβάλετο is aor., mid., ind., 3rd pers., sg. of περιβάλλω, meaning "to put on clothes, implying the clothing being completely around—'to clothe'" (L&N, 524). The writer of Matthew says Christ depicts Solomon *clothed* in his appearance with τῇ δόξῃ αὐτοῦ in a way that is visible to the eye. Louw-Nida cites Matt 6:29 as an example.

29. The verb εἶδον means "to perceive by sight of the eye" (Kittel, "Εἶδος, Εἰδέα (ἰδέα)," 2:279). Dodd writes, "In xii. 41 we have a reference to the vision of Isaiah described in ch. vi of his book. Isaiah says bluntly, 'I saw the Lord.' John, in accordance with

of Luke previously described this sight as τὸ εἶδος τοῦ προσώπου αὐτοῦ in 9:29.[30] Peter, in agreement with the synoptic accounts, will later describe the experience of the event as a reception of glory from God—λαβὼν γὰρ παρὰ θεοῦ πατρὸς τιμὴν καὶ δόξαν (2 Pet 1:17).

Caird cautions readers of the Fourth Gospel to "hesitate before attributing to John any Greek usage, however well attested in the LXX, which he knew to be unintelligible to those whose only language was Greek."[31] Even if one can demonstrate that one category of usage of δόξα in the NT agrees with or reflects usage in the LXX, this does not necessarily mean that John used the term in the manner of the other NT writers, especially if his concern was for Greek readers of the Gospel and not simply Jewish readers. Although Jewish readers would have been familiar with the LXX background to the term, a Greek might not have such linguistic history or literacy. However, it will become apparent that the term could be understood by a Greek by the usage of the term within the Gospel of John and the localized contexts of the passage units in which the author places the term.

The Use of Δοξάζω and Δόξα in John's Gospel

William Cook suggests δόξα / δοξάζω has three usages in the Johannine corpus: 1) brightness or splendor (e.g. Rev 15:8; 21:11, 23); 2) great power or strength (e.g., John 2:11; 11:40; 12:41; and 3) majesty and honor (e.g.

---

the general tendency of contemporary Judaism, says *eiden ten doxan autou*. Clearly, therefore, *doxa* here means the manifestation of God's presence and power, *kavod* or *yeqarah*" (Dodd, *Interpretation*, 207).

30. The noun εἶδος refers to "'What is visible' (in a man or object): 'figure,' 'appearance;' (Kittel, "Εἶδος, Εἰδέα (ἰδέα)," in *TDNT*, 2:373); or "the shape and structure of [something] as it appears to someone, *form, outward appearance*" (BDAG, 280). BDAG cites the passage as one of its examples.

31. Caird, "The Glory of God in the Fourth Gospel," 275. Caird continues by making a case for a Greek-speaker's understanding of the Fourth Gospel's writer's use of δόξα: "No Greek reader of the LXX could fail to notice that it was written in translation Greek, in a Greek written, so to speak, in a foreign accent. Many of its words and idioms would sound strange to him. But that is not to say that they would be unintelligible. He would recognize that the translators had been proceeding by analogy, and by recognizing the underlying analogies he would decipher their meaning. Δοξάζεσθαι, used intransitively to mean 'to display one's importance, greatness, or glory,' is an LXX neologism. But from Classical Greek it is possible to cull an impressive list of analogies which might have persuaded the translators that this usage either already existed or at least had every right to exist" (276).

John 1:14; 17:1, 5, 24; Rev 1:6; 7:12; 19:1).[32] More narrowly than Cook, Paul Robertson recognizes at least two senses of the use of "glory" in the Gospel of John: "The ministry of Jesus and the passion are tied together under the theme of glory. They are a declaration of the character of God. Although God's glory was manifested in the ministry of Jesus, *there was always a sense in which the glory was yet to come.*"[33] Robertson's suggestion opens the way for seeing three aspects of the use of "glory" in the Fourth Gospel as indicative of works of the Father evidenced *in* and *through* Christ.

First, there seems to be "glory" present before the passion in the presentation of the Father. Jesus manifests the power and majesty of God the Father through his works. For example, in John 10:37–38, Jesus said, "If I am not doing *the works of my Father*, then do not believe me; but if I do them, even though you do not believe me, believe *the works*, that you may know and understand that *the Father is in me and I am in the Father*." It is evident that the works provide *evidence* of God the Father working in Christ—sufficient evidence for the works to offer *reasons* for belief in Christ (τοῖς ἔργοις πιστεύετε) and *knowledge* for understanding what the evidence signifies (ἵνα γνῶτε καὶ γινώσκητε ὅτι ἐν ἐμοὶ ὁ πατὴρ κἀγὼ ἐν τῷ πατρί). The works themselves are not simply Jesus imitating the workings of the Father. Instead, Jesus points to the mysterious union of the Father and Jesus, in which the Father is present in the person of Jesus (ἐν ἐμοὶ ὁ πατὴρ) and Jesus is present in the person of God the Father (κἀγὼ ἐν τῷ πατρί).[34] As John Calvin notes, "This discourse does not relate to the

---

32. Cook, "The 'Glory' Motif in the Johannine Corpus," 293.

33. P. E. Robertson, "Glory in the Fourth Gospel," 126 (italics mine).

34. *TDNT* suggests that this use of ἐν in John emphasizes "religious fellowship" that might be termed "mystical" in one sense, something that is "reciprocal," but distinct from Pauline usage (Oepke, "Ἐν," in *TDNT*, 2:543). BDAG seems to be clearer in its explanation of the nature of the fellowship: "In Paul. or Joh. usage, to designate a close personal relation in which the referent of the ἐν-term is viewed as the controlling influence: *under the control of, under the influence of, in close association with* (cp. ἐν τῷ Δαυιδ εἰμί 2 Km 19:44): of Christ εἶναι, μένειν ἐν τῷ πατρί (ἐν τῷ θεῷ) J 10:38; 14:10f . . . In Paul the relation of the individual to Christ is very oft. expressed by such phrases as ἐν Χριστῷ, ἐν κυρίῳ etc., also vice versa" (BDAG, 327). Both entries cite John 10:38 multiple times among their examples for this use of the dative. While the persons remain distinct (cf. John 1:1–3), and the Son is submissive to the Father (cf. 5:19; 8;28; 14:10), the mysterious union is such a close personal relation/association that one cannot distinguish the "controlling influence" between the Son and the Father. Yet this indicates still that the Father works through the Son, and his influence is displayed through the Son.

unity of essence, *but to the manifestation of Divine power in the person of Christ, from which it was evident that he was sent by God."*[35]

Second, glory is present in both the crucifixion and the resurrection. In the *crucifixion*, Jesus manifests God's love through his love for his own (13:1–2; 14:23–24; 15:9, 10, 12, 13) through the accomplishment of redemption (19:30). Seemingly, at the turning of water into wine at the wedding of Cana (John 2:1–12), the writer of the Fourth Gospel hints at the manifestation of love through Christ's redemption by foreshadowing Christ's death leading to the pouring out of water at the departure of the bridegroom through blood on the cross.[36] It is at the wedding that Jesus first manifests his δόξαν as a display of the glory of the Father (2:11). The writer returns to this idea with the departure of Judas to betray Christ so that Christ is delivered over to his death. In this, God is glorified in Christ (13:31, 32).[37]

The ideas in John 13:31–32 have great importance within their place in the Gospel of John relative to John 17:4 and the argument I am advancing. If ἐδοξάσθη ἐν αὐτῷ . . . ἐδοξάσθη ἐν αὐτῷ . . . δοξάσει αὐτὸν ἐν αὐτῷ . . . δοξάσει αὐτόν is revelation of the Father through Jesus, it would be reasonable to consider these verses are one reference point for the completed work in 17:4. As Caird writes, "Thus when John put into the mouth of Jesus the words ὁ θεὸς δοξάσει αὐτὸν ἐν αὐτῷ, he could confidently expect his reader whether Jews or Greeks, to understand that God had made a full display of his glory in the person of the Son of Man."[38] Similarly, in agreement and with direct reference to 17:4, Carson notes,

---

35. Calvin and Pringle, *Commentary on the Gospel According to John*, 422.

36. Hengel, "The Interpretation of the Wine Miracle at Cana: John 2:1–11," 14–15; Tabb, "Jesus's Thirst at the Cross: Irony and Intertextuality in John 19:28," 338–51.

37. Lincoln sees Christ's death in view in these statements (*The Gospel According to Saint John*, 386), and Borchert sees both death and resurrection in view (*John 12–21*, 97). However, I would agree with Carson when he writes, "God is glorified in Jesus' temporal obedience, sacrifice, death, resurrection and exaltation—one event; Jesus is glorified in the same event, in the eternal presence and essence of his heavenly Father, partly because by this event he re-enters the glory he had with the Father before the Word became incarnate (1:14), before the world began (17:5). The entire event displays the saving sovereignty of God, God's dawning kingdom" (Carson, *The Gospel According to John*, 483). The broad and open-ended temporary nature of the future in the phrase καὶ ὁ θεὸς δοξάσει αὐτὸν ἐν αὐτῷ seems to account for the cross, resurrection, and ascension, whereas the clauses in 13:31 refer to Christ's obedience and the cross. The *homoioteleuton* that occurs in 13:32 accounts for the variant witness to a smoother reading of opening clause of 13:32. Metzger, *A Textual Commentary on the Greek New Testament*, 206; also Ensor, "The Glorification of the Son of Man," 230–31.

38. Caird, "The Glory of God in the Fourth Gospel," 277.

"Jesus, by perfectly revealing the Father to human beings, has brought glory to the Father (17:4)."[39]

In the *resurrection*, the glory of God is evident in God's ability to raise the dead. The Son of God indicates that the glory of God (the Father—through and in the incarnate Jesus Christ) is manifest *visibly* in the resurrection of Lazarus: "Jesus said to her, 'Did I not tell you that if you believed you would see the glory of God?'" (ὄψῃ τὴν δόξαν τοῦ θεοῦ, 11:40).[40] The author introduces this idea by framing death as something that will lead to the δόξαν of God (11:4). In the development of thought in the Fourth Gospel, God the Father raises the dead and gives them life (5:21) and has granted Jesus authority to raise his own life (10:18).

Third, δόξα / δοξάζω refers to Christ returning to his display of glory in heaven (17:1, 5, cf. 7:39; 12:16).[41] Christ is returning to his pre-existent glory (17:5; cf. 1:1; 12:41).

By examining additional uses of δοξάζω, found 23x in John's Gospel,[42] five ideas about the concepts of "glory" and "glorify" are clarified. First, John 7:39 uses ἐδοξάσθη to speak of Jesus ascending and receiving the glory he had prior to his incarnation (cf. 17:5), for it concerns the giving of the Spirit. The giving of the Spirit only comes when Jesus leaves this earth to return to the presence of his Father in heaven (cf. John 15:26; Acts 1:5), save the temporary filling of the Spirit for the disciples in John 20:22. The Acts narrative places the coming of the Spirit after the ascension of Christ to heaven and his seating at the right hand of the Father (Acts 3:13). John 7:39 speaks of Christ being glorified and does not refer to the Father being glorified. Instead, it is the Father who will glorify

---

39. Carson, *The Gospel According to John*, 482 (italics mine).

40. The verb, ὄψῃ, 2nd. per., sg, fut., act. mid. of ὁράω, as indicated above, refers to something able to be grasped visibly.

41. Robertson believes that the request for the re-establishment of his pre-incarnate glory with the Father implies "he did not possess on earth the full glory he had in the beginning" (*Grammar*, 127). It seems that it would be more accurate to say that Christ did not possess on earth *the manifestation of* the full glory he had in the beginning. Robertson, following Strachan, immediately says, "In the death of Jesus the power and presence of God was *manifested* supremely" (emphasis mine). Quoting Strachan, he says, "The Cross is the complete manifestation of God's glory, revealing his goodness or love to the utmost, yet not complete unless that love is accepted and reproduced in men's lives" (Robertson, *Grammar*, 127–28; ref. Strachan, 206).

42. I will exclude discussion of the Spirit glorifying the Son, for it is outside of the scope of this work. Similarly, I will not discuss the use in John 17 so as not to beg the question of the meaning of 17:4.

Christ in the ascension, restoring to him the visible glory he had prior to the incarnation.

Second, John 8:54 uses both δοξάσω and δοξάζων in the sense of "to present oneself or another as praiseworthy."[43] It uses the noun to speak of the result of the verb: "If I glorify [present as praiseworthy] myself, my glory [the renown, majesty, or praiseworthiness] is nothing. It is my Father who glorifies [presents as praiseworthy] me."[44] More specifically, the Christ, in his voluntary humility, is not making *himself* praiseworthy in the acts of making his divinity known to others.[45] Instead, the Father is making the divinity of Christ known so that he is presenting Christ as praiseworthy as God. Even so, this verse does not speak of Christ bringing glory to the Father, but of the Father bringing glory to Christ. Yet 8:55 demonstrates that such glory leads to the knowledge of God the Father.[46]

Third, John 12:23 uses δοξασθῇ to speak of one of the events of "the hour," which, in this passage, refers to the work of the cross. This is evident as "the hour" of glorification (12:23), the hour in which Christ will refuse to make a plea to be rescued (12:27). It also is evident in Christ's immediate discourse with the parable of the dying kernel of wheat (12:24) and the losing of one's life (12:25). This is the same period in which Christ will be "lifted up from the earth" (12:32)—a reference to being lifted up onto the cross to die, as the prior referents of 3:14 and 8:28 show.

---

43. This is my explanation of the concept found in 8:54. To bring glory to oneself is to bring focus to oneself that intends to invoke the praise of another. For the term can mean "praise" or "honor." Balz and Schneider cite John 8:54 as an example of "the critical sense of honoring oneself" (Balz and Schneider, "δοξάζω," *EDNT*, 348). See also L&N, "δοξάζω; δόξα," 429.

44. Michaels also notes, "He is here basically repeating what he said in verse 50, using the verb 'glorify' in place of the expression 'to seek glory'" (Michaels, *John*, 529).

45. Both Burge and Whitacre recognize that the question in 8:53, "Who do you make yourself out to be?" (τίνα σεαυτὸν ποιεῖς) has the force of "What are you making of yourself here?" or "Who are you making yourself out to be?" The question is "antagonistic and aggressive" (Burge) and questions what Jesus is promoting (Whitacre) (Burge, *John*, 263; Whitacre, *John*, 229). Thus, in 8:54 Jesus responds to a question about apparent self-promotion or the appearance of claiming himself to be praiseworthy. The refutation of self-praise or self-praiseworthiness is in view: "Jesus refutes any suggestion that he has promoted himself. He well understands that any self-praise, any self-glory, independent of the glory of God, *means nothing*" (Carson, *John*, 356).

46. As Lincoln surmises, "Jesus, however, is not in the business of self-aggrandizement, of having to make himself something he is not . . . The issue is that of how the one true God is known. Now that Jesus has come, God is to be known through *the revelation that takes place in him*. To refuse Jesus, therefore, is also to forfeit any genuine knowledge of God (Lincoln, *The Gospel According to Saint John*, 275–276; italics mine).

Yet the glorifying of the Son and the glorifying of the Father occur either in tandem, in sync, and/or synonymously with one another.[47] The Father glorifies his name (12:28) in the purpose for which Christ has come—to die rather than be delivered from the hour of death (12:27). However, this event is part of "the hour . . . for the Son of Man to be glorified" (12:23). The Father will bring praise to his name as God by glorying the Son of Man as the Son goes to the cross to fulfill his purpose in death.

The Father also speaks of having glorified his name already.[48] In the Fourth Gospel, God's glory is evident in Christ (1:14; 7:18; 11:4). As Christ makes praiseworthy the Father through his words and acts, so the Father makes himself praiseworthy in those same acts—"I have glorified it"—even as he makes praiseworthy Christ. The glorification work of the Father in Christ in 8:54 and 11:4 seems to serve as two reference points for the Father working in Christ prior to the cross and resurrection in order to bring glory to himself. The Father makes the divinity of Christ known through his words and deeds, and Christ in turn makes the Father known majestically above all.

Fourth, returning again to 13:31–32 and inserting "make praiseworthy" as the conceptual idea of "glorify," in a similar manner to 12:23, 13:31 speaks of God the Father being glorified (ἐδοξάσθη) in Christ—"in him." God the Father will be made praiseworthy in making Christ praiseworthy in his death. However, a result of being glorified—εἰ[49]—is that God the Father will glorify himself (δοξάσει), seemingly speaking of the resurrection of Christ, (e.g., "in himself . . . at once"). The work of Christ on the cross and in the resurrection brings glory to the Father.

Fifth, broader in scope than 12:23 and 13:31, 14:13 uses δοξασθῇ when speaking of the Father being glorified by the disciples' reliance on the Son through prayer. The dependency of the disciples demonstrates the all-sufficiency of Christ and his divine ability to do what the disciples ask without limits (e.g., ὅ τι ἂν . . . τοῦτο ποιήσω). But the power displayed

---

47. Michaels proposes, "On the assumption that the glorification of God's name is the same as the glorification of Jesus himself, 'the Son of man' (v. 23), it appears that the promise, 'I will glorify again,' refers to Jesus' 'hour' now at hand" (Michaels, *John*, 694).

48. "It is, perhaps, more natural to interpret the statement as meaning that the Father's name has been glorified in *the revelation that has taken place through the ministry of Jesus* ('I have glorified it'), and that now the *revelation* is about to be climaxed in the obedience of the Son on the cross and in his exaltation by the Father" (Beasley-Murray, *John*, 212; italics mine).

49. The writer leaves the apodosis unstated yet implied, so as to create an "if/then" result clause.

by and through Christ is that of the Father (cf. John 5:19, 30a; 10:37-38). The Father is demonstrated to be praiseworthy "in the Son" (ἐν τῷ υἱῷ). The Son, in working on behalf of the prayer-dependent disciples, makes the power of the Father known to the disciples so that the Father is manifested as glorious in his working. John 15:8 adds that the Father is glorified (ἐδοξάσθη) through the fruit borne by the disciples by means of their dependence on Christ. The fruit points back to the greatness of the Father who gave the power of Christ to answer the prayer done in his name.[50]

Thus, it is certain that Christ glorifies the Father because the Father is working in Christ to bring Christ glory. The Father will glorify Christ as Jesus goes to the cross in concert with the purpose of his coming in his incarnation (12:23, 27). Jesus manifests the Father as glorious for purposing redemption for humankind in him (cf. 1:29, 13; 8:54; 11:4). The Father will glorify Christ by raising him from the dead, showing the power of God over death. Christ will manifest the Father as all-powerful (13:31). The Father, likewise, will be glorified in Christ in the ascension of Christ (7:39) and in the resulting Spirit-wrought fruit of good and powerful works in the lives of the disciples (15:8).

Yet it remains that in the past that the Father already has glorified his name within the Fourth Gospel (12:23-24). Thus, δόξα /δοξάζω refers to more than Christ's mission to the cross.

Van der Merwe, looking at the uses of δόξα and δοξάζειν via discourse analysis sees a chiastic pattern in the use of the noun and verb forms of "glory" in John 17:1-5.[51] Following the pattern of Malatestra, he suggests the following chiasm:[52]

A   δόξασόν σου τὸν υἱόν (17:1)
B   ὁ υἱὸς δοξάσῃ σέ (17:1)
C   ἡ αἰώνιος ζωὴ (17:3)
B1 ἐγώ σε ἐδόξασα (17:4)

---

50. "Since the fruit of believers is a consequence of the Son's redemptive work, the result of the vine's pulsating life (15:4), and the Son's response to the prayers of his followers (14:13), it follows that their fruitfulness brings glory to the Father through the Son" (Carson, *John*, 518). Morris's comments would agree with my conclusion and the conclusion drawn by Carson: "The disciples will surely glorify the Father by their continual fruit-bearing; since they cannot bear fruit of themselves (v. 4) their fruitfulness is evidence of the Father at work in them and thus it glorifies him" (Morris, *John*, 597).

51. Van der Merwe, "The Glory-Motif in John 17:1-5: An Exercise in Biblical Semantics," 229-31.

52. Van der Merwe refers to Malatesta, "The Literary Structure of John 17 (Two Folding Charts)," 190-214.

A1 δόξασόν με σύ (17:5)

On the basis of the proposed structure, the outer frame of the chiasm interprets δοξάζειν from the perspective in which the Son is glorified (A-A¹). The inner frame of the chiastic structure interprets δοξάζειν from the perspective of the glorification of the Father (B-B¹). For van der Merwe, then, "the pattern indicates that the δοξάζειν theme revolves around the ἡ αἰώνιος ζωὴ theme. Thus, the glorification of the Father and of the Son has to be interpreted from the perspective of ἡ αἰώνιος ζωὴ."[53] Van der Merwe suggests ἡ αἰώνιος ζωὴ provides "the main theological setting" for interpreting δοξάζειν.[54]

If van der Merwe's conclusions are correct, it would give support to the idea that Christ glorifies God through revelation, for eternal life comes through the knowledge (γινώσκωσιν) of the Father and the Son (17:3). Although van der Merwe includes proleptic ideas in his view of 17:4, he does come to such conclusions.[55] He would translate the δόξα clause in 17:4 as "I have perfectly revealed your identity and greatness on earth."[56]

Conclusion on the Use of Δοξάζω and Δόξα

The glorification of God the Father of which Jesus speaks occurs prior to John 17 within his public and private ministries in John 1:18–12:50 and 13:1–16:33, respectively. Jesus is revealing the Father by his works. The display of δόξα makes the greatness of the Father known through Christ. In the full narrative of the Fourth Gospel, such knowledge leads to eternal life for those who place faith in Christ.

---

53. Van der Merwe, "Semantics," 231.

54. Van der Merwe, "Semantics," 231. Van der Merwe defines "setting" as "the theological environment from which a word or a concept is to be interpreted due to the influence the theological environment will have on the understanding and interpretation of that particular word or concept" ("Semantics," 231).

55. Van der Merwe states, "δοξάζειν in verse 4 can be taken as referring to Jesus' obedient revelation of the Father's identity (σου τὸ ὄνομα [v 6] and ὅτι τὰ ῥήματα ἃ ἔδωκάς μοι [v 8]). Therefore, in a dynamic-equivalent translation, ἐγώ σε ἐδόξασα (v 4) can be translated as 'I have perfectly (qualified by τελειώσας) revealed your identity and greatness' (see vv 7–8). Because of the close relationship between the 'glorification' of the Father and that of the Son is the identification of the Father's identity here an allusion of the Son's glorification" (Van der Merwe, "Semantics," 244–45).

56. Van der Merwe, "Semantics," 247.

The idea of δόξα as a visible display of God is consistent with the use of δόξα in the LXX. John mirrors the senses of the LXX. The LXX draws its concept of δόξα from δοκέω translating the כָּבוֹד of the MT.

ANALYSIS OF "ON THE EARTH" (ΕΠΙ ΤΗΣ ΓΗΣ)

The second half of the first clause in 17:4 seems to reference Jesus's earthly ministry. At question is the significance of this clause to Jesus's provision of glory.

I will consider the use of ἐπὶ τῆς γῆς in certain OT passages that formulate an echo with John 17:4. I also will explore the concept of glorifying God the Father on earth as a theme carrying over to the Gospel of John from the OT (i.e., Gen 11:4, 8, 9; 1 Kgs 8:27).

I will examine also other ideas within the Fourth Gospel supporting "on the earth" as a phrase that references Jesus's incarnational and earthly ministry. I will consider the words of Jesus that point to reflective ideas both in his public ministry and private ministry. I will explore the works (signs, miracles) of Jesus performed in public that demonstrate Jesus is revealing the Father through his works. "Earth" (γῆς) is not John's usual word for speaking of the inhabitable sphere. John's preferred word for the inhabitable sphere of this present world is κόσμος. But κόσμος refers also to inhabitants (3:16) and a structural system 12:25.[57]

---

57. BDAG notes eight usages of κόσμος in the Scriptures, five of which are evident in the Gospel of John: (1) "the sum total of everything here and now, *the world, the (orderly) universe*," citing John 1:10b; 17:5, 24; and 21:25 as examples; (2) "planet earth as a place of inhabitation, *the world . . . as the habitation of humanity*," citing John 12:25 and 16:21 as examples; (3) "planet earth as a place of inhabitation . . . [the] *earth, world* in contrast to heaven," citing John 1:9, 10a; 3:17a, 19; 6:14; 9:5a, 39; 10:36; 11:27; 12:46; 13:1a; 14:19; 16:28ab; 17:11a, 12, 18; 18:37, 36ab; (4) "humanity in general," citing John 1:29; 3:17b; 5:14; 7:4; 8:12, 26; 9:5; 12:19, 47a; 14:22, 31; 17:6, 21, 23; 18:20, and citing John 3:16, 17c; 6:33, 51; and 12:47b as "of all humanity, but especially of believers, as the object of God's love;" (5) "the system of human existence in its many aspects, *the world . . .* and everything that belongs to it, appears as that which is hostile to God, i.e. lost in sin, wholly at odds w. anything divine, ruined and depraved," citing John 1:10; 7:7; 8:23; 12:25, 31a, 31b; 13:1; 14:17, 27, 30; 15:18, 19abcd; 16:8, 11, 20, 33ab; 17:9, 11b, 14abc, 15, 16ab, 18b, 25; 18:36. William Arndt et al., BDAG, 561–63. The third usage above—"planet earth as a place of inhabitation . . . [the] *earth, world* in contrast to heaven"—demonstrates that the writer of the Fourth Gospel can speak of the earth with a term synonymous to γῆς. In contrast to the 105 usages of κόσμος, forms of γῆς appear only eleven times in the Fourth Gospel in addition to 17:4 if one discounts 8:6. The usages are "land" (or "countryside" or "ashore," 3:22; 6:21; 21:8, 9, 11), of the earthly sphere in contrast to heaven (3:31 [3x]), "ground" (12:24, 32). Even though the writer uses ἐπὶ τῆς γῆς in 6:21, it is evident that the use differs from 17:4, for it speaks of a boat

The Use of ἐπὶ τῆς γῆς in the LXX

Of 288 uses in the LXX, there seem to be seven distinct ways the writers of the Hebrew Bible and the Apocrypha use ἐπὶ τῆς γῆς.[58] First, writers use the term to indicate *in/over/of the land*. The references are to a specific geographical location, like Egypt or Canaan, or the general places in the sense of "anywhere" on the earth.[59]

Second, there are uses constructed as ἐπὶ προσώπου τῆς γῆς or ἐπὶ προσώπου πάσης τῆς γῆς—literally, "on the face of the earth" or "on the face of all of the earth." Idiomatically, these ideas communicate "on the earth," in multiple senses, including *on the surface* (Amos 5:8), *toward the ground* (Gen 48:12), *among mankind* (Gen 48:16), *in the land* (2 Chr 6:31), *on the face of the ground* (Jer 25:33, 32:19 in LXX-Swete, and 32:33

(τὸ πλοῖον) reaching the shore (γῆς).

58. Of the 288 uses, eighteen times writers use ἐπὶ προσώπου τῆς γῆς or ἐπὶ προσώπου πάσης τῆς γῆς: Gen 7:23; 11:4; 41:56; Deut 7:6; 14:2; 2 Sam 14:7; 2 Chr 6:31; Sir 38:8; Amos 5:8; Jer 8:2; 16:14; 32:26, 33; Ezek 34:6; 38:20; 39:14; Dan 4:22; 8:5. The phrase also appears in the accusative an additional 149x as ἐπὶ τὴν γῆν or ἐπὶ πᾶσαν τὴν γῆν. These usages do not lend themselves to a possible echo, so they are excluded from this examination. Psalm 57:6, 12 (56:6, 12 LXX), and 108:5 (107:6, Swete, Rahlfs; 107:5, Brenton) possibly are exceptions. But the differences between ἐπὶ πᾶσαν τὴν γῆν and ἐπὶ τῆς γῆς would make an echo unlikely.

59. Gen 12:10; 19:28, 31; 26:1, 22; 34:21; 41:31; 41:56; 42:6; 43:1; 45:6, 7, 26; 47:27; Exod 8:23; 9:5, 22 (in which the *land of Egypt* is implied), 23 (not reflected in ESV); 10:6, 12; 20:12; 23:26; 33:16; 34:12, 15; Lev 20:2; 22:24; 25:10, 18; 26:5; Num 14:14; 22:5; 33:55; 35:32; Deut 4:14, 25; 40; 5:16, 33; 7:13; 8:10; 11:9, 21a, 25; 12:1a, 10, 19; 15:11; 23:20 [ESV; 23:21 LXX]; 25:15; 28:8, 11; 30:18, 20; 31:13; Josh 24:15; 1 Sam 23:23; 1 Kgs 8:27, 40; 10:12; 17:7; 2 Kgs 11:3; 2 Chr 6:28, 20:29; 22:12; 32:31; 1 Esd A 5:49 (LXX-Swete edition; 5:50 in LXX-R and Brenton); 1 Macc 13:32; 14:11, 13; 15:29; Ps 101:6 [100:6 LXX]; Odes 2:13; Job 1:10; 37:17; Hos 2:23 (2:25 in LXX-Swete); 4:1, 2; Amos 5:2; 9:15; Zech 9:16; Isa 4:2; 5:8; 6:12; 7:22; 14:1, 2; 16:4; 26:10; 38:11; Jer 3:16; 4:5; 5:30; 9:3 (9:2 in LXX-R), 24 (9:23 in LXX-R); 14:2 (based on parallelism with "Jerusalem," and not "on the ground" as in LXX English translations—Lexham, Brenton—and the ESV, NRSV); 14:8, 13; 25:5; 50:20 (27:20 in LXX in all traditions, but 50:20 in MT); 51:27 (28:27 in LXX); 35:7 (42:7 LXX), 15 (42:15 LXX); 41:2 (48:2 LXX); Ezek 12:15, 22; 28:25; 33:24, 27, 29; 36:17, 28; 37:25; Dan 4:10 (4:7 in LXX in Swete and Brenton; 4:10 in Rahlfs); 9:6. On Exod 8:23, modern English versions do not reflect the ἐπὶ τῆς γῆς of the Rahlfs, Swete, or Brenton traditions, but follow the MT, which has no equivalent terms for ἐπὶ τῆς γῆς [וְשַׂמְתִּי פְדֻת בֵּין עַמִּי וּבֵין עַמֶּךָ לְמָחָר יִהְיֶה הָאֹת הַזֶּה]. On Exod 8:19, the MT of Exod 8:19 is reflected in 8:19 of the Rahlfs tradition, and 8:23 of the Swete and Brenton traditions. The Rahlfs tradition adds τὸ σημεῖον, which seems to be reflected in the ESV, NASB, NIV, NRSV, CSB, NET, and NLT. Also, on Isa 8:11, the Rahlfs' LXX has εἶπα Οὐκέτι μὴ ἴδω τὸ σωτήριον τοῦ θεοῦ ἐπὶ τῆς γῆς, οὐκέτι μὴ ἴδω ἄνθρωπον. However, the Brenton and Swete editions have Εἶπα, οὐκέτι οὐ μὴ ἴδω τὸ σωτήριον τοῦ Θεοῦ ἐπὶ γῆς ζώντων, οὐκέτι μὴ ἴδω τὸ σωτήριον τοῦ Ἰσραὴλ ἐπὶ γῆς, οὐκέτι μὴ ἴδω ἄνθρωπον.

in LXX-R and Brenton), and *inhabited world* or *in all the inhabited places of the world* (Jer 25:26 [38:26 in the LXX] and Ezek 34:6).

Third, some uses of ἐπὶ τῆς γῆς, often translated as "on the earth" or "upon the earth," indicate a concept of *among humankind, in this present world,* or *in all the inhabited world*. These include references to the Lord obliterating humankind such that only eight persons remain (Gen 7:23b), or the sense of, "of finite existence," referring to man (Ps 10:18).[60] Or it is used in the sense of in the present world as opposed to heaven (Odes 5:10; 4 B:10 in LXX-Swete).[61]

Fourth, ἐπὶ τῆς γῆς sometimes stands in contrast to heaven above. It can have the closely related sense of "in the entire world" or "in the entire earthly sphere," as in Job 41:33 (41:24 in LXX-Swete and Brenton, and 41:25 in LXX-R).[62]

Fifth, the Genesis writer uses ἐπὶ τῆς γῆς repeatedly as the place of the accomplishment of God's works in creation in Gen 1, 2, and 3 with the idea that ἐπὶ τῆς γῆς is the place of the accomplishment of God's purposes for humankind in this present creation—both fruitfulness and dominion. This is the sphere in which God's initial dealings with man take place and where the hope of redemption is accomplished, as pronounced

---

60. Ps 9:39 in LXX-R and LXX-Swete; Ps 9:38 in Brenton. In the *NETS*, the translations "on the face of the whole earth" (Gen 7:23b) and "so that man on the earth may not add to brag" (Ps 9:38) reflect these ideas.

61. Other references in this category include Num 12:3; Deut 11:21c; 12:1c; Josh 23:14; 2 Sam 7:9; 1 Kgs 8:23; 1 Chr 1:10; 17:8, 21; 22:8; 1 Chr 29:30; Jdt 13:18; 2 Macc 15:5; Ps 46:8 (Ps 45:8 Brenton, 45:9 Swete, 45:10 Rahlfs; see also ἐν τῇ γῇ in LXX 45:11 in Rahlfs and τῆς γῆς in LXX 45:10 in Rahlfs); Ps 140:11 (although ESV/RSV have "in the land;" 139:12 in LXX-R and LXX-Swete, and 139:11 in Brenton); Odes 5:9 (2x) (4 B:9 in Swete); Odes 5:18 (4 B:18) (2x); Odes 11:11 (LXX-R, 7:11 in LXX-Swete); Prov 30:24 (in LXX-R and Brenton, but Prov 24:59 in LXX-Swete); Eccl 8:14, 16; Job 1:3, 8; 2:3; 8:9; 14:5; 20:4; 22:8; Job 37:12; Sir 36:22 (36:17 in LXX-R); 49:14; Pss. Sol. 17:2, 28 (in LXX-R; 17:27 in LXX-Swete); Isa 23:9; 24:14, 17; 26:9 (2x), 18, 21; 42:4; 62:7; 65:16; Jer 23:5; 25:29, 31 (with the term μέρος added to the clause, 32:17 in LXX-Swete, and 32:31 in LXX-R and Brenton editions); 27:11 (34:9 in LXX-Swete, and 34:11 in LXX-R and Brenton); Bar 1:11; 3:16, 20, 31 (3:37 LXX in Brenton, 3:38 in Swete and Rahlfs); Ezek 1:15; 28:18; 38:12 (ἐπὶ τὸν ὀμφαλὸν τῆς γῆς, lit. "upon *the navel* of the earth"); 38:20b; Dan 2:10; 3:1 (in LXX-Swete and LXX-R only, and not reflected in Brenton); 7:23.

62. The *NETS* seems to agree with its translation of Job 41:25a as, "There is nothing on the earth like it." See also Josh 2:11; 1 Kgs 8:27; 1 Chr 29:11; 2 Chr 6:14, 18; Esth 1:1g (LXX-R, Brenton = A7); Ps 73:9 (Ps 72:9 LXX); Ps 73:25 (72:25 LXX); Eccl 5:2 (5:1 LXX); Sir 39:31; Amos 8:9; 9:6b; Joel 2:30 (Joel 3:3 in LXX-R); 3 Macc 2:12.

in Gen 3:15.[63] The later usage in Job 7:1 makes a reference to Gen 3 and the curse upon the ground.

Viable OT Uses of ἐπὶ τῆς γῆς in John 17:4

The various uses of ἐπὶ τῆς γῆς in the LXX traditions provide options for identifying an allusion, echo, or fulfillment with respect to one or more OT passages and John 17:4. However, not all of the options are viable, especially those indicating surface and those indicating a position over/in/of the land. The content of John 17:4 and the lack of use of προσώπου rules out such uses as options. Yet there remain three options that could be the OT background of John 17:4:[64] (1) Genesis 1–2 as a composite whole that focuses on the earth as the sphere of man as an agent of God and his will; (2) Sir 38:6–8, due to the broad similarity with the majority of the words in John 17:4; and (3) Ps 48:10 and its reference to the praise of the name of the Lord on the earth within the larger context of Ps 48.

"On the Earth" as Place of Accomplishment of Genesis 1 and 2 Purposes

There is a refrain of ἐπὶ τῆς γῆς throughout Gen 1. As the days of creation pass, the activities of the creation take place within the sphere of ἐπὶ τῆς γῆς (Gen 1:11, 17, 22, 26, 28; 2:5; 3:1, 14). Whether ἐπὶ τῆς γῆς refers to activity on the land or in the realm of earth in contrast to "the heavens" (τὸν οὐρανὸν, Gen 1:1), the echo remains the same. Similarly, the further uses of ἐπὶ τῆς γῆς in 6:1, 4, 5, 6, 12, 17 reinforce the idea that humankind has not done what is pleasing in the sight of the Lord within the created realm.[65] Humankind has not maintained the stewardship of subduing

---

63. See also Gen 1:11, 17, 22, 26, 28; 2:5; 3:1, 14; 4:12, 14; 6:1, 4, 5, 6, 12, 17; 7:4, 6, 10, 12, 17, 18, 19, 21a, 23a, 24; 9:16, 17; 10:8, 32; Deut 3:24; 4:10, 32, 36, 39 (ditto?); Ps 48:10 (47:11 in LXX-Swete and LXX-R, and 47:10 in Brenton); Job 7:1.

64. Exod 33:16 has a δόξα term in it that could make the verse a candidate for the background of 17:4. But the verse speaks of the honoring of Moses and the people of the land (Israel), and not of glorifying God. So this is possible, but not probable.

65. "By recurring reference to mankind (*'ādām*) in 6:5–7, the passage focuses on the source of his grief . . . But his is not regret over destroying humanity; paradoxically, so foul has become mankind that it is the necessary step to salvage him . . . God indicates that unbridled human sin has become his source of anguish. Yet this anguish does not reflect impotent remorse; it entails also God's angry response at the injury inflicted by human rebellion," Mathews, *Genesis 1—11:26*, 343.

the earth and multiplying upon it—and thus of remaining obedient to the commands given for man ἐπὶ τῆς γῆς in the creation account.

The narrative of the removal of the entirety of humankind from the earth proceeds with ἐπὶ τῆς γῆς in focus (7:4, 6, 10, 12, 17, 18, 19, 21a, 23a, 24). Each of the aforementioned references in Gen 7 refers to the location of floodwaters in judgment. The ἐπὶ τῆς γῆς scenes are the setting of the destruction of humankind rather than the place in which man and woman enjoy both God's creation and fellowship with God. That enjoyment of God and his creation was pleasing in the sight of God, for God blesses them (1:28— וַיְבָרֶךְ אֹתָם אֱלֹהִים, cf. 2:3) and identifies their creation, work, and things they enjoy as "good" (2:9; 1:31—טוֹבa, 12; cf. 2:18).

The judgment scenes of ἐπὶ τῆς γῆς serve as the counterpart to the goodness of the "earth" in the creation narrative. Whereas all ἐπὶ τῆς γῆς was created as "good" in Gen 1 and continued in "good," now that which is ἐπὶ τῆς γῆς is not good; therefore, it is no longer in position to bring glory to the Creator actively.

In the Genesis account, the Lord promised one to come who would deliver the earth from its curse such that it will be released from judgment (Gen 3:15; cf. Rom 8:18–25). From John 17:4, hearing an echo in Gen 7 is just as viable as hearing an echo in Gen 1, for ἐπὶ τῆς γῆς now is the sphere where the Lord has been rejected rather than glorified—where no one does what God commands them to do. In John 17:4, the echo points to one who now comes to do what humankind is failing to do by the time of Noah's day—to do ἐπὶ τῆς γῆς what glorifies God and to restore the joy and fellowship humankind enjoyed in the Creation before the fall.

"On the Earth" as the Place of God's Healing

In the NRSV, Sir 38:8 reads, "God's works will never be finished; and from him health spreads over all the earth" (καὶ οὐ μὴ συντελεσθῇ ἔργα αὐτοῦ, καὶ εἰρήνη παρ αὐτοῦ ἐστιν ἐπὶ προσώπου τῆς γῆς). While the concept of healing seems to be foreign to the context of John 17, it is evident that John put much weight on the healing power of Christ within the signs to point to his Messiahship.[66] Therefore, one cannot overlook the possibility

---

66. The writer of the Fourth Gospel records four healing miracles: (1) The royal official's son (4:46–54), (2) the sick man at Bethesda (5:1–16), (3) the man born blind (9:1–14), and (4) raising Lazarus from the dead (11:1–44). Several writers have called attention to the significance of Jesus as healer in the Fourth Gospel: Guthrie, "The Importance of Signs in the Fourth Gospel," 72–83; Kim, "The Christological and

of an echo hailing from Sir 38:8 when one sees parallels to the terms of John 17:4 in the larger context of Sir 38:6–8.

Table 3. Sir 38:6–8 LXX Compared to John 17:4 GNT

Sir 38:6–8 LXX	John 17:4 GNT
⁶καὶ αὐτὸς ἔδωκεν ἀνθρώποις ἐπιστήμην ἐνδοξάζεσθαι ἐν τοῖς θαυμασίοις αὐτοῦ· ⁷ἐν αὐτοῖς ἐθεράπευσεν καὶ ἦρεν τὸν πόνον αὐτοῦ, ⁸μυρεψὸς ἐν τούτοις ποιήσει μίγμα· καὶ οὐ μὴ συντελέσῃ ἔργα αὐτοῦ, καὶ εἰρήνη παρ' αὐτοῦ ἐστιν <u>ἐπὶ</u> προσώπου <u>τῆς γῆς</u>.	ἐγώ σε ἐδόξασα <u>ἐπὶ τῆς γῆς</u> τὸ ἔργον τελειώσας ὃ δέδωκάς μοι ἵνα ποιήσω
⁶And he **gave** skill to human beings that he **might be glorified** in his marvelous works. ⁷By them the physician heals and takes away pain; ⁸the pharmacist **makes** a mixture from them. God's **works** will never **be finished**; and from him health spreads **over all the earth.**	I **glorified** you **on earth, having accomplished the work** that **you gave me to do.**

Concerning the comparability of Sir 38:1–15 to John 17, Sirach's subject matter concerns the honoring of physicians as the instruments of God. They are instruments of healing who have the power of God (38:2,

---

Eschatological Significance of Jesus' Miracle in John 5," 413–24; Kok, "The Healing of the Blind Man in John, 36–62; McColl and Ascough, "Jesus and People with Disabilities: Old Stories, New Approaches," 1–11; Metzner, "Der Geheilte von Johannes 5—Repräsentant des Unglaubens," 177–93; Pilch, "Jesus as Healer," https://www.baylor.edu/ifl/christianreflection/HealthArticlePilch.pdf; Rhodes, "Signs and Wonders: Disability in the Fourth Gospel," 53–75; Thomas, "Healing in the Atonement: A Johannine Perspective," 22–39; Thompson, "Healing at the Pool of Bethesda: A Challenge to Asclepius?" 65–84; Uzukwu, "The Disabled in the Gospel of John: An Exegetical Study of John's Account of Jesus' Healing in John 5:1–47 and 9:1–41, and its Implications for Contemporary African Society," 39–67; Van Dyke, "Miracles of Jesus in the Gospel of John," 15–30; Waterson, "The Miracles of Healing in the Fourth Gospel," 21–26; Wynn, "Johannine Healings and the Otherness of Disability," 61–75. Especially see Thompson ("Signs and Faith in the Fourth Gospel," 89–108), who concludes events in the Fourth Gospel "[show] both that healing could be used as an image of salvation, and that healing was also part of salvation" (100), and "through the signs God is at work restoring to health the very world which was made through the Logos who became incarnate as a human being" (104).

9, 12–15). God is the source of healing (38:9), but physicians, with their use of medicines, are the secondary cause of healing.

Within the subject matter, three things are important to note. First, in Sir 38:5, the writer of Sirach makes a reference to Exod 15:22–27. He appeals to the healing of the bitter waters at the beginning of Israel's sojourn in the wilderness in order to make a case of healing as a work of God. Implicitly, the writer frames Moses as a physician who acts as the Lord's instrument to heal the bitter waters.[67] If the author of the Fourth Gospel has in view Sir 38 while penning John 17:4, he again would be depicting Jesus as one greater than Moses, as he does throughout the gospel account (cf. 1:17, 45, 51; 3:14–16; 5:46; 6:32; 7:22–23; 9:28–29). Jesus would be the greater *physician* as the instrument of God's healing acts.

However, such a suggestion seems to be without merit. There is great disparity in the comparable content in John. The subject matter of John 17 reveals Christ as the great *intercessor*, and concerns God's glorification through his Son, the Son's disciples, and the unity of the future church.

Second, the writer of Sirach depicts healing as a continuation of God's work in creation. The work of God in the physician, like that in the Creation account, intends to spread over the entire earth. As some see John 17:4 as a fulfillment of the work of creation,[68] the concept of healing as a work of creation would lend to reading John 17:4 as a reference to Sir 38.

Yet identifying the "work" of John 17:4 with the "works" in the Fourth Gospel is unfounded.[69] The concepts are separate, with "works" especially referring to the miraculous signs in the Gospel of John. Moreover, it might be better to recognize that the writer of Sirach refers to Gen 2:1 without suggesting the writer of the Fourth Gospel then draws from both Sir 38 and Gen 2.

Third, the comparable words themselves have few grammatical agreements beyond sharing the same roots. The comparable terms are not the same case, tense, or number in any of the eight terms sharing the same roots. For example, ἔδωκεν in Sir 38:6 is aorist, active, indicative,

---

67. See Thompson, "Signs of Faith," 100, for discussion of God as healer in Exodus 15.

68. Stephen J. Bedard, "The Johannine Creation Account);" Brown, "Creation's Renewal in the Gospel of John," 274–75; Coloe, "Theological Reflections on the Creation in the Gospel of John," 5–6; ibid, "The Structure of the Johannine Prologue and Genesis 1," 54–55. Hengel, "The Old Testament in the Fourth Gospel," 393–94. The many aforementioned authors recognize an echo of Gen 2:1 in John 17:4.

69. I will provide extended discussion on this in chapter 5.

MAKING GOD KNOWN PUBLICLY AND PRIVATELY

third person, singular from δίδωμι, whereas δέδωκάς in John 17:4 is perfect, active, indicative, second person, singular, agreeing in voice, mood, and person. However, ἐνδοξάζεσθαι in Sir 38:6 is a present, middle/passive, infinitive from ἐνδοξάζομαι, whereas ἐδόξασα in John 17:4 is aorist, active, indicative, first person, singular from δοξάζω, showing no agreement between the terms other than a root.

In Sir 38:8, ποιήσει is future, active, indicative, third person, singular from ποιέω, but ποιήσω in John 17:4 is aorist, active, subjunctive, first person, singular, agreeing only in person between the two terms. Sir 38:8 has συντελέσῃ, an aorist, passive, subjunctive, third person, singular verb from συντελέω, a compound of συν- and τελέω, and thus a derivative of τελέω. However, John 17:4 has τελειώσας, an aorist, active, participle, nominative, masculine, singular verb from τελειόω, a different verb than τελέω, which negates an echo between the two verbs.

Again, in Sir 38:8, one reads ἔργα, a nominative, neuter, plural noun, but in John 17:4 one reads ἔργον, an accusative, singular, neuter noun. The difference is similar to the difference between "works" and "the work" in John's Gospel. Because John makes distinct use between ἔργα and ἔργον, it seems unlikely that an echo is present between the very similar sounding terms, derived the same word, but differing in case and number.

Finally, in terms of grammatical accord, the counterpart term to ἐπὶ τῆς γῆς in Jn. 17:4 is ἐπὶ προσώπου τῆς γῆς in Sir 38:8. While ἐπὶ τῆς γῆς does have a range of usages that include "on the face of the earth" (e.g., surface or inhabited world), it seems that Jesus speaks of "this present world," indicating an age or epoch related to the period of his incarnational ministry rather than "surface" or "every geographical location," as in Sir 38:8. The existence of a verbal echo between Sir 38:8 and John 17:4 is possible but improbable, because the two concepts in the comparable terms are not similar.

"On the Earth" as a Fulfillment of Ps 48:10

In Ps. 48:10 (LXX-R 47:11, LXX-Brenton 47:10), one reads, οὕτως καὶ ἡ αἴνεσίς σου ἐπὶ τὰ πέρατα τῆς γῆς ("Thus, also, your praise is to the ends of the earth").[70] The LXX αἴνεσίς means "praise,"[71] and reflects the Heb. תְּהִלָּה, translated as both "praise" and "glory" in the MT.[72] It is possible, therefore, to render Ps 48:10 as "Thus, also, your *glory* is to the ends of the earth." Although different terms, αἴνεσίς and δόξα have a semantic overlap that would allow one to hear the synonymous concept in the alternative term.

The terms ἡ αἴνεσίς σου translate תְּהִלָּה, a term used for both "glory" and "praise."[73] Although different in terminology than John 17:4—ἐδόξασα vs. αἴνεσίς—the concepts are very similar. In Ps 48:10, the praise "*of you*" (σου)—the praise directed toward the name of God—extends ἐπὶ τὰ πέρατα τῆς γῆς. In John 17:4, Jesus brings glory to "you" (σε) to the extent of ἐπὶ τῆς γῆς.

Although it would seem that ἐπὶ should be translated with respect to geographic distance because of τὰ πέρατα (i.e., "to"), it is possible that it could speak of a location (i.e., "on") for that is within the semantic range of the term.[74] However, the sharing of the same meaning of terms is not required for an echo. Thus, ἐπὶ can mean "to" in Ps 48:10 and "on" in John 17:4 and still constitute an echo. When Jesus therefore says ἐπὶ τῆς γῆς ("on the earth"), his hearers could well connect John 17:4 to Ps 48:10 and recall "to the [ends of the] earth."

Structurally, Psalm 48 divides into four strophes: vv. 1–2, 3–8, 9–11, 12–14.[75] The first strophe considers the Lord's beautification of Zion with

---

70. The NET Bible suggests differently, "The praise you receive as far away as the ends of the earth is worthy of your reputation, O God," placing the emphasis on the reception of the praise by the Lord rather than the world-wide communication, and flattening the parallelism between כְּשִׁמְךָ ("as your name") and תְּהִלָּתְךָ כֵּן ("so your praise"). However, most English translations are reflective of the MT, in which both the name of אֱלֹהִים and the praise of that name reach the ends of the earth. The psalmist considers the *extent* of the honoring of God's name, and not the *worth* of the name. The New English Translation of the Septuagint (*NETS*) reads, "Like your name, O God, so also your praise is to the ends of the earth. Full of justice is your right hand" (570).

71. BDAG, 27.

72. *HALOT*, 1692.

73. *HALOT*, 1692. BDB defines the range of meaning of the term as "*praise, adoration, thanksgiving, paid to* [God]" (*Enhanced* BDB, 239).

74. BDAG indicates the range of ἐπὶ includes, "marker of location or surface, answering the question 'where?' *on, upon, near,*" and "marker of movement to or contact with a goal, *toward, in direction of, on,*" (363).

75. Terrien divides Psalm 48 into "five strophes or regular triads made of bicola, except for the tricolon of the final verse (v. 15)," vv. 1–3, 4–6, 7–8, 9–11, 12–14. He views vv. 7–8 as "the center of the whole poem, and that it serves as the core hinge that holds together two integrated themes: divine majesty and the aesthetics of defensive

his presence on the earth. The Lord's presence calls the worshiping community to extol his greatness.[76] The second strophe concerns the establishment of Zion against threatening armies. Zion will stand forever by the power of God (v. 8). The defender of the city is God himself, identified as both לְמִשְׂגָּב (v. 3) and צְבָאוֹ (v. 8).

In strophe three, the writer meditates on the Lord's mercy (חַסְדֶּךָ, v. 10) being in the temple of the Lord's presence in Zion. The meditation leads to praise of the Lord's righteous judgments in Zion and all of the earth. Similarly, the psalmist invites Israel to observe Zion while walking through her. The observation centers on the undefeatable ramparts of the city. By calling Israel to look at the strength of Zion—strength from the Lord's presence in Zion—the psalmist seeks to establish God as the only true God in the hearts and minds of the generations to come.

In all of the strophes, the Lord's exaltation of Zion by his presence in her is central. It is the exaltation of Zion that leads the community to make the Lord known as king. Such a context also allows the reader to recognize the significance of three elements. (1) The psalm is *incarnational* in its context, focusing on God's dwelling *in* Zion, *on* Mt. Zion, and *in* the citadels. This is not an allegory, for the kings of the earth see and tremble (vv. 5–6). This is not to speak of a fully embodied presence of the Lord, but of a presence on earth rather than in heaven.[77] (2) The psalm concerns *God's name being known* to all people. This includes

---

architecture." Terrien, *The Psalms*, 381. However, it is common to divide the Psalm into four strophes of vv. 1–3, 4–8, 9–11, 12–14. McCann, "The Book of Psalms: Introduction, Commentary, and Reflections," 4:870–74; Kidner, *Psalms 1–72*, 179–81; Goldingay, *Songs from a Strange Land*, 110–21. Goldingay and McCann largely base their structure on the character of God within each strophe or subsection. I would divide the Psalm into four strophes of vv. 1–2, 3–8, 9–11, and 12–14, thematically grouping v. 3 with vv. 4–8 because of their focus on the Lord's role in defending Zion from her enemies. In contrast, vv. 1–2 speaks of the beauty of Zion. For a similar structuring of Psalm 48, see John Goldingay, *Psalms*, 82–85.

76. The pronominal suffix of אֱלֹהֵינוּ is first person, plural, indicating that the psalmist is speaking to the worshiping community.

77. VanGemeren speaks similarly, writing, "Only because of God's condescension to dwell on Mount Zion may she be called beautiful in her elevation . . . and 'the joy of the whole earth' (v. 2; cf. 50:2; Lam 2:15). The beauty and joy are not inherent in Mount Zion, because it is surrounded by higher mountains offering a better panoramic view. The godly had a special feeling about Jerusalem that is beautifully and sensitively expressed in this psalm. They looked on the city, mountain, and temple as symbols of God's presence with his people. Therefore, the psalmist uses the geographical/spatial references to express the joy of God's people with the blessed presence of God. Von Rad calls this revelation of God's identification the kenosis of the OT: the beauty of Yahweh's condescension to the needs of his people." VanGemeren, "Psalms," 362.

being known in the city (v. 1) and all the earth (v. 2), "[making] himself known" (v. 3); the people speaking as eyewitnesses in order to tell others of what they have both seen and heard (v. 8); and proclaiming the greatness of Zion and her King to a second generation (vv. 13–14). (3) The intent of God being known *to the next generation* is so that the Lord also might be the God of the next generation and of subsequent generations if each generation is faithful to do as the psalm writer instructs. This is a passing of the faith. One could say that the psalmist intends for one generation to *disciple* the next generation with respect to the greatness of God and Zion.

Each of the above elements—incarnation, revelation, and concern for the faith of generations yet future—are represented in John 17. The incarnate Christ has worked "on the earth" as the Word made flesh (cf. 1:14). He has revealed the name of God publicly and privately (17:3). The prayer itself seeks the unity of the coming generations with the present generation—the later generation that will come to believe in the same God as the disciples present with Christ.

It would therefore seem that there is metalepsis involved in placing ἐπὶ τῆς γῆς in the mouth of Christ in John 17:4.[78] The writer intends for the audience to hear ἐπὶ τῆς γῆς as an echo of Ps 48:10 within the context of the entirety of Ps 48. The ἐπὶ τῆς γῆς of John 17:4 should invoke thoughts of an incarnational, revelatory, discipleship context in which God dwells in Zion and will fortify her against her enemies. The greatness of Zion that comes from God's presence within her is truth for the generation to come.

The complete fulfillment of Ps 48 looks toward an eschatological Zion. But the echo informs the understanding of John 17:4. The work of God among his people is *revelatory*. God is made known and Zion is beautified by God being revealed in her midst. He is praised for his exaltation of Zion on the earth by means of his incarnational, revelatory presence.

---

78. "Metalepsis is a rhetorical and poetical device in which one text alludes to an earlier text in a way that evokes resonances of the earlier text *beyond those explicitly cited*. The result is that the interpretation of a metalepsis requires the reader to recover unstated or suppressed correspondences between the two texts." Hays, *The Conversion of the Imagination*, 2. Hays also writes, "When a literary echo links the text in which it occurs to an earlier text, the figurative effect of the echo can lie in the unstated or suppressed (transumed) points of resonance between the two texts . . . Allusive echo functions to suggest to the reader that text B should be understood in light of a broader interplay with text A, encompassing aspects of A beyond those explicitly noted."

Similarly, therefore, in appealing to Ps 48, John 17:4 references a work *on the earth* for which Christ glorifies the Father. It would appear that this work, too, is *revelatory*.

Conclusion on ἐπὶ τῆς γῆς

It would seem that the writer of the Gospel of John reaches into the OT to draw ἐπὶ τῆς γῆς into John 17. In doing so, John 17 portrays the Fourth Gospel's Logos and Son of God figure as one who intends to succeed *on the earth*—in the present human realm and present creation—where humankind failed. Humankind lived in a place prepared for humankind to fulfill God's purposes for the present creation to be a realm of rule, work, rest, and blessing—ἐπὶ τῆς γῆς—and then experienced judgment in that same realm—ἐπὶ τῆς γῆς. Christ comes to bring glory to God in the same realm—ἐπὶ τῆς γῆς, with perfect completion of the stewardship given to him by the Father. Jesus makes a claim to fulfill what was intended in the creation ἐπὶ τῆς γῆς.

John 17 also makes a double-reference to the OT, drawing also upon the ἐπὶ τῆς γῆς of a Zion psalm in Ps 48:10. In Psalm 48, the ἐπὶ τῆς γῆς is heard within a revelatory, incarnational, discipleship context—a context very similar to that of John 17. Speaking in 17:4, Christ points to himself as the one who has mediated the incarnational presence of God in Zion, who has made God known to the peoples, and who intends for God to be known to generations in Israel to come. Christ's use of ἐπὶ τῆς γῆς is not a complete fulfillment of Ps 48:10, but a partial fulfillment pointing to an eschatological Zion that will experience God's full presence within her.

CONCLUSION

The phrase ἐγώ σε ἐδόξασα ἐπὶ τῆς γῆς speaks of the revelatory work of Christ. The Fourth Gospel's use of ἐδόξασα in the first part of the evangelist's narrative is within the range of the ways in which the LXX uses δόξα. In John 17, Christ draws upon the *display* aspect of δόξα, intending the praiseworthiness of God to be made known by the words and works of Christ.[79]

---

79. Köstenberger, observing John's transposition of Isaianic material, proposes, "Speaking of glory, while John does not record the Synoptic account of the transfiguration, he contends that Jesus's glory was visible throughout his ministry, not merely at

That the work of ἐδόξασα takes place ἐπὶ τῆς γῆς reinforces the revelatory nature of ἐδόξασα. That is, ἐπὶ τῆς γῆς denotes the sphere established for humankind to bring δόξα to God through obedience to the mandates of the creation account. The repeated judgment upon sin ἐπὶ τῆς γῆς (rather than simply in an ethereal and/or eschatological realm) demonstrates that humankind has not brought glory to God on the earth. God is displeased with those ἐπὶ τῆς γῆς and their works.

It then is Christ, who comes in full obedience to the Father, who has displayed works and proclaimed words ἐπὶ τῆς γῆς that make the Father known. Christ's words point to the future display of the glory of God through God's full presence in Zion. Jesus is the one present in Zion in the Fourth Gospel.

The Lord intends to display his glory to the entire earth. This physical world and the earth's inhabitants will see this glory and be transformed by it. The idea that the entirety of this present earth will be full of the display of the glory of God runs through the entire OT (Num 14:21; Ps 72:19; Isa 6:3; 11:9; 49:26; Jer 16:21; 31:34; Ezek 21:5; 25–26, 28–30, 38:23; 35, 39; Hab 2:14). In becoming flesh and maintaining perfect obedience to God, Jesus begins to make the δόξα of God known ἐπὶ τῆς γῆς.

---

certain events (1:14). Properly conceived, all of Jesus's ministry was characterized by divine, heavenly glory from beginning to end, and the cross constituted the climax of the glorification of the Son, the place where Jesus was exalted both physically and spiritually." Köstenberger, "John's Appropriation of Isaiah's Signs Theology: Implications for the Structure of John's Gospel," 378.

4

The Book with Two Completions

INTRODUCTION

I AM ARGUING THAT the completed work of which Christ speaks in John 17:4 is *revelation of God the Father*. Important to this argument is the understanding that Christ speaks of a work in the past when he says, "I glorified," "having accomplished," "you gave," and "to do," and that such work was given to him in eternity past even though it was yet future to the time of its decree. It is future only in terms of the completion with respect to the pronouncement of the decree by the Father. This does not in any way imply or infer that the "work" in question is future to the time of the Christ's speaking of the words of John 17:4 or from the perspective of the author of the Fourth Gospel. I am arguing that the verbs in 17:4 intend to indicate that the work is completed *perfectively* rather than *proleptically*.

By speaking of perfective and proleptic concepts, I am beginning a discussion on what the tenses of Koine Greek verbs intend to communicate.[1] To do so I will consider the verbal aspect of each of the verbs in

---

1. When speaking of what John has written in the Koine, one might question what influence Jesus's speaking of Greek had on the choice and tense-form of the verb John chose to use in a given passage. At issue is whether or not a Semitism is influencing the text received. First, *all scholars do not agree on when a term reflects a Semitism*. As Marlowe writes, "So there is a gray area, in which there is some room for disagreement in marginal cases. One scholar may consider an expression to be a Semitism while another doubts whether it is right to classify it as such. Nevertheless, all scholars agree that various Semitisms are abundantly present in the New Testament." Marlowe, "The Semitic

John 17:4 rather than simply tense-form or *Aktionsart*.[2] I am seeking to

Style of the NT." Second, *scholarship is not in agreement on whether the NT came from an Aramaic source*, and if so, to what degree. As Marlowe also writes, "Some scholars are inclined to think that much of the New Testament was originally written in Hebrew or Aramaic, and that the Semitisms of the Greek text are a consequence of the translation of these original sources, in which Hebrew or Aramaic idioms were reproduced literally... Other scholars prefer to explain the Semitisms of the New Testament as a consequence of peculiarities in the Greek commonly spoken by bilingual Jews in the first century. Other scholars believe that the Semitic style of the New Testament is best explained as a kind of 'Biblical' style which Jewish authors or preachers of the era would have used, not so much in their ordinary speech, but in their writing and in preaching, after the model of the Septuagint. Probably there is some truth in all of these explanations" (Marlowe, "Semitic Style"). The lack of clarity in identifying a Semitism and the role of such devices in the development of the NT text rules out its consideration for influencing the terms I will explore in this chapter. Third, the degree to which Jesus spoke Aramaic is uncertain, and his speaking may reflect the influence of multiple languages. As Turner writes: "It is not inconceivable that, whatever the language of Jesus, it was influenced by all those spoken in Galilee at that time, viz. Hebrew, Aramaic, Greek, and perhaps Latin. It was Biblical Greek, of a kind not very different from the Septuagint—a branch of the Koine, but very different from what we read in the Egyptian rubbish heaps or on the papyrus of more literate people. Since 1949, intense study of vocabulary and syntax seem to me to establish that there was a distinguishable dialect of spoken and written Jewish Greek. That is to say, the biblical language was more than a written product of those whose mother tongue was Semitic and who floundered in Greek because they knew so little of it that they must copy Semitic idioms as they penned it. I am not the first to suggest that the Greek of the OT was a language distinct from the main stream of the Koine yet fully understood by Jews. Perhaps, as Gehman suggests, those who used this dialect of Greek were bilingual; it may have been a temporary phase in the history of the language, representing a period of transition for those Jews who were passing from a Semitic speaking to a Greek speaking stage, and coinciding with the New Testament period. However, as works of a much later date, like the Testament of Abraham, exhibit exactly this kind of diction, I do not think it was merely transitional. Certainly, it was not artificial. Biblical Greek is so powerful and fluent, it is difficult to believe that those who used it did not have at hand a language all ready for use. This, I submit, was the normal language of Jesus, at least in Galilee—rather a separate dialect of Greek than a form of the Koine, and distinguishable as something parallel to classical, Hellenistic, Koine and Imperial Greek." Turner, Grammatical Insights into the New *Testament*, 183, cited in Marlowe; see also Voelz, "Semitic Influence on the Greek of the New Testament," 115–29. Fourth, *all conclusions would be speculative, having no idea what word or words Jesus used*. Even if Jesus did speak Aramaic, without knowing the Aramaic verb, it is difficult to determine anything concerning (1) the reason for the choice of the verb in the GNT, (2) and whether or not the choice of the aorist reflects the Aramaic verb or overrides/departs from the Aramaic tense-form equivalent for stylistic or theological reasons.

2. Without here introducing discussions in New Testament Greek Grammars and specialized studies on aspect within one NT book (save Barnard's study using Luke's Gospel and Decker's study using Mark's Gospel, both referenced below), the following works characterize the development of the understanding of Aktionsart and verbal aspect since the publications of Porter in 1989 and Fanning in 1990 (both referenced below): Baugh, *Introduction to Greek Tense Form Choice in the Non-Indicative Moods*; Barnard, "Is Verbal Aspect A Prominence Indicator?," 3–29; Brookins, "A Tense

demonstrate that "completed" (τελειώσας) has a *perfective* or *completed* aspect, and not so-called "proleptic" aspect. I will argue that a proleptic view is dependent upon an antiquated, tense-form view of the aorist of τελειώσας. After considering the modern discussion of verbal aspect theory, tense-forms, and time, I will seek to make the case for viewing τελειώσας as perfective in *aspect* and also past in its communication of time. Briefly I will discuss the differences between τελειώσας in 17:4 and Τετέλεσται in 19:30 and the significance thereof. I will conclude (1) "completed" is perfective and (2) with respect to Τετέλεσται (a) the two different verbs, τελειώσας and Τετέλεσται, intend to communicate different types of telic conclusions and (b) the completion of which Τετέλεσται rather than τελειώσας speaks of the atoning work of Christ.

However, before making the greater argument and drawing conclusions regarding the terms in question, I will provide a diagrammatical analysis of John 17:1–5, 19:28, and 19:30. The explanation of the analysis intends to establish early some of the elements of the grammatical argument for a reflective view of the completed work.

Discussion: Rethinking the Grammaticalization of Time in Greek Indicative," 147–68; Campbell, *Advances in the Study of Greek*; Campbell, *Basics of Verbal Aspect in Biblical Greek*; Campbell *Verbal Aspect, the Indicative Mood, and Narrative*; and Campbell, *Verbal Aspect and Non-Indicative Verbs: Further Soundings in the Greek of the New Testament*; Carson, "An Introduction to the Porter/Fanning Debate, 21–25; Decker, *Temporal Deixis of the Greek Verb in the Gospel of Mark with Reference to Verbal Aspect*; Decker, "The Poor Man's Porter: A Condensation and Summarization of *Verbal Aspect in the Greek New Testament, with Reference to Tense and Mood*, by Stanley E. Porter;" Ellis, Aubrey, and Dubis, "The Greek Verbal System and Aspectual Prominence," 33–62; Fanning, "Approaches to Verbal Aspect in New Testament Greek: Issues in Definition and Method," 46–62; Fanning, "Greek Presents, Imperfects, and Aorists in the Synoptic Gospels," 157–90; Fanning, *Verbal Aspect in New Testament Greek*; Huffman, *Verbal Aspect Theory and the Prohibitions in the Greek New Testament*; Lamb, "Verbal Aspect, Aktionsart, and the Greek New Testament," 95–130; Levinsohn, *Discourse Features of New Testament Greek*; McKay, *Greek Grammar for Students*; McKay *A New Syntax of the Verb in New Testament Greek*; McKay, "Aspect in Imperatival Constructions in New Testament Greek," 201–26; Merkle, "Abused Aspect: Neglecting the Influence of a Verb's Lexical Meaning on Tense-Form Choice," 57–74; Merkle, "Response to Porter," 83; Naselli, "A Brief Introduction to Verbal Aspect in New Testament Greek," 17–28; Picirilli, "The Meaning of the Tenses in New Testament Greek," 533–55; Porter, *Idioms of the Greek New Testament*; Porter, *Verbal Aspect in the Greek of the New Testament, with Reference to Tense and Mood*; Porter, "What More Shall I Say? A Response to Steve Runge and Benjamin Merkle," 75–79; Runge, *Discourse Grammar of the Greek New Testament*; Runge, "Markedness: Contrasting Porter's Model with the Linguists Cited as Support"; "Response to Porter," 81–82; Runge and Fresch, eds., *The Greek Verb Revisited*; Voelz, "Present and Aorist Verbal Aspect," 153–64. Useful bibliographies may be found in Lamb, "Verbal Aspect," 124–26, and Naselli, "A Brief Introduction," 27.

DIAGRAMMATICAL ANALYSIS OF JOHN 17:1–5 WITH EXPLANATION OF SYNTAX

17:1 Ταῦτα ἐλάλησεν Ἰησοῦς
    καὶ ἐπάρας τοὺς ὀφθαλμοὺς αὐτοῦ εἰς τὸν οὐρανὸν
εἶπεν,
Πάτερ, ἐλήλυθεν ἡ ὥρα·
δόξασόν σου τὸν υἱόν,
    ἵνα ὁ υἱὸς δοξάσῃ σέ,
17:2 καθὼς ἔδωκας αὐτῷ ἐξουσίαν πάσης σαρκός,
    ἵνα πᾶν ὃ δέδωκας αὐτῷ δώσῃ αὐτοῖς ζωὴν αἰώνιον.
17:3 αὕτη δέ ἐστιν ἡ αἰώνιος ζωὴ
    ἵνα γινώσκωσιν σὲ τὸν μόνον ἀληθινὸν θεὸν
    καὶ ὃν ἀπέστειλας Ἰησοῦν Χριστόν.
17:4 ἐγώ σε ἐδόξασα ἐπὶ τῆς γῆς
    τὸ ἔργον τελειώσας ὃ δέδωκάς μοι ἵνα ποιήσω
17:5 καὶ νῦν δόξασόν με σύ, πάτερ,
    παρὰ σεαυτῷ τῇ δόξῃ ᾗ εἶχον πρὸ τοῦ τὸν κόσμον εἶναι παρὰ σοί.

In verse 1, the main clause is a compound sentence in which the subject is Ἰησοῦς and the two independent clause verbs are ἐλάλησεν ("he spoke") and εἶπεν ("he said"). Yet temporally, εἶπεν is subordinate to ἐλάλησεν, occurring after the completion of the words spoken in John 13–16. The participle, ἐπάρας, carries a temporal sense, for just prior to the prayer to follow, Jesus was speaking to the disciples; he lifts his eyes to speak to God. Jesus lifts his eyes toward heaven after the Upper Room discourse; the intercession occurs then.

The content of the prayer, following εἶπεν, because with the vocative Πάτερ. The remainder of the sentence simply recognizes the arrival of the aforementioned hour—ἐλήλυθεν ἡ ὥρα—as recognized by the perfect, active, indicative of ἔρχομαι. The main sentence follows, as the aorist indicative δόξασόν is the main verb of the initial part of the prayer's request: "Father . . . glorify your Son." The ἵνα clause with the subjective δοξάσῃ indicates purpose. The Son's request for the Father to glorify his Son intends for the Son to glorify the Father. The second person personal pronoun, σέ, is the direct object of the ἵνα clause. The writer will pick up the σέ directly again in v. 3b and 4a, and with σύ and [παρὰ] σοί in 5a and

5b. The address of the Father in the second person comes through the verbs ἔδωκας (2a), δέδωκας (2b), ἀπέστειλας (3c), and δέδωκάς (4b).

Harris suggests καθὼς leads verse 2 with a causal sense.³ The request for glorification seeks to fulfill the given stewardship the Son has with authority over all *persons*, for πάσης σαρκός is the grouping from which the Son identifies πᾶν ὃ δέδωκας αὐτῷ δώσῃ αὐτοῖς ζωὴν αἰώνιον—"to everyone whom you have given to him, he might give to them eternal life." The πάσης σαρκός is broad, referring to all persons on the earth, whereas πᾶν ὃ δέδωκας is narrow, referring to the disciples. The wording of 17:2a—ἔδωκας αὐτῷ ἐξουσίαν πάσης σαρκός—harkens back to 1:12b, in which there is a similar narrowing: ὅσοι δὲ ἔλαβον αὐτόν, ἔδωκεν αὐτοῖς ἐξουσίαν τέκνα θεοῦ γενέσθαι, τοῖς πιστεύουσιν εἰς τὸ ὄνομα αὐτοῦ.

The ἵνα clause in verse 2 again occurs with the subjunctive—δώσῃ, indicating purpose. The Son has authority over all persons in order that to the ones given by the Father he might give to them specifically (αὐτοῖς) eternal life.

Verse 3 begins a new sub-topic with the δέ clause; it is a simple connecting conjunction. The ἐστιν carries the sense of "is the essence of," explaining the ζωὴν αἰώνιον of verse 2. The ἡ seems to be attributive. But it is significant in pointing back to the previously mentioned ζωὴν αἰώνιον, although the clause reverses the order of the words to αἰώνιος ζωή.⁴

The third ἵνα clause co-coordinates the definition indicated by ἐστιν and ἡ: ἵνα ὁ υἱὸς δοξάσῃ σέ ... ἵνα πᾶν ὃ δέδωκας αὐτῷ δώσῃ αὐτοῖς ζωὴν αἰώνιον ... ἵνα γινώσκωσιν σὲ τὸν μόνον ἀληθινὸν θεὸν καὶ [ἵνα γινώσκωσιν] ὃν ἀπέστειλας Ἰησοῦν Χριστόν—"in order that the Son might glorify you ... in order that all who you gave to him he might give life eternal ... in order that they might know you, the only true God, and [in order that they might know] [the one] whom you sent, Jesus Christ." The Son purposes to glorify the Father, which is to grant life eternal to the ones whom the Father has given to him, which is for those given to know both the Father—the only true God—and (καὶ, with ἵνα γινώσκωσιν being implied as a carryover from the parallel line) Jesus Christ—the sent one from God. Making known the Father and the Son is what the Son purposes to

---

3. Harris, *John*, 286.

4. Michaels observes, "The definition reverses the order of 'life eternal' (ζωὴν αἰώνιον, the normal word order in John's Gospel, v. 2) to 'the eternal life' or 'that eternal life' (ἡ αἰώνιος ζωή, v. 3), creating a kind of chiasm ('life eternal ... eternal life'), with the definite article noting the previous reference. Michaels, *The Gospel of John*, 859. Michaels references *BDF*, §252.

bring glory to the Father. The Father must glorify the Son in order for the Son to accomplish this purpose. This clarifies—ἐστιν ἡ—eternal life as knowledge of the Father and Son in truth. The Son is ὃν ἀπέστειλας—the one the Father sent (see also 17:8, 18, 21, 23, and 25).[5]

The fourth ἵνα clause in 17:4 seemingly coordinates with the previous three. The English texts tend to translate 17:4 as two clauses, smoothing out the ἵνα clause as "you gave me to do." Yet the ἵνα introduces a third clause—a purpose clause: "in order that I might do [it.]" The "it" is implied by the ἵνα—Jesus *purposed* to do the work given, completing it. The previous three ἵνα clause point to the work as making the Father and Son known in salvation (eternal life) as the way the Son glorifies the Father.

The ἐγώ σε ἐδόξασα is emphatic with respect to the Son: "I . . . I glorified." It also is emphatic in moving the direct object σε before the verb ἐδόξασα. "I glorified *you*."

The temporal adverb, νῦν, leading verse 5, stands in contrast to ἐγώ σε ἐδόξασα . . . τὸ ἔργον τελειώσας. The Son has glorified the Father with his completed work.[6] As a result of completing the work that brings the

---

5. In the Fourth Gospel, the Son is the sent one from the Father in 3:34; 4:34; 5:23, 24, 30, 36, 37, 38; 6:29, 38, 39, 44, 57; 7:16, 18, 28, 29, 33; 8:16, 18, 26, 29, 44; 9:4; 10:36; 11:42; 12:44, 45, 49; 13:16, 20; 14:24; 15:21; 16:5; 17:3, 8, 18, 21, 23, 25; 20:21. Consistent with the argument of this work, references to Jesus as the sent one of the Father dramatically drop off in frequency of use after John 17, appearing only once after the passion narrative (20:21). John 17 is the climax of understanding Jesus as the sent one of the Father—and the one sent by the Father on the mission to reveal the Father and provide eternal life. As Köstenberger surmises, "The Fourth Gospel's portrayal of Jesus' mission centers on Jesus' provision of salvation (often called the "giving of life;" cf. 3:16–17; 6:53–58; 10:10; 17:2) and the forgiveness of sin (cf. 1:29, 36; cf. also 20:23). Even Jesus' signs transcend the actual works of Jesus, functioning as a revelation of the nature of Jesus' sender, the Father, and of the authenticity of Jesus' representation of his sender." Köstenberger, *The Missions of Jesus and the Disciples According to the Fourth Gospel*, 215. See also, Haenchen, "Der vater, der mich gesandt hat," 208–216.

6. In this context, νῦν indicates "a time shortly before or shortly after the time of the discourse—'just now, presently'" (L&N, 633). This is evident as the glorification of Christ that will be expressed in his pre-existent form does not begin concurrently with the request or immediately following it. BDAG suggests, "In the [aorist], mostly in contrast to the past, [it is] denoting that an action or condition is beginning in the present" (BDAG, 681). Similarly, with respect to the Gospels' (especially Johannine?) use of νῦν as "the Divine Hour," Stählin writes, "in particular, mention should be made of the νῦν of the exodus of Jesus, which is given distinctive form in Jn. (12:27; 13:31; 16:5; 17:13) and which Lk shows to be a significant turning-point with his peculiar formula (→ n. 12) ἀπὸ τοῦ νῦν: 12:52; 22:18 and par. (cf. Mt. 23:39: [ἀπ᾿ ἄρτι]); 22:69 and par. In the last of these passages Jesus anticipates His glorification and even His coming again in a paradoxical ἀπὸ τοῦ νῦν, cf. the 'transfiguration' in Jn. 12:27 ff.: Now even in this state of

Father glory, the time has arrived for the Father to glorify the Son with the work that will bring the Son glory. The νῦν = ἐλήλυθεν ἡ ὥρα (v. 1), as the reversal of the vocative terms shows:

Πάτερ, ἐλήλυθεν ἡ ὥρα· δόξασόν σου τὸν υἱόν
νῦν δόξασόν με σύ, πάτερ

The remainder of each clause has (1) a temporal reference drawing a significance to the time of the earthly ministry of Christ after the Upper Room Discourse; (2) a request for glorification with δόξασόν (aor., act., imper., 2nd pers., sg.); (3) Jesus as the direct object using the articular predicate nominative τὸν υἱόν in 17:1 and the personal pronoun με in 17:5; and (4) a form of the personal pronoun σύ, identifying the Son in relation to the Father in the genitive in 17:1—"the Son of you" and serving as the emphatic subject of δόξασόν in 17:5—"*You*, you glorify me." The emphatic δόξασόν με σύ in 17:5 stands in contrast to the emphatic ἐγώ σε ἐδόξασα of 17:4, pointing to the further significance of the νῦν: *I* glorified you . . . now [is the hour for] *you* to glorify me.[7]

The παρὰ σεαυτῷ . . . παρὰ σοί—"beside yourself . . . beside you"—indicates that the glory of which Christ speaks concerns his ascension—a return to the glory he shared with Father although a distinct person from the Father. That glory is the pre-existent glory of the Son—ᾗ εἶχον πρὸ τοῦ τὸν κόσμον εἶναι: "that which I had before the world [came] to be." The reference seems to be to John 1:1 (e.g., Ἐν ἀρχῇ). Having glorified the Father by revealing him, the Son, who left his pre-existent glory in order to complete the work of the Father, having completed that work, now seeks to return to that glory after his coming suffering and crucifixion.

---

humiliation, the exaltation begins" (Stählin, "Νῦν (ἄρτι)," *TDNT*, 4:1112-13). Although Stählin does not cite 17:5, the verse falls within his concept of the use of the adverb as it falls within the "state of humiliation" in which "the exaltation begins" (cf. 13:1; 17:7, 13). Significantly, therefore, the placing of νῦν here in the discourse draws a distinction between what is to come (e.g., the glorification of Christ via the road through the crucifixion) and what he has completed. The "exodus of Jesus" follows what is already completed and is not part of that completed work.

7. Michaels suggests "the result is a kind of chiasm":
    a "Glorify your Son (v. 1a)
        b "So that the Son might glorify you" (v. 1b)
        b' "I have glorified you" (v. 4)
    a' "And now glorify me" (v. 5)

(Michaels, *The Gospel of John*, 861). For more on the structure of John 17 and its significance toward the interpretation of the high priestly prayer with argumentation for a reflective view of John 17:4, see Becker, "Aufbau, Schichtung," 56-83.

Rather than 17:4 being anticipatory of the cross, 17:5 is anticipatory of the resurrection of Christ in route to the ascension.[8]

DIAGRAMMATICAL ANALYSIS OF JOHN 19:28 WITH EXPLANATION OF SYNTAX

Μετὰ τοῦτο
εἰδὼς ὅτι ἤδη πάντα τετέλεσται,
ἵνα τελειωθῇ ἡ γραφή,
ὁ Ἰησοῦς λέγει, Διψῶ.[9]

In 19:28, ὁ Ἰησοῦς λέγει, Διψῶ is the main clause as the only independent clause in the sentence. The verb λέγει (pres., act., ind., 3rd pers., sg.) is the only indicative verb corresponding to a nominative subject, whereas εἰδὼς is participial, and τελειωθῇ functions in the subordinate purpose clause.

Μετὰ τοῦτο refers to the crucifixion events of 19:16b–27, as the neuter of the demonstrative pronoun encompasses all in the immediate context. Only after the work of atonement is complete will the words of Jesus follow.

The diagrammical analysis demonstrates that εἰδὼς is subordinate to λέγει, and not to Μετὰ τοῦτο. Jesus speaks with the full understanding that all things were complete. The temporal adverb ἤδη is relative to the Μετὰ τοῦτο, i.e., "Now—that is, after the events of 19:16b–27." The finished work here—τετέλεσται—is πάντα—all things. The πάντα of 19:28 is a more encompassing term than the τὸ ἔργον . . . ὃ δέδωκάς μοι ἵνα ποιήσω of 17:4. The πάντα appears in conjunction with the Μετὰ τοῦτο . . . ἤδη, suggesting strongly that the τὸ ἔργον is not associated with the completion of the events of 19:16b–27; the writer of the Fourth Gospel easily could have written, Μετὰ τοῦτο εἰδὼς ὁ Ἰησοῦς ὅτι ἤδη τὸ ἔργον τετέλεσται, ἵνα τελειωθῇ ἡ γραφή, λέγει (or earlier in 17:4, πάντα τελειώσας ὃ δέδωκάς μοι ἵνα ποιήσω). As I will argue below, τετέλεσται (3rd pers., sg., perf., act., ind. of τελέω) indicates πάντα is completed *with continuing results.*

---

8. The writer of John speaks previously of the resurrection of Christ in 2:19–22, 10:17–18, and 11:25a, *explicitly.* Implicitly, the resurrection of the Son is within each promise of the Son to raise others from the dead (5:21; 6:40, 41; 11:25b–26), only being able to do so if he himself will be alive and stronger than death.

9. Deliberately I have moved the position of ὁ Ἰησοῦς in order to place the subject and main verb together so that I might show the clauses relative to the main clause.

The ἵνα clause points to the purpose for which Jesus will say, "I thirst." Jesus intends to complete the prophetic Scripture—ἡ γραφή which says, "I thirst," referring to either Ps 22:15 or 69:21.[10] Only after the three relative clauses are inserted, including the purpose clause, does the writer complete the predicate of the sentence with λέγει. In this way, (1) the relative clauses build the tension that will climax in the act of speaking, and (2) the mental ruminations of ὁ Ἰησοῦς involved in speaking the words are known prior to the speaking; they are seen as contributing to the choice of words. That the writer uses ὁ Ἰησοῦς and not the personal pronoun—"he"—shows that the τελειωθῇ of the ἵνα clause intends to draw attention to Jesus.[11]

DIAGRAMMATICAL ANALYSIS OF JOHN 19:30 WITH EXPLANATION OF SYNTAX

ὅτε οὖν ἔλαβεν τὸ ὄξος
εἶπεν, Τετέλεσται,
    καὶ κλίνας τὴν κεφαλὴν
παρέδωκεν τὸ πνεῦμα.

John 19:30 leads with two conjunctions, the first—ὅτε—being adverbial and temporary, placing the acts of 19:30 temporally after the giving of the wine.[12] The second conjunction—οὖν—relates the results of drinking the wine within the time scheme of ὅτε.[13] It directs the reader back to the fulfillment of Scripture in 19:28. In order to fulfill Scripture, Jesus must drink the sour wine and must do so prior to finishing his last words.

Although the first clause is dependent upon the second, with εἶπεν being the first main verb of the compound sentence, the first clause is antecedent or co-relative to the second in time.[14] Similarly, Jesus's handing

---

10. Below I give detailed exegesis to 19:28, so I will not enter such here.

11. I will argue this below.

12. As a conjunction, with indicative verbs, like ἔλαβεν, ὅτε is a "marker of a point of time that coincides with another point of time" (BDAG, 731).

13. Although commonly οὖν "serves to indicate a transition to [something] new ... [especially] in the Gospel of John *now, then, well*," the more likely use here is inferential, "denoting that what it introduces is the result of or an inference [from] what precedes, *so, therefore, consequently, accordingly, then*" (BDAG, 736–37).

14. Elsewhere John's Gospel uses ὅτε οὖν in this manner in 2:22; 4:45; 6:24; 13:12, 31; 19:6, 8; 21:15.

over of his Spirit is the main clause upon which καὶ κλίνας τὴν κεφαλὴν depends. Even the bowing of the head proves to be within the express will of God.

Two indicative verbs—εἶπεν (aor., act., ind., 3rd., sg. of εἶπον) and παρέδωκεν (aor., act., ind., 3rd., sg. of παραδίδωμι)—follow the reception of the wine. The use of παραδίδωμι is concentrated in John's passion narrative.[15] The concentration is common in the passion narrative in each of the Gospels,[16] drawing attention to the authority of God and Christ over Jesus's own time of death: Jesus delivers over his spirit in death in accord with the completion of all things, the fulfillment of Scripture, after drinking the prophesied sour wine, and bowing his head. He is not finally delivered over to death by those delivering him to the authorities (18:2, 30; 19:11, 16); he delivers himself (cf. John 10:17–18). The writer pushes παρέδωκεν back in the compound sentence as the climax of Τετέλεσται. The "handing over" of the spirit communicates the death.

EXEGETICAL CONSIDERATIONS WITH RESPECT TO ΕΔΟΞΑΣΑ, ΤΕΛΕΙΩΣΑΣ, ΔΕΔΩΚΑΣ, AND ΠΟΙΗΣΩ

The writer of the Fourth Gospel uses four Greek verbs in John 17:4: ἐδόξασα, τελειώσας, δέδωκάς, and ποιήσω. I will consider the basic exegetical concepts of each verb below.

ἐδόξασα

The first verb in 17:4, ἐδόξασα ("I glorified"), is aorist tense, active voice, and indicative mood.[17] It is first person and singular in number in agreement with its subject, ἐγώ ("I"). It is a finite verb, whose root is δοξάζω, meaning, "to glorify."[18] English translations attempt to capture the aorist,

---

15. Eight of the Fourth Gospel's fifteen uses of the verb occur in the passion narrative: 18:2, 5, 30, 35, 36; 19:11, 16, 30. The other uses are in 6:64, 71; 12:4; 13:2, 11, 21.

16. The use of παραδίδωμι in the passion narrative accounts for fifteen of Matthew's thirty-one uses (15/31), thirteen of Mark's twenty uses (13/20), and eight of Luke's seventeen uses (8/17). As a whole, 83 of 119 NT uses of the verb occur in the Gospel accounts (83/119).

17. Here I am using "tense" to discuss time in an *Aktionsart* sense. Later I will distinguish between "tense" as the *tense-form* of a verb, and *aspect*.

18. "δοξάζω," BDAG, 258.

active, indicative in various ways, including "I glorified" (ESV, NASB, NET, NRSV), "I have brought . . . glory" (NIV, NLT), and "I have glorified" (KJV/NKJV, CSB). Each of the translated ideas carry a past tense idea with respect to time, and some seem to indicate a perfective aspect understanding of the Greek verb by the use of the helping verb "have" in their English translations.

τελειώσας

The verb τελειώσας is aorist tense, active voice, and participial in mood, from τελειόω, meaning *to finish, complete, or perfect*. As a participle, it is a verbal adjective, having the characteristics of both a verb and an adjective.[19] It is in the nominative case, indicating that it is the subject of the clause. It is singular in person and masculine in gender in agreement with the subject, ἐγώ. It is an adverbial participle, relating to the preceding verb, ἐδόξασα, and having a direct object in its participial phrase, τὸ ἔργον—"the work" in question in this full paper. English translations of the verb include, "having accomplished" (ESV, NASB), "by completing" (NET, NLT, CSB), "by finishing" (NET, NIV, NRSV), and "I have finished" (KJV/NKJV). The translated ideas range from perfective to undefined concepts in their time and aspects.

δέδωκάς

The only non-aorist verb in 17:4 is δέδωκάς. It is the perfect, active, indicative, second person, singular form of δίδωμι, meaning, "to give."[20] The person and number agree with the implied subject, "You," referring to God the Father, the one Jesus addresses as σε earlier in the verse, and by direct address as Πάτερ in 17:1. This verb has a pronoun modifier as an indirect object: μοι ("to me").

Translations in English of the use of this verb in 17:4 include "have given" (NASB, NKVJ) and "you gave" (ESV, NET, NRSV, NIV, CSB, NLT). Only the NASB and NKJV translate the verb with a perfective idea. The other translations suggest the verb denotes a past idea. This seems much more reflective of the Greek perfect tense, which writers use to describe

---

19. Mounce, *Basics of Biblical Greek Grammar*, 236.
20. "δίδωμι," BDAG, 242.

a verbal action completed in the past with an ongoing, continued, or enduring results in the present with respect to the speaker/writer.[21]

ποιήσω

Like ἐδόξασα and τελειώσας, ποιήσω is an aorist verb. It is aorist, active, and subjunctive in mood, first person, and singular in number, from ποιέω, meaning "to do."[22] Following the adverbial purpose conjunction ἵνα, ποιήσω is first person within the purpose clause because it refers to the purpose of Christ, the speaker, who is the subject. This is not reflected in the English translations, which tend to simplify the readability of the Greek purpose clause with the English infinitive, "to do."[23] Yet the Greek should be translated, "In order that I might do it."

Concerning the subjunctive mood, Mounce notes, "The subjunctive does not describe what is, but what may (or might) be. In other words, it is the mood not of reality but of *possibility* (or *probability*)."[24] Similarly Wallace writes, "The subjunctive is used to grammaticalize *potentiality*. It normally does so in the realm of *cognitive probability*, but may also be used for *cognitive possibility* (overlapping with the optative) or *volitional intentionality* (overlapping with the imperative)."[25] The writer of the Gospel of John seems to communicate that ποιήσω speaks of a work that is potential with respect to δέδωκάς.

THE PREVIOUS AORIST UNDERSTANDING OF ΤΕΛΕΙΩΣΑΣ

From the late nineteenth century through much of the twentieth century, it was common to understand Greek verbs in terms of tenses that communicate a sense of time. Robertson demonstrates this earlier perspective in his Greek grammar when speaks of "the three kinds of action expressed in terms of tense." He explains, "These ideas (punctiliar, durative, perfected state) lie behind the three tenses (aorist, present, perfect) that run through all the moods. The forms of these tenses are meant to

21. Mounce, *Basics*, 223.
22. "ποιέω," BDAG, 839.
23. This is consistent in the ESV, CSB, KJV/NKJV, NASB, NIV, NLT, and NRSV.
24. Mounce, *Basics*, 288.
25. Wallace, *Greek Grammar Beyond the Basics*, 463.

accentuate these ideas."[26] Slightly a decade later, Dana and Mantey express the significance of tense to Koine Greek students a century ago:

> No element of Greek language is of more importance to the student of the New Testament than the matter of tense. A variation in meaning exhibited by the use of a particular tense will often dissolve what appears to be an embarrassing difficulty, or reveal a gleam of truth which will thrill the heart with delight and inspiration. Though it is an intricate and difficult subject, no phase of Greek grammar offers a fuller reward. The benefits are to be reaped only when one has invested sufficient time and diligence to obtain an insight into the idiomatic use of tense in the Greek language and an appreciation of the finer distinctions in force.[27]

As indicated in Robertson's comments above, grammarians perceived the aorist tense to indicate an action punctiliar in time in the past. "The aorist refers to the past simply (the simple occurrence of an event at some past time, considered a as momentary act), and is the ordinary tense of narration ... the perfect brings the past into connection with the present time, and represents an action as a completed one, in relation to the present time," writes Winer.[28] Robertson too noted, "The aorist stem presents action in its simplest form (ἄ- οριστος, 'undefined'). This action is simply presented as a point by this tense. This action is timeless."[29]

Each of the Greek tenses (aorist, present, and perfect) and their states (punctiliar, durative, and perfective), were thought to be pure and distinct in their communication of time. There was very little thought of the perfect overlapping with the aorist, or the aorist overlapping with the future, etc. Winer posits,

> Strictly and properly speaking, no one of these tenses can ever stand for another, as commentators in so many ways have maintained: where such an interchange seems to exist, either it exists in appearance only, there being in point of fact some assignable

---

26. Robertson, *Grammar*, 842.
27. Dana and Mantey, *A Manual Grammar*, 176–77.
28. Winer, *A Treatise on the Grammar of New Testament Greek: Regarded as a Sure Basis of New Testament Exegesis*, 330–31.
29. Robertson, *Grammar*, 842. Robertson's ideas stemmed from his thoughts on the evolution of the Greek language: "There were originally two types of verb-roots, the punctiliar and the durative. The tense called aorist (ἀόριστος, 'undefined action') is due to the use of the punctiliar verbs (the idea of a point on a line). The present tense comes out of the durative verb-root. But it is worth repeating that tenses are a later development in the use of the verb" (344).

reason (especially of a rhetorical kind) why this tense is used on no other; or else it must be ascribed to a certain inexactness belonging to the popular language, through which the relation of time was not conceived and expressed with perfect precision."[30]

Thus, for Winer, and those with similar sentiments, the aorist was punctiliar with respect to time, only. If there was a different use of the aorist, it was only in appearance, because the fact of a writer's employment of the aorist indicated that only a punctiliar idea should be expressed in that clause of that verb.[31] The only other possibility is that the colloquial understanding of Greek by the first century writer allowed for a use of a tense other than the time assigned to it. Seemingly, such a "popular" understanding of the Greek language was not accessible to modern readers.

In the same era, Machen expressed the common understanding of distinct, non-overlapping categories of aorist verbs, saying,

> The aorist is like the imperfect in that it refers to past time. But the imperfect refers to continuous action in past time, while the aorist is the simple past tense. Thus the imperfect means *I was loosing*, while the aorist means I loosed. It will be remembered that in present time this distinction between the simple assertion of the act and the assertion of continued (or repeated) action is not made in Greek (λύω, therefore, means either *I loose* or *I am loosing*). But in past time the distinction is very carefully made; the Greek language shows no tendency whatever to confuse the aorist with the imperfect.[32]

Like his contemporaries, Machen viewed the aorist as wholly distinct from other tenses—the imperfect in this example. The aorist denoted the past only, as a "distinction is carefully made" in the expression of time in the past tense.

---

30. Winer, *A Treatise*, 330–1.

31. Against the aorist carrying any perfective sense, almost with finitude Winer states, "There is no passage in which it certainly can be proved that the aorist stands for the perfect" (Winer, *A Treatise*, 344). He cites John 17:4 as an exceptional example of a case in which the aorist might stand in place of the perfect, suggesting a perfective aspect to the verb (345). He continues by saying, "But in all these instances the action is merely represented as having occurred, as filling a point of past time, as simply and absolutely past" (344). Yet one also should bear in mind that Winer is reading the aorist, active, *indicative* of the Byzantine text of John 17:4—'Ἐγώ σε ἐδόξασα ἐπὶ τῆς γῆς· τὸ ἔργον ἐτελείωσα ὃ δέδωκάς μοι ἵνα ποιήσω—and not the aorist, active, *participle* τελειώσας of the NA/UBS GNT.

32. Machen, *New Testament Greek for Beginners*, 81–82.

Yet the understanding of the aorist tense occasionally expressed by the grammars seemed to allow for a "proleptic" idea of the aorist tense, at least in theory. Seemingly in an attempt to preserve hard lines between the aorist and any other tense, Winer recognizes a proleptic aorist, but in appearance only, keeping with what he said previously (above): "It is only in appearance that the aorist stands for the future," he writes. "The aorist is never used in this manner where there is no antecedent sentence."[33] Other grammars and commentaries must have proposed a proleptic aorist too, for in his 1884 commentary on Rom 8:30, Meyer writes of the glorification term, "Paul selected the proleptic aorist."[34] The small allowance for a future use of the aorist tense[-form] would have provided grammatical warrant for viewing a verb such as τελειώσας as proleptic.[35]

THE DEVELOPMENT OF THE UNDERSTANDING OF THE AORIST VIA AKTIONSART IN THE PERIOD FROM ROBERTSON UP TO FANNING AND PORTER

As the grammars' discussions of tense and time interacted with theories of *Aktionsart*, the understanding of the time of the aorist tense became a discussion of the aorist tense-form—that the aorist did not intend so much to communicate a *time* of action, but a *kind* of action. In general, earlier movement of thinking in terms of *Aktionsart* instead of time resonated with the explanations of Dana and Mantey:

> The distinctive function of the verb is to express action. Action as presented in the expression of a verbal idea involves two elements, time of action and kind of action. That is, the action may be described as occurring at a certain time, and must be

---

33. Winer, *A Treatise*, 345–46. For certain Winer was speaking of a proleptic use of the aorist, for he cites the use of δοξάζω (the aorist, active, indicative, third person, singular form, ἐδόξασεν) in Rom 8:30 as an exception to the rule: "In Rom. Viii. 30, ἐδόξασε (sic.) is used because he in regard to whom God has accomplished the δικαιοῦν has already obtained from him the δοξάζεσθαι also, though the reception of the δόξα as an actual reception belongs to the future" (346). Later Winer makes his position clear in another example: "The aor. ἐδοξάσθη, Jo. xv. 8, is now explained by Tholuck more correctly than before: it is the proleptic aorist, as in [Eph.] ii. 6, Rom. Viii. 30" (347).

34. Meyer, *Critical and Exegetical Handbook to the Epistle to the Romans*, 337.

35. As evidenced by the history of interpretation of John 17:4, a proleptic idea within τελειώσας long precedes the grammars of the nineteenth century. It may be that the grammarians, following the commentators, posited a proleptic idea on theological grounds rather than exegetical-lexical-linguistic grounds.

> described, if intelligible, as performed in a certain manner. Tense deals with these two aspects of verbal expression, kind of action being the chief idea involved, for *time is but a minor consideration in the Greek tenses* . . . The important element of tense in Greek is kind of action. This is its fundamental significance . . . For this element of tense recent grammarians have adopted the German term *aktionsart*, "kind of action." The character of an action may be defined from either of three points of view; it may be continuous, it may be complete, or it may be regarded simply as occurring, without reference to the question of progress. There are, therefore, three fundamental tenses in Greek: the present, representing continuous action; the perfect, representing completed action; and the aorist (ἀόριστος, without limits, *undefined*), representing indefinite action.[36]

Although *Aktionsart* begins to supplant the time idea—with its clear lines of demarcation between each tense's type of time—it comes with its own distinct, non-overlapping concepts of the kinds of actions the Greek verbs are communicating. The concept of "completed action" now belongs wholly to a "perfect" *Aktionsart*, and "undefined [action]" now belongs to the aorist, apparently on the basis of, or being more consistent with the term itself, which means, *without* (ἀ-) definition, limit, or boundary (ὁριστος).

A. T. Robertson

Robertson's interpretation of *Aktionsart*, which precedes Dana and Mantey's, attempts to associate the kind of action with the verbal root. So each verb inherently carries a kind of action that influences the time of its tense-form:

> *Aktionsart* ("kind of action") must be clearly understood. The verb-root plays a large part in the history of the verb. This essential meaning of the word itself antedates the tense development and continues afterwards . . . [The] matter of the kind of action in the verb-root (*Aktionsart*) applies to all verbs. It has long been clear that the "tense" has been overworked and made to mean much that it did not mean.[37]

---

36. Dana and Mantey, *A Manual*, 177–78.
37. Robertson, *Grammar*, 823.

For Robertson, "The verb itself is the beginning of all."[38]

Yet Robertson saw (and maintained) the confusing understanding of *Aktionsart* in association to time, even though he attempts to maintain distinctions between durative and completed *Aktionsart*. He noted,

> Instead of 'punctiliar' (*punktuelle Aktion*, Brugmann), others use 'perfective . . .' But this brings inevitable confusion with the perfect tense. All verbs may be described as 'punctiliar' (*punktuell*) and 'non-punctiliar' (*nicht-punktuell*). But the 'non-punctiliar' divides into the indefinite linear (durative) and the definite linear (completed or perfect). The notion of perfect action as distinct from point action came later.[39]

In attempting to apply his unclear concept of *Aktionsart* to verbs in the aorist tense, Robertson maintained the punctiliar-time notion germane to the aorist-as-tense model. In doing so, the *Aktionsart* aorist becomes a "point-action" aorist (kind of action) with accented emphasis on a period of the action (time) that modified the verbal root. Robertson reasons,

> It is not merely true that three separate kinds of action are developed (punctiliar, durative, perfected), that are represented broadly by three tenses in all the modes, though imperfectly in the present and future tenses of the indicative. The individual verb-root modifies greatly the resultant idea in each tense. This matter can only be hinted at here, but must be worked out more carefully in the discussion of each tense. The aorist, for instance, though always in itself merely point-action, "punctiliar," yet may be used with verbs that accent the beginning of the action or the end of the action. Thus three distinctions arise: the unmodified point-action called "constative," the point-action with the accent on the beginning (inceptive) called "ingressive," the point-action with the accent on the conclusion called "effective."[40]

---

38. Robertson, *Grammar*, 823.

39. Robertson, *Grammar*, 823. Robertson attempts to demonstrate his three-fold explanation of Aktionsart with terms that sound very similar to the three-fold explanation of tense: "The three essential kinds of action are thus momentary or punctiliar when the action is regarded as a whole and may be represented by a dot (.), linear or durative action which may be represented by a continuous line ——, the continuance of perfected or completed action which may be represented by this graph ●——. The distinction between punctiliar and perfected action is not clearly drawn in the verb-root itself. That is a later refinement of tense" (823).

40. Robertson, *Grammar*, 828–29.

Again, for Robertson, where the verbal root and verbal tense once were in full agreement, with the tense only appropriate to roots that accepted the tense, the *Aktionsart* theory explained how verses that should have been punctiliar in tense and root now displayed a durative idea in the root even though being in the aorist *Aktionsart*. The tense still determined the *Aktionsart*. Robertson reiterates this idea later, writing, "The aorist tense, though at first confined to verbs of punctiliar sense, was gradually made on verbs of durative sense. So also verbs of durative action came to have the tenses of punctiliar action. Thus the tenses came to be used for the expression of the ideas that once belonged only to the root."[41]

James Moulton

Moulton, also a contemporary of Robertson, advances and clarifies the *Aktionsart* discussion within his commentary. Differently than seeing the *Aktionsart* of verbs in pristine, separate categories akin to the tense-as-time category distinctions, Moulton finds overlap in the categories, and of the aorist and perfect in particular, noting, "We must add the aorists and perfect as formations essentially parallel."[42] Moulton considered "aorists and perfect[s] as formations essentially parallel." But in aorists and perfects, *Aktionsart* was "appropriate" to the conjugation of the two tenses (rather than "tense-form" at that point in the understanding of Koine Greek). However, *Aktionsart* was not considered something that was consistent throughout the conjugations, but "naturally blurred by later developments."[43]

In agreement with Robertson, for Moulton the aorist represents punctiliar action with three possible formations: *Ingressive* (or "point of entrance"), *Effective* (or "point of completion"), and *Constative* (or "[point of looking] at a whole action simply as having occurred without distinguishing any step in its progress").[44] Yet for Moulton, some aorists and perfects, like ἔθην, were stems of "pure verb-roots" that could be punctiliar, durative, or both in their function. He proposes,

---

41. Robertson, *Grammar*, 830. "All aorists are punctiliar in statement," says Robertson later. "The 'constative' aorist treats an act as punctiliar which is not in itself point-action. That is the only difference" (832).

42. Moulton, *Prolegomena*, 109.

43. Moulton, *Prolegomena*, 109.

44. Moulton, *Prolegomena*, 109.

Other conjugations are capable of making both present and aorist stems, as ἔθην compared with ἔβην, γράφειν with τραπεῖν, στένειν with γενέσθαι. In these the pure verb-root is by nature either (a) 'punctiliar,' (b) durative, or (c) capable of being both. Thus the root of ἐνεγκεῖν, like our bring, is essentially a 'point' word, being classed as 'Effective:' accordingly it forms no present stem. That of φέρω, *fero*, bear, on the other hand, is essentially durative or 'linear,' and therefore forms no aorist stem.[45]

That Moulton still is thinking of the meaning of verbs more with respect to *time of action* than kind of action is evident in his understanding of the aorist of τελέω. Comparing the Greek of the NT to that of the ancient Greek writer, Polybius, Moulton observes, "The NT use of τελέω, again, differs widely from that of Polybius, where the perfective compound (συντ.) greatly predominates: in NT the simplex outnumbers it fourfold. Moreover the aorist in the NT is always punctiliar ("finish"): only in Gal 5:16 is the constative 'perform' a possible alternative."[46] Because Moulton uses a time concept in speaking of the *Aktionsart* of verbs in general and of the aorist in particular (and of the aorist of τελέω as an example), the grammar's view of the aorist remains open to the other *time* concepts within an *Aktionsart* framework.

Nigel Turner, Frank Stagg, Charles Smith

Other grammars propagate imprecision on *Aktionsart* and time. Turner, still speaking primarily in tense categories in 1963, declares, "The timeless aor. is a suitable tense to express this projection of the future into the present as if some event had already occurred."[47] Based on Nigel's comments, it would appear that there is a *proleptic* aorist, and that it is both timeless—"The *timeless* [aorist]," and future—"projection of the *future*."

---

45. Moulton, *Prolegomena*, 109–10. Moulton resolves the problem of a missing aorist stem on the basis of a durative concept or Aktionsart. It was not that the stem communicated the aspect, but that the Aktionsart inherent in the verb determined whether or not the verb would have a form in one tense (tense-form) or not. This is in great contrast to recent scholarship's insight that aspect determines whether or not the tense-form will have a mood.

46. Moulton, *Prolegomena*, 118. The Polybius reference is to Purdie, "The Perfective 'Aktionsart' in Polybius," 63–153. Moulton later, again, considers an example of τελέω in the aorist, saying, "For the effective aorist, we may compare durative τελεῖν 'fulfil, bring to perfection (2 Co 12:9 "my power is being perfected in weakness") with the aorist τελέσαι 'finish' (Lk 2:39 etc.): for constative in Gal 5:15" (130).

47. Turner, *A Grammar of New Testament Greek*, 73–74.

Similarly, in 1972, when Stagg wrote his now classic, "The Abused Aorist," he indicted many well-known scholars for describing the nature of the aorist's action as "point action."[48] He attempts to provide a helpful correction with an appeal to "semantics," proposing

> "[A]orist" is a term happily suited to the primitive form which it labels. It is "a-oristic," i.e., undetermined or undefined. The aorist draws no boundaries. It tells nothing about the nature of the action under consideration. It is 'punctiliar' only in the sense that the action is viewed without reference to duration, interruption, completion, or anything else. What is 'aoristic' belongs to semantics and not necessarily to the semantic situation. The aorist can properly be used to cover any kind of action: single or multiple, momentary or extended, broken or unbroken, completed or open-ended. The aorist simply refrains from describing.[49]

The appeal to semantics places the signifying nature of what is "aorist" within the verb itself or the verbal root. It is an appeal a "primitive form" for verbs—a form preceding the other *tense*-forms. The action-circumstance in which the verb occurs is not what determines the meaning of the aorist. It is in the sense of stating something happened on will happen (e.g., "open-ended").

Even with Stagg's improvement upon the understanding of the aorist, as late as 1981, Charles Smith, while largely expressing ideas on the aorist similar to Stagg's and discussing "aspect," misunderstands the aorist. This is not immediately evident when he proposes,

> In the matter of 'aspect' the purpose of the aorist is to be invisible. The term *means* 'no boundary,' 'without horizon,' 'nonspecific,' 'noncommittal,' 'indefinite,' etc. The whole point of the aorist is to *refrain* from saying anything about the nature of the action . . . *As it relates to the matter of aspect*, the aorist is transparent, it leaves the verbal idea 'naked' by adding *nothing* to the basic vocabulary concept. It merely labels or titles the act.[50]

---

48. Stagg, "The Abused Aorist," 222. Stagg also writes condemningly of several scholars: "To cite a few, the following are among those who have built theology or biblical interpretation upon what to this writer is a misunderstanding of the nature of the aorist: F. W. Beare, W. Bousset, R. H. Charles, J. Jeremías, R. Law, Leon Morris, J. A. Sanders, R. Schnackenburg, and A. N. Wilder . . . Raymond E. Brown and C. H. Dodd may be cited among those who reflect a basic understanding of the aorist and yet succumb to the fallacy that it normally indicates 'point action'" (222).

49. Stagg, "Abused Aorist," 223.

50. Smith, "Errant Aorist Interpreters," 206–7.

Here, Smith's identification of the aspect as "indefinite" is consistent with Stagg's marking of the tense-form of the aorist as "undefined."

However, Smith, quite in contrast to the imprecise language on aorist and *Aktionsart* of previous grammarians, seeks to be as precise as possible in describes what the aorist does and does not do. His article proposes eight propositions on the aorist, four of which intend to render tense an insufficient means of speaking of the function of the aorist: (1) (Stagg's #1) The aorist does not refer to past time, (2) (#3) it neither identifies nor views action as punctiliar, (3) (#4) it does not designate once-for-all action, (4) (#6) it is not the opposite of the present imperfect or perfect.[51] These proposals would seem to have advanced the discussion of the aorist.

Yet three other proposals unintentionally deny an aspect understanding of the aorist: (1) (#2) The aorist does not indicate completed action, (2) (#5) it does not designate the kind of action, and (3) (#7) it does not occur in classes or kinds. With concepts of "time" (#1) and tense (#6) removed from understanding and the *kind* of action also removed from consideration, Smith only can conclude "the aorist may describe any action or event."[52]

Buist Fanning and Stanley Porter

A significant change in the understanding of the aorist in the NT dawns with the back to back publications of Fanning and Porter on verbal aspect.[53] Their discussions (and the nearly thirty years of volumes of debates over their differing views of aspect that have followed) were not directed at the aorist alone. But the aorist receives much treatment in their volumes and various subsequent publications by Porter, Fanning,

51. Smith, "Errant," 207–20.
52. Smith, "Errant," 207–26.
53. Fanning, *Verbal Aspect*; Porter, *Verbal Aspect*. Between the time of Smith's article ("Errant") and Porter's publication, McKay contributes much to the discussion on aspect. However, scholars on NT Greek verbal aspect frame the current discussion as a debate between Fanning and Porter. So I will retain the same emphasis. The debate contains much of McKay's work. See also, Fanning, "Approaches," 46–62; Porter, *Linguistic Analysis*, 159–217; Schmidt, "Review of *Verbal Aspect in New Testament Greek* by Buist Fanning," 714–18; Silva, *Biblical Words and Their Meanings*, 183–211; Silva, *God, Language and Scripture*, 111–17; Silva, "A Response to Fanning and Porter on Verbal Aspect," 74–82; Silva, Review of *Verbal Aspect in New Testament Greek*, by Buist Fanning, and *Verbal Aspect in the Greek New Testament: With Reference to Tense and Mood*, by Stanley Porter, 179–83.

and others, based on the original works of Porter and Fanning. The debates served to bring greater clarity to the different concepts of tense, *Aktionsart*, and aspect.[54]

Fanning defines *Aktionsart* as a description of "how the action actually occurs" that "reflects the external, objective facts of the occurrence," and "focuses on something outside the speaker."[55] This is something lexically expressed in the lexical form or prefixes and suffixes of the verb.[56]

Aspect "involves a way of viewing the action" that reflects the subjective conception or portrayal by the speaker" and "focuses on the speaker's representation of the action."[57] Rather than being expressed lexically, it is expressed grammatically by the tense-inflexions and tense-stems of the Greek verbs.[58] Aspect "reflects the focus or viewpoint of the speaker in regard to the action or condition which the verb describes."[59] It is a perspectival view, rather than a view of how the action occurs actually (like *Aktionsart*), which shows how the author regards the action as having occurred, "or the portrayal of the occurrence apart from the actual or perceived nature of the situation itself."[60] Fanning elaborates:

> To be more specific, aspect is concerned with the speaker's viewpoint concerning the action in the sense that it implicitly sets up a relationship between the action described and a reference-point from which the action is viewed. The crucial aspectual distinction is whether this reference-point is internal or external to the action. The action can be viewed from a reference point *within* the action without reference to the beginning or

---

54. Runge, however, believes "Most discussions about the Greek verb within NT studies have been hampered by how Porter initially framed the debate in 1989" (Runge, "Markedness," 56). He argues that Porter has erred on his concepts of markedness because Porter assumes a model for which he does not provide adequate definition or discussion (51). "He builds a plausible, logical argument, but one that lacks linguistic support" (50). In a similar vein, Swart is critical of framing the discussion of NT Greek Verbal Aspect as a debate between the views of Porter and Fanning, saying, "Focus on the differences between the opposing views of Porter and Fanning has tended to hamper the application of aspect theory to the analysis of texts and the exploration of its exegetical implications (Swart, "Non-past referring Imperfects in the New Testament: A Test Case for an Anti-Anti-Anti-Porter Position," 1086).

55. Fanning, *Verbal Aspect*, 31.
56. Fanning, *Verbal Aspect*, 31.
57. Fanning, *Verbal Aspect*, 31.
58. Fanning, *Verbal Aspect*, 31.
59. Fanning, *Verbal Aspect*, 84.
60. Fanning, *Verbal Aspect*, 84–85.

end-point of the action but with focus instead on its internal structure or make-up. Or the action can be viewed from a vantage point *outside* the action, with focus on the whole action from beginning to end, without reference to its internal structure. Thus, aspect has nothing inherently to do with temporal sequence, with procedural characteristics of actual situations or of verbs and verb-phrases, or with prominence in discourse.[61]

Fanning's definition largely, but not exclusively, moves the focus of the discussion of the Greek verb away from time within the verb. Fanning's view of aspect includes concepts carried over from tense-as-time discussions, and from verbal meaning and functioning as *Aktionsart* discussions. But Fanning develops the discussion of the verb by focusing on the viewpoint of the writer. Fanning argues that aspect interacts closely with features such as the procedural character of the verb and the verbal-phrase and cannot be analyzed apart from analyzing these other contextual features.[62]

Therefore, for Fanning, the aorist and all tense-forms offer the writer's perspective of an action rather than a punctiliar *kind* of action (*Aktionsart*), or a punctiliar or undefined *time* of action (tense). Following McKay,[63] Fanning proposes the aorist "presents an occurrence in summary, viewed as a whole from the outside, without regard for the internal make-up of the occurrence."[64] This is the only concept that is inherent and unchanging within the aorist, regardless of the tense-form's voice or mood. As Fanning indicates, "Other nuances of meaning (instantaneous occurrence, completed action, ingressive action, etc.) come from combinations of the aorist [aspect] with the lexical nature of the verb or from other features of the context—and these 'combinatory variants' or functions of the aorist in interaction with other features must be studied—but the aorist itself does not bear these meanings."[65]

Thus, the aorist indicative may have a constative or complexive use, but "makes a summary reference to a past action or a state as a whole without emphasis on any of the actual features which may be involved in the internal constituency of the occurrence." The focus is not on a

61. Fanning, *Verbal Aspect*, 85.
62. Fanning, *Verbal Aspect*, 85.
63. McKay, "Aspect in Imperatival Constructions."
64. Fanning, *Verbal Aspect*, 97.
65. Fanning, *Verbal Aspect*, 97–98.

time-point reference but on the whole-occurrence.[66] So the constative aorist might be employed in a durative or instantaneous situation, but such senses "depend on the lexical character of the verb and other features" and not on the aorist itself.[67] Similarly, if the aorist use is ingressive, it might take "a summary view of the entire situation, denoting the past existence of the subject in the state, or a summary of repeated past state" in a constative sense, or it might "denote the whole action from beginning to end" in a narrative sequence.[68]

Pertaining to a consummative or effective use of the aorist in which a writer emphasizes the end-point of an action instead of the beginning-point, the aorist will view the action as a whole, seeing both end-points and denote the completion of the action—a reaching of the termination of the action.[69] With respect to a proleptic aorist, there is a "rhetorical transfer of viewpoint" in which the writer envisions an event yet future as though it had already occurred.[70] The writer either looks at an occurrence from a future viewpoint within an if/then clause, or "in a statement which by context seems to point to the future, and the aorist is used to portray a future occurrence as if it were already done."[71]

Again, the aorists in these examples do not speak to the time or kind of action apart from other lexical or contextual features. The prolepsis is only future because of its placement within a conditional clause or a "context" that "seems to point to the future."[72] The aorist itself only summarizes holistically that an occurrence has reached completion as the writer considers it from a future perspective.[73] For Fanning, the writer

---

66. Fanning, *Verbal Aspect*, 256.
67. Fanning, *Verbal Aspect*, 259.
68. Fanning, *Verbal Aspect*, 262–63.

69. Fanning, *Verbal Aspect*, 263–65. It is worth noting that Fanning recognizes a possible overlap between the consummative use of the aorist and the Greek perfect tense, which was long held to be a perfective use of the verb (265n144).

70. Fanning, *Verbal Aspect*, 269.
71. Fanning, *Verbal Aspect*, 269.
72. Fanning, *Verbal Aspect*, 272.

73. Within his analysis of examples of the proleptic-aorist, Fanning cites John 13:31 and Rom 8:30. In John 13:31, Fanning prescribes "the sense of perfect of confidence" to the proleptic aorist—that is, "occurrences which have not yet started or, having started, have not been completed but which the circumstances show to be inevitable or for some other reason are viewed as certain" (*Verbal Aspect*, 274). Fanning does not indicate whether he refers to the first or second use of ἐδοξάσθη in the verse, or both uses. But for either use I would not agree that this is an example of a proleptic aorist, for Christ speaks of what is now (Νῦν) in comparison to what is future (καὶ ὁ θεὸς δοξάσει

is summarizing the whole of the occurrence as he speaks of the event reaching its terminus.

Porter, holding to a different theory of verbal aspect than that of Fanning, introduces his first monograph on verbal aspect with the words, "The major assertion of this work in biblical Greek linguistic is that the category of synthetic verbal aspect—a morphologically-based semantic category which grammaticalizes the author/speaker's reasoned subjective choice of conception of a process—provides a suggestive and workable linguistic model for explaining the range of uses of the tense forms in Greek."[74] Verbal aspect, for Porter, "is a synthetic semantic category (realized in the forms of verbs) used of meaningful oppositions in a network of tense systems to grammaticalize the author's reasoned subjective choice of conception of a process."[75] The Greek verbal aspects are three in Porter's model: *Perfective* (Aorist), *Imperfective* (Present/Imperfect), and *Stative* (Perfect/Pluperfect).[76]

αὐτὸν ἐν αὐτῷ, καὶ εὐθὺς δοξάσει αὐτόν). The future, active, indicative of δοξάζω stands in contrast to the temporal adverb + aorist, passive, indicative of "Νῦν ἐδοξάσθη" and the conditional subordinate clause, εἰ ὁ θεὸς ἐδοξάσθη ἐν αὐτῷ. The writer is not comparing the certain future to an as-if-it-is-certain-future. Instead, the employment of the future contrasts to what is not yet future. Similarly, Fanning prescribes "aorist of 'divine decree'" to Rom 8:30: "The writer views the future event as certain because of God's predestination of it in eternity past or else portrays a course of action just determined in the councils of heaven but have not worked out on earth: the aorist refers to the future working out, but it is seen as certain in light of God's decree" (274). In this example, I would suggest that the proleptic aorist of ἐδόξασεν is certain, because it seems that the subject of the passage is *God's love in Christ for the elect in every stage of salvation*, and "glorified" speaks of a stage within the plan of salvation which is yet future (e.g., glorification), in contrast to *stages* that are in the past (e.g., *foreknew, predestined, called, justified*). Keeping with Fanning's own concept of the aorist, the other factors of each verse's context determine the aspect of the aorist. (Benjamin Merkle concludes a similar idea on the role of aspect and context: "Verbal aspect only gives us the basic perspective of how the author views the action of the verb but does not necessarily take into consideration contextual features [the pragmatic or affected meaning . . . It is necessary to consider not only the aspect of the verb but also other factors that might have influenced an author to choose a particular tense-form"]. Merkle, "The Abused Aspect: Neglecting the Influence of a Verb's Lexical Meaning on Tense-Form Choice," 60–61.) More importantly, Fanning does not discuss John 17:4 under the concept under the aorist participle as a "consummative" aorist—one in which "the context stresses in some way the actual performance of an action in contrast to mere attempt" (415). To be sure, τελειώσας is an aorist participle. But Fanning does not find a proleptic use of this participle, as so many commentators have concluded on John 17:4.

74. Porter, *Verbal Aspect*, xi.

75. Porter, *Verbal Aspect*, 88.

76. Porter utilizes the "tense" concepts—*present, future, imperfect, aorist, perfect, pluperfect*—only to avoid confusion within his monograph's discussion of what then

Although Porter's theory utilizes terms from traditional tense models, in Porter's theory verbs do not grammaticalize time: "Tense categories in Greek are not time based, but aspectually based . . . Aspect is not properly speaking a temporal category, but it is related to tense (and attitude) in the sense that all three of these categories are concerned with processes which occur in time and the realm of time is their semantic domain."[77] Elsewhere Porter writes,

> My hypotheses can be stated simply, although the monograph attempts at great length and in significant detail to defend the positions taken. I believe that, rather than indicating absolute (past, present, future) temporal distinctions, the so-called verbal tense-forms in Geek grammaticalize the author's reasoned subjective choice of how to conceive of a process or event . . . I argue that verbal aspect is the essential semantic component of tense-form usage in Greek, rather than absolute tense, and that this is true in both the indicative and nonindicative moods.[78]

Porter desires to move the conversation of aspect away from time with respect to tense forms.

Expectedly, Porter greatly differentiates verbal aspect from *Aktionsart*. *Aktionsart* refers to the kind of action of a verb.[79] It is "procedural or lexical aspect" rather than "grammatical aspect, the aspect that is morphologically encoded in the tense-forms."[80] Comparing views of the place of *Aktionsart* in the concept of aspect (or its relationship to verbal aspect) held by other grammarians, Porter says of himself, "Porter minimizes the role of Aktionsart and considers it to involve a (problematic) debate

---

was a newer paradigm. He explains, writing, "To avoid the tense terminological difficulties . . . the traditional tense-form names are retained to represent the formal paradigms as abstracted constructs that developed early in Greek usage and are now hallowed by tradition. But consistent functional names for the representative verbal conceptions of action must be devised as well. The following have been selected: perfective (» » Aorist), imperfective (» » Present/Imperfect), stative (» » Perfect/Pluperfect). These terms are recognizably taken from Slovonic linguistics, and not only provide possibilities for dialogue in general linguistic theory (e.g. typology), but they seem to provide descriptive labels which encapsulate the essential semantics of each aspectual category" *Verbal Aspect*, 89.

77. Porter, *Verbal Aspect*, 98.
78. Porter, *Linguistic Analysis*, 161.
79. Porter, *Verbal Aspect*, 86.
80. Porter, *Linguistic Analysis*, 184.

about lexis, not aspect, and hence to be unimportant for defining aspectual semantics."[81]

Key to Porter's understanding of verbal aspect are the concepts of *markedness* and *prominence*. Markedness concerns "a number of different means by which more or less significant elements might be identified, including (but not exclusive of) frequency of appearance and things related to morphology.[82] Prominence is "motivated markedness." Prominence "involves marked features that are (by whatever means) shown to be motivated in a particular context, so that a given dimension of a text is brought to the fore."[83] The markedness of a verb can be (1) *material*—what the tense-form paradigm does to the verb stem; (2) *implicational*—which either (a) evidences fewer irregularities as a verbal category or (b) shows amalgamation of Middle/Passive voices; (3) *distributional*—tense frequency; or (4) *semantic*—e.g. verbal opposition, conceptual description, planes of discourse, or systemic network.[84]

The aorist tense-form is the least heavily marked among the traditional tenses.[85] It formed the basis for carrying a narrative when a Greek-speaker narrated events.[86] As such it is "aspectually *perfective*, occurring in past contexts as the background narrative tense."[87] Instead of describing punctiliar time or an action of scope, the aorist describes a series of *complete* events.[88] Porter agrees with Fanning and Campbell that "the

81. Porter, *Linguistic Analysis*, 202. See also, Porter, *Verbal Aspect*, 87. Porter is complementary of McKay for differentiating *Aktionsart* "as a lexical distinction" from verbal aspect (Porter, *Linguistic Analysis*, 164). He is highly critical of Wallace's view of aspect which "[equates] Aktionsart, which is concerned with how an action 'actually happened,' with aspect" (*Linguistic Analysis*, 184, referring to Wallace, *Greek Grammar Beyond the Basics*. Also, he is critical of Fanning and Campbell for "confusing discussion of aspect and its central role by their attention to Aktionsart and, to a large extent, making their discussion focus upon Aktionsart" (*Linguistic Analysis*, 202–3). Tresham thinks that Porter has understated the closeness of some traditional grammars' understanding of *Aktionsart* to that of aspect (Tresham, "Aspect and *Aktionsart* in Greek Grammars," 17).

82. Porter, *Linguistic Analysis*, 141.

83. Porter, *Linguistic Analysis*, 141. See also Porter, "Prominence: A Theoretical Overview," 45–74.

84. Porter, *Verbal Aspect*, 178–81.

85. Porter, *Verbal Aspect*, 178–81.

86. Porter, *Verbal Aspect*, 198.

87. Porter, *Verbal Aspect*, 198, italics mine.

88. Porter, *Verbal Aspect*, 206, italics mine. Porter seems to agree with McKay, who says, "The Aorist is the 'residual aspect, used when the speaker or writer had no special reason to use any other" (McKay, "Syntax," 46; cited in Porter, *Verbal Aspect*, 207).

aorist tense-form encodes *perfective* aspect."⁸⁹ Porter indicates that this is most evident when analyzing contexts that utilize both the aorist and the imperfect.⁹⁰

Although he expresses with certainty that the aorist is aspectually *perfective*, Porter supports the use of the aorist in a future (e.g. *proleptic*) reference. Yet he recognizes that "most of the examples cited by grammarians are the apodoses of conditional or conditional-like statements . . . and are better treated as logical future-referring statements" (Porter, *Verbal Aspect*, 232). Porter, therefore, completely divests the aorist of denoting time or kind of action. The "future aorist" only is future if it is in a clause in which a condition will be fulfilled in the future, or in which the context demands a completion that is yet future.⁹¹

Therefore, Porter's theory of the aorist as an aspect that indicates the speaker's viewpoint via markedness advances the discussion of the aorist. For Porter, the aorist verbs of John 17:4 would be *backgrounding* the "glorified" (ἐδόξασα—aorist, active, indicative), "completed" (τελειώσας—aorist, active, participle), and "to do" (ποιήσω—aorist, active, subjunctive) of Jesus's words (and thus of "the work"). Although imperfect, δέδωκάς, following the relative pronoun ὅ and the particle τελειώσας, to which it corresponds, also would be backgrounded. Since τελειώσας does not occur in the apodosis of an if/then clause, it only could be proleptic for Porter if the remainder of the context reveals it to be logically future.

---

89. Porter, *Linguistic Analysis*, 199, italics mine.

90. Porter cites Luke 6:1ff.; 24:13, and John 10:19ff.: "[In] Luke 6:1ff . . . the incident of the plucking and eating of the grain is introduced with two Imperfects. The details of the encounter with the Pharisees are then recorded with Aorists, with the concluding point of the story introduced with the Imperfect (v. 5). A similar pattern is found in Luke 24:13. In contrast John 10:19ff. records a division that occurs. The fact that there was a schism is recorded with the Aorist, and the details are elucidated with Imperfects. The most common pattern throughout the NT, and within Greek literature as a whole, is to find an alteration of tenses" (Porter, *Verbal Aspect*, 207). In the examples above, Porter's point is to show that writers indicate the foreground or main events ("the details" in both examples) in a narrative sequence by using the *imperfect*, and events that introduce or provide setting to a narrative are spoken of using the *aorist* because they are less prominent from the speaker's point of view.

91. Concerning the aorist participle, Porter proposes, "As has been seen, there is nothing inherent in the Participle that forbids its reference to a subsequent action in relation to the main verb of the sentence. In fact, it would appear that the perfective aspect of the Aorist, since it grammaticalizes an event as a complete process, would be suitable not only for antecedent and coincidental reference but for subsequent reference as well" (Porter, *Verbal Aspect*, 385).

THE ADVANCEMENT OF THE UNDERSTANDING OF THE AORIST FROM CAMPBELL FORWARD

Constantine Campbell

Campbell's forays into verbal aspect advance the discussion beyond the place of *Aktionsart* within aspect in Biblical Greek. Campbell simplifies the definition of verbal aspect to the concept of *viewpoint*: "An author or speaker views an action, event, or state either from the *outside* or from the *inside*. The view of an action, event, or state from the outside is called the *perfective* aspect, while the view from the inside is called the *imperfective* aspect."[92] Perfect aspect views the action as a whole, presenting an action "in summary form—*this happened, that happened*—without reference to how it happened and without viewing it as though happen*ing*."[93] It views action "from a distance."[94] In contrast, imperfective aspect presents an action "as unfolding or in progress—this was happening, that happens—without reference to the whole action."[95] It views actions "up close."[96]

Like many grammarians before him, he recognizes a difference between aspect and *Aktionsart*, defining the latter as "how an action actually takes place—what sort of action it is."[97] Thus, for Campbell, a significant distinction between aspect and *Aktionsart* is that aspect is a subjective category based on an author's choice, but *Aktionsart* is an objective category based "in reality."[98]

Campbell is careful to distinguish between *verbal semantics* (or *grammatical* semantics, as opposed to *lexical* semantics) and *pragmatics*—the former referring to the unchanging and uncancelable values encoded in the verbal form and the latter referring to the expression of semantic values in context and in combination with other factors.[99] The

---

92. Campbell, *Basics of Verbal Aspect in the Greek*, 19. See also, Campbell, *Verbal Aspect in the Indicative Mood*, 8; Campbell, *Verbal Aspect and Non-Indicative Verbs*, 6.
93. Campbell, *Advances in the Study of Greek*, 106–7.
94. Campbell, *Advances in the Study of Greek*, 106.
95. Campbell, *Advances in the Study of Greek*, 107.
96. Campbell, *Advances in the Study of Greek*, 107.
97. Campbell, *Basics of Verbal Aspect*, 22.
98. Campbell, *Verbal Aspect in the Indicative Mood*, 11.
99. Campbell, *Basics of Verbal Aspect*, 22–23. Elsewhere Campbell elaborates: "*Semantics* refers to the core grammatical values of a linguistic item; the values of verbal items being of primary interest. The semantic value is the uncancelable essence of meaning ... that is inherent to the verb form in questions. *Pragmatics* here refers to the

aspect of any one tense-form does not change because it is a *semantic* value. But the *Aktionsart* of a tense-form can change based on the lexeme used in a tense, the context, and what happened in reality, because it is a *pragmatic* value.[100] Aspect and *Aktionsart* work together in understanding verbal action in Campbell's theory and method.[101]

According to Campbell, an aorist verb always will be perfective in aspect, even though its *Aktionsart* might be punctiliar, iterative, or ingressive, for its aspect in uncancelable but its *Aktionsart* is cancelable.[102] Therefore, the aorist always presents events in summary form, without viewing the manner in which the actions happened—it is an outside or external viewpoint of the action.[103] Writers employ the aorist when they wish to employ *remoteness*—a metaphorical (and semantic) value of distance. Such remoteness may be past, present, or future temporally.[104]

Methodologically speaking, Campbell provides a four-step process to exegete a verb in its context:

> First, the semantic values of the verb are to be identified (e.g., perfective aspect). Second, the type of lexeme must be taken into account (e.g., punctiliar). Third, relevant elements of the context are considered (e.g., a repeated action is implied). Finally, the *Aktionsart* is determined based on predictable patterns of the combinations of the previous three elements (e.g., iterative *Aktionsart*).[105]

---

way in which language is used in context. It has to do with linguistic performance and implicature, which will vary depending on lexical, stylistic, grammatical, and deictic interactions, and thus cancelable features" (*Verbal Aspect in the Indicative Mood*, 24).

100. Campbell, *Basics of Verbal Aspect*, 23.

101. Campbell, *Advances in the Study of Greek*, 120–21; Campbell, *The Basics of Verbal Aspect*, 62–63.

102. Campbell, *The Basics of Verbal Aspect*, 62–63.

103. Campbell, *The Basics of Verbal Aspect*, 34; Campbell, *Advances in the Study of Greek*, 119; Campbell, *Verbal Aspect in the Indicative Mood*, 103.

104. Campbell, *Basics of Verbal Aspect*, 37.

105. Campbell, *Advances in the Study of Greek*, 120–21; Campbell, *The Basics of Verbal Aspect*, 62.

Campbell diagrams his process in this manner:[106]

| 1. Semantics Aspect? Spatial Value? | + | 2. Lexeme Punctiliar? Stative? Transitive? etc. | + | 3. Context Time reference? Duration? Logic? etc. | = | 4. Aktionsart Past progressive? Iterative? Stative? |

Using the above scheme, Campbell proposes six *Aktionsart* implicatures for the aorist: *Summary, Punctiliar, Ingressive, Gnomic, Present,* and *Future*.[107]

As stated above, in all uses of the aorist, Campbell's first step will denote a perfective aspect indicating remoteness, e.g.:

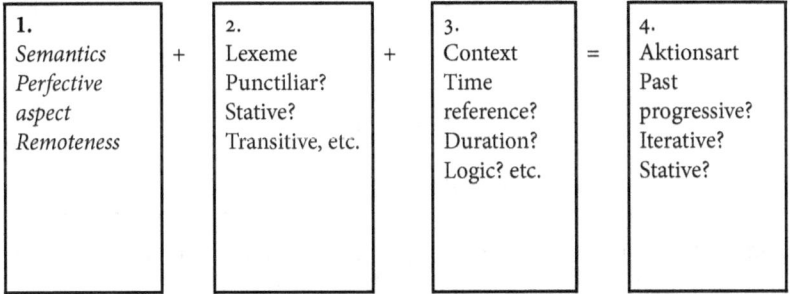

| 1. Semantics Perfective aspect Remoteness | + | 2. Lexeme Punctiliar? Stative? Transitive, etc. | + | 3. Context Time reference? Duration? Logic? etc. | = | 4. Aktionsart Past progressive? Iterative? Stative? |

For example, the perfective aspect can combine with any non-punctiliar or non-stative lexeme to create a *summary Aktionsart* as long as the context allows for a summary sense:[108]

---

106. Campbell, *Advances in the Study of Greek*, 121. With respect to participles, pragmatically aorist participles express actions antecedent to the leading verb. "The action of the leading verb occurs after the action of the aorist participle" (*Basics of Verbal Aspect*, 94).

107. Campbell, *Advances in the Study of Greek*, 122. Campbell indicates that the present and future *Aktionsarten* of the aorist tense-form are special functions of the aorist rather than strictly two *Akitionsart* forms.

108. Campbell, *Advances in the Study of Greek*, 122–23; Campbell, *The Basics of Verbal Aspect*, 86. Campbell cites John 1:17 as an example: ὅτι ὁ νόμος διὰ Μωϋσέως ἐδόθη, ἡ χάρις καὶ ἡ ἀλήθεια διὰ 'Ιησοῦ Χριστοῦ ἐγένετοι- "for although the law *was given* though Moses, grace and truth *came* through Jesus Christ" (*The Basics of Verbal Aspect*, 86).

| 1. Semantics Perfective aspect Remoteness | + | 2. Lexeme Non-punctiliar/ non-stative | + | 3. Context Allows summary | = | 4. *Aktionsart* *Summary* |

Similarly, the perfective aspect can combine with a punctiliar lexeme to create a *punctiliar Aktionsart* as long as the context allows for a punctiliar sense:[109]

| 1. Semantics Perfective aspect Remoteness | + | 2. Lexeme Punctiliar | + | 3. Context Allows punctilarity | = | 4. *Aktionsart* *Punctiliar* |

Similar methodology would apply to ingressive, gnomic, and present aorists.

Concerning the future aorist, the aorist tense-form still records remoteness. Any lexeme may be present in a Future Aorist, and a Future-referring context is what establishes a Future *Aktionsart*.[110]

---

109. Campbell, *Advances in the Study of Greek*, 123; Campbell, *The Basics of Verbal Aspect*, 86–87. Campbell cites John 19:34 as an example: ἀλλ' εἷς τῶν στρατιωτῶν λόγχῃ αὐτοῦ τὴν πλευρὰν ἔνυξεν, καὶ ἐξῆλθεν εὐθὺς αἷμα καὶ ὕδωρ—"But one of the soldiers *pierced* his side with a spear, and at once blood and water came out" (*The Basics of Verbal Aspect*, 87).

110. Campbell, *Basics of Verbal Aspect*, 90. Contrary to many past grammarians, Campbell does not cite Rom 8:30 as an example of a future (proleptic) aorist, but as a *gnomic* aorist, on the basis that ἐδόξασεν has a non-punctiliar/non-stative lexeme, and the context allows for a universal or timeless aspect (147). He translates the verse gnomically: "And those he predestines, he calls, and those he calls, he also justifies, and those he justifies, he also glorifies" (147). I disagree with Campbell, for, as shown above, the "context" concerns stages of salvation, starting in eternity past with the foreknowledge of God ("fore*knew*"), then chronologically proceeding through predestination ("predestine*d*"), summoning ("calle*d*"), justification ("justifie*d*"), and glorification ("glorifie*d*"). Again, to be clear, I am not suggesting that the verb encodes the future. I am saying that the context—the type-logic of the subject of Rom 8:30—demands a future referring stage. Also significant is that Campbell cites John 13:31 as a present aorist, in keeping with my discussion of 13:31 above (*Basics of Verbal Aspect*, 88). Campbell

| 1. Semantics Perfective aspect Remoteness | + | 2. Lexeme Any | + | 3. Context Future referring | = | 4. Aktionsart *Future aorist* |

It seems that Campbell's theory and method would rule out John 17:4 as containing any future aorists. The first term, ἐδόξασα, although seemingly stative, does not have a context that refers to the future. The ἡ ὥρα of 17:2 is coupled with ἐλήλυθεν to indicate a thought immediately before the speaker's eyes.[111] The imperative δόξασόν in 17:1 and 17:5 have indeterminate *Aktionsart* even though the aorist tense-form renders it to have a perfective aspect.[112] Thus, one cannot conclude that they contribute to a future context, even though the cross will be upon Jesus soon. The temporal adverb, νῦν, seems to demand a more immediate, present context for ἐδόξασα. That is, the hour is upon Jesus presently with respect to the prayer, so seemingly—according to Campbell's theory—"glorify" is not inherently future. The request for pre-existent glory indicates the verb points toward the future.

The aorist participle, τελειώσας, would speak of a work antecedent to ἐδόξασα. It too is perfective in its aspect, with a seemingly non-punctiliar lexeme and without a future context. It seems to have a summary context, for it is not punctiliar, present-referring, setting a new direction, or speaking universally.

The aorist subjunctive, ποιήσω, depicts a particular activity, one that is concrete, and it does so in a summary fashion.[113] The *doing* of the ὃ δέδωκάς is *particular*, concerning a specific activity—τὸ ἔργον, for a specific person—μοι. It too is perfective in aspect as an aorist and lacks a future context based on δέδωκάς. As a perfect tense-form verb, according

---

does not discuss John 17:4 as a future aorist.

111. Campbell, *The Basics of Verbal Aspect*, 105; Campbell, *Verbal Aspect, the Indicative Mood*, 193.

112. Campbell's research concludes the aorist imperative has little to do with *Aktionsart*. See *Verbal Aspect and Non-Indicative Verbs*, 84–91.

113. *Verbal Aspect and Non-Indicative Verbs*, 56–57.

to Campbell's theory, δέδωκάς would be imperfective aspectually, with heightened proximity.[114]

Therefore, according the Campbell's theory, the aspectual forces of the verbs would render John 17:4 as, "I presently have glorified you perfectively (from my perspective) on the earth so that you are glorified statively (in reality), having completed perfectively (from my viewpoint) the whole of the work, in summary, which you—from my perspective—perfectively gave to me specifically, particularly, in order that potentially I might do it perfectively (from my viewpoint)." Campbell's discussion moves the aorist participle τελειώσας away from any possible proleptic reading.

Nicholas J. Ellis, Michael G. Aubrey, and Mark Dubis

Ellis, Aubrey, and Dubis offer a proposal that advances the study of verbal aspect of the aorist by demonstrating that the Greek verbal system matches the structure of verbs with the functioning of the verbs.[115] They argue that the Greek language positions itself as a morphological system of a three-part aspect, as opposed to a morphology system based on tense. They emphasize what they term, "verbal prominence" (or more specifically, "grammatical prominence"), suggesting that Greek demonstrates aspectual prominence over tense prominence and mood prominence.[116] Aspectual prominence does not cancel the role of tense or mood. As Ellis explains,

> [Grammatical] prominence does not mean that the prominent category (whether tense, aspect, or mood) is dominant to the exclusion of the other two categories. It also does not mean that one category is more important than the other two, or that the other become irrelevant . . . Grammatical prominence involves the extent to which one of these categories provides the primary or central concept for how a particular verbal system is arranged. The prominent category functions as a sort of organizing principle for the other two categories.

---

114. *Verbal Aspect and Non-Indicative Verbs*, 195–211.

115. Ellis, "Aspect-Prominence, Morpho-Syntax, and a Cognitive-Linguistic Framework for the Greek Verb," 122–60; Ellis, Aubrey, and Dubis, "The Greek Verbal System and Aspectual Prominence: Revising Our Taxonomy and Nomenclature," 33–62.

116. Ellis, "Aspect-Prominence," 124; Ellis, Aubrey, and Dubis, "Greek Verbal System," 34. The three writers do not emphasize "voice" in a traditional sense of our understanding of verbs as having tense, *voice*, and mood. Instead they recognize three verbal parameters in most languages: *tense, aspect, and mood*.

For Ellis, verbal aspect concerns "a situation's internal structure, usually in terms of being bounded (self-contained) or unbounded (uncontained)," or "an event's internal temporal structure ... the manner and extent to which time unfolds within a situation."[117]

A key to Ellis, Aubrey, and Dubis' conclusions is that Greek primarily grammaticalizes aspect within its morphological meaning and structure. Greek encodes aspect-prominence within its morphology, resulting in an aspectual system of *Perfective*, *Imperfective*, and *Combinative* aspects.[118]

What past grammars have termed, "verbal root," Ellis will identify as "lexical core." The lexical core has an aspectual marker as the prominent grammatical feature. The lexical core combines with aspect markers to form the aspect stem. In this theory, the most basic grammaticalized feature of the Greek verb is its *aspect stem*. Ellis represents the formation of the aspect stem as demonstrated in the following table.

Table 4. Ellis' Overview of Morphological Features of Greek Verbs

	Aspect Stem			
Tense Indicator (indicative mood only)	Imperfective Aspect Marker	Lexical Core	Perfective Aspect Marker	Personal Endings

In this model, beginning with the lexical core, verbal prominence has the tendency of moving "from the inside out, with the more-prominent, more foundational, and generally less static elements located closer to the lexical core, and the less-prominent and more variable elements located on the periphery of the verbal form."[119] Important to this theory are 1) that any lexeme can utilize all three aspectual stems and 2) the prominent verbal category will be both pervasive and obligatory. Ellis has proposed that the non-indicative moods—subjunctive, imperative, optative, infinitive, and participle—grammaticalize aspect pervasively, appearing in all Greek verbs.[120] In contrast to aspect, tense appears in

117. Ellis, "Aspect-Prominence," 125.

118. Ellis, "Aspect-Prominence," 133. "Combinative" is so-labeled because it combines the semantic categories of the other two aspects. Synonymously, it could be denoted as the "perfect" or "stative" aspect.

119. Ellis, "Aspect-Prominence," 133.

120. Ellis identifies infinitives and participles each as a "form" rather than as a "mood."

the indicative mood only, but aspect is obligatory throughout the entire Greek verbal system.[121]

Using Ellis, Aubrey, and Dubis' paradigm, I will consider the verbal aspect of the three aorist tense-form verbs in John 17:4—ἐδόξασα, τελειώσας, and ποιήσω. The verb ἐδόξασα being aorist, active, indicative in tense-form, has a past perfective tense indicator, ε. Its lexical core is δοξάζ-. The σ is a perfective aspect marker and has combined with ζ to produce a σ. It has the personal ending α for the first person, singular form. One might diagram the aspect in the manner demonstrated in the following table.

Table 5. Morphological Features of ἐδόξασα

			Perfective Aspect Stem		
	Tense Indicator (indicative mood only)	Imperfective Aspect Marker (prefix)	Lexical Core	Perfective Aspect Marker (suffix)	Personal Endings
Past Perfective (Aorist)	ε	∅	δοξάζ	σ	A

The *perfective* aspect stem is the lexical core + σ, which is δοξάζ + σ. This aorist form is also past with respect to tense, indicated by the marker ε. The writer of the Fourth Gospel views "glorified" as a perfective whole that was completed in the past relevant to the time of Jesus speaking.[122]

The verb τελειώσας is the aorist, active, participial form of τελειόω, meaning *to finish, complete, or perfect*. Because the participle tense-form is non-indicative, no tense indicator appears; tense remains limited to the indicative mood. The verb form does not have a prefix that would mark an imperfective aspect. Its lexical core is τελειο-, with a lengthening of the ω before the σ. The *perfective* aspect stem is the lexical core + σ, or τελειο- + σ. The personal ending –ας indicates the nominative, masculine singular.

---

121. Ellis, "Aspect-Prominence," 135–36. Ellis also notes proposes, "Mood is not expressed at all with infinitives and participle, and the past/nonpast distinction expressed by the Greek augment prefix disappears entirely outside of the indicative mood" (136).

122. "For those rare times when a perfective event needs to be communicated with a perfective aspect, the 'aorist' form is chosen" (Ellis, "Aspect-Prominence," 155).

Table 6. Morphological Features of τελειώσας

		Perfective Aspect Stem			
	Tense Indicator (indicative mood only)	Imperfective Aspect Marker (prefix)	Lexical Core	Perfective Aspect Marker (suffix)	Personal Endings
Past Perfective (Aorist)	ø	ø	τελειο	σ	Ας

Ellis's aspectual schema indicates that τελειώσας is perfective in its aspect. The aspect presents the state of affairs of this verb "as an undifferentiated whole, as complete, including the end points."[123] As ἐδόξασα is the main event of John 17:4, the participle τελειώσας precedes the time of ἐδόξασα. As a participle, τελειώσας acts adverbially to modify the meaning of ἐδόξασα.[124] A participle of means, it explains the working of ἐδόξασα.[125]

Therefore, the completion of which τελειώσας speaks is a *past perfective* event because it logically—that is, *grammatically*—precedes the past perfective tense of the aorist indicative of ἐδόξασα. Jesus claims a perfectively completed glorification in the past (as grammaticalized in the verb) on the basis of a previous perfective *completion* (τελειώσας) of a given work.

The final verb in John 17:4, ποιήσω, is aorist, active, subjunctive of ποιέω—*to work or to do*. In Ellis' model, one would diagram the aspect as demonstrated in the following table.

---

123. Buth, "Participles as Pragmatic Choice," 275.

124. Ellis's understanding of the Aorist participle agrees with Mounce: "The aorist participle indicates an action occurring prior to the time of the main verb" (Mounce, *Basics of Biblical Greek*, 237). Buth writes similarly, "*Prototypically*, the time of the aorist participle is prior to the main event," (Buth, "Participles as Pragmatic Choice," 275, italics mine).

125. A participle of means "indicates the means by which the action of a finite verb is accomplished; *defines* or *explains* the controlling verb; usually *follows* the verb" (Wallace, *Greek Grammar*, 758). Wallace further notes, "Sometimes means blends imperceptibly into cause, especially with aorist participles. In such instances, the participle may be used for an action that is both antecedent and contemporaneous to the controlling verb" (758).

Table 7. Morphological Features of ποιήσω

	Perfective Aspect Stem				
	Tense Indicator (indicative mood only)	Imperfective Aspect Marker (prefix)	Lexical Core	Perfective Aspect Marker (suffix)	Personal Endings
Past Perfective (Aorist)	ø	ø	ποιε	σ	Ω

The verb does not have a tense indicator because it is not the indicative mood,[126] and it lacks the imperfective marker. Its lexical core is ποιε, with the final vowel lengthening to indicate the subjunctive. The perfective aspect marker is σ present. The personal ending ω indicates the first person, singular form of the verb.

The subjective mood indicates probability even though the aspect is perfective. From the speaker's viewpoint, the clause, ἵνα ποιήσω ("in order that I might do it") indicates a probable event to be perfectively executed.

Concerning δέδωκάς, one must consider the morphological differences between μι-verbs and ω-verbs as one discusses the verbal aspect of this derivative of δίδωμι. Ellis points out three such differences.[127] First, whereas the imperfective aspect is the default morphological form for ω-verbs, is does not serve as such for μι-verbs. The imperfective aspect uses the prefixed reduplication. Second, the personal endings—which are outside of the aspect stem—are different, as represented by the μι of the first person, singular ending in the non-past forms. Third, reduplication in the imperfective aspect prefix is formed with an iota instead of an epsilon.

The three aspects remain the same for μι-verbs: imperfective, perfective, and combinative. The μι-verbs still encode tense in a past/non-past system. Ellis provides a chart of the analysis of the verbal aspect of μι–verbs using δίδωμι as his example:[128]

---

126. Similar to Ellis, Mounce writes, "There is no concept of absolute past or present time in the subjunctive," (Mounce, *Basics of Biblical Greek*, 289).

127. The discussion to follow on δίδωμι comes from Ellis, Aubrey, and Dubis, "The Greek Verbal System," 55.

128. Ellis, Aubrey, and Dubis, "The Greek Verbal System," 52.

Table 8. Tense and Aspect for μι-Conjugation verb δέδωκάς as a First Singular Active Indicative Verb

Non-Past Tense (with Primary Endings)						
	Tense Indicator	Imperfective Aspect Prefix (Reduplication)	Lexical Core	Perfective Aspect Suffix	Personal Endings (Active 1 Sg)	Final Form
Non-Past Imperfective	∅	δι	δω	∅	μι	Δίδωμι
Non-Past Perfective	∅	∅	δω	σ	ω	Δώσω
Non-Past Combinative	∅	δε	δω	κ	α	Δέδωκα
Past Tense (with Secondary Endings)						
	Tense Indicator	Imperfective Aspect Prefix (Reduplication)	Lexical Core	Perfective Aspect Suffix	Personal Endings (Active 1 Sg)	Final Form
Past Imperfective	ε	δι	δο	∅	ον	ἐδίδουν
Past Perfective	ε	∅	δω	κ	α	ἔδωκα
Past Combinative	(ε)	δε	δω	κ	ειν	ἐδεδώκειν

Per Ellis's chart, it is evident that δέδωκάς (perfect, active, indicative, *second* person, singular form of δίδωμι) would follow the analysis of δέδωκα (perfect, active, indicative, *first* person, singular form).[129] Thus, it is a non-past combinative aspect verb, having no tense indicator,[130] and having both imperfective (prefix) and perfective (suffix) aspect markers combining with its lexical core: δε (reduplication) + δω (lexical core) + κ. It has the second person, singular number ending –ας.

As a verb of combinative aspect, δέδωκάς reflects "the perfective nature of the completed verbal event and the imperfective nature of its ongoing relevance."[131] It is perfectively completed ("have given") but with

---

129. The verb δίδωμι simply means "to give" in this context. See entry for "δίδωμι" in Montanari, *The Brill Dictionary of Ancient Greek*, α–κ, 521.

130. Ellis notes, "One might question why we view the reduplicated δι and δε as well as the κ as markers of aspect rather than markers of tense... Although this should become clearer as we move forward, we will note here that it is the augment that is absent in the non-indicative paradigms (where tense is absent), not the reduplication or κ/σ suffixes. Thus we argue that it is the augment that expresses tense, not the other features (which instead express aspect)" (Ellis, Aubrey, Dubis, "The Greek Verbal System," 42).

131. Ellis, Aubrey, Dubis, "The Greek Verbal System," 48; Ellis, "Aspect Prominence," 143.

relevance to the accomplishment of the work yet future communicated, which the subjunctive ποιήσω reflects. As Ellis concludes, "Semantically speaking, the non-past combinative ('perfect') forms refer to an event that is completed at the time of speaking, though it has present relevance."[132] It marks the "present relevance" of an event.[133]

In sum, according to the work of Ellis, Aubrey, and Dubis, the aspects of the three aorist and one perfect tense-forms verbs would render John 17:4 as, "I have glorified you perfectively [in past time] on the earth, [by] having completed the whole of the work (from my viewpoint) perfectively [because this logically precedes "have glorified"] which you (from my perspective) perfectively gave to me at a point in the past with relevance until I did what I was to do perfectively." Similar to Campbell's discussion, Ellis, Aubrey, and Dubis's work excludes the possibility of the aorist participle τελειώσας offering a proleptic idea.[134]

---

132. Ellis, Aubrey, Dubis, *The Greek Verbal System*, 60.

133. Ellis, "Aspect Prominence," 134.

134. To be fair, Ellis, Aubrey, and Dubis do not give discussion to a "proleptic" aorist, because it would not be possible for an *aorist* (perfective-*past* aspect) to be "future." Aspectually, the future tense form is not so much referring to the future as it is a form encoding the non-past perfectively. Therefore, although they do not consider Rom 8:30 in one of their examples—either to support or deny a proleptic possibility in the NT or in John 17:4 specifically—it would seem that the ἐδόξασεν of Rom 8:30 is past-perfective aspectually. It has the same aorist, active, indicative tense-form, the past perfective tense indicator ε, the lexical core δοξάζ-, and the σ perfective aspect marker. The only difference is the personal ending—εν for the third person, singular form. The *perfective* aspect stem is the lexical core + σ, which is δοξάζ + σ. As stated earlier in the above analysis, this aorist form also is past with respect to tense, indicated by the marker ε. Paul views "glorified" as a perfective whole that was completed in the past *concurrent* to the time of *foreknew, predestined, called,* and *justified*. All the events were perfectively completed; they were perfectively completed when "foreknew" was perfectively completed. This would remove a future glorification concept in my "stages" theory also, for Paul would not be speaking of simultaneous stages, but of concurrent acts in eternity past. Foreknew, predestined, called, justified, and glorified each would have been perfectively completed in the past time. This conclusion, based on the work of Ellis, Aubrey, and Dubis, would also define an "inaugurated eschatology" view of Rom 8:30 differently than Ortlund. Ortlund concludes that Paul speaks of "what has happened now . . . We are glorified in the sense that we become what we once were in Eden" (Dane Ortlund, "Inaugurated Glorification: Revising Romans 8:30," 130). He writes, "Believers are decisively 'glorified' no less than they are already 'justified.' The point of the five verbs in Rom. 8:29–30 is not to outline a linear progression of individual salvation in temporal sequence, but to exalt the benefits that come, both now and later, through faith in Christ." I would agree with Ortlund with respect to the equal sense and states of "glorified" and "justified." But based the conclusions of Ellis, Aubrey, and Dubis, I cannot see that Paul speaks of "later." Paul speaks of "glorified" as an event completed perfectively in the past. In Rom 8:30, ἐδόξασεν is not an "ingressive aorist,"

Timothy Brookins

Brookins offers the most current proposal of understanding verbal aspect of Greek verbs.[135] I will interact with him only briefly because his theory (1) does not pertain strictly to aspect and (2) is relevant only to the *indicative* mood. The only indicative verb in John 17:4 is ἐδόξασα, and my greater concern lies with the *participle* τελειώσας.

Brookins seeks to make a case for the grammaticalization of time in Greek verbs in the indicative mood on the basis of cognitive-linguistic theories of perspective, mental space, and conceptual blending. Brookins proposes:

> The cognitive-linguistic theories of perspective, mental space, and conceptual blending are able to account for the selection of verb forms more convincingly than both the no-time position and the conventional tense position, in the one case because these theories expose the so-called exceptions as being nothing of the kind and, in the other case, because they provide a theoretical framework that offers the qualifications the conventional explanation has lacked.[136]

Disagreeing with Campbell, Brookins does not think that spatiality can substitute for temporality as an encoded value in Greek verb morphology. He denies any claim that time is not grammaticalized in the morphology of indicative verbs. Instead, both aspect and time are encoded in Greek verbs. He prefers to understand the six tense-forms of the indicative mood as grammaticalizing anteriority (imperfect, aorist, perfect, and pluperfect), contemporaneity (present), and posteriority (future).[137] *Aspect* is what differentiates the structure of the action indicated by the four tenses that grammaticalize anteriority.

One of Brookins's assumptions is that an objectivist view of language is passé, such theory having been destroyed by both Continental philosophy and cognitive linguistics.[138] By this he means two things. First, "language never corresponds strictly with reality but only represents

---

as Ortlund concludes (132). The very concept of a "proleptic aorist" seems false based on the grammaticalization of aspect within the tense-form.

135. Brookins, "A Tense Discussion," 147–68.
136. Brookins, "A Tense Discussion," 149.
137. Brookins, "A Tense Discussion," 150.
138. Brookins, "A Tense Discussion," 151.

it."[139] Second, "listeners do not simply decode in one-to-one fashion the thoughts expressed but rather construct them, often moving beyond the expressed elements to channel the message."[140] For Brookins, meaning primarily is cognitive rather than a matter of relationships.[141]

Understanding that some linguistic units are understood only with respect to temporal or spatial context, Brookins suggests that deixis or "conceptual origo"—whether personal (*I, you*), spatial (*here-there, this-that, come-go*), and temporal (*now-then*)—is not anchored in "the embodied situation" but elsewhere.[142] The person who grounds a given speech event may be the speaker, but the subject of conceptualization might be the listener or a third party. Brookins provides an example from Phil 3:19, "whose glory was in their shame," noting, "It is doubtful that Paul's opponents in [this example] thought that their '*glory* was in their *shame*;' rather what *they* considered 'glory' the *speaker* considered 'shame.'"[143]

In another example, Brookins demonstrates that time shifts relative to mental space: "Last night you were leaving tomorrow and now you are leaving the day after tomorrow! What am I supposed to believe?"[144] Brookins reasons,

---

139. Brookins, "A Tense Discussion," 151.

140. Brookins, "A Tense Discussion," 151. I disagree with the premise of the philosophical and linguistic undermining of an objectivist view of language, for the simple fact that Brookins expects readers of the article to understand his words *objectively*—that is, as he intends to communicate his ideas via his words—and to interpret them as such. Brookins undermines his own assumption. Also, how a listener decodes thoughts is a subjective response to language communication. Whether or not a listener decodes correctly—e.g., *objectively*—what is heard is not an appropriate consideration of how the language of the author works. *Decoding*, or *interpreting*, is the work of the reader or hearer. It is the work of looking at the *encoding* of the author and attempting to *un*-code what is encoded. The very idea of decoding assumes something objective exists with the language communication. That a hearer or reader might then choose to construct one's own meaning in addition to or apart from what is encoded does not change the original encoding.

141. Brookins, "A Tense Discussion," 151.

142. Brookins, "A Tense Discussion," 154.

143. Brookins, "A Tense Discussion," 157. In the article, Brookins provides forty-eight examples in order to demonstrate that conceptual origo is anchored in a place other than the embodied situation of the speaker personally, spatially, or temporally.

144. Brookins, "A Tense Discussion," 159. Brookins credits this example to Boogart and Janssen, "Tense and Aspect in Geeraerts and Cuyckens," 803–28, esp. 809, citing Janssen. In the printed example in Brookins' article, he erroneously writes, "What *I* am supposed to believe" rather than "What *am* I supposed to believe."

In this example, the Base space is the time of speech. But the Viewpoint space shifts, first, from the perspective of "last night," at which time the addressee was planning to leave "tomorrow" (which is today relative to the Base space), to "now," at which time the addressee planned to leave "the day after tomorrow" (which is the day after tomorrow relative to the Base space). What results is a blended scenario, in which "last night" existed as a past event (hence the past tense "were leaving") and yet the same event is said to occur "tomorrow."[145]

With this and his many other examples Brookins argues that events described often take place in "mental spaces" that are anchored in a place other than the "embodied present." The "originary viewpoint" for an action may (1) be a future mental space, from which point the action is viewed as either present or past, or (2) originate in the past and, from that perspective, view some event as present, or as future but still prior to the (speaker's) present, or as future and contemporaneous with the (speaker's) present.[146] For Brookins, mental space is as important as morphology and temporal reference. In the indicative mood, past-tense forms encode mental space *anterior* actions and states, the present *contemporaneous* actions and states, and the future *posterior* actions and states.[147]

Therefore, although there is a shift in perspective from the I (ἐγώ) who glorified God the Father by having completed the work, the giving of the work is not grounded in the speaker, but in the listener; "in order that I might do it" stems from the giving of the Father. Yet the aorists still would indicate *anterior* actions.

---

145. Brookins, "A Tense Discussion," 160.

146. Brookins, "A Tense Discussion," 164.

147. Ibid. Brookins uses Rom 8:30 as an example of the verb tense needing to be understood relative to a shift in mental space or viewpoint: "And those whom he justified, these he also glorified [ἐδόξασεν]" (NRSV). He writes, "In [Rom. 8:30], ἐδόξασεν could perhaps be debated: because of Paul's two-age, 'already–not yet' perspective on God's work in Christ, it may be difficult to adjudicate between a proleptic aorist, in which the future serves as the Viewpoint space and the subject looks back, and a simple aorist, in which the Viewpoint is anchored in the present. But, especially because Paul exhibits marked eschatological restraint in the undisputed letters, we should almost undoubtedly prefer the former construal: from the viewpoint of the future, ' . . . he glorified'" (161). Yet in his very last conclusion to his work, he leaves open for Pauline theologians to discuss the "when" of certain "salvation-historical or "eschatological occurrences," citing Rom 8:30 as the example that needs to be discussed. Brookins, therefore, is uncertain about a "proleptic" aorist in a traditional sense, and his theory does not seem to support proleptic aorist readings. He does give one example of a proleptic present in Gal 3:8 of which he seems certain (161–62).

ASPECT AND ΤΕΛΕΙΩΣΑΣ VS. ΤΕΤΕΛΕΣΤΑΙ

At question still remains the relationship between τελειώσας (John 17:4) and τετέλεσται (19:30), especially as one considers whether the former intends to foreshadow the latter, or whether the latter stands as an echo or fulfillment of a so-called *proleptic* aspect of the former. As Ellis, Aubrey, and Dubis's theory provides the most current and comprehensive scheme for understanding aspect, I will utilize their research toward a resolution of the meaning each of term.[148] As concluded above, it is certain the aorist usage of each term indicates that a writer may use either term to speak *perfectively* of a completion or end. Each term can be used to indicate past time, but the form of Τετέλεσται indicates that τελέω may be used combinatively.

Nevertheless, the meaning and relationship of τελειώσας and Τετέλεσται cannot be resolved completely by observation of verbal aspect alone, for the lexical meaning only is evident once the term is placed in the context of the surrounding words. Verbal aspect, as exegesis of the grammar, is the beginning step, to be followed by the determination of the term in light of usage(s) in context.

NT Use of τελειόω

The NT uses forms of τελειόω 23x.[149] Forms appear 2x in Luke-Acts, 5x in the Gospel of John, 1x in the Pauline corpus (Phil 3:12), 9x in Hebrews, 1x in James, and 4x in 1 John. It does not appear at all in Matthew and Mark, or the Petrine literature and Jude. The uses favor the Johannine

---

148. I am adopting Ellis, Aubrey, and Dubis' theory for three reasons: (1) It uses every structural part of the Greek verb and gives each part significance with respect to communicating the verb's aspect, whether the part is the verbal root/lexical core, prefix, tense indicator, suffix, or personal ending; stem, prefixes, suffixes, and personal endings all are accounted for within a theory of aspect. (2) The theory does not require exceptions for some tense forms; instead, what would be so-called exceptions in other theories are accounted for by the morphological features (e.g., there is no need for an aorist to communicate a future idea as an exception, or for other special categories for a verb that does align with the tense-form or aspect's normal or natural usage). (3) The theory still retains a place for tense in the tense form, recognizing "tense" in the indicative. Overall, the theory appears to be more encompassing than that of earlier theories, accounting for the aspectual use of the full structure of the verb in each tense-form.

149. Luke 2:43; 13:32; John 4:34; 5:36; 17:4, 23; 19:28; Acts 20:24; Phil 3:12; Heb 2:10; 5:9; 7:19; 7:28; 9:9; 10:1, 14; 11:40; 12:23; Jas 2:22; 1 John 2:5; 4:12; 4:17; 4:18.

Literature (9x—5x in John and 4x in 1 John) and Hebrews (9x). Of the twenty-three uses, these are the characteristics:

1. There is only one use of τελειόω in a present tense-form: τελειοῦμαι, pres., pass., ind., 1ˢᵗ, sg., in Luke 13:32.
2. The use of τελειοῦμαι in Luke 13:32 is also the only use of the passive "voice" with a tense-form other than the aorist or perfect.
3. Ten (10x) of the uses are in the *active voice*, 9x aorist tense-form and 1x perfect tense-form. Thirteen (13x) of the uses are passive, 1x present, 4x aorist, and 8x perfect. Four (4) of the perfect passive tense-form usages are in 1 John.
4. Eight (8x) uses are in the *indicative* and are always singular in number. Plural forms always are used outside of the indicative mood.
5. Seven (7x) of the uses are *participles*, 2x active and 5x passive. The two (2x) active uses are found in the aorist tense-form only. The passive tense-form is used with the perfect 4x and the aorist only 1x.
6. Four (4x) of the uses are in the *subjunctive*. The subjunctive uses always are in the aorist tense-form, and each active use is in the first person while each passive use is in the third person.[150]
7. Four (4x) of the uses are *infinitives*, and each of these uses is in the aorist tense-form and active voice.
8. The aorist tense-form favors the active voice 9x of 13x. The perfect tense-form prefers the passive 7/8 times.

Here are examples of each of the various tense-form usages according to the aspectual markings of Ellis, Aubrey, and Dubis:

---

150. There are only two tenses that form the subjunctive, the present and the aorist (Mounce, *Basics of Biblical Greek*, 289).

Table 9. Morphological Diagramming of τελειόω Verbs in the NT

Scripture Verse	Traditional Tense-form	Aspect	Tense Indicator (indicative mood only)	Aspect Stem			Personal Endings
				Imperfective Aspect Marker (prefix)	Lexical Core	Perfective Aspect Marker (suffix)	
Luke 2:43	Aor., act., part.	Past perfective			τελειο	σ	αντων
Luke 13:32	Pres., pass., ind.	Non-past imperfective			τελειο		μαι
John 4:34	Aor., act., subj.	Past perfective			τελειο	σ	ω
John 17:23	Perf., pass., part.	Non-past imperfective		τε	τελειο		μένοι
John 19:28	Aor., pass., subj.	Past perfective			τελειο	Θη	η
Acts 20:24	Aor., act., inf.	Past perfective			τελειο	σαι	
Phil 3:12	Perf., pass., ind.	Non-past imperfective		τε	τελειο		μαι
Heb 5:9	Aor., pass., part.	Past perfective			τελειο	θε	ς[151]
Heb 7:19	Aor., act., ind.	Past perfective	ε		τελειο	σ	εν
Heb 10:14	Perf., act., ind.	Non-past combinative		τε	τελειο	κε	(ν)[152]
Jas 2:22	Aor., pass., ind.	Past perfective	ε		τελειο	θη	η

The chart reveals that uses of τελειόω include past perfective, imperfective non-past, and combinative non-past aspects, with past tense being indicated in the indicative occasionally. This is consistent with the Johannine usage of the verb:

151. Mounce explains the nom. masc. form: "The case ending is sigma, the ντ drops out because of the sigma, and the epsilon lengthens to compensate for the loss" (*θε+ ντ + ς ▸ θες ▸ θεις) (Mounce, *Basics of Biblical Greek*, 261).

152. Mounce explains the change in form: "The tense formative changes from κα to κε, much like the change in the first aorist from σα to σε" (Mounce, *Basics of Biblical Greek*, 224).

Table 10. Morphological Diagramming of τελειόω Verbs in John and 1 John

Scripture Verse	Traditional Tense-form	Aspect	Tense Indicator (indicative mood only)	Aspect Stem			Personal Endings
				Imperfective Aspect Marker (prefix)	Lexical Core	Perfective Aspect Marker (suffix)	
John 4:34	Aor., act., subj.	Past perfective			τελειο	σ	ω
John 5:26	Aor., act., subj.	Past perfective			τελειο	σ	ω
John 17:4	Aor., act., part.	Past perfective			τελειο	σ	ασ
John 17:23	Perf., pass., part.	Non-past imperfective		τε	τελειο		μένοι
John 19:28	Aor., pass., subj.	Past perfective			τελειο	θη	η
1 John 2:5	Per., pass., ind.	Non-past imperfective		τε	τελειο		ται
1 John 4:12	Perf., pass., part.	Non-past imperfective		τε	τελειο		μένη
1 John 4:17	Per., pass., ind.	Non-past imperfective		τε	τελειο		ται
1 John 4:18	Per., pass., ind.	Non-past imperfective		τε	τελειο		ται

The Johannine use also reveals that when speaking of God's love in the believer (1 John 2:5; 4:12, 17, 18), τελειόω is imperfective aspectually and not perfective, for the work is not complete, contrary to older, tense-form views of the perfect-tense. Similarly, the working of God to completely unite believers mysteriously is spoken of as imperfective aspectually, for the speaker does view the yet-to-be-completed work as something finished or done in time past.

In contrast, when Christ speaks of his work (τὸ ἔργον, 4:36 and 17:4) and works (τὰ [γὰρ] ἔργα . . . τὰ ἔργα, 5:36) that are completed and to be completed, he speaks of them in a perfective sense, aspectually. The author of the Johannine literature writes with clear distinction between imperfective non-past and perfect past uses of τελειόω. This is evident even in the use of the aorist, passive, subjunctive in John 19:28, which I will discuss below.

NT Use of τελέω

The NT uses forms of τελέω 28x.[153] Forms appear 7x in Matthew, 5x in Luke-Acts, 2x in the Gospel of John, 5x in the Pauline corpus, 1x in James, and 8x in Revelation. Forms do not appear at all in Mark, the Petrine literature, or Jude. The uses favor the Johannine Literature (10x—2x in John and 8x in Revelation). Of the twenty-eight uses, these are the characteristics:

1. The use of τελέω in the second person always is active and plural, whether present or aorist. It never appears in the second person in the perfect.

2. Perfect-tense forms always are singular and indicative, whether active or passive.

3. There are eight (8x) uses in the subjunctive, and the subjunctive only is used with the aorist. Five (5x) times the subjunctive appears with the passive, and 3x with the active.

4. In addition to the subjunctive use, the aorist appears with the indicative 9x, the infinitive 1x, and the participle 1x.

5. It appears in the aorist tense-form 18x—10x active and 8x passive.

6. It appears in the present tense-form 5x—4x active and 1x passive.

7. It appears in the perfect tense-form 3x—1x active and 2x passive.

8. It is used in the future tense-form only in the 3rd pers., pass., ind. 2x—1x each in the singular and plural.

---

153. Matt 7:28; 10:23; 11:1; 13:53; 17:24; 19:1; 26:1; Luke 2:39; 12:50; 18:31; 22:37; John 19:28, 30; Acts 13:29; Rom 2:27; 13:6; 2 Cor 12:9; Gal 5:1; 2 Tim 4:7; Jas 2:8; Rev 10:7; 11:7; 15:1, 8; 17:17; 20:3, 5, 7.

Here are examples of each of the various tense-form usages according to the aspectual markings of Ellis, Aubrey, and Dubis:

Table 11. Morphological Diagramming of τελέω in the NT

Scripture Verse	Traditional Tense-form	Aspect	Tense Indicator (indicative mood only)	Aspect Stem			Personal Endings
				Imperfective Aspect Marker (prefix)	Lexical Core	Perfective Aspect Marker (suffix)	
Matt 7:28	Aor., act., ind.	Past perfective	ε		τελε	σ	εν
Matt 10:23	Aor. Act., subj.	Past perfective			τελε	σ	ητε
Matt 17:24	Pres., act., ind.	Non-past imperfective			τελε		ει
Luke 12:50	Aor., pass., subj.	Past perfective			τελε	σθ	η
Luke 18:31	Fut., pass., ind.	Non-past perfective			τελε	(σ)θησ	ται
Luke 22:37	Aor., pass., inf.	Past perfective			τελε	σθηναι	
John 19:28	Perf., pass., ind.	Non-past combinative		τε	τελε	σ	ται
Rom 2:27	Pres., act., part.	Non-past imperfective			τελε	ουσ	α
2 Cor 12:9	Pres., pass., ind.	Non-past imperfective			τελε		ται
2 Tim 4:7	Perf. Act., ind.	Non-past combinative		τε	τελε	κα	α
Rev 10:7	Aor., pass., ind.	Past perfective	ε		τελε	σθη	η

Similar to the NT use of τελειόω, the chart above reveals that uses of τελέω include both past and non-past perfective, non-past imperfect, and combinative non-past aspects, with past tense being indicated in the indicative occasionally. This is consistent with the Johannine usage of the verb:

Table 12. Morphological Diagramming of τελειόω in the NT

				Aspect Stem			
Scripture Verse	Traditional Tense-form	Aspect	Tense Indicator (indicative mood only)	Imperfective Aspect Marker (prefix)	Lexical Core	Perfective Aspect Marker (suffix)	Personal Endings
John 19:28	Perf., pass., ind.	Non-past combinative		τε	τελε	σ	ται
John 19:30	Perf., pass., ind.	Non-past combinative		τε	τελε	σ	ται
Rev 10:7	Aor., pass., ind.	Past perfective	ε		τελε	σθη	η
Rev 11:7	Aor. Act., subj.	Past perfective			τελε	σ	σιν
Rev 15:1	Aor., pass., ind.	Past perfective	ε		τελε	σθη	η
Rev 15:8	Aor., pass., subj.	Past perfective			τελε	σθ	σιν
Rev 17:17	Fut., pass., ind.	Non-past perfective			τελε	(σ)θησ	ονται
Rev 20:3	Aor., pass., subj.	Past perfective		τελε	σθ	η	
Rev 20:5	Aor., pass., subj.	Past perfective		τελε	σθ	η	
Rev 20:7	Aor., pass., subj.	Past perfective		τελε	σθ	η	

The usage by the Johannine writer reveals a favoring of the past perfective aspect in Revelation, and only in the Apocalypse does one find tense-markers to indicate past tense. In contrast, both uses in the Fourth Gospel are non-past combinative in aspect. That is, τετέλεσται, in both John 19:28 and 19:30, reflects the perfective nature of the completed verbal event and the imperfective nature of the ongoing relevance of the different verbal events in the two verses.

Comparably, if one juxtaposes the Fourth Gospel writer's use of τελειόω and τελέω, one sees a stark contrast in their aspects:

Table 13. Morphological Diagramming of Τελειόω in the Fourth Gospel

Scripture Verse	Traditional Tense-form	Aspect	Tense Indicator (indicative mood only)	Aspect Stem			Personal Endings
				Imperfective Aspect Marker (prefix)	Lexical Core	Perfective Aspect Marker (suffix)	
John 4:34	Aor., act., subj.	Past perfective			τελειο	σ	ω
John 5:26	Aor., act., subj.	Past perfective			τελειο	σ	ω
John 17:4	Aor., act., part.	Past perfective			τελειο	σ	ασ
John 17:23	Perf., pass., part.	Non-past imperfective		τε	τελειο		μένοι
John 19:28	Aor., pass., subj.	Past perfective			τελειο	θη	η

Table 14. Morphological Diagramming of Τελέω in the Fourth Gospel

Scripture Verse	Traditional Tense-form	Aspect	Tense Indicator (indicative mood only)	Aspect Stem			Personal Endings
				Imperfective Aspect Marker (prefix)	Lexical Core	Perfective Aspect Marker (suffix)	
John 19:28	Perf., pass., ind.	Non-past combinative		τε	τελε	σ	ται
John 19:30	Perf., pass., ind.	Non-past combinative		τε	τελε	σ	ται

Whereas the writer uses τελειόω in both past perfective and non-past imperfective aspectual senses, he uses τελέω only in a combinative aspectual sense. As seen by the previous charts on the uses of each verb throughout the NT, the Fourth Gospel's use does not mean that τελειόω may not be used combinatively, or that it may not be used for past perfective and non-past imperfective aspectual ideas. It only means that the writer chose the different verbs for different aspectual purposes in the

Fourth Gospel. Τελέω, only in the form of τετέλεσται (3rd pers., sg., pres. pass., ind.), is used to indicate a perfective aspect, but with ongoing relevance; Τελειόω is used to indicate a past perfective aspect without ongoing relevance (or, in the lone case of John 17:23, a non-past imperfective aspect). The comparison of the aspects of the two is helpful for (1) comparing the use of τελειόω in John 17:4 to the use of τελέω in John 19:30, since the presence of the latter often is used to explain the former,[154] and (2) understanding the use of both verbs in John 19:28 (with 19:30).

In John 17:4, τελειώσας, the aorist, active, participle of τελειόω, is past perfective in aspect. The writer intends to communicate that an event is completed. As argued above, one also discerns that the verb is past with respect to time relevant to the main verb of the clause. The completion or finish is in the past, perfectively. But τετέλεσται, the 3rd person, singular, perfect, active, indicative of τελέω, indicates a past perfective aspect *with continuing results*. Whereas a past time and perfective aspect is indicated by the first verb, the second verb does not have a time marker, based on its local deixis, and it intends to indicate that the results of what was done perfectively are in view. The first verb, τελειώσας, does not communicate anything in an ongoing sense, and thus neither does it allude to or foreshadow the work indicated by the second term, τετέλεσται—a term from a different verbal root altogether.

John 19:28 says, "After this, Jesus, knowing that all was now finished (τετέλεσται), said (to fulfill [τελειωθῇ] the Scripture), 'I thirst'" (ESV). It would appear that the Fourth Gospel's writer intends to indicate that "all things" (πάντα) being finished perfectively has ongoing results in the

---

154. See again Chapter 2 in this present work for many examples.

present.[155] However, the Scriptures would be fulfilled perfectively with-

---

[155]. I suggest that the ongoing results of τετέλεσται concern *the completion of the work of redemption as commissioned by the Father (John 10:17-18, 27-30), in fulfillment of all that the OT Scriptures foretell of salvation (1:17, 45; 5:39, 46-67), but without presently manifesting the full eschatological experience of the final salvation (which the ongoing results cannot yield prior to the return of the Son to share the glory he previously held with the Father, cf. 17:5, 24), but with the assurance that they will be manifested (1:51; 5:29).* With respect to the ongoing results of τετέλεσται, Morris sees the term as "ambiguous," referring possibly to Jesus' life being finished "i.e., that he was at the point of death." Yet, he proposes further, "this is part of the meaning but it is highly improbable that it is the whole meaning. More important is the truth that Jesus' work was finished. He came to do God's work, and this meant dying on the cross for the world's salvation. This mighty work of redemption has now reached its consummation." Morris, *The Gospel According to John*, 720, ft. nt. 77. Thus, for Morris, the writer of the Fourth Gospel includes all that redemption entails in the completion represented by τετέλεσται. Carson, wrongly equating *"teleioō"* and *"tetelestai,"* includes the entire prophetic scope within what is fulfilled, writing, "In fulfillment formulae, John elsewhere uses the verb preferred by others, *plēroō* ('to fulfil'), but here resorts to *teleioō* (more properly 'to complete'). Almost certainly this is because he is drawing attention to the use of the same verb in the preceding clause ('that all *was* now *completed,' tetelastai*) and in v. 30 ('It is finished,' *tetelestai*). The completion of his work is necessarily the fulfillment of Scripture and the performance of the Father's will. Jesus' cry *I am thirsty*, the final instance of his active, self-conscious obedience in the Fourth Gospel, and so tied to 'It is finished,' thus represents 'not the isolated fulfilling of a particular trait in the scriptural picture, but the perfect completion of the whole prophetic image'" (Carson, *John*, 620). Lindars suggests τετέλεσται, in 19:28, means "to bring to a completion what is appointed in Scripture for Jesus as the agent of God's will" (Lindars, *The Gospel of John*, 580). Similar to Carson, Lindars wrongly says τετέλεσται is "not to be distinguished from John's usual teleioun," even though it is evident that John employs two different verbs. His comments on 19:30 only indicate that he sees the verb referring to victorious completion. Köstenberger, also having a victorious "climax" reading of 19:30, writes of τετέλεσται, "Jesus triumphantly announces the completion of his mission entrusted to him by the Father at what may be considered the lowest point of his life, his death by crucifixion" (Köstenberger, *John*, 551). This follows his understanding that τετέλεσται in John 19:28 "marks the point immediately prior to Jesus' death at which everything that brought Jesus to the cross in keeping with God's sovereign plan had taken place" (550). Elsewhere Köstenberger also writes, "John 19:28-29 most likely represents an allusion to Ps. 69:21: 'They . . . gave me vinegar for my thirst . . .' The allusion may involve the entire psalm in its portrayal of the righteous sufferer . . . The choice of *teleiōthē* rather than *plērōthē* in 19:28 seems to be a function of the presence of *tetelestai* immediately preceding in 19:28 and following again in 19:30 . . . Jesus' cry there, 'I thirst,' fulfills the entire prophetic pattern of Scripture rather than merely matching an isolated trait of the psalmist's portrayal of the righteous sufferer." Köstenberger, "John," 502. Michaels sees a difference between a work already completed in 17:4 and the τετέλεσται in 19:30, which "encompasses [4:34 and 17:4] and more embracing as well 'everything that was happening to him' (18:4) from the moment of the arrest in the garden up to the present.'" Michaels, *The Gospel of John*, 964. Michaels also sees the full scope of the prophetic panorama contained within the ongoing results of τετέλεσται.

out comment on the ongoing results in the present.[156]

The writer then follows in John 19:30 with the words, "When Jesus had received the sour wine, he said, 'It is finished' (Τετέλεσται), and he bowed his head and gave up his spirit" (ESV). Consistent with 19:28, Jesus speaks perfectively of his entire earthly ministry with ongoing results. The work is finished perfectively, which the context of his death shows with finality. Yet it is completed in such a way that the writer views ongoing significance to the verb.

Contextual Uses of τελειόω and τελέω within the NT

The different aspectual senses of the two verbs in question invite me to explore whether there is a difference in the types of *completions* or *finishes* denoted by the two verbs. Or, in other words, why does the Gospel writer prefer τελειόω for a past perfect aspect and τελέω for a combinative aspect? Is the writer recognizing a different meaning in the terms even though both verbs are used in both past perfective and non-past imperfective aspects in the NT?

It is common for NT lexicons to give τελειόω and τελέω very similar meanings based on the use of the verbs in Hellenistic Greek and inductive reasoning from the occasional uses of the verbs in the NT.[157] For example, BDAG suggests of τελειόω (1) *to complete an activity, complete, bring to an end, finish, accomplish*; (2) *to overcome or supplant an imperfect state of things by one that is free from objection, bring to an end, bring to its goal/accomplishment*; (3) *as a term of mystery religions, [to] consecrate, initiate; in the passive: be consecrated* (citing Phil 3:12 and Heb 2:10; 5:9; and 7:28 as examples).[158] Specialized uses of the second sets of meanings include (a) "completion or perfection"; (b) "bring to a full measure, fill the measure of" (without citing any biblical examples, but only citing ancient Greek examples); and (c) "*fulfill* of prophecies, promises, etc., which arouse expectation of events or happenings that correspond to their wording" (citing only John 19:28 as an example from Scripture).

However, on τελέω, which is a separate entry, BDAG proposes its range of meaning as (1) *to complete an activity or process, bring to an end,*

---

156. The ἵνα + the subjunctive τελειωθῇ indicates the idea, "in order that ... would be."

157. Even in a major dissertation study given to τελέω in Ancient Greek, the writer does not distinguish τελέω from τελειόω. See Waanders, *The History of ΤΕΛΟΣ and ΤΕΛΕΩ in Ancient Greek*.

158. BDAG, 996.

finish, complete; (2) *to carry out an obligation or demand, carry out, accomplish, perform, fulfill, keep*; and (3) *to pay what is due, pay* (citing Matt 17:24; Luke 20:22; and Rom 13:6 as examples).[159] The definitional ranges of meaning of the two terms are largely synonymous, varying only in the *occasional* use of the former "as a term of mystery religions to consecrate" and the later as "pay."

TDNT lists both terms under the same heading, noting first of this word-group,

> *It is hard to pin down the original sense.* Already in the Iliad it ranges from "fulfilment" (mostly τέλος θανάτοιο of the death which overtakes a man, e.g., Hom. Il., 3, 309) to "military post," "detachment," 10, 56. 470; 11, 730 == 18, 298; the idea of ritual correctness is also important esp. in the deriv. → τέλειος and τελήεις. Hence most etym. dict. think several terms have come together in τέλος, esp. * quelos קֶלֶב "turning-point" (πέλομαι, though this is not certain) and * telos, "promotion," "achievement" (τελα-, ταλα-), cf. Boisacq, Hofmann, s.v., Schwyzer, I, 512 (only πέλομαι). The post-Homeric and almost exclusively poetic τέλλω "to fulfil" is itself not wholly clear.[160]

Specifically concerning the use of the verb τελέω outside of the Bible, TDNT notes,

> The older form is τελείω, found, e.g., in Hom.; it arose out of * τελεσξω ... τελέω is a very ancient, important, and widespread term which in the prose and common speech of the post-class. period was increasingly supplanted by practically equivalent compounds like ἐκ-, συν- ... and διατελέω, so that the simple form could have a lofty sound.[161]

---

159. BDAG, 997–98. Of the first definition, it cites John 4:34; 5:36; 17:4; and 19:28 as example of such usage.

160. Delling, "Τέλος, Τελέω, Ἐπιτελέω, Συντελέω, Συντέλεια, Παντελής, Τέλειος, Τελειότης, Τελειόω, Τελείωσις, Τελειωτής," in *TDNT*, 8:49, italics mine. *EDNT* indicates "Τελειόω as a causative [verb] (with virtually the same meaning as → τελέω) is used of *complete* (metaphorically, Acts 20:24: 'one's course'), *bring to an end* (e.g., Luke 2:43: 'the days'), *place in a certain (final) condition* and thus *make complete / perfect* ... but also to *fulfill* (Scripture)" (Balz and Schneider, *EDNT*, 344). By the same token, *EDNT* says "Τελέω, often indistinguishable from → τελειόω, refers to bring to an end, complete ... [and] is largely synonymous with → πληρόω" (346). Louw-Nida groups the two verbs under one entry, meaning, "to cause to happen for some end result—'to make happen, to fulfill, to bring to fruition, to accomplish, fulfillment'" (L&N, 162).

161. Delling, "Τέλος," in *TDNT*, 8:57.

Thus, *TDNT* immediately links together the two verbs as one idea, later giving only the slightly strong sense of "totality" to the meaning of τελειόω:

> The verbs τελέω and τελειόω coincide in the NT especially in the sense "to carry through," "to complete . . ." Whereas this is the chief meaning of τελέω, the thought of totality is stronger in the case of τελειόω . . . The findings suggest for τελέω the meanings of τέλος, "goal," "issue," "end . . ." and for τελειόω those of τέλειος, "whole," "complete," "perfect."[162]

TDNT regards NT usage of τελειόω as (1) to fulfill or to carry out a required course in the sense of a received commission, (2) the completeness or perfection of the love of God or of the Christian in love, (3) a "special use" in Hebrews that means "to put someone in the position in which he can come, or stand, before God . . . whether in the narrower sense as a priest who may perform his cultic functions before God or in the broader sense as a non-priest" (citing Heb 7:19; 10:1, 20), and (4) a cultic sense in which one reaches consummate perfection in the saving work of Christ.[163]

TDNT identifies varied occasional uses of τελέω grouped largely under three ideas. First, there are uses related to perfection, such as "[coming] to perfection" (2 Cor 12:9), "carrying out" a will (Gal 5:16), accomplishing judgment (Luke 12:50), "[carrying] through [Paul's] course" to success, "[executing]" the judgment of God and fulfilling God's secret plan until they are "accomplished" (Rev 15:1; 10:7; 11:7, respectively), or the "[putting] into effect" the plan of God and "[carrying] out" his will—ideas completed aspectually imperfective. Second, it is used in the since of "finished," as in the "stereotyped conclusion" of Matthew's "five sermon-complexes" (Matt 7:28; 11:1; 13:53; 19:1; 26:1) and of "the conclusion of divinely appointed time" (Rev 20:3, 5, 7)—ideas that seem to be completed perfectively. Third, it means "to pay what one owes" (Matt 17:24; Rom 13:6).[164] Once sees that a lexicon again views the terms largely as synonymous.[165]

---

162. Delling, "Τέλος," in *TDNT*, 8:84.
163. Delling, "Τέλος," in *TDNT*, 8:83.
164. Delling, "Τέλος," in *TDNT*, 8:59-60.
165. *TDNT* attempts to explain Τετέλεσται in 19:30 by means of its usage in 19:28: "The word from the cross in Jn. 19:30 is explained by v. 28: Everything that God commissioned Jesus to do has been 'completed,' the saving work whose earthly completion according to Jn. is at the cross." It relates the use of the verb here to the first idea above, in the sense of a "carrying out" or drawing near to perfection. Yet the choice of category

Louw and Nida, grouping together the verbs as a word-group, simplify the range of meaning as "to bring an activity to a successful finish— 'to complete, to finish, to end, to accomplish.'" Yet they note, "There are no doubt certain subtle distinctions, particularly of emphasis, in the series τελέω, ἐκτελέω, ἀποτελέω, ἐπιτελέω, συντελέω, and τελειόω, but it is not possible to determine with precision the particular distinctions on the basis of existing contexts, though possibly ἐκτελέω and ἀποτελέω emphasize more finality, while ἐπιτελέω may focus upon the resulting purpose."[166] LSJ likewise categorizes all uses under a simplified idea of "[to] make perfect, complete."[167]

In the *Exegetical Dictionary of the New Testament*, Hübner suggests τελειόω has "virtually the same meaning as → τελέω" and "is used of *complete . . . bring to an end . . . place in a certain (final) condition* and thus *make complete / perfect . . .* but also to *fulfill* (Scripture)."[168] Τελέω, he also writes, is "often indistinguishable from → τελειόω," and refers to "*bring to an end, complete.*" "Τελέω . . . is largely synonymous with . . . πληρόω" in cases referring to the fulfillment of Scripture. Hubner recognizes too that it can be used when referring to paying taxes (cf. Matt 17:24; Rom 13:6).[169]

If one charts the verbs in the NT, one notices that the vast majority of the NT uses of τελειόω are used to speak of *completion with respect to something in the life of a person—either for a person to bring a deed to completion, or for something to be brought to completion with a person.*

---

reveals that Delling did consider the lexical idea of the verb to carry the full sense of its meaning rather than the context to carry the meaning. For the last cry of Jesus from the cross accomplishes perfectively what Jesus is to do. But Delling identifies the range of meaning with a host of imperfective uses. Seemingly, he must do this because he concludes as a whole that the thought of totality is stronger in the case of τελειόω and cannot now have a stronger sense in a form of τελέω. But in doing so, he avoids saying what is obvious—that there is a perfective sense of the verb τελέω in 19:30, equating it with his range of meaning for τελειόω (Delling, "Τέλος," in *TDNT*, 8:59).

166. L&N, 657.
167. LSJ, 1770.
168. Hübner, "τελειόω," in *EDNT*, 344.
169. Hübner, "τελέω," in *EDNT*, 346.

Table 15. Use of τελειόω in the NT

Verse	Verb	Greek Text	English Text (ESV)	Item of Completion
Luke 13:32	τελειοῦμαι	τῇ τρίτῃ τελειοῦμαι	The third day I finish my course	Jesus's work of casting out demons and performing cures[170]
John 4:34	τελειώσω	τελειώσω αὐτοῦ τὸ ἔργον	To accomplish his work	Jesus's commissioned work from the Father
John 5:36	Τελειώσω	τὰ γὰρ ἔργα ἃ δέδωκέν μοι ὁ πατὴρ ἵνα τελειώσω αὐτά	For the works that the Father has given me to accomplish	Jesus's commissioned work from the Father
John 17:23	Τετελειωμένοι	ἵνα ὦσιν τετελειωμένοι εἰς ἕν	That they may become perfectly one	The mysterious union of believers with one another
Acts 20:24	τελειῶσαι	ὡς τελειῶσαι τὸν δρόμον μου καὶ τὴν διακονίαν ἣν ἔλαβον παρὰ τοῦ κυρίου Ἰησοῦ	If only I may finish my course and the ministry that I received from the Lord Jesus	The course of ministry to which the Lord commissioned Paul
Phil 3:12	Τετελείωμαι	Οὐχ ὅτι ἤδη ἔλαβον ἢ ἤδη τετελείωμαι	Not that I have already obtained this or am already perfect	The final sanctification of the Apostle Paul
Heb 2:10	τελειῶσαι	τὸν ἀρχηγὸν τῆς σωτηρίας αὐτῶν διὰ παθημάτων τελειῶσαι	Should make the founder of their salvation perfect through suffering	The moral impeccability of Christ
Heb 5:9	τελειωθείς	καὶ τελειωθεὶς ἐγένετο	And being made perfect, [Christ] became	The moral impeccability of Christ—his "reverence" (5:7, εὐλαβείας) and "obedience" (5:8, ὑπακοήν)
Heb 7:19	ἐτελείωσεν	οὐδὲν γὰρ ἐτελείωσεν ὁ νόμος	For the law made nothing perfect	The law's (in)ability to make priests reach God's standard of righteousness

---

170. The translators of the ESV take liberty in translating the object of τελειοῦμαι as "course" when the object is unstated. The "course" is a reference to Jesus's earlier statement of the work of casting out demons and curing people for two days.

Heb 7:28	Τετελειωμένον	τὸν νόμον υἱὸν εἰς τὸν αἰῶνα τετελειωμένον	Appoints a Son who has been made perfect forever	The moral impeccability of Christ
Heb 9:9	Τελεῖσαι	μὴ δυνάμεναι κατὰ συνείδησιν τὸν λατρεύοντα	That cannot perfect the conscience of the worshiper	The making of a person's conscience morally righteous
Heb 10:1	τελειῶσαι	οὐδέποτε δύναται τοὺς προσερχομένους τελειῶσαι	It can never … make perfect those who draw near	The (in)ability of the law to make a worshiper morally acceptable to God
Heb 10:14	Τετελείωκεν	μιᾷ γὰρ προσφορᾷ τετελείωκεν εἰς τὸ διηνεκὲς τοὺς ἁγιαζομένους	For by a single offering he has perfected for all time those who are being sanctified	The moral righteousness of the believer by the work of Christ
Heb 11:40	τελειωθῶσιν	ἵνα μὴ χωρὶς ἡμῶν τελειωθῶσιν	That apart from us they should not be made perfect	The final sanctification of the believer
Heb 12:23	Τετελειωμένων	καὶ πνεύμασι δικαίων τετελειωμένων	And to the spirits of the righteous made perfect	The status of heavenly souls in final moral sanctification
Jas 2:22	ἐτελειώθη	καὶ ἐκ τῶν ἔργων ἡ πίστις ἐτελειώθη	And faith was completed by his works	The completion of the faith of Abraham
1 John 2:5	Τετελείωται	ἡ ἀγάπη τοῦ θεοῦ τετελείωται	The love of God is perfected	The full working of God's love in the believer
1 John 4:12	Τετελειωμένη	ἡ ἀγάπη αὐτοῦ ἐν ἡμῖν τετελειωμένη ἐστιν	His love is perfected in us	The full working of God's love in the believer
1 John 4:17	Τετελείωται	ἐν τούτῳ τετελείωται ἡ ἀγάπη μεθ' ἡμῶν	By this is love perfected with us	The full working of God's love in the believer
1 John 4:18	Τετελείωται	ὁ δὲ φοβούμενος οὐ τετελείωται ἐν τῇ ἀγάπῃ	And whoever fears has not been perfected in love	The full working of God's love in the believer

Across various aspects, the NT uses forms of τελειόω to express Jesus's completion of his works (Luke 13:32; John 4:34; 5:36), God's completion of the believers' mysterious union with one another (John 17:23), the completion of the final course of ministry and the final sanctification of the Apostle Paul (Acts 20:34; Phil 3:12), the completion of the moral impeccability of Christ (Heb 2:10; 5:9; 7:28), the ability or inability of the law to complete the moral righteousness and sanctification of believers (Heb 7:19; 9:9; 10:1) or the status of the believers sanctified completely (Heb 10:14; 11:40; 12:23), the completion of the faith of Abraham as true faith (Jas 2:22), and the completion of the full working of God's love in the believer (1 John 2:5; 4:12; 4:17, 18).

This idea holds true when one considers Luke 2:43 and John 17:4. In Luke 2:43 one reads of the ending of the days of the Feast of the Unleavened Bread. Grammatically speaking, the completion in question refers to the ends of the "days" of the feast: καὶ τελειωσάντων τὰς ἡμέρας—"And when the feast was ended." Although this is a reference to an impersonal item—"days"—the action completed is the participation of the Israelites in the Feast of the Unleavened Bread, or rather, the worshipper completed their obligation to the days of the feast until the next year.

Similarly, in John 17:4—the verse in question in this full work—Christ speaks of completing the work given to him by the Father. It is a deed finished by the person of Christ.

Differently, the NT uses τελέω to speak of the completion of words, of lusts, or of the working of God in judgement, and it could consistently be translated in English by the verb "to fulfill." There is not a strong difference between what is denoted or connoted between τελειόω and τελέω even if one uses the English translations of "complete" and "fulfill." Rather, it appears the two similar terms signify "the end of a work in, upon, or by a person or persons" and "the filling to the full measure of words, lusts, and eschatological working of God.

Table 16. Use of τελέω in the NT in the Sense of Fulfillment

Verse	Verb	Greek Text	English Text (ESV)	Item of Completion
Matt 7:28	τελειοῦμαι	Καὶ ἐγένετο ὅτε ἐτέλεσεν	And when Jesus finished these sayings	Completions of the words of Jesus's discourse
Matt 11:1	ἐτέλεσεν	Καὶ ἐγένετο ὅτε ἐτέλεσεν ὁ Ἰησοῦς διατάσσων τοῖς δώδεκα μαθηταῖς αὐτοῦ	When Jesus had finished instructing his twelve disciples	Completion of the words of Jesus's discourse
Matt 13:53	ἐτέλεσεν	Καὶ ἐγένετο ὅτε ἐτέλεσεν ὁ Ἰησοῦς τὰς παραβολὰς ταύτας	And when Jesus had finished these parables	Completion of the words of Jesus's discourse
Matt 19:1	ἐτέλεσεν	Καὶ ἐγένετο ὅτε ἐτέλεσεν	Now when Jesus had finished these sayings	Completion of the words of Jesus's discourse
Matt 26:1	ἐτέλεσεν	Καὶ ἐγένετο ὅτε ἐτέλεσεν	When Jesus had finished all these sayings	Completion of the words of Jesus's discourse
Luke 2:39	ἐτέλεσαν	Καὶ ὡς ἐτέλεσαν πάντα τὰ κατὰ τὸν νόμον κυρίου	And when they had performed everything according to the Law of the Lord	The requirements of the law are *completed*—the observers of the law fulfill everything the laws in question require
Luke 18:31	τελεσθήσεται	καὶ τελεσθήσεται πάντα τὰ γεγραμμένα διὰ τῶν προφητῶν τῷ υἱῷ τοῦ ἀνθρώπου	And everything that is written about the Son of Man by the prophets will be accomplished	The things written in the OT prophets are fulfilled
Luke 22:27	τελεσθῆναι	λέγω γὰρ ὑμῖν ὅτι τοῦτο τὸ γεγραμμένον δεῖ τελεσθῆναι ἐν ἐμοί	For I tell you that this Scripture must be fulfilled in me	The things written in the OT are fulfilled
Acts 13:29	ἐτέλεσαν	ὡς δὲ ἐτέλεσαν πάντα τὰ περὶ αὐτοῦ γεγραμμένα	And when they had carried out all that was written of him	What is written of Judas in OT is fulfilled

Rom 2:27	τελοῦσα	καὶ κρινεῖ ἡ ἐκ φύσεως ἀκροβυστία τὸν νόμον τελοῦσα	Then he who is physically uncircumcised but keeps the law	The law is *obeyed*— its requirements are fulfilled by the one obedient to it
Jas 2:28	τελεῖτε	εἰ μέντοι νόμον τελεῖτε βασιλικὸν κατὰ τὴν γραφήν	If you really fulfill the royal law according to the Scripture	The law is fulfilled
Rev 10:7	ἐτελέσθη	καὶ ἐτελέσθη τὸ μυστήριον τοῦ θεοῦ	The mystery of God would be fulfilled	Announced mystery fulfilled
Rev 11:7	τελέσωσιν	καὶ ὅταν τελέσωσιν τὴν μαρτυρίαν αὐτῶν	And when they have finished their testimony	*Prophetic* witness finished
Rev 15:1	ἐτελέσθη	ὅτι ἐν αὐταῖς ἐτελέσθη ὁ θυμὸς τοῦ θεοῦ	For with them the wrath of God is finished	Wrath of God fulfilled
Rev 15:8	τελεσθῶσιν	καὶ οὐδεὶς ἐδύνατο εἰσελθεῖν εἰς τὸν ναὸν ἄχρι τελεσθῶσιν αἱ ἑπτὰ πληγαὶ τῶν ἑπτὰ ἀγγέλων	And no one could enter the sanctuary until the seven plagues of the seven angels were finished	Plagues of judgment fulfilled
Rev 17:17	τελεσθήσονται	χάρη τελεσθήσονται οἱ λόγοι τοῦ θεοῦ	*Until the words of God are fulfilled*	Words of God fulfilled
Rev 20:3	τελεσθῇ	ἄχρι τελεσθῇ τὰ χίλια ἔτη	Until the thousand years were ended	1000 years fulfilled
Rev 20:5	τελεσθῇ	ἄχρι τελεσθῇ τὰ χίλια ἔτη	Until the thousand years were ended	1000 years fulfilled
Rev 20:7	τελεσθῇ	Καὶ ὅταν τελεσθῇ τὰ χίλια ἔτη	And when the thousand years are ended	1000 years fulfilled

The vast majority of uses (19 of 28) concern a sense of fulfillment. Yet six other uses outside of the Fourth Gospel seems to have difference contextual ideas, including paying taxes:

Table 17. Use of τελέω in the NT in a Sense other than Fulfillment

Verse	Verb	Greek Text	English Text (ESV)	Item of Completion
Matt 17:24	τελειοῦμαι	Ὁ διδάσκαλος ὑμῶν οὐ τελεῖ [τὰ] δίδραχμα	Does your teacher not pay the tax?	The temple tax[171]
Luke 12:50	τελεῖ	Ἐλθόντων δὲ αὐτῶν εἰς Καφαρναοὺμ προσῆλθον οἱ τὰ δίδραχμα λαμβάνοντες τῷ Πέτρῳ καὶ εἶπαν, Ὁ διδάσκαλος ὑμῶν οὐ τελεῖ [τὰ] δίδραχμα	I have a baptism to be baptized with, and how great is my distress until it is accomplished!	Jesus's judgment on the cross from God
Rom 13:6	τελεῖτε	διὰ τοῦτο γὰρ καὶ φόρους τελεῖτε	For because of this you also pay taxes	Payment of taxes to the government
2 Cor 12:9	τελεῖται	ἡ γὰρ δύναμις ἐν ἀσθενείᾳ τελεῖται	For my power is made perfect in weakness	God's power in the believer weakened by a physical ailment
Gal 5:16	τελέσητε	καὶ ἐπιθυμίαν σαρκὸς οὐ μὴ τελέσητε	And you will not gratify the desires of the flesh	Yielding to a desire of the remnants of the believer's Adamic nature
2 Tim 4:7	τετέλεκα	τὸν δρόμον τετέλεκα	I have finished the race	Paul's finishing of his ministry commission

Although less evident, in each of the above examples, the sense of "fulfill" would represent the verb τελέω accurately. For to pay a tax is to

---

171. Blomberg notes, "All Israelite males over the age of twenty paid this tribute annually for the upkeep of the Jerusalem temple. The practice stemmed from the commands of Exod 30:13 and 38:25–26; later developments are reflected in Josephus (*Ant.* 18.9.1; *J.W.* 7.6.6) and the Mishna (*Seqal.*)." (Blomberg, *Matthew*, 269). On this tax, Nolland understands the tax as a customary collection: "A custom had arisen, and was being defended in Jesus' day as a requirement of the Law, of levying an annual temple tax on males over twenty to finance offerings in the temple made on behalf of the whole people. Provision was made for collecting the tax locally and sending the gathered monies on to Jerusalem," (Nolland, *The Gospel of Matthew*, 723–724). The tax, as a required collection, had to be completed, or rather *fulfilled* by the tax-payer. That is, the amount of the tax obligation owed by a person was fulfilled by given the amount due. That seems to be the concept of the idea of "pay." Also, Moulton and Milligan give two examples of the use of τελέω with reference to paying taxes that come c. 1 BC–1 AD—ἀφ᾽ ὧ ἐστιν τῶν μὴ τελούντων ἱερά ἔθωη, "from this are to be exacted those priestly corporations which are exempt from the tax" (citing P. Petr. III. 59b3 [census paper, 3rd century BC], and τελοῦντες λαογραφίαν Ὀξυρυγχίτου ἄνδ(ρες), "Men paying poll-tax in the Oxyrhynchite nome" (citing P. Oxy. IX 12102, c. 1 BC–1 AD), (Moulton and Milligan, *The Vocabulary of the Greek Testament Illustrated from the Papyri and Other Non-Literary Sources*, 630). Moulton and Milligan's other examples—including the use of τετέλεσται to introduce receipts—are from AD 111 and beyond and are not helpful as background material.

fulfill a required financial obligation of a known amount (cf. Matt 17:24; Rom 13:6). Jesus awaits the judgment of God to be fulfilled (or completed) in him (cf. Luke 12:50). Yielding to temptation is to "gratify" or fulfill those desires, and the completion of a commission is to fulfill all duties of a stewardship. I would suggest, too, that 2 Cor 12:9 utilizes "perfected" only as an editorial choice. Easily one understands that the Lord's power is not lacking within the person of God, but it is actualized in a greater sense during a period of physical weakness than during a period of physical strength. One comes to get a measure of God's power in weakness rather than while trying to rely on one's own strength. Or, God's power is *fulfilled* in the weakness of a believer in a way it is not fulfilled in a season of physical health or strength.[172]

The idea then of "fulfilled" also fits the two uses of τελέω in the Gospel of John in 19:28a and 19:30, translated as "finished" in the both the ESV and NRSV in both verses:

Table 18. Use of τελέω in John 19:28, 30

Verse	Verb	Greek Text	English Text (ESV)	Item of Completion
John 19:28a	τετέλεσται	Μετὰ τοῦτο εἰδὼς ὁ Ἰησοῦς ὅτι ἤδη πάντα τετέλεσται	After this, Jesus, knowing that all was now finished	The divine course of action leading to Jesus's death[173]
John 19:30	Τετέλεσται	Ἰησοῦς εἶπεν Τετέλεσται	He said, "It is finished!"	All that pertains to Jesus's atoning death

Jesus *fulfilled* all that the Father willed for his course of life that led to his suffering and atoning death (cf. John 4:34; 5:30; 6:38-40; 14:31;

---

172. On the use of τελεῖται, Garland suggests, "His weakness becomes the vehicle by which God's grace and Christ's power is most fully manifested to himself and to others. Furnish correctly points out that Paul is not saying that weakness is power. Instead, he is saying that 'the weaknesses that characterize his life as an apostle—of which the Corinthians are very much aware and from which he neither seeks nor expects relief—represent the effective working of the power of the crucified Christ in his ministry' [Furnish]. What makes Paul seem so weak to some paradoxically allows the power of Christ to work through him all the more." Garland, *2 Corinthians*, 525. Garland cites Furnish, *II Corinthians*, 551–52. Similarly, Harris writes, "But if weakness is recognized, his power will be sought and granted. Then it will operate at the same time as the weakness and find unhindered scope in the presence of that weakness. 'My risen power *finds its full scope and potency* in your acknowledged weakness.'" Harris, *The Second Epistle to the Corinthians*, 864, italics mine.

173. Carson notes, "Jesus' knowledge *that all was now completed* is the awareness that all the steps that had brought him to this point of pain and impending death were in the design of his heavenly Father, and death itself was imminent" (Carson, *John*, 619).

17:8). The use of τελέω intends to signal to the reader a fulfillment of that which Jesus was commanded to do (12:49, 50; 14:31).

One then might ask, however, if τελέω signals fulfillment, why the writer used τελειόω in 19:28b for what appears to be the fulfillment of the words of Scripture. The question is especially significant in light of the Fourth Gospel's consistent use of forms of πληρόω to indicate the fulfillment of Scripture (John 12:38; 13:18; 15:25; 17:12; 18:9, 32; 19:24, 36).

Carson proposes that the change in verb selection reflects the author's pointing to the use of the same verb in the preceding clause and then again in 19:30.[174] However, although the verbs are related, they are not the same verb, not sharing the same lexical core. Instead, it would seem that the writer intends to distinguish the apparent "fulfillment" in 19:28b from the fulfillments in 19:28a and 19:30 and the fulfillments indicated by the use of πληρόω.

I would suggest that the writer of the Gospel of John's use of τελειωθῇ in 19:28b is consistent with his use of τελειόω verbs in the Fourth Gospel and the NT.[175] That is, the writer intends to communicate a *completion with respect to something in the life of a person—either for a person to bring a deed to completion, or for something to be brought to completion with a person*. In this case, Scripture—as it pertains to Christ fulfilling what the OT spoke of his suffering and death—was brought to completion with respect to the *person* of Christ. By using the different verb, the writer takes the emphasis away from the words and places the focus on the *Person*—the one who is suffering on the cross as one rejected by his own (John 1:10–11; 5:43; 12:37; 15:25), taking away the sins of the world as the Lamb of God (1:29, 35), and giving his life to draw his sheep to himself and to the Father (6:44, 51, 65; 10:27; 11:50; 12:32; 15:13; 18:14). This *Person* of the "I am" statements in the Fourth Gospel is the loci in which the Scripture is fulfilled. This verb does not intend to indicate the fulfillment of words (e.g., τελέω) or point the reader back to an OT

---

174. "In fulfillment formulae, John elsewhere uses the verb preferred by others, *plēroō* ('to fulfil'), but here resorts to *teleioō* (more properly 'to complete'). Almost certainly this is because he is drawing attention to the use of the same verb in the preceding clause ('that all *was* now *completed*,' *tetelestai*) and in v. 30 ('It is finished,' *tetelestai*). The completion of his work is necessarily the fulfillment of Scripture and the performance of the Father's will" (Carson, *John*, 620).

175. In 19:28b, τελειωθῇ is the 3rd pers., sg., aor., pass., subj., of τελειόω. It is perfective in its aspect. The subjunctive grammaticalizes the potentiality of coming completion or fulfillment.

context (e.g., πληρόω). Instead, the use of τελειωθῇ in 19:28b points the reader to the Christ himself.

CONCLUSION

In John 17:4, the use of τελειώσας is perfective aspectually and past time relative to the main verb ἐδόξασα. Its aorist tense-form indicates its perfective aspect. It is not forward-pointing, or in any sense proleptic based on its form or based on the most immediate context of the additional perfective aspect verbs and the one imperfect, combinative-aspect verb in 17:4.

Any sense of τελειώσας carrying the possibility of a proleptic idea is based on an older concept of the workings of aorist tense-form verbs, whether that be punctiliar, undefined, or completed in past time. Use of the aorist, active, indicative ἐδόξασεν in Rom 8:30 does not justify the use of the aorist in a proleptic sense. The past-tense prefix with the perfective aspect excludes the possibility of a future intent by the writer. The only basis for viewing τελειώσας as proleptic is theological: writers impose the theme of the atonement in John on 17:4 without clear exegetical warrant.

What the Fourth Gospel's writer intends to communicate in 17:4 is that Christ has performed a commission task completely, perfectively, in past time, without any reference to enduring or continuing results into the present. That verb does not point toward Τετέλεσται in 19:30; there is no justifiable reason for the verb of the τελειο- lexical core to foreshadow the verb of the τελε- lexical core. The τελειόω-verb indicates the completion of a deed with respect to Christ's person.

Differently, the use of Τετέλεσται in 19:30 is a completion or ending in a *fulfillment* sense. Christ fulfills all concerning the plan of God to bring him to the cross to suffer and accomplish the atoning death for his own.

In John 17:4, Christ completes a commissioned task in the past. In John 19:30, Christ fulfills a task more encompassing than that which was completed in past time in 17:4. Two different endings take place in 17:4 and 19:30. John 19:28 reminds readers of the Fourth Gospel to give focal emphasis to the *Person* in whom all work in the atonement is fulfilled, as prophesied in the OT.

5

The Work of the Words and Works

As evidenced in the second chapter of this present work, there is not uniform agreement on the identity of "the work" of John 17:4. There is much leaning toward a view that sees a completed mission or obedience being complemented by a view of a proleptic completion of the work of the cross. As Keener writes, "That Jesus glorified the Father 'on the earth' (17:4) refers to the whole of his earthly ministry . . . In the cross, he finished the work the Father called him to do (cf. 4:34; 19:30), though his followers still need to be 'completed' or perfected in unity (17:23)."[1] Lincoln's comments on 4:34 too, similar to Keener's, are prototypical in that they reference 19:30 in support of their idea that the "work" in 4:34 (and 17:4) refers to the crucifixion: "The food that sustains Jesus is the mission he has been given by God, who is frequently characterized as the one who sent Jesus. His mission is also designated elsewhere as doing the will and completing the work of God (cf. e.g. 5:30, 36; 6:38–40; 9:4; 10:37–8; 17:4), and his death on the cross will signal its completion (19:30)."[2]

It is common to frame or filter the idea of "the work" in John 17:4 through John 4:34. As Klink comments on 4:34,

> It is important to note that Jesus aligns his needs with "the one who sent me" (τοῦ πέμψαντός με). Jesus is so exclusively defined by the Father and his "sending" that even food is made subsidiary. That is why Jesus claims to do another's "will" (θέλημα) and

---

1. Keener, *The Gospel of John*, 1005.
2. Lincoln, *The Gospel According to Saint John*, 179–180.

"work" (ἔργον), terms used exclusively in the Fourth Gospel for the Father's work of salvation. It is never the work of Jesus or his disciples; it is always the work of the Father (cf. 17:4). Jesus is so dependent on the Father that the Father's will and work is food to him, and he is actually hungry for it, actually craving its accomplishment (cf. Deut. 8:3). Jesus' "life" was sustained ultimately by God.[3]

While I do agree that there seems to be a relationship between τὸ ἔργον in 4:34 and τὸ ἔργον in 17:4, it is important to make the case for τὸ ἔργον in 17:4 to stand on its own as an act other than the crucifixion.

In seeking to argue that the completed work of Christ in John 17:4 is not the atoning act of the crucifixion of Christ, I now will turn to explain what "the work" (τὸ ἔργον) is. Chapter Five will contrast and compare diverse views of "the work" in John in 17:4. I will seek to explain how "the work" (17:4b) relates to "glory on the earth" (17:4a). In terms of the meaning of "glorified" in 17:4 only, I will show that the Father is glorified by the Son via a specific, singular work. I intend to demonstrate that "the work" differs from "works" in the Fourth Gospel, addressing proposals of the relationship between the two terms and concepts.

EXEGESIS OF ΤΟ ΕΡΓΟΝ IN JOHN

The noun ἔργον ("work") refers to "that which displays itself in an activity of any kind, deed, or [an] action."[4] Such deeds or actions can be in reference to God the Father or Jesus, or "the deeds of humans, exhibiting a consistent moral character."[5] It also may refer to "that which one does as regular activity, *work, occupation, task*."[6] The related verb ἐργάζομαι ("to work") means "to engage in activity that involves effort, work," or "to do or accomplish something through work."

Both the noun, (τὸ) ἔργον, and the verb, ἐργάζομαι, appear in the Gospel of John. In the Fourth Gospel, the writer makes twenty-eight uses

---

3. Klink, *John*, 248.
4. BDAG, 390.
5. BDAG, 390.
6. BDAG, 391. BDAG locates the uses in John 4:34 and 17:4 within this range of meaning.

of forms of τὸ ἔργον.[7] He also makes eight uses of ἐργάζομαι.[8] Of the twenty-eight uses of the noun, it appears in the singular only six times, with the use of τὸ ἔργον in both 4:34 and 17:4 being singular uses.[9] Only 4:34, 6:29, and 17:4 reflect articular uses in the singular form in order to speak of a specific work, or "the work."

The uses of τὸ ἔργον largely appear together among eight dialogues or discourses within the Fourth Gospel, and often in proximity to a form of ἐργάζομαι: John 3:19–21 (3x + εἰργασμένα in 3:21), 5:20–36 (3x + ἐργάζεται and ἐργάζομαι in 5:17), 6:28–29 (2x + ἐργάζεσθε, ἐργαζώμεθα, and ἐργάζῃ in 6:27, 28, and 30), 7:3–7:7 (2x), 8:39–41 (2x), 9:3–4 (2x + ἐργάζεσθαι 2x in 9:4), 10:25–38 (6x), 14:10–12 (3x). Only the uses in 4:34, 7:21, 15:24, and 17:4 stand alone without multiple uses of "work"/"works" or a near use of ἐργάζομαι in a dialog or discourse.

The uses within the grouping have further distinguishing marks that will help clarify the use of τὸ ἔργον in 17:4. Some of the uses refer to *the evil deeds or activities of people*. For example, Jesus will speak of people loving darkness due to their evil (πονηρὰ) actions (ἠγάπησαν οἱ ἄνθρωποι μᾶλλον τὸ σκότος ἢ τὸ φῶς· ἦν γὰρ αὐτῶν πονηρὰ τὰ ἔργα, 3:19–20). They do not wish for the light (of righteousness) to expose the evil nature of their workings.[10] Jesus also can speak of testifying about the works of the world being evil (again using πονηρὰ: ὅτι ἐγὼ μαρτυρῶ περὶ αὐτοῦ ὅτι τὰ ἔργα αὐτοῦ πονηρά ἐστιν, 7:7). Or the works in question can be of the historical Abraham (8:39—Εἰ τέκνα τοῦ Ἀβραάμ ἐστε, τὰ ἔργα τοῦ Ἀβραὰμ ἐποιεῖτε), or the devil-generated works of Jesus's contemporaries who are opposed to him (8:41—ὑμεῖς ποιεῖτε τὰ ἔργα τοῦ πατρὸς ὑμῶν, cf. 8:44).

A different set of uses concerns *the works of God (the Father)*, whether subjective or objective. For example, in 5:20, Jesus speaks of "all" works "that he himself [the Father] is doing" (πάντα . . . ἃ αὐτὸς ποιεῖ) as an antecedent idea to the greater works the Father will show to him (καὶ

---

7. John 3:19, 20, 21; 4:34; 5:20, 36 (2x); 6:28, 29; 7:3, 7, 21; 8:39, 41; 9:3, 4; 10:25, 32, 33, 37, 38; 14:10, 11, 12; 15:24; 17:4).

8. John 3:21; 5:17 (2x); 6:27, 28, 30; 9:4 (2x).

9. The other four references are 6:29; 7:21; 10:32; 10:33.

10. Whitacre writes, "[The] image is of a person involved in some activity that is morally neutral or even virtuous. This person does not come to the light because it would expose that what was considered virtuous is actually evil. This latter interpretation best fits this context, and we know it was held very early because some manuscripts, including p66 (from about A.D. 200), read, 'He does not come to the light lest his deeds be exposed, that they are evil' (*hina mē elenchthē ta erga autou hoti ponēra estin*)," (Whitacre, *John*, 92–93).

μείζονα τούτων δείξει αὐτῷ ἔργα). In 6:28 the crowd following Jesus speaks of "the works of God" (τὰ ἔργα τοῦ θεοῦ)—that is, the works God requires of them. To this Jesus will give a reply in 6:29 of "the work of God" (τὸ ἔργον τοῦ θεοῦ)—the work God requires—being belief in Jesus.[11] Jesus also speaks of works from the Father (10:32—ἔργα καλὰ ἔδειξα ὑμῖν ἐκ τοῦ πατρός) and works of his Father (10:37—τὰ ἔργα τοῦ πατρός μου), both uses seeming to be genitives of source—works that find their origin in God the Father. Similarly, making a possessive use of the genitive, Jesus speaks of the Father doing "*his* works" (14:10—τὰ ἔργα αὐτοῦ).

John 5:36 is particularly important to observe when discussing "works" because of the verbal similarities between 5:36 and 17:4:

5:36b-c: τὰ γὰρ ἔργα ἃ δέδωκέν μοι ὁ πατὴρ ἵνα τελειώσω αὐτά, αὐτὰ τὰ ἔργα ἃ ποιῶ

17:4b-c: τὸ ἔργον τελειώσας ὃ δέδωκάς μοι ἵνα ποιήσω

A form of every term in John 17:4 appears in 5:3, including *work/works* (τὰ ἔργα/ τὸ ἔργον), *complete* (τελειώσω/ τελειώσας), *which he gave/which you gave* (ἃ δέδωκέν/ ὃ δέδωκάς), *to me* (μοι), *in order that* (ἵνα), and *do* (ποιῶ/ ποιήσω). One notable difference, however, is that in 5:36 he speaks of *works* (plural—τὰ ἔργα) the Father gives to him to complete (τὰ γὰρ ἔργα ἃ δέδωκέν μοι ὁ πατὴρ ἵνα τελειώσω αὐτά). In 17:4 the writer speaks of a singular work—τὸ ἔργον.

On 5:36, Carson identifies the plural *works* from God the Father as a referent to the whole of Jesus's commission:

> The works (plural, *contra* NIV) which the Father has given Jesus to finish, and which he is in process of completing, testify that the Father has sent him. These "works" include all of Jesus' ministry, including the "signs..." which point to the climactic work, the work of redemption achieved in the cross and exaltation of the Lamb of God. Anyone who has followed John's Gospel this far will know that these works are not some mere demonstration

---

11. Klink suggests a reason for the toggle between "work" and "works" in the two verses that is related to the work being of God the Father. He writes, "The singular work of the Christian is Faith in the Son who was sent from the Father... Any work *for* God must involve faith in *his* Son... The duties and responsibilities of humanity are entirely eclipsed by this one task of trusting in the person and work of the Son. It is likely for this reason that Jesus kept the word 'work' alongside the call to faith in his response to the crowd's question. There is a work to be done, but it belongs to God, both Father and Son... Faith, then, is to trust in the work of God accomplished in Jesus Christ" (Klink, *John*, 328).

that Jesus is a notable human being, perhaps a prophet, following the conclusion of Nicodemus (3:2). The argument in this verse turns on the exposition of the Father/Son relationship found in 5:19–30. All that Jesus does is nothing more and nothing less than what the Father gives him to do. The works he does are thus peculiarly divine: they are the works of God.[12]

Importantly, Carson proposes that a reader "who has followed John's Gospel this far" will have observed the *works*—they will have observed "all of Jesus' ministry," which is inclusive of the "signs" (cf. 2:1–11; 4:46–54).

It seems evident that the "works" in 5:36 refer to visible, tangible acts of Jesus based on the discourse in which it is found for three reasons. First, the discourse arises in response to Jesus performing a miracle on the Sabbath (5:16) and calling God his Father (18). Second, the miracle and its origin receive constant reference in the dialog: "nothing of his own accord" (19), "only what he sees the Father doing" (19), "greater *works* (ἔργα) than *these* will he show him" (20—μείζονα τούτων δείξει αὐτῷ ἔργα), "I can do nothing on my own" (30). Third, the works in question act as visible witnesses to those watching Jesus that he is the sent one from God (36; and bearing witness in 31, 32 [2x], 33); these are actions observed. As Lincoln comments,

> [This] witness consists of the works that the Father has given me to complete, the very works that I am doing, works such as the healing of vv. 1–9 which had provoked this particular controversy in the first place. The signs Jesus does are included in the testimony of his works and are properly understood when they are seen as bearing witness to the divine origin of Jesus' mission, to his commissioning as the Father's representative. Their witness about him is that the Father has sent me. Jesus will repeat the emphasis on the witness of his works in 10:25 and will then point out in 15:24 that they also play a condemnatory role for those who do not believe.[13]

Borchert writes with similar thought about the works as witnessing miracles:

> So Jesus moves from human testimony to the more significant witness of his "works" (erga). This term is used in the Gospel to describe the powerful acts of Jesus done on earth in cooperation with the Father (5:36; cf. 5:20; 9:4; 10:25, 32, 37–38; 14:10–11;

---

12. Carson, *John*, 261–62.
13. Lincoln, *The Gospel According to Saint John*, 206.

15:24). These works are not to be seen as ends in themselves but testify to the fact that Jesus is on a mission ("sent") from the Father.[14]

As works that should lead to belief rather than opposition, the works act as signs pointing to the working of God and Christ's divinity. The Fourth Gospel emphasizes the witnessing nature of the works Jesus performs (5:36; 7:3-4; 10:25, 32-33, 37-38; 14:10-11). The works point some toward Christ as the divine Son of God while others look at the same works and reject the Son (cf. John 1:9-12). It would seem then that the "works" of God refer to *the sign-miracles Jesus performs in the Fourth Gospel*.

ΤΑ ΕΡΓΑ AS SIGNS

"One notable feature of the Gospel of John is the presentation of Jesus's ministry in a series of distinctive signs (20:30-31)," writes John Painter.[15] "Sign" (or often in the plural, "signs" in John) translates σημεῖον (or the plural, σημεῖα).[16] It is common for scholars to identify six or seven "signs" in the Gospel of John: Turning water into wine (2:1-11), healing the nobleman's son (4:46--4), healing the lame man (5:1-15), feeding the multitude (6:1-15), healing the blind man (9:1-41), and raising Lazarus from the dead (11:1-44).

However, there is not uniform agreement on the number of signs beyond the six in the list above minus the clearing of the temple (2:12-17). For additional signs' lists for the Gospel of John have included the following nine: (1) cleansing the temple (2:12-17), (2) Jesus's parabolic saying about the serpent in the wilderness (3:14-15), (3) Jesus's walking on water (6:16-21), (4) the anointing of Jesus (12:1-8), (5) the triumphal entry (12:12-16), (6) the washing of the disciples' feet (13:1-11), (7) Jesus's crucifixion and resurrection (18:1-19:42), (8) the post-resurrection appearances (20:1-21:25), and (9) the miraculous catch of fish (21:1-14).[17]

---

14. Borchert, *John 1-11*, 245.

15. Painter, "The Signs of the Messiah and the Quest for Eternal Life," 239.

16. The term has a range of meaning that includes "a sign or distinguishing mark whereby something is known, *sign, token, indication*" (BDAG, 920). But BDAG lists all Fourth Gospel references to "sign" under the concept of "an event that is an indication or confirmation of intervention by transcendent powers, *miracle, portent*" in general, and under "miracle" specifically (BDAG, 920). BDAG thus evaluates John's use of sign/σημεῖον as equivalent to the Synoptics and Acts' concept of "miracle."

17. Köstenberger, *Theology of John's Gospel*, 329.

The variation in identification of signs is due in part to whether or not one views only the six miraculous happenings directly and immediately identified as "signs" as the only signs (cf. 2:11; 4:54; 7:31; 6:14, 26, 30; 9:16; 11:48).

In an attempt to argue for only six signs, Köstenberger develops criteria for identifying signs in the Fourth Gospel based on a survey of the explicitly identified signs. First, *a sign is a public work of Jesus*, which Köstenberger concludes on the basis the consistent use of σημεῖον with the verbs ποιέω ("do"), εἶδον ("see") or δείκνυμι ("show"), and never the verb ἀκούω ("hear"). That is, the "'signs' in John are therefore *works* of Jesus, not mere words." They are works done before audiences inclusive of unbelievers, which Köstenberger proposes is evident in the summary statement toward the end of Jesus's *public* ministry: "Though he had done so many signs before them, they still did not believe in him" (John 12:37).[18]

Second, *a sign is explicitly identified as a sign in John's Gospel*. Köstenberger strongly believes this is the only way to identify a "sign."[19] Third, *signs, with their concomitant symbolism, point to God's glory displayed in Jesus, thus revealing Jesus as God's authentic representative*. Köstenberger notes,

> That the signs are works of Jesus that reflect God's glory can already be seen in John's account of the first sign: "What Jesus did here in Cana of Galilee was the first of the signs through which he revealed his glory; and his disciples put their faith in him" (2:11). The reader of John's gospel is almost certainly expected to draw the connection between this statement and the earlier assertion found in the introduction to the gospel: "The Word became flesh and made its dwelling among us. We have seen his glory, the glory of the one and only Son, who came from the Father, full of grace and truth" (1:14). John thus presents Jesus's signs as vehicles through which God's glory is revealed in Jesus."

Köstenberger's criterion allows him to include the cleansing of the temple as a sign, for John's Gospel explicitly identifies it as a sign (cf. 2:12–21).[20] It also allows him to exclude Jesus walking on water as a sign even though

---

18. Köstenberger, *Theology of John's Gospel*, 326–27. Köstenberger quotes the NIV of John 12:37 with emphasis while making his case: "Even after Jesus had performed so many signs *in their presence*, they [i.e., 'the Jews'] still would not believe in him" (327).

19. Köstenberger, *Theology of John's Gospel*, 326–27.

20. Lee finds Köstenberger's inclusion of the cleansing of the temple and exclusion of Jesus's walking on water among the signs to be "unusual" among commentators. Lee, "'Signs' and 'Works:' The Miracles in the Gospels of Mark and John," 90.

many have viewed it as a sign. It also allows him to exclude the crucifixion and resurrection as signs.

It would seem to me that Köstenberger's three-fold criterion is narrow. This seems especially so concerning Jesus's walking on water. Just as Köstenberger proposes to know what is "certainly expected" in the mind of the reader with respect to the first sign, I propose that one reading in John 6:30—"So they said to him, 'Then what sign do you do, that we may see and believe you? What work do you perform?'"—within such close proximity to Jesus walking would find irony in the questions. The reader immediately would harken back to the episodes of the feeding of the five thousand *and* the walking on water. Seemingly the writer strategically places the episode of the walking on water *between* the feeding of the five thousand and the discourse on the bread of life for at least such a purpose. One recognizes the Exodus typology in the comparison of the *two* signs to the crossing of the Red Sea and the giving of "manna in the wilderness"—which occurs first immediately after the crossing of the Red Sea in Exodus 16—within the Fourth Gospel's presentation of Christ as the greater Moses (cf. John 6:31–23; see also 1:17, 45; 3:14–16; 5:46; 7:19–23; 9:28–29).

Similarly, Köstenberger determines "the signs' function is primarily to authenticate the one who performs them as God' true representative."[21] Or as he defines "sign" after applying his three-fold signs-criterion to John's Gospel, a sign "is a symbol-laden, but not necessarily 'miraculous,' public work of Jesus selected and explicitly identified as such by John for the reason that it displays God's glory in Jesus who is thus shown to be God's true representative (cf. 20:30–31)."[22] If one removes the necessity of explicitly identifying the signs by the designation "signs," the crucifixion and the resurrection would qualify as "signs" under his broader definition. In saying this, I am recognizing too that the writer of the Fourth Gospel is not explicit in communicating all symbolic meanings, including the symbolism related to the Second Exodus and Jesus being portrayed as the greater Moses. Readers should not constrain the writer of John to be explicit with his ideas when one can discern much in the whole narrative, like the reference to the Red Sea crossing in John 6.

Köstenberger excludes the crucifixion and resurrection additionally on the basis that (1) they are the reality to which the other signs point;

---

21. Köstenberger, *Theology of John's Gospel and Letters*, 113.
22. Köstenberger, *Theology of John's Gospel and Letters*, 328.

(2) the "signs" are preliminary in nature; (3) the connection between the crucifixion, resurrection, and John 20:30 is not explicit; and (4) it would have appeared to be inappropriate to the writer of the Fourth Gospel and Jesus's disciples to place the crucifixion and resurrection in the category of "signs" with the other recognized signs.[23] On this fourth objection, Köstenberger assumes the correctness of his own criteria while arguing the case against categorizing an item within the criteria. So I would dismiss this objection as fallacious and assuming. Again, Köstenberger cannot be certain that the earliest disciples would have found identifying the crucifixion and resurrection as signs would have been blasphemous; in the Gospel of John, only Jesus's claim of deity appears as blasphemous, and even that is only to those opposed to him.

Moreover, it is evident that the entirety of the Fourth Gospel intends to point to Jesus's claim to be the Messiah (cf. John 20:30-31). The entire account intends to signify, including the crucifixion and resurrection. I would agree that the signs are preliminary in nature, because (1) Jesus and the writer of John's Gospel indicate that the sign of the cleansing of the temple points to the crucifixion and resurrection (cf. John 2:21-22), (2) the signs are attended by discourses and discussions that point toward the crucifixion and the resurrection (2:18-20; 5:21-22, 25; 6:39, 44, 50, 54, 58; 10:15 [after John 9:1-40]; 11:25-26, 50-53), and (3) all of the events explicitly designated as "sign" occur in the first half of John's Gospel (1:19-12:50), not during the private ministry to the disciples in which there is much more development in Jesus's teaching on his ministry, the ministry of the Father and the Spirit, and on the events to come. But the preliminary nature of the designated signs does not exclude the possibility of undesignated "signs" in the narrative, including signifying event like Jesus's washing of the disciples' feet (13:1-12) or of the catch of 153 fish that signified to Peter the identity of the resurrected Christ (21:1-14).

Once the possibility of "sign(s)" being broader than six specific events exists, one can categorize the sign-events as several of the many "works" to which Jesus refers to himself as doing and to them as bearing witness of him (John 10:25, 37-38). Even if one does not see a case for the "signs" being broader than those so explicitly designated, a relationship between "works" and "signs" still exists.

For example, in John 5:20, Jesus indicates that he will do the "greater works" of the Father as a result of the Father revealing them to him. These

---

23. Köstenberger, *Theology of John's Gospel and Letters*, 328-29.

works will cause observers to "marvel"—possibly in a manner in proportion to their objection to Jesus's *sign* of healing of the lame man in 5:1–15.[24] Jesus implicitly refers to the sign of the healing of the lame man as a work lesser than the works to come. At that work, the Jews did "marvel" (7:21).

Again, in 9:3, Jesus speaks of the "works of God" (τὰ ἔργα τοῦ θεοῦ) being displayed in the man born blind. That work in turn is the healing of the blind man so that he gains sight. Some of the Pharisees will refer to this work as one of the "signs" (σημεῖα) Jesus performs that would argue against him being a sinner before God (9:16). The works of God performed by Jesus reveals itself as the sign of the opening of the eyes man born blind and as one of many other "*such* signs" (τοιαῦτα σημεῖα).[25]

Thus, it is evident that the *signs* and *works* in the Fourth Gospel may be used to speak of Jesus's miracles. The terms are not used exclusively to refer to miraculous events, for the cleansing of the temple is not a miracle (cf. 2:18, 23; 3:2).[26] Yet the miraculous events are among the works Jesus does, for he does exclusively what he sees his Father doing when he does his works (5:19, 20; 10:32, 37). The works would therefore include all of the signs. Nevertheless the works include the non-miraculous, such as Jesus's proclamation of knowledge of the guileless Nathaniel and his location prior to their first encounter (1:47–49), revelation of his messiahship to the woman at the well in Samaria (4:1–26, 28–29), teaching in the temple (7:14–19; 8:12–20), triumphal entry and reception of worship

---

24. The healing of the lame man is identified as one of "many signs" in 7:31. See Köstenberger, *Theology of John's Gospel*, 324 and 327.

25. Bertram proposes that ἔργα θεοῦ has a specific limited reference to miracles of Christ in the Fourth Gospel: "It is only in the NT, however, that along with the reference to the wonderful works of God we have a clear awareness of His saving work and activity on the basis of the divine will to redeem which is consistently attested in all the individual works. If the concept of the ἔργα θεοῦ corresponds to a comprehensive view of the work of salvation, it is not surprising that it is for the most part lacking in the Synoptic tradition. Only in Mt. 11:2 do we read that John the Baptist in prison hears of the acts of Jesus . . . The Baptist cannot evaluate them as acts of Christ . . . and therefore he cannot regard them as the work of salvation. On the other hand, the concept of God's saving acts through Christ is common in John's Gospel: 5:20, 36; 7:3, 21; 9:3, 4; 10:25, 32, 37, 38; 14:10, 11, 12; 15:24. These statements relate to individual works done by Jesus. *As miracles, they bear witness to Jesus and to the salvation which He brings*" (Georg Bertram, "Ἔργον, Ἐργάζομαι, Ἐργάτης, Ἐργασία, Ἐνεργής, Ἐνέργεια, Ἐνεργέω, Ἐνέργημα, ΕὐεργεσίαΕὐεργετέω, Εὐεργέτης," in *TDNT*, 2:642, italics mine).

26. In contrast, Loren Johns and Douglas Miller think σημεῖον is used exclusively for the miraculous in the Fourth Gospel. Johns and Miller, "The Signs as Witnesses," 526.

as the King of Israel (12:12–19), dismal of Judas and preparation of the disciples (13:30–38), and all other things Jesus performs in the Gospel of John.

ΤΟ ΕΡΓΟΝ IN 17:4 AS A COMMISSION DISTINCT FROM ΤΑ ΕΡΓΑ

While it is evident that τὰ ἔργα often relates to the signs and other acts of Jesus, the use of τὸ ἔργον in 17:4 (and 4:34) seems to have a different referent. This suggestion stands in contrast to views of equating "the work" and "works," but in line with viewing the works—particularly as expressed in John 5:36—as Jesus's commission. That is, "works" refers to all Jesus does, but "the work" has a unique focus in relationship to the "works."[27]

There are six occurrences of τὸ ἔργον in the Gospel of John: 4:34; 6:29; 7:21; 10:32, 33; 17:4. Only the uses in 4:34 and 17:4 appear to refer to an undefined "work" (singular). The other uses refer to a defined work (singular), or a defined work singular with the "works" in view. The context of each verse reveals these uses.

For example, in John 6:27–29, Jesus initiates a discussion on "works" by inviting the crowd to work (ἐργάζεσθε) for food that will provide eternal life. Metaphorically, the food should endure in a manner that the manna of Moses's day did not. But it is a gift that cannot be earned, for the Son of Man provides it.[28] It is not a work Jesus claims he must do, but a work he commands the people to do.

With misunderstanding, the people respond to Jesus's teaching by asking about "the works of God" (τὰ ἔργα τοῦ θεοῦ), missing both that (1) Jesus indicated that the Son of Man would give them the food for

---

27. On 5:36, where Jesus speaks of the "works" the Father has given him to accomplish, Klink understands "The works are so surrounded by the Father (i.e. given by and completed for) that the Son serves as intermediary. The 'works' of Jesus, therefore, must be understood to refer to Jesus' entire mission" (Klink, *John*, 293). Similarly, on the basis of the discussion of "works" in 5:17, 19–20, Ridderbos concludes, "[Works] refers to the content of Jesus' entire mission, his miracles, *and his words*" (Ridderbos, *The Gospel of John*, 203, italics Ridderbos).

28. "The continuing discourse shows that the 'food' is Jesus himself, but the idea is not so much that Jesus endures forever as that, because this food endures, the life it sustains goes on into eternity . . . If they ought to 'work for' the food that endures unto eternal life, they must also recognize that it is the Son alone who can give it" (Carson, *John*, 284).

eternal life and (2) that Father's seal of approval is on the Son of Man and not upon their own works. Yet the response also reveals they understood that the responsibility of "the works" was their own, and not that of Jesus, even though the food given would be his to give.

In order to clarify all misunderstanding, Jesus identifies "the work" (τὸ ἔργον)—the one work needed in opposition to multiple "works" on the part of the hearers. While they wish to provide works to offer to God, "the work" he requires is belief. Upon belief, the Son of Man will give eternal life, for the hearers will have "worked" for the food in the correct way. "The work" specified is belief, and it is required of the hearers. Thus, it does not qualify for consideration as "the work" of Jesus, singular *and* undefined.

Similarly, Ἓν ἔργον in John 7:21 makes reference to a known miraculous event—the healing of the lame man on the Sabbath—as indicated by the echo of ὑγιῆ (7:23; cf. 5:6, 9, 11, 14, 15).[29] The healing of the lame man, along with Jesus's claim to be equal to the Father, is the act the writer of John identifies as the motivation for the Jews' desire to kill Jesus (5:18). The "one work," although singular in number, is specified rather than undefined, being one of the "signs." The use of ἔργον in this verse is dissimilar to the uses in 4:34 and 17:4.

Again, in 10:32 and 33 there is a question about the miracles—the *signs*. When the Jews attempt to stone Jesus, Jesus speaks of "many good works" (Πολλὰ ἔργα καλὰ). The singular ἔργον reference in 10:32—not reflected in the ESV—comes as a term appositional to ποῖον ("which"). The full clause, διὰ ποῖον αὐτῶν ἔργον ἐμὲ λιθάζετε, questions the work among the *works* (plural) or *signs* Jesus has performed before the eyes of the Jews (10:31).[30] The "good work" (καλοῦ ἔργου) which the Jews reference in reply also concerns the performed sign that has led to intent to kill Jesus (cf. 5:18), even though they attribute the desire to stone him to what they perceive to be blasphemy. Therefore, like the use in 7:21, the singular term has a definite antecedent event that identifies it with the signs rather than with an undefined "work" for Jesus to accomplish.

---

29. Salier, *The Rhetorical Impact of the Sēmeia*, 86–87.

30. Lincoln agrees: "Jesus has carried out many honourable or noble deeds, which have benefited others, have displayed his unique power, and have been for God's glory, and so he demands to know which of them merits his death ... His question allows the opposition to make explicit the reason for wanting to stone him" (Lincoln, *The Gospel According to Saint John*, 306).

In contrast to the singular uses of ἔργον in 6:29, 7:21, 10:32 and 33, the writer of John describes ἔργον in 4:34 as "the will of the one who sent me" (τὸ θέλημα τοῦ πέμψαντός με). "The one who sent me" is a reference to the Father (cf. 5:37; 6:44; 8:16; 12:49; 14:24). By speaking with the Samaritan woman, gradually *revealing* himself to her as the promised messiah, and gradually making her aware of her need to drink his water of life, Jesus is partaking of the food of God—of what God the Father wills for him to do. "His work" (αὐτοῦ τὸ ἔργον, contra τὸ ἔργον in 17:4) in the scene is to reap the fields that are ready for harvest—the very thing he has done with the Samaritan woman.

According to the narrative of John 4, the will of the Father—the divine will for Jesus—includes no less than the following actions, the final five which are revelatory with respect to Jesus and the Father:

1. Departing for Galilee and passing through Samaria (3-4).[31]
2. Landing in Sychar in proximity to Jacob's well (5-6a).
3. Near the sixth hour, resting from the weariness of his journey from Judea, including sitting (6b-f).
4. Asking the woman for a drink in the absence of the disciples (7).
5. Answering the woman's question with respect to giving initial revelation of his identity via inquiry (e.g. "*who* it is [τίς ἐστιν] that is saying to you," v. 10).
6. Moving the discussion to revelation about himself with respect to the water of the well and the water of eternal life (e.g., "that *I* will give [ἐγὼ δώσω] him," v. 14).[32]
7. Commanding the woman to call her husband so that he could enter into a discussion that would reveal him as one sent from God (e.g., "Sir, I perceive that you are a prophet,"—v. 19).
8. Giving the woman *knowledge*—ὃ οὐκ οἴδατε ... ὃ οἴδαμεν—that will lead to worship of the Father in spirit and truth (vv. 22-24). This includes revelation of (1) the Father's locale of worship (i.e., true temple), (2) the Father's reception of truthful worship (e.g., "true worshipers ... in truth"), (3) the Father's desire for true worshipers,

---

31. Michaels sees the use of ἔδει ("must") as geographical rather than theological (*The Gospel of John*, 235). Even so, the will of the Father is for a journey on a route that went through Samaria.

32. The ἐγὼ δώσω is emphatic.

(4) the non-corporal character of God (the Father), and (5) the non-corporal God's requirement for true worshipers.

9. Revealing himself as the Christ (26).[33]

In all this, the food of Jesus includes making known the Father in truth.

It is apparent from the response of the Samaritans that Jesus accomplished the will of the Father with respect to the woman at the well. The Samaritans become the immediately approximate referent for the fields ready for harvest.[34] Among the Samaritans is the woman from the well. On both the woman and the townspeople who return, Jesus performs the food-work of reaping—of gathering in persons from among all people on the earth.[35]

The establishment of ἔργον in 4:34 as the work of Christ revealing himself to all persons as messiah so that they might believe on him does not now demand that the use of ἔργον in 17:4 correspond to this work. However, the conclusion on 4:34 related to belief and eternal life is helpful when considering the work in 17:4, for conclusions on 17:4 should not contradict known themes and ideas within the Fourth Gospel.

Yet the private, intercessory discourse of John 17 provides a vastly different context than the public dialogues of John 4. Extremely important is the idea of *revelation* repeated explicitly three times in John 17:

1. And this is eternal life, *that they know you*, the only true God, and Jesus Christ whom you have sent (17:3).

---

33. The Ἐγώ εἰμι is emphatic, and consistent with other uses related to Jesus's revelation as the divine Son of God in the Fourth Gospel (cf. 6:20, 35, 41, 48, 5; 8:12, 18, 24, 28, 55; 9:9; 10:7, 9, 11, 14; 11:25; 13:19; 14:6; 15:1, 5; 18:5, 6, 8).

34. As Michaels observes, "It is fair to conclude that this harvest corresponds in some way to the salvation promised in [Jesus's] references to the Father's search for 'true worshipers' to worship 'in Spirit and in truth' (vv. 23–24) . . . The reader knows that the disciples do not, that the townspeople are on their way back to the well even as Jesus speaks (v. 30), and that if the disciples look they will see them coming into view . . . Jesus is telling his disciples that the 'harvest' he has in mind is a harvest of souls, not of grain, and that its time has come . . . The "harvest" consists of Samaritans" (Michaels, *The Gospel of John*, 262–63).

35. "This saying [4:34] calls attention to what is significant about his encounter with the Samaritan woman and indeed about all of his activity: he does God's will and finishes God's work. Jesus is the true Son of God, living out the obedience that was expected of the people of Israel, who were not to 'live on bread alone but on every word that comes from the mouth of the LORD' (Deut 8:3) . . . Israel was to be a source of God's salvation for the whole world, and this is now coming to fulfillment, beginning with the Samaritans." Whitacre, *John*, 110.

2. *I have manifested your name* to the people whom you gave me out of the world. Yours they were, and you gave them to me, and they have kept your word (17:6).[36]

3. *I made known to them your name, and I will continue to make it known,* that the love with which you have loved me may be in them, and I in them (17:26).

The idea of *revealing the Father* to the disciples is consistent with "glory" being a term associated with revelation of God—of God being praiseworthy in the sight of others. It also would be consistent with the past and perfective completion act of Christ if one understands that Jesus's incarnation intends to reveal the Father (cf. 1:14, 18).[37]

In accomplishing the work of salvation in John's narrative, Jesus's making known the name of the Father cannot be underestimated. Akala points out the significance of Jesus revealing the Father's name through the Johannine narrative:

> In 5:43, the Son's coming is mentioned by Jesus himself for the first time in the narrative when he declares that he has come in his Father's "name" or authority. The Father's act of giving the Son his name signifies full agency and authority of the Son. The theme of the Son and Father sharing the divine name also develops in the narrative: Jesus has come (5:43; 12:13), performs signs (10:25), and keeps the disciples (17:12) all in the Father's name; Jesus also glorifies (12:28), and manifests the Father's name (17:6; 26). In addition, believing in the Son's name is necessary for receiving the Father's salvation (1:12; 2:23; 3:18;

---

36. The *name* of a person represents the nature of the person whom it designates (BDAG, 712).

37. Although commentators have made much of the clause in 1:18, ὁ ὢν εἰς τὸν κόλπον τοῦ πατρὸς ἐκεῖνος ἐξηγήσατο, Michaels suggests one should translate ἐξηγήσατο as "told about." That is, Jesus "told about" God. He suggests this on the basis that ἐξηγήσατο "can be a rather straightforward, even colorless, term for reporting something or telling a story" (cf. Luke 24:35; Acts 10:8; 15:12, 14; 21:19). He recognizes the term also "can be a technical term for delivering revelations from the gods or authoritative interpretations of sacred writings" (following Büchsel, *TDNT*, 2:908; BDAG, 349). Michaels prefers the former idea, noting that the NT and early Christian literature lack evidence for the latter technical use. However, Michael yet concludes that the concept of Jesus as the ἐξηγήσατο of God is significant: "But it is not for that reason unimportant; the assertion that Jesus 'told about' God presupposes that he is the exception to the principle laid down in the first half of the verse. Because he himself is God, and 'right beside the Father,' he (and he alone) has seen God and can therefore 'tell about' God. This he will do in the narrative to follow, though not immediately" (Michaels, *The Gospel of John*, 93).

20:31), both Father and Son answer prayers made in the Son's name (14:13–14; 15:16; 16:23–24, 26), and the disciples will be persecuted because of the Son's name (15:21).[38]

The revelation of the Father—which is to reveal his "name"—permeates the incarnational ministry of Jesus in the Fourth Gospel.

I would suggest that Jesus's triple emphasis on revealing the Father/the Father's name in John 17 points to "the work"—the work that perfectively completed the commission given to Christ by the Father in the past (past with respect to the time of the intercessory prayer) that makes God praiseworthy. The derivatives of the revelation of the Father in John 17 point to this conclusion, as the very work of Christ intends to point back to the Father as the sending agent. This is manifested by four means in John 17.

First, the very things that Jesus is, has, and does point to God the Father as the source: "Now they know that everything that you have given me is *from you*" (17:7). Second, the conversations, teachings, public and private discourses, and dialogues act as revelation of the Father as the sender of Jesus: "For I have given them the words *that you gave me*, and they have received them and have come to know in truth *that I came from you*; and they have believed *that you sent me*" (8). Third, the request for the Father to keep present and future disciples in his name has revelation of the Father to the world as its goal: "So *that the world may believe that you* have sent me" (21), and "so *that the world may know that you* sent me and loved them even as you loved me" (23). Fourth, the continuing ministry of Christ provides assurance of knowledge of the Father and salvific-love by him to the disciples (25, 26).

When Jesus, therefore, says that eternal life is to know the one true God (ἵνα γινώσκωσιν σὲ τὸν μόνον ἀληθινὸν θεὸν), he places revelation of the Father at the center of salvation. If the will of God for Jesus concerns a harvest of souls that comes through revelation of his messiahship, it does not come apart from the revelation of God's name. Rather, they are one and the same (John 5:19, 30; 7:16; 8:28; 10:38; 14:10, 20). For Jesus to offer salvation, he must reveal the God who saves as the object of belief: "[Whoever] believes *him who sent me* has eternal life" (5:24). Jesus clarifies this very idea for Philip in John 14:6–10:

> Jesus said to him, "I am the way, and the truth, and the life. No one comes to the Father except through me. If you had known

---

38. Akala, *The Son-Father Relationship*, 163.

me, you would have known my Father also. From now on you do know him and have seen him." Philip said to him, "Lord, show us the Father, and it is enough for us." Jesus said to him, "Have I been with you so long, and you still do not know me, Philip? Whoever has seen me has seen the Father. How can you say, 'Show us the Father'?"

Jesus, the embodiment of *the way to, the truth of,* and *the life in* the Father (14:6), makes known (γνώσεσθε, γινώσκετε—14:7; ἔγνωκάς—14:9) and visible (ἑωράκατε—14:7; ἑώρακεν—14:9) the Father in himself so that the works Jesus performs reveal the Father who is at work in him. That "the work" of revelation of the Father (17:4) precedes the work of the crucifixion (19:16–30) is consistent too with the different intentions of τελειώσας and Τετέλεσται (19:30).

CONCLUSION: WHAT IS THE WORK?

"The work" in 17:4 differs from the "works" that Jesus performs throughout the Gospel of John. The "works" (σημεῖον) show themselves to refer to the signs of Jesus. At least seven of these are marked throughout John 1–12 (2, 4, 5, 6, 6, 9, 11). Additional signs that are not explicitly designated as such may include Jesus' washing of the disciples' feet (13)—which signifies the effect of the crucifixion as much as does healing one lame or one blind, and the catch of the miraculous fish that makes the identity of the Lord known to Peter (21). Seemingly, the resurrection is a sign confirming the reality of the deity of Christ in Jesus and his complete union with the Father and with the disciples (cf. 14:20).

The "works," as encompassing all that the Father reveals to the Son and all that the Son does exclusively, is a category broader than "signs." The works encompass all words and works of Christ in 1:19–21:23 (cf. 12:50). "The work" of 17:4 also differs from the narrow "the work" of 4:34 related to salvation; in 4:34 the "food" relates to the revelation of Christ for belief unto salvation while in John 17 the "work" concerns revelation of the Father.

The work in John 17:4 uniquely situates itself in John as that which brings glory to the Father, is completed in the past and perfectively, and was given as a stewardship in eternity past.[39] The completion of the work

---

39. Moloney concludes, "Jesus fulfills his mission, not in condemnation, but in rendering eternal life possible by making God known." Moloney, *Johannine Studies*, 453. More specifically, he later says, "Jesus has perfected the task the Father gave him to do:

Christ relates to the context of John 17, particularly to the goal of making known the name of the Father. The revelation of the Father through the incarnate Logos is the climax to which the prologue of John points as the emphasis of the Fourth Gospel: the end of the Word becoming flesh is that the God invisible to the naked eye now becomes manifest or "told about" (1:18). The remainder of the Fourth Gospel returns repeatedly to the idea of the Father being revealed in the person, words, and works of Jesus (5:45; 8:19; 10:37–38; 11:4 with 11:40; 14:7).

Jesus completing the work of revealing the Father fits within the three-year frame of the time of the narrative of John 17:4. In the next chapter I will argue that the Gospel of John gives evidence for this in its use of the term "Father" when speaking of God.

---

he has made God known" (457).

6

The Absentee Father

BY THE TIME THE reader reaches John 17, Jesus has revealed many things about God the Father in his explicit statements about the Father, revealing the glory of the Father (1:14) and making the Father known (1:18): (1) The Father loves the world and sent the Son to save the world rather than condemn it (3:1–17; 6:32–33); (2) The Father seeks worshipers in Spirit and in Truth (4:24); (3) The Father raises the dead and gives life (5:21); (4) the Father commits judgment of people to the Son, the Father has life in himself (5:26); (5) the Father is invisible and undisclosed toward all people (5:37); (6) the Father, sharing the essence of the Son, secures those who respond with belief to the voice of Christ (10:30–31); (7) the Father will glorify himself in the Son (13:31–32); (8) the Father will send the Spirit to those who follow Christ (as teacher and witness), will love those who love Christ, and will dwell in those who love Christ (14:16–17, 21, 23, 26; 15:26; 16:1–4, 33); (9) the Father sanctifies believers (15:2–3; 17:17); and (10) the Father will give the believers what they ask for according to the name of Christ (16:23).

In doing the express will of the one who sent him (10:30; 12:49; 14:31) and in doing only what he sees the Father doing (5:19, 20; 8:28; 10:37, 38; 14:10, 11, 12, 24), *every* act of Jesus—every work, "sign," and word reveals the Father:[1] the Father has the power to change water to

---

1. I am arguing that the acts reveal the Father *through* Christ. I am not suggesting that the Father took these acts upon himself in his role as the Father. The distinction between the persons of the Father and Son is evident from John 1:1—"with God ... was God"—and maintained throughout John's Gospel.

wine and desires a pure temple of worship (ch. 2); the Father seeks a harvest of salvation of people from among the Samaritans (ch. 4); the Father shares in the healing of a lame man (ch. 5); the Father shares in the feeding of the 5000, has the ability to walk on water, and demands faith for salvation (ch. 6); the Father gives the Spirit for providing water to give eternal life (ch. 7); the Father shares in the opening of the eyes of a man born blind (ch. 9); the Father shares in the raising of Lazarus from the dead, weeps over the death of Lazarus, and commands the removal of Lazarus's grave clothes (ch. 11); the Father shares in serving the disciples by the washing of their feet and gives them a new commandment (ch. 13); the Father shares in offering peace to the disciples in anticipation of the departure of Jesus and will share in the answer of prayers done according to the name of the Son (ch. 14); and the Father shares in Christ's overcoming of the world (ch. 16).

If the writer gives this large swath of the content of the Fourth Gospel to a focus on God the "Father," one should wonder why references to the Father dramatically decrease in John 18–21.[2] That is, if the Gospel of John is intentional in speaking of the Father in great volume in John 1–16—more than the total uses in the Synoptic Gospels combined[3]—then is it also intentional in going almost silent on speaking of God as "Father" in John 18–21? If it is true that "choice implies meaning,"[4] then

---

2. Van Eerden would seem to agree with this interest: "Seven chapters include ten or more occurrences of the term while the remaining chapters have six or less. There is a fairly even distribution between the two major halves of the book, with the public ministry containing sixty-one examples while the second half of the Gospel accounts for fifty-seven. Of these latter fifty-seven the bulk of πατήρ references is found, as one might suspect, in the Farewell Discourse (esp. chaps. 14–16). The high concentration of πατήρ in the Farewell Discourse, with chap. 14 having almost twice the number of any other chapter, leads to the common observation that πατήρ as a designation for God is primarily—if not exclusively—found on the lips of Jesus. This is essentially borne out when looking at the high frequency chapters. It is within the expansive dialogues-turned-monologues, located in chaps. 5, 6, 8, and 10, that the vast majority of the instances of πατήρ are contained. *What is of particular interest, then, is when John deviates from this pattern.*" Van Eerden, "John's Depiction of God as Father," 52–53.

3. There are sixty-five uses of πατήρ for God "the Father" in the Synoptic Gospels. There are forty-four in Matthew (5:16, 45, 48; 6:1, 4, 6 [2x], 8, 9, 14, 15, 18 [2x], 26, 32; 7:11, 21; 10:20, 29, 32, 33; 11:25, 26, 27 [3x]; 12:50; 13:43; 15:13; 16:17, 27; 18:10, 14, 19, 35; 20:23; 23:9; 24:36; 25:34; 29:29, 39, 42, 53; 28:19). There are four in Mark (8:38; 11:25; 13:32; 14:36). There are seventeen in Luke (2:49; 6:36; 9:26; 10:21[2x], 22 [3x]; 11:2, 13; 12:30, 32; 22:29, 42; 23:34, 46; 24:49).

4. Runge, *Discourse Grammar of the Greek New Testament*, 5. As relates to communication, Runge proposes, "The choices we make are directed by the goals and objectives of our communication. The implication is that if a choice is made, then there

the choice to emphasize or diminish the use of πατήρ concerns meaning related to the prominence or minimization of the role of the Father in a passage or section of Scripture, or the content of a given discourse. The writer of the Fourth Gospel make choices to identify Jesus with the Father, to increase the frequency of use of πατήρ in John 13–17, and to decrease dramatically the use of πατήρ in John 17–21.

I propose the disappearance of the virtual Father in John 18–21 is related to the completion of Jesus's "work." As the Father has been revealed, he no longer needs to be in focus; he is known in a general sense, for Jesus has made him known (cf. 1:14, 18; 5:17–18; 10:30–31; 14:8–11).

This chapter only intends to consider the frequency of use of πατήρ for God the Father in the Gospel of John, how the frequency of use differs in John 1–16 and John 18–21, and the significance of the change in frequency with respect to the role of God the Father in the story of the Fourth Gospel. This chapter does not intend to consider any other aspect of the use of πατήρ with respect to the portrayal of "the Father" as God in the fourth Gospel. Many other studies have been given to that task.[5]

BRIEF CONSIDERATION OF THE SIGNIFICANCE OF THE FATHER IN THE GOSPEL OF JOHN

Thompson draws out the significance of God as "Father" in the Gospel of John and the complexity of the relationship of the identity of the "Father" to Jesus the "Son" when she observes,

> Indeed, John so emphasizes the unique character of the relationship between the Son and the Father that it is not unreasonable to ask whether it is even possible to talk about God as Father apart from talking about Jesus the Son . . . Although the very emphasis

---

is meaning associated with the choice . . . If I chose to do X when Y and Z are also available options, this means that I have at the same time chosen not to do Y or Z" (6).

5. Anderson, "The Having-Sent-Me Father," 33–57; D'Angelo, "Intimating Deity in the Gospel of John," 59–82; Cowan, "The Father and Son in the Fourth Gospel," 115–35; Fisher, *God the Father in the Fourth Gospel*; Köstenberger, *A Theology of John's Gospel and Letters*, 361–80; Lee, "Beyond Suspicion?," 140–50; Lee, "The Symbol of Divine Fatherhood," 177–87; O'Day, "Show Us the Father," 11–17; Meyer, "'The Father:' The Presentation of God in the Fourth Gospel," 255–73; Park, *Discourse-Analytic Significance of the Use of "Father" as God's Title in John's Gospel*; Reinhartz, "Introduction: 'Father' as Metaphor in the Fourth Gospel," 1–10; Thompson, *The God of the Gospel of John*; Thompson, "The Living Father," 19–31; Thompson, *The Promise of the Father*; Tolmie, "The Characterization of God in the Fourth Gospel," 57–75; Van Eerden, "John's Depiction of God the Father."

on the unity and inseparability of Father and Son offers a real challenge to the discrete delineation of the Father apart from the Son, it does so only if the question is framed as follows: "What does the Fourth Gospel say about the Father apart from what it says about the Son?" To phrase the question that way, however, already suggests that the question is misconstrued, for it is only in relation to the Son that God is "Father." It is not merely the designation of God as "Father" but the corollary reference to Jesus as "Son" that delineates the meaning of each.[6]

While Thompson's emphasis above seems to be on the figure of the Son, her question about the separate content concerning the Father and Son in John's Gospel is important.[7] The Father receives discussion in John that is massive in quantity and scope.

Some 43% of the uses of πατήρ for God the Father within the Fourth Gospel are concentrated in the Farewell Discourse (John 13–17): 52 of 120, or 1 use per every 2.31 verses. Park finds this significance to be important to the plot-line of John's Gospel, concluding, "The macro-level analysis shows that the use of 'Father' is concentrated in John 14–17, which is the didactic peak (or the thematic climax) of the entire Gospel . . . The concentrated use of the term in the didactic peak alerts readers that they have reached the thematic climax of the story."[8] The story climaxes with a great focus of the working of the Father and then references to the Father almost disappear from the story. The change in concentration seems intentional.

Köstenberger also notes the significance of the Farewell Discourse's characterization of God as Father, the "intricate connection" between God the Father and Jesus, and the implications of their relationship for believers in Jesus:

> With regard to Jesus, the Father: (1) has handed all things over to him (13:3; 17:2); (2) has sent him (13:3, 20; 15:21; 16:5, 28, 30; 17:3, 8, 18, 25); (3) will glorify him (13:31, 32; 17:1, 5, 22); (4) reveals himself through him (14:6–11; 17:6, 11, 14, 26); (5) is in him (14:10–11, 20); (6) tells him what to say and do (14:10, 24,

---

6. Thompson, *God in the Gospel of John*, 71.

7. Thompson proposes "Father" should not be thought of as a synonym for "God." In her findings, θεός and πατήρ are used with great distinction of significance in the Fourth Gospel. But that God is "Father" in First Century Judaism is apparent even in the responses to Jesus by the characters in the Gospel of John (5:18; 8:41; 10:33). See discussion in Thompson, *God in the Gospel of John*, 57–79.

8. Park, *Discourse-Analytic*, iii.

31; 15:10, 15); (7) grants his requests (14:16); (8) is greater than he (14:28); (9) loves him (15:9; 17:23, 26); (10) gives people to him (17:6, 9); and (11) is one with him (17:10, 11, 21-22). With regard to believers, the Father: (1) has adequate space for them in his "house" (14:2); (2) will send the *paraklē*[set macron over e]*tos* to them (14:16, 26; 15:26); (3) will love them (14:21, 23; 16:27); (4) will come and stay with them (14:23); (5) will prune them in order that they may bear more fruit (15:2); (6) will grant their requests (15:23; 16:23); (7) will protect them from the evil one (17:15); and (8) will enable them to be one (17:21-22).[9]

It is certain from Köstenberger's simple, purely inductive analysis above that the Father's role in the Farewell Discourse is extremely significant to the Fourth Gospel's theology proper (especially as it concerns his role as sovereign ruler of history and all mankind), and theologies of the Trinity, salvation of humankind, last things, the Person and work of the Spirit (and his presence with/within believers), sanctification in Christ, prayer, and the believers' union with Christ and one another. The Father is a prominent player in the redemption of humankind, and to reduce his role in the narrative seemingly would have significance to many of the themes and teachings repeated in the evangelist's story.

Thompson, too, in a manner similar to Köstenberger, summarizes the work of the Father, but across the entirety of the Gospel of John, writing,

> The Father seeks true worshippers (4:23); works (5:17, 19-20); loves the Son (5:20; 10:17; 15:9; 17:23, 26); shows the Son what he is doing (5:20); raises the dead and gives life (5:21); gives authority to the Son to have life (5:26) and execute judgment (5:27); gives his works to the Son (5:36); sent the Son (5:37, 38; 6:29, 39, 57; 8:16, 18, 26; 11:42); testifies to Jesus (5:37; 8:18); set his seal on the Son of man (6:27); gives true bread from heaven (6:32); gives "all" to the Son (6:37; 13:3; 17:2, 7); "draws" people to him and teaches them (6:44-45, 65); judges (8:16); instructs Jesus (8:28); is with Jesus (8:29); seeks Jesus's glory (8:50, 54); knows the Son (10:15); consecrated the Son (10:36); hears the Son (11:41); honors those who serve Jesus (12:26); glorifies his name (12:28); will come and "make his home" with believers (14:23); will send the Holy Spirit (14:26); prunes the vine (15:2); loves the disciples (16:27; 17:23); glorifies Jesus (17:1; 24);

---

9. Köstenberger, *Theology of John's Gospel*, 376.

"keeps" what has been given to the Son (17:11, 15); and sanctifies believers in the truth (17:17).[10]

From her inductive analysis, Thompson makes a special note of two items: (1) The actions of God as Father are distinctly and peculiarly concentrated toward and through Jesus the Son, and (2) God's activity with relationship to the Son is all-encompassing and comes to expression in statements regarding God's life-giving powers and activity in past, present, and future.[11]

BRIEF CONSIDERATION OF SELECT VERSES RELATED TO THE FATHER

I wish to consider briefly five verses or sets of verses that point to the importance of God the Father in the development of the Fourth Gospel's narrative and theology. These verses are only a select sample of scores of verses that one might consider. It is beyond the scope of this chapter to give detailed exegesis of these verses, for exegetical study will not add to my line of argument.

John 1:18 and 3:16—μονογενής

John presents Jesus as the "one and only [Son]" (μονογενής) from the Father. The picture seems to place importance on the relationship between the two persons: "Analogous to the human phenomenon of a father cherishing his only son, this description conveys a special relationship of love and trust."[12] Jesus's role as μονογενής is significant to the entire salvation story in the Fourth Gospel and exists solely because of the relationship of the Son to the Father. *Jesus is the one and only Son of God the Father.*[13]

---

10. Thompson, *God in the Gospel of John*, 69.
11. Thompson, *God in the Gospel of John*, 69.
12. Köstenberger, *Theology of John's Gospel*, 371.
13. In contrast, on 1:14, Lindars also notes that the articular "of *the* Father" is decisive for understanding *monogenēs* as "only-begotten." *The Gospel of John*, 96.

John 4:34—ὁ πέμψας με [πατήρ]

Unique to the Johannine writer, the phrase, ὁ πέμψας με [πατήρ] ("the Father who sent me"), is also used as a way to refer to God.[14] The phrase, "the Father who sent me," makes the Father the subject and initiator of the Son's activity and makes the Son the emissary of the Father's commissioning activity.[15] As Köstenberger writes, "The emphasis on the Father as the one who sent Jesus and who testifies of him casts him as the one who authorizes and authenticates Jesus's messianic mission."[16] This phrase, too, occurs twenty-three of its twenty-four times prior to John 17—95.8% of its uses.

John 6:57—ὁ ζῶν πατήρ

In the Fourth Gospel, the Father is the source of life, and as the ὁ ζῶν πατήρ ("the living Father"), he is the source of life in the Son.[17] Because he gives life to the Son, the Son has life from the Father; it is the Father who is mediating eternal life through the Son (John 5:26; 14:6). Both eternal life (3:16; 5:21; 6:37–39, 40, 45; 14:23) and the alternative judgment of death (5:22; 8:16) have *the Father* as their source.

---

14. Van Erden, "John's Depiction," 7. Van Erden counts twenty-seven usages of the term, while I count twenty-four (4:34; 5:23, 24, 30, 37; 6:38, 39, 44; 7:28, 33; 8:16, 18, 26, 29; 9:4; 12:44, 45, 49; 13:2; 14:24; 15:21; 16:5; 20:21). I question two examples that are general references that refer to the Father obliquely: 7:18 and 13:16. I also suggest eight of the uses refer to "the Father" directly rather than Van Erden's conclusion of seven (5:23, 37; 6:44; 8:16, 18; 12:49; 14:24; 20:21).

15. Thompson, *God of the Gospel of John*, 93.

16. Köstenberger, *Theology of John's Gospel and Letters*, 371.

17. Thompson, *God in the Gospel of John*, 72. She further writes, "The occurrence of the phrase 'living Father,' rather than 'living God,' is not simply an incidental variant attributable to Johannine style or preference. Rather, the epithet embodies within it the conviction that, as the eternally existent, living God, God alone is the source of all life, an aspect of God's activity that is illuminated by an image drawn from the human sphere of paternal relationship, particularly since that life is bestowed through the Son. The affirmation that God is "Father" cannot be separated from the affirmation that God is the source of life nor from the conviction that the life of the Father has been given to, and comes to human beings through, the Son. Consequently, within the Gospel of John, the commonplace that God is the living God appears within polemic contexts (chs. 5 and 6) precisely as the warrant for the claims about the life-giving work of Jesus, the Son. John is not interested in the Unmoved Mover but in the living life-giver" (76).

John 5:17–18 and 10:29–30—ὁ πατήρ μου

Jesus' claims to deity and subsequent incurring of the Jews' desires to kill him at 5:17–18 and 10:29–30 only arise in relation to the Father. At 5:17, Jesus speaks of Ὁ πατήρ μου as part of the explanation for his working on the Sabbath. The writer indicates that the μου is possessive in a sense that is greater than a collective "our Father" (Πάτερ ἡμῶν, cf. Matt 6:9),[18] or of the implied collective in the vocative address of Luke 11:2, "Father" (Πάτερ). The claim is to make God ἴδιον—"one's own."[19]

The exact same phrase in 10:29—ὁ πατήρ μου—which was understood as a reference to deity by the Jews in 5:18, now receives a reinforcement with Jesus's claim to perfect oneness with the Father in working: ἐγὼ καὶ ὁ πατὴρ ἕν ἐσμεν (10:30). While Jesus responds to his opponents with a question about the work from the Father they are rejecting, the Jews rightly perceive the claim to the essence of deity that is inherent in Jesus's claim to being one with the Father in his working. That is, being a mortal man (ἄνθρωπος ὤν), he makes himself God (ποιεῖς σεαυτὸν θεόν).[20]

John 14:6–10—ἡ ὁδός

The very works of Jesus intend to be "the way" by which those who believe on him are able to have access to God the Father (14:6–7). John 14:6 seems to be a cryptic reference to the Most Holy Place and the way through the tabernacle's furniture and behind the veil to access God—that is, *the Father*—who resided above the mercy seat behind the wings of the

---

18. "Even Jesus' use of *my Father* adds to the pointedness of what he is saying. In corporate worship Jews sometimes spoke of God as 'our Father,' but the individual way Jesus spoke of God as his own father displayed the unique Father-Son relationship Jesus claimed as his own. Jesus' opponents instantly grasp the implications of his remark, including the fact that he was *calling God his own Father*. Perceived infractions against Sabbath laws were serious, and might provoke murderous intent; but a man *making himself equal with God* was challenging the fundamental distinction between the holy, infinite God and finite, fallen human beings. *For this reason the Jews* (*cf.* notes on 1:19; 5:10) *tried all the harder to kill him*" (Carson, *John*, 249).

19. Michaels' comments on this verse demonstrates reasoning similar to my own: "All [the Jews] seem to hear is the expression, 'my Father.' That, perhaps together with his use of the emphatic "I" (*kagō*) is what provokes them. From it they conclude three things: that Jesus is referring to God, that he is claiming God as 'his own Father,' and therefore that he is claiming to be 'equal to God'" (Michaels, *The Gospel of John*, 303).

20. The NIV and NET bibles attempt to clarify the sense of the terms by inserting the concept of a *claim* to be God. But the wording is slightly stronger than this, and it is stronger than the wording in 5:18, for it is a direct claim to deity.

cherubim.²¹ Jesus, the "bread" (cf. Exod 25:23-30; 37:1-9) and "light" (cf. Exod 25:31-40; 37:17-24) would be the way through the veil to God *the Father* in his death (cf. Exod 26:1-33; Matt 27:51; Mark 15:38; Luke 23:45; Heb 10:20). As the "way," Jesus "mediates" knowledge of *the Father*.²²

NUMERICAL REPRESENTATION AND EVALUATION OF ΠΑΤΗΡ IN THE FOURTH GOSPEL

The writer of John uses πατήρ in the singular and plural 136x in 112 verses according to UBS5. There are no uses in John 9, 19, or 21.²³ The lone usage in John 7 is the plural τῶν πατέρων in 7:22, referring to the patriarchs in ancient Israel.

Sixteen times (16x) the writer uses πατήρ for figures other than God the Father:

- 1x for Jacob the patriarch in 4:12
- 5x to refer to the patriarchs or ancestors of Israel in general in 4:20; 6:31, 49, 58; 7:22
- 1x for the nobleman (whose child Jesus healed) in 4:53
- 1x for Joseph, the husband of Mary the mother of Jesus and thought to be the biological father of Jesus by the Jews in the Fourth Gospel
- 3x for Abraham the patriarch, specifically in 8:39, 5, 56
- 5x for the devil in 8:38, 41, 44 [3x]

The 120x uses of πατήρ for God the Father distribute in frequency across the chapters in the Fourth Gospel in this manner: Chapter 1 (2x); 2 (1x); 3 (1x); 4 (3x); 5 (14x); 6 (11x); 7 (0x); 8 (12x); 9 (0x); 10 (13x); 11 (1x); 12 (5x); 13 (2x); 14 (23x); 15 (10x); 16 (11x); 17 (6x); 18:1 (1x);

---

21. In the OT, the way to the presence of the Father was through the tabernacle, behind the veil, to where the high priest would go once a year with blood (Exod 30:10; Lev 16:15, 34; Heb 9:1-10). The priest was going to God [the Father?]. That *way* to God ceased with the death of Christ (Heb 9:11-12). I am suggesting that the writer of the Gospel of John makes an allusion to that annual high-priestly ritual when he identifies Christ as "the way."

22. Thompson, *God in the Gospel of John*, 88.

23. John 9 does not use πατήρ. However, John speaks of the Father by the synonymous terms "God" (9:3, 16, 24, 29, 31 [3x], 33), and "him who sent me" (9:4). There is no direct mention of the Father in John 19, but the idea of God as "Father" is intrinsic to the term "Son of God" (19:7).

19 (0x); 20 (4x); 21 (0x). In order of frequency, the writer uses πατήρ for God the Father twenty-three (23) times in John 14, fourteen (14) times in John 5, thirteen (13) times in John 10, twelve (12) times in John 8, eleven (11) times in both John 6 and 16, ten (10) times in John 15, six (6) times in John 17, five (5) times in John 12; four (4) times in John 20, three (3) times in John 4, two (2) times in both John 1 and 13, one (1) time each in John 2, 3, and 11, and zero (0) times in John 7, 9, 19, and 21 (as previously stated). There is an average use of 5.7143x per chapter (e.g., 120 uses / 21 chapters).

However, the 120x uses of πατήρ for God the Father are distributed over 17 chapters in actual use. This averages to 7.0588x uses per chapters in actual usage when removing the null usages of John 7, 9, 19, and 21 (e.g., 120 uses / 17 chapters).

Table 19. πατήρ for God the Father Across the 21 Chapters of John 1:1–21:25

John 1—21 as a Whole	Seventeen Chapters of Actual Appearances
5.71x per chapter	7.06x per chapter

John 1–12 Compared to John 13–21

If one further examines the uses of πατήρ for God the Father in John 1–12 in comparison to John 13–21, one finds 63x in John 1–12 for an average of 5.25x per chapter as a whole (63 uses/12 chapters), and 6.3x per chapter removing the null chapters of John 7 and 9 (63 uses/10 chapters). One also finds 57x in John 13–21 for an average of 6.33x per chapter as a whole (57 uses/9 chapters), and 8.14x per chapter removing the null chapters of John 19 and 21 (57 uses/7 chapters).

Table 20. πατήρ for God the Father Across John 1–12 Compared to John 13–21

The Book of Signs John 1-12		The Book of Glory John 13-21	
63x		57x	
Across 1–12 as a Whole	Across the Ten Chapters of Actual Appearance	Across 13–21 as a Whole	Across the Seven Chapters of Actual Appearance
5.25x per chapter	6.30x per chapter	6.33x per chapter	8.14x per chapter

As a whole, the 120 uses of πατήρ for God the Father are distributed across the 867 verses of John 1:1–21:25. Thus, in terms of the entirety of the Fourth Gospel, πατήρ for God the Father averages one use (1x) per every 7.225 verses in John 1–21. If one divides John by the common designations of "The Book of Signs" (1–12) and "The Book of Glory" (13–21), πατήρ for God the Father averages one use per every 9.11 verses in John 1–12, and one use per every 5.14 verse in John 13–21.[24]

Table 21. πατήρ for God the Father Across the 867 verses of John 1:1–21:25

One Use Per Every 7.3 Verses in John 1–21	
The Book of Signs John 1-12	The Book of Glory John 13-21
1x use per every 9.11 verses 63 uses in 574 verses total	1x use per every 5.14 verses 57 uses in 293 verses total

The 120 uses of πατήρ for God the Father distributes over 96 verses of actual use. The is an average of 1.25x per verse in actual usage.

John 1–16 Compared to John 18–21

Differently than dividing John as 1–12 and 13–21, for this analysis it seems wise to examine uses of πατήρ for God the Father in John 1–16 in comparison to John 18–21. Jesus's statement concerning the completed work occurs in John 17, in which he is addressing the Father directly. The direct addresses in John 17 are not counted among the work completed

---

24. There are 574 verses in John 1–12 (Book of Signs), not including 7:53–8:11, and 293 verses in John 13–21 (Book of Glory).

in the narrative of John 1–16. As addresses directly to the Father, they should not be considered in an analysis of John 17–21, for they are not revealing anything to the disciples, the Jews, or crowds about the Father; the revelation is solely to the reader. Therefore, if one removes six uses (6x) of πατήρ for God the Father in John 17, where Jesus speaks to God the Father in the vocative (17:1, 5, 11, 21, 24, 25), and refers only to what is (1) prior to the prayer in John 1–16—the period in which the work of 17:4 would have been complete and (2) after the prayer in John 18–21, the statistics are even more revealing than the comparisons of John 1–12 to 13–21.

There are 703 verses in John 1–16 (prior to Jesus directly addressing the Father in John 17) in which there are 109 uses of πατήρ for God the Father. This is an average of 6.82 uses per chapter for John 1–16 as a whole, and an average of 7.79x per chapter in actual usage when removing the null chapters of John 7 and 9. It is an average of 1x per every 6.44 verses in John 1–16.

In contrast, the are 138 verses in John 18–21 (after Jesus directly addresses the Father in John 17) in which there are only five uses of πατήρ for God the Father (4x in John 20 [with 3x of these in 20:17], 1x in 18, and 0x in 19 or 21). This amounts to an average of 1.25x per chapter for the whole of John 18–21, and an average of 2.50x actual uses per chapter when removing the null chapters of John 19 and 21. The distribution of the uses is 1x per every 27.6 verses, with 80% of the uses in John 20 and 60% of the uses in John 20:17 alone.

Table 22. πατήρ for God the Father Across John 1–16 Compared to John 18–21

	John 1–16 (703 Verses) Use Toward the Completed Work of John 17:4	John 18–21 (138 Verses) Use After the Completed Work of John 17:4
Total Number of Uses	109x	5x
Average Use Per Chapter as Whole	6.82	1.25x
Average Use Per Chapter in Actual Appearance	7.79	2.50x
Distribution of Use Per Verse Across Chapters as Whole	1x per 6.44 verses	1x per 27.6 verses

CONCLUSION

As stated in Chapter 1, it is evident that references to God as "Father" decrease significantly after John 17.[25] The 6.82x/7.79x average use of πατήρ for God the Father per chapter in John 1–16 reduces dramatically to an average use of 1.25x/2.50x in John 18–21. Whereas "the Father" (πατήρ), when used for deity, would appear on average once every 6.44 verses in John 1–16, it would only make an appearance once every 27.6 verses in John 18–21.

The dramatic change in the use of πατήρ in reference to God the Father support the thesis of the completed work as revelation. That is, the references to the Father disappear almost completely in John 18–20 because Jesus revealed the Father in 1:19–16:33.[26]

What is evident is that Jesus did come to reveal God the Father—he is the μονογενής from the Father (1:14) and the sole person to reside in the bosom of the Father so as to be able to "tell about" the Father to all—the people of the earth—people who never have seen the Father. By explaining the Father, he is explaining God to those who never have seen God (1:18; 5:37; 6:46). He completes that work by the end of John 16 such that he can speak of it as completed in John 17:4. It seems that the writer assumes in John 18–21 that the disciples have grasped the deity of the Son and the Father (cf. 14:7–9 and "You believe I am from God").

If the Father is diminished in his role in the narrative, it would seem that the Son's role as Judge and Sent One might be diminished simultaneously, for they share the same words, works, will, essence, and glory, even though they are separate persons. One might suspect this diminishing of roles unless the Father has been so revealed throughout the narrative that it is a foregone conclusion that he is in the background of all Jesus wills to say and do and that, in some sense, he also is in the foreground within the person of the Son. That is, even in the diminished references to the Father, we are watching the manifestation of the previously-revealed Father via the obedient Son.

Do references to Christ the Son of God therefore increase in John 18–21? Such a study is beyond the focus of this present work. What is

---

25. Akala also recognizes the shift in the frequency of usage of Father terms in the Fourth Gospel, although she does not relate the reduction in usage to a completed work in John 1:19–16:33. Akala, *The Son-Father Relationship*.

26. The drop in the amount of discourse by Jesus seems to argue for the position of this paper. That is, if it were important to reveal the Father, Jesus would have continued with as much discourse as previous chapters.

evident is that God "the Father" fades into the background, and the focus of the betrayal, trials, sufferings, crucifixion, resurrection, and post-resurrection appearances all concern the Son. Seemingly he has completed one work of revealing the Father in John 1–16. He then completes the necessary sacrifice and overcoming of death for the redemption of his own to be completed—to be *finished* (cf. 19:30).

A final support of the conclusion of the intentional diminishing of terms for "the Father" after the completed work comes in comparison of the crucifixion account in John compared to that of the Synoptics. Of the seven last sayings of Christ from the cross, there is no direct address to Father by Jesus from the cross in John, even though John witnesses to three of the seven sayings. In contrast, the only saying in Matthew (27:46), and the parallel Mark (15:34), is a direct address to God the Father: "My God, My God, why have you forsaken me?" Also, of the three sayings within the Gospel of Luke, two are direct addresses to the "Father:" "Father, forgive them, for they know not what they do" (Πάτερ, ἄφες αὐτοῖς, οὐ γὰρ οἴδασιν τί ποιοῦσιν, Luke 23:34), and "Father, into your hands I commit my spirit" (Πάτερ, εἰς χεῖράς σου παρατίθεμαι τὸ πνεῦμά μου, Luke 23:34, 46).

Although the Father is available to Jesus via direct address in the Fourth Gospel (cf. John 11:41; 12:27, 28; 17:1, 5, 11, 21, 24, 25), Jesus makes no direct address to the Father on the cross at all in this gospel account. One knows, however, that Christ does address his Father on the cross directly in history, for the other Gospel record such words. The writer of John, in contrast to Matthew, Mark, and Luke, removes the Father from the scene of the cross because the work of revealing the Father is completed. The final work of the Son, and the hope thereof, is the concern of the writer in John 18–21.

Conclusion

WHAT I HAVE ARGUED in this work is that Jesus's words in John 17:4 concern a work that Christ completed in full in his earthly ministry prior to his prayer in John 17. That is, the phrase "completed the work you have called me to do" concerns Christ's commission to reveal the Father to the world. That work is the first part of Christ's message of good news in the Fourth Gospel, as God is the object of faith of that message (cf. 17:3). Making God known is what Jesus's public and private ministry intended to do. As the writer of the Gospel of John structures his narrative, it is only after the completion of this work that the story turns to the final work of the atonement with Christ as the primary Person in focus.

HISTORICAL READINGS

In order to make a case for this view of the completed work in 17:4, one is required to go against the most prevalent view of this work in the history of interpretation. The vast majority of commentary writers hold to a *proleptic* reading of John 17:4—that Jesus's words refer to his work of suffering and dying on the cross for sin in the place of sinners. Such a reading seems to be in line with the Fourth Gospel's general themes related to the atonement and with the Fourth Gospel's own purpose statement: "But these [signs Jesus did] are written so that you may believe that Jesus is the Christ, the Son of God, and that by believing you may have life in his name" (20:3). The literary goal of John's Gospel is for the readers to place faith in the one who died and rose again—the Son of God who went to the cross.

However, quite often those writers who espouse proleptic views do so while also holding to a reflective view of 17:4. They see that "completed" seems to refer to a past work, but then they appeal to the Fourth

Gospel's thematic idea of the cross in order to hear a proleptic idea in the mouth of Jesus. The proleptic reading then takes on a life of its own without the writers making strong exegetical attempts to support such a reading; those who have commented on the "work" seem to repeat what those before them have said rather than offering a historical-grammatical analysis that would give weight to a proleptic reading. Augustine, Aquinas, Charles Simeon, and D. A. Carson's works on the Gospel of John, as they attempt to wrestle exegetically and contextually with the "work" to come to proleptic readings, are significant exceptions to the prevailing practice. In church history, there have been several writers who have held to a form of the reflective reading, even though all reflective readings do not resemble the conclusions I have drawn in this work.

GLORY ON THE EARTH AS REVELATION

The Johannine writer can speak of Jesus saying ἐγώ σε ἐδόξασα in part due to the Fourth Gospel's use of δόξα in a manner consistent with one of the uses of δόξα in the LXX. It is in the LXX that one finds δόξα employed for a display of God that is visible—one that can be seen. Translating the term כָּבוֹד of the MT, the Fourth Gospel writer follows the ancient LXX writers. Although the Synoptics each have an account of the transfiguration of Christ, which Peter later describes as *"glory* from the Father" (Matt 17:1–8; Mark 9:2–8; Luke 9:28–36; 2 Pet 1:17), the Gospel of John, which focuses on Christ bringing glory to the Father, has no similar account.

The completed work glorifies the Father ἐπὶ τῆς γῆς—"on the earth." The repetitive use of ἐπὶ τῆς γῆς in the early chapters of Genesis allows for an echo between Gen 1, 2, 6, and 7, and John 17:4. The ἐπὶ τῆς γῆς of the Genesis writer is the sphere of the Creator's purposes for humankind. The creation account finds its climax in the creation of man and woman to have dominion "on the earth." This same sphere is the focus of the judgment of the flood in Gen 7. Christ, however, succeeds in the realm of the earth where mankind failed. He brings glory to God through the obedience to God that man was unable to do.

Moreover, as much as John 17 provides a revelatory, incarnational, discipleship context for Christ's words in 17:4, so too Ps 48:10 offers the front end of an echo via a revelatory, incarnational, discipleship context for ἐπὶ τῆς γῆς. As the speaker in 17:4, Christ reveals the flower of what is concealed in seed-form in Ps 48. He will mediate the incarnational presence of God in Zion, bodily, as the God-man; he will make God known to the peoples, visibly and fully; and he will make God known to future generations in Israel, all as promised by prophecy in the psalm. The Johannine writer, seeing a partial fulfillment of Ps 48:10 in Christ's use of ἐπὶ τῆς γῆς, points the reader to the eschatological Zion in which God's full presence will dwell on the earth.

DIFFERENT TELIC WORKS

The previous understanding of aorist verbs in terms of tense, tense-form, *Aktionsart*, and aspect each influenced the interpretation of τελειώσας in John 17:4. Going beyond all discussions of the aorist as punctiliar, durative, time-of-action, or even proleptic in certain cases, Constantine Campbell first proposes a theory of verbal aspect that places a proleptic reading of the aorist out of the realm of possibility; the aorist always presents events in summary form, focusing on the remoteness of the action.

Ellis, Aubrey, and Dubis's theory of verbal aspect argues that Greek primarily grammaticalizes aspect within its morphological meaning and structure. Following their scheme, I observe τελειώσας is perfective in its aspect. It precedes the time of ἐδόξασα, explaining the working of ἐδόξασα as its modifying participle. It therefore cannot be proleptic; it only can speak of a *past perfective* event because grammatically it precedes the aorist of ἐδόξασα. Aspectually, the completion of which τελειώσας speaks is a completed glorification in the past.

The writer of the Fourth Gospel uses τελέω only in a combinative aspectual sense. In 19:30, the author uses τετέλεσται in order to indicate a perfective aspect, but with ongoing relevance. John's Gospel portrays Jesus speaking perfectively with continuing results during his three-year ministry on earth. The difference in the two verbs argues against a verbal echo or allusion to 17:4 by 19:30, or a foreshadowing of the latter verse by the former verse. Instead, τελειόω speaks of *completion with respect to something in the life of a person*—a deed finished by the person of Christ. Differently, τελέω, speaking of *the completion of words, lusts, or of the working of God in judgement*, intends to indicate that Jesus *fulfilled* all things that the Father willed for his course of life that led to his suffering and atoning death. The completion to which Jesus refers in 17:4 is a subset of the completion to which he refers in 19:30.

Although the field of verbal aspect is evolving and we are still very much near the infancy of studies in verbal aspect of the Koine Greek text, it is doubtful that the conclusions that I have drawn in this paper—conclusions based on Ellis, Aubrey, and Dubis's theory—will be overturned. Their theory seemingly accounts for all aspects of the components of the verb and for time, foregrounding, and backgrounding. John 17:4, following the latest theories of verbal aspect, shows a perfectively completed *work*. That work, different from the works, or signs and other ministry of Jesus in John, is singular: *it is to make the Father known.*

THE DISAPPEARANCE OF THE FATHER

Considering the density with which the writer of John speaks of God the "Father," it is significant that references to "Father" dramatically drop from use after John 17. I suggest that the change in frequency of use of πατήρ further serves to support the theory that Christ's work is to reveal the Father: once he has revealed the Father, he does not need to speak of him continually. Instead, the focus turns to Christ as the Person of the Trinity who will complete the final work of redemption. In the Fourth Gospel, in contrast to the Synoptic Gospel accounts, the unique absence of a direct address to the Father from the cross by Christ additionally supports that John 18–21 intends to show the glory of the Person of Christ rather than the glory of the Father, even though the glory of one brings glory to the other.

READING THE GOSPEL OF JOHN

Rightly understanding John 17:4 as reflective rather than proleptic allows for a reading strategy in the Gospel of John. After the prologue (1:1–18) and prior to the epilogue (John 21), John's Gospel has two major parts: the work of Christ to reveal the Father in 1–17 and the work of Christ to fulfill the plan of redemption in 18–20. The entirety of the Gospel of John intends to enable belief in the Christ so that the reader might gain eternal life, and the unit on the work of the revelation of the Father has scores of statements contributing to the fulfillment of the plan of redemption. But it is in reading the Fourth Gospel as a work in which the Son is obedient to complete both works that one most sees the Father being glorified in his one and only Son and the Son being glorified in his Father. As Jörg Frey writes, "Jesus ultimately reveals the Father in his whole mission and history, in his way to the cross, and in what is visualized in the cross of Jesus is God's saving love . . . Thus, reading this Gospel is the process in which the Father is revealed in his true character and in his ultimate intention."[1]

Bultmannian Readings

Such a reading strategy addresses the concerns of both Bultmannian and Barthian approaches to John's Gospel—one that "rightly recognizes the theological intention of the Gospel, without classifying its statements simply as 'time conditioned' or explaining and thereby relativizing them as 'historical' or 'cultural,'" and avoids relativizing "problematic aspects of Johannine theology, such as the polemical statements about the 'Jews.'"[2] If Jesus intends to reveal God, the national Jewish rejection of Jesus's claim to Messiahship, as portrayed in the Fourth Gospel, is a rejection of the God whom the characters claimed to worship and for whose temple and Sabbath they claimed zeal. In light of 17:4, "The Jews," or anyone else taking up issues with Jesus's claims in John's Gospel, run into a problem of God making himself known in every word and work of Jesus. The God of the glory of Moses's tabernacle has given a work to Jesus to complete. "The Jews," Greeks,[3] and Romans[4] who failed to grasp Jesus's identity in the narrative rejected God's express intention to make himself known from the time of Jesus's first appearance at the Jordan until he handed over his spirit. *In history*, God was making himself known.

Source Criticism

Launching from John 17:4 also address macro-level source-critical concerns. One might suggest that "the Gospel of John can scarcely be regarded as a text 'made from a single mold,' as a completely homogeneous literary unity."[5] However, the emphasis on the Father—significantly with

---

1. Frey, *The Glory of the Crucified One*, xxviii–xxix.
2. Frey, *The Glory of the Crucified One*, 6.
3. See 12:20 with 12:35–40.
4. See 19:23–24.
5. Frey, *The Glory of the Crucified One*, 19. This is not Frey's position, for he concludes "one can scarcely expect source criticism to provide the key for the interpretation of the Fourth Gospel."

the distributive use of πατήρ—argues for a homogeneous unit. It seems that the writer or editor of John constructed the work so that chapters 18 and 20 would fit within the intentional structuring revealed by John 17:4. Possibly, another option would be that the writer or editor was careless in writing chapters 18 and 20, trying to match the two chapters in the passion and resurrection narratives with the public and private ministries' narrative while also making a connection to the wealth of appearances of πατήρ in 1–16. At best, starting with 17:4 suggests a unity of 1–16 and 18–21. At worst, launching one's reading of John from 17:4 would show how difficult is the work to make a plausible source theory for 18–21.

Eschatology and Christology

With respect to John's eschatology, the hope of God dwelling in Zion finds fulfilment within the incarnate person of Jesus on every page of the Fourth Gospel. From his baptism through him sitting with the Samaritans, healing people on the Sabbath, feeding five thousand, offering himself as the living bread through whom living waters will come, etc., one sees in Jesus glimpses of what it will mean for God the Father to take up residence in the New Jerusalem. When he pitches his tent in the future (cf. 1:18), anyone who has believed in Jesus will experience in fullness Zion's light (9:1–39), Zion's shepherding (10:1–21), Zion's life (11:17–44), Zion's King's coronation (12:12–18), and Zion's love and cleansing (13:1–15; 31–35). The objects of Jesus's earthly ministry, like the man born blind (ch. 9), experienced the fulfillment of the prophecy of God dwelling in Zion among them. It was limited in scope, due to Jesus's return to the Father. But it will become a complete reality when he returns for his own, not leaving them orphans (14:18), but bringing them to be with him in his Father's presence (17:24).

Within this mystery and fulfillment reading, it is tempting to read the fulfillment of God dwelling in Zion through Jesus back upon the earthly concerns of the opening chapters of Genesis. In this reading, John 17:4 would allow the reader to hear the echo of Ps 48 influencing a tabernacle reading of the Creation account and the post-flood account. The one who appears as God dwelling in Zion "on the earth" incarnate originally dwelt with Adam and Eve in the garden "on the earth" and with Noah's generation "on the earth" after the floodwaters subsided.

Interpretations of Genesis that view the Garden of Eden as a tabernacle of God in Gen 1–2 should consider this strategy of reading John's Gospel.

In the same way, it also might be tempting to hear the echo of Genesis 1 influencing an earthly reading of the New Jerusalem/ Zion account. The New Zion will be earthly even as the dwelling among men by Jesus was "on the earth." *Amillennial* readings of the Gospel of John will not hold: "On the earth" is where God will dwell in Zion.

Finally, at the level of the full story, whether each statement of ἐγώ εἰμί in the mouth of Jesus is a revelation of the OT God of Exod 3:14 is without question. Every word and work of Jesus in John's Gospel intends to make God the Father known. The repeated use of ἐγώ εἰμί certainly raises the question of the style of the Johannine writer—why did he choose such an emphatic way to express the first person when other stylistic options exist, if not for the purpose of pointing back to the God who spoke to Moses? Micro-level concerns about individual ἐγώ εἰμί sayings and whether a particular instance is a reference to Exod 3:14 requires exegesis of the individual pericope to resolve. However, I strongly suspect that the macro-level story of God appearing in the incarnate Jesus and the micro-level stories of the ἐγώ εἰμί statements are congruent as part of one compositional content.

LIMITATIONS AND FURTHER STUDY

I cannot determine if John should be read as actual history with respect to community motives behind the text. If it is a choice between myth and history upon the text as received, then the strategy reads John as a historical account of God seeking to accomplish a mission through Jesus. However, if it is a choice between history in a received text and history as re-constructed by a post-Easter Johannine community, the strategy does not help. While this analysis assumed a document claiming to present the truth about God in a truthful recording of history, i.e., "on the earth," this is only an assumption. The strategy cannot resolve the problem of historical communities or the identity of the writer. Only when truth is presupposed can one do that.

Stated differently, the current reading strategy does not address compositional concerns with respect to Johannine communities. Instead, I am in agreement with any reader who understands that a writer, writers, editor, and/or editors included 17:4 in the final shaping of the text we receive as "John." That writer or editor included the verse so that one would read the story of John 1–21, structurally, as 1–16, 17, and 18–21, regardless of the social forces or political motivations behind the text. This strategy assumes the text before us "as is"—as composed—and does not address the process of composition. It only addresses the given content of the composition. That composition is the story of God in Jesus dwelling among his people on the earth as he will in the New Zion in fullness—in order to reveal the Father to those given to Jesus to be drawn to him.

Doxa (δόξα) and *Shekinah* (שְׁכִינָה)

A question raised by the Fourth Gospel's δόξα concepts is whether or not it is referring to the Hebrew concept of *Shekinah* (שְׁכִינָה). James Marshall proposed such over a century ago, writing,

> We turn now to the NT where the word שְׁכִינָה occurs both transliterated and translated. There can be no reasonable doubt that the Greek word σκηνή (= "tabernacle") was from its resemblance in sound and meaning used by bilingual Jews for the Heb. *Shekinah*; e.g. in Rev 21:3 "Behold the σκηνή of God is with men, and he will *tabernacle* (σκηνώσει) with them." The allusion is equally clear in Jn 1:14 "The Logos ... tabernacled (ἐσκήνωσεν) among us, and we beheld his glory."[6]

Reasoning in a very similar manner, R. A. Stewart also argues for an equating of *doxa* and *Shekinah*, even though he recognizes כָּבוֹד as the term translated by δόξα. As he notes,

> The glory of God (*kābôd* in the Heb. Bible, *doxa* in LXX and NT) is another name for the Shekinah . . . The term is postbiblical, but the concept saturates both Testaments. It underlies the teaching that God dwells in his sanctuary (Ex. 25:8, *etc*.), or among his people (Ex. 29:45f., *etc*.) . . . The resemblance between the Heb. word and Gk. *skēnē*, *etc*., may suggest the *shekinah* motif in Jn. 1:14 (*eskēnōsen*, 'dwelt') and Rev. 21:3 (*skēnē*, 'dwelling').[7]

As evidenced by Stewart's equating of *Shekinah* with δόξα via the LXX translation of כָּבוֹד, there is no express textual basis within the Hebrew Bible by which to equate the *Shekinah* term with a Biblical concept. The

---

6. Marshall, "Shekinah," in *A Dictionary of the Bible*, 489.
7. Stewart, "Shekinah," 1091.

Targums, the Talmud, Midrash, and other Jewish writings outside of the Hebrew Bible use the term within their Aramaic contents, even though the term itself is Hebrew.[8]

Walter Elwell and Barry Beitzel are among those who see a legitimate basis for equating "Shekinah" with a visible display of God's glory (i.e. δόξα). Even though they recognize the absence of the term in both the Hebrew Bible and the New Testament, they reason from the Rabbinic equating of the term for "dwelling" with כבוד. They propose,

> Although the word is not itself used in either Testament, it clearly originates in OT passages which describe God as *dwelling* among a people or in a particular place ... In its narrower uses the term is applied to the "shekinah glory," the visible pillar of fire and smoke that dwelled in the midst of Israel at Sinai (Ex 19:16-18), in the wilderness (40:34-38), and in the temple (1 Kgs 6:13; 8:10-13; 2 Chr 6:1, 2) ... The rabbinic sources used the term more widely than with specific reference to this OT phenomenon alone. In the Targums "shekinah," "glory of God," and "word of God" are used synonymously. Shekinah became a comprehensive term for any form of the presence of God; it could be used as a designation for God or as a circumlocution for references to the face or hand of God. Only in the later rabbinic sources does the Shekinah become a separate entity created by God as an intermediary between God and man.[9]

One example of the Targums' understanding of *Shekinah* occurs in comments on Gen 9:27 in which the statement of God dwelling among his people becomes the *Shekinah* dwelling with God's people: "God enlarge Japheth, may he [God] dwell in the tents of Shem." W. A. Vangemeren notes, "The Aramaic Tg Onkelos renders this verse: 'He will cause his Shekinah to dwell in the dwelling-place of Shem.'"[10]

The *Shekinah* also took on the characteristic of light in the Rabbinic literature: "A Gentile asked the patriarch Gamaliel (c. 100): 'Thou sayest that wherever ten are gathered together the Shekinah appears; how many

---

8. "The term 'Shekinah,' which is Hebrew, whereas 'Memra' and 'Yeḳara' are Aramaic, took the place of the latter two in Talmud and Midrash, and thus absorbed the meaning which they have in the Targum, where they almost exclusively occur. Nevertheless the word 'Shekinah' occurs most frequently in the Aramaic versions, since they were intended for the people and were actually read to them, and since precautions had therefore to be taken against possible misunderstandings in regard to the conception of God" (Kaufmann and Kohler, "Shekinah").

9. Elwell and Beitzel, "Shekinah," 1943.

10. Vangemeren, "Shekinah," 466.

are there?' Gamaliel answered: 'As the sun, which is but one of the countless servants of God, giveth light to all the world, so in a much greater degree doth the Shekinah' (Sanh. 39a)."[11] As writers equated *Shekinah* with light, δόξα references in the NT became associated with the *Shekinah*: "Since the Shekinah is light, those passages of the Apocrypha and New Testament which mention radiance, and in which the Greek text reads δόξα, refer to the Shekinah, there being no other Greek equivalent for the word."[12]

The interchangeable nature of the terms was due, in part, from the overlap in the usage of the term in the Jewish literature, as Joseph Greene notes: "The meanings of God's presence and dwelling existed on a continuum that were related but not equated with the glory cloud."[13] Greene elaborates, saying,

> In both biblical and contemporary usage, the meaning of God's "presence" and God's "glory" overlap, so that in some contexts they are used interchangeably (Exod 33:18-23; Num 16:16-19; 20:6-9; Ps 26:8). The same overlap applies to God's "dwelling" and "presence" (Deut 12:11-12; Pss 26:8; 132; Jer 7:9-15; Zech 2:10-11), which then yields an overlap of God's "dwelling" and "glory" (Exod 29:43-45; 2 Chr 6:1-2; Ps 26:8). This overlap reflects and complicates the intersection of the semantic domains of the specific Hebrew and Greek lexemes that often convey "glory" (כָּבוֹד/δόξα), "presence" (לְפָנֵי/πρόσωπον) and/or "dwelling" (שָׁכַן/κατοικέω); moreover, the Bible communicates these three concepts with lexemes other than these Hebrew/Greek lexeme pairings. This biblical overlap of terminology produces a similar ambiguity in contemporary discussions.[14]

Thus, it would seem that it is possible for one to equate שְׁכִינָה and δόξα and then conclude that Jesus is making the *Shekinah* seeable and approachable in his incarnate nature within the Fourth Gospel. Certainly if it is the *Shekinah* that comes to dwell among the people, then Christ is making the *Shekinah* known. However, in light of the semantic overlaps,

---

11. Cited in Kohler, "Shekinah." Kohler cites another example in which "Shekinah" is the equivalent of the display of God: "The emperor (Hadrian) said to Rabbi Joshua b. Hananiah, 'I desire greatly to see thy God.' Joshua requested him to stand facing the brilliant summer sun, and said, 'Gaze upon it.' The emperor said, 'I can not.' 'Then,' said Joshua, 'if thou art not able to look upon a servant of God, how much less mayest thou gaze upon the Shekinah?' (Ḥul. 60a)."

12. Ibid.

13. Greene, "Did God Dwell In The Second Temple? Clarifying The Relationship Between Theophany And Temple Dwelling," 768.

14. Ibid.

it might be wise to say it is possible that the Johannine writer is speaking of the *Shekinah* because this was a concept familiar to a Jewish audience via the Rabinnic literature even though "*Shekinah*" is not in the corpus of the Hebrew Bible. Again here, more study is necessary in order to make a definitive statement.

ἐκ τῆς γῆς

Although the use of ἐκ τῆς γῆς and ἐπὶ τῆς γῆς seem to have distinct, separate usages in the LXX, a few references need more exploration to see if what the LXX has translated by ἐκ τῆς γῆς also is rendering the idea communicated by ἐπὶ τῆς γῆς in John 17:4. Genesis 19:5 and Ps 148:7 might be good starting points for such comparisons.

So-Called "Prophetic Perfect" in Hebrew and So-Called "Proleptic Aorist" in Greek

In addressing the issue of the possibility of the Greek verbs reflecting the translation of the spoken Aramaic, one may wish to explore whether the LXX translates Prophetic Perfect verbs in the Hebrew Bible with the aorist. The translation of Prophetic Perfect verbs with aorist verbs would not necessarily make a case for a "proleptic" verb in the Greek NT. One would have to assume that the writer of the Gospel of John is translating a spoken Prophetic Perfect by Jesus in the verbs in 17:4, 19:28, and 19:30.

If one could demonstrate the plausibility of the idea that John uses the aorist as the basis for his translation of the Prophetic Perfects in OT quotations in the Fourth Gospel, such an analysis would also need to explore what the verbal aspect of the NT Greek verb is doing with the aspect of the OT Hebrew verb, and it would have to assume such where the OT is quoted by the NT writers other than the Johannine writer.

Good may have provided the first part of a model for such analysis in work on comparing Hebrew and Greek verbal systems.[15] However, such a study might be moot as Rogland's research concludes that so-called Prophetic Perfects in Hebrew are not "prophetic" (or proleptic), but can be explained by *Qatal* clauses (1) speaking of a past with respect to a reference-time in the future, (2) in past tense sentences within

---

15. Good, *The Septuagint's Translation of the Hebrew Verbal System in Chronicles*, 43–70.

future-coming speeches, and (3) in events which occurred in a vision.[16] Following Good with additional research, Carver also concludes that "Prophetic Perfect" does not accurately describe the phenomenon one sees in the Hebrew text.[17]

Reading the Fourth Gospel

Christ as Agent

John 1:1–18—the Prologue—informs the reader that John is a story about how one comes to know God the Father (1:1 "with God" and 1:18 "made him known"). Yet it reveals the role of Christ as *agent* of Creation (cf. 1:2, 10). A reading of John 1–16 as the revelation of the Father gives much greater significance to Christ as agent of creation. As Whitaker notes,

> The description of Wisdom as the master worker at God's side at creation (Prov 8:22–31) is now echoed in John's declaration that the *Word* was the agent of all creation (1:3). As agent he is distinct from the Creator. God the Father is viewed throughout the Gospel as the ultimate source of all, including the Son and the Spirit. But life did not simply come *through* the Word but was *in* the Word (1:4). Only God is the source of life, and it is a mark of Jesus' distinctness and deity that the Father "has granted the Son to have life in himself" (5:26).[18]

Much discussion of 1:1–3 tends to focus on the deity of Christ, largely in response to the errors of Arius (and the Watchtower Society), and the resulting Christological creedal formulation, or on the full humanity of Christ in response to seeing John as a pro-Gnostic text or text dependent upon Gnostic ideas.[19] The Johannine emphasis seems to be on *agency* as a means of revelation of the God of Creation (cf. John 3:18–19).

Throughout the Fourth Gospel, believing the revelation of *God* gives one access to become a child of God (1:12–13; 5:24). The object of such belief is the Father, but it also is Christ. One Person is ultimate, the other

---

16. Rogland, *Alleged Non-Past Uses of Qatal in Classical Hebrew*. See also, Hatav, "Review of Alleged Non-Past Uses of Qatal in Classical Hebrew," 302–304.

17. Carver, "A Reconsideration of the Prophetic Perfect in Biblical Hebrew."

18. Whitacre, *John*, 51.

19. Bultmann proposed that the Prologue (John 1:1–18) was Gnostic in its origin. Kysar, "Rudolf Bultmann's Interpretation of the Concept of Creation in John 1, 3–4," 77–85.

is penultimate. Within a Biblical Theology of the full plan of redemption, Christ the Son is penultimate in honor, where his Father is ultimate (cf. 1 Cor 15:27–28). In revealing the Father, the Son seeks to show that the Father is the object and goal of worship (cf. 4:21–24). Thus it seems that if one fails to receive salvation due to not believing in the name of the Son and because one's works are evil, such failure is in opposition to seeing that the works of one receiving salvation are done in *God* (3:21).[20] Such statements in the Fourth Gospel, when read in light of Christ revealing the Father, seem to steer away from emphasizing the deity of Christ in salvation—that one is mysteriously united in the Divine Son of God. Instead, such statements in the Fourth Gospel would appear to be emphasizing what is done for the believer *in God* the *Father* in salvation.

Additionally, such concepts would seem to add clarity as to why the rejection of the Son incurs the wrath of the Father: it is for the rejection of the Son's revelation of the Father in truth that one incurs the Father's wrath (cf. 3:18, 33, 36). One is rejecting that God the Father exists ("true"), to which existence Christ bore witness and which existence the reception of the Spirit verifies through the words of Christ (3:34).

The Visibility of God the Father

Following the OT revelation, John emphasizes the invisibility of God the Father. Yet in a very different sense, the Father is completely visible through the Son (1:18; 5:37; 6:46; 12:45; cf. Exod 33:20; Col 1:15; 1 Tim 6:16; 1 John 4:12, 20). In 8:19, one thus sees the vicious absence of the knowledge of God as Jesus condemns the Jewish leaders, for the Father is standing before them in Jesus and they cannot see him.

Similarly, in John 1:29, a primary identity of Jesus concerns the atonement, even as much as it concerns his deity: *he is the Lamb who will offer himself as the substitutionary sacrifice for human sins.* Until 1:29, Jesus's identity is associated with the Father and his glory (1:1–18). Jesus offers life, but the means is unknown. The focus turns to him being the Lamb, even though later he will reiterate divinity through the "I am" statements. The writer of the Fourth Gospel will identify him as the giver of the Spirit and the "Son of God" immediately following this (1:33–34). The work of atonement brings to focus the giving of the Spirit and the

---

20. "*The Father* is Jesus' characteristic way of referring to God (*e.g.* 2:16; 11:41; 12:27–28; 17:1)" (Carson, *John*, 223).

divinity, or rather, the focus on God the Father helps us see the role of Christ as Spirit-giver and Son more significantly.

In 6:14, the author gives Jesus the title, "the Prophet." This and terms like "Savior," "Lamb," and "Christ" are references and allusions to OT personalities, or antitypes of OT types (cf. 1 Sam 2:35; 2 Sam 22:3; Pss 2:2; 17:7; 20:6; 106; 21; 132:17; Isa 19:20; 43:3, 11; 45:15, 21; 53:1–12). Through Jesus, these terms are putting a face on God the Father so that he might be visible to them; the Father is the one revealing the will of God through Jesus, saving the world through Jesus, providing a substitutionary sacrifice through Jesus, and appointing an anointed one. The people receive the revelation of Jesus but say "the prophet" rather than "the Father," because Jesus meets the requirements of these figures. Yet it is Jesus who says to Philip, "Have I not been with you?" in response to the request to show the Father (14:7; see also 8:38, 42).

In another example in 10:28, the disclosure of the Father is the issue for the Jews seeking to stone Jesus. In the Fourth Gospel, at this point, it seems that the perceived blasphemy concerns the revealing of the Father. The reader, however, reads what the Pharisees cannot understand—that the Father is in Jesus. Even as one gives further exploration to these concepts, one might consider that the *signs*' primary focus might not be to point to Christ's deity, identity as Messiah, or identity as Savior. Instead, the signs would be for Jesus to reveal God the Father—of having the very identity and approval of God the Father in his acts and words (cf. 4:51).

"The Hour" Statements

Understanding that Jesus is revealing the Father as his work may add understanding to the "the hour" arrival statements in the Fourth Gospel—2:4; 7:30; 8:20; 12:23; 27; 13:1; 16:25; 17:1.[21] Seemingly, what has not yet come or remains undisclosed is the revelation of the Father through Christ—a revelation that will lead to Christ's death. Even though the revelation of the Father has been coming through Christ from the beginning of the Fourth Gospel, the cross and resurrection will reveal God in a unique way.

---

21. The Fourth Gospel has several eschatological "hour" statements also: 4:23; 5:28; 16:2, 32. These, awaiting post-resurrection revelation of Christ, are outside of the further study statements here.

The Upper Room Discourse

In John 14–16, the hope of the discourse rests on the oneness of the Son and the Father—that the Son is making the Father known and has made him known (14:6–11).[22] This is most evident (1) in the initial discussion about the Father's "house" in 14:1–2 and (2) as Jesus reveals a Vinedresser role of the Father in sanctification in John 15:1–8.[23] Although less seems to be said directly of the Father than of Jesus in 15:1–8, reading John 1–16 as the completion of the work to reveal the Father would place stress on the role of the Vinedresser.[24] The initial sense of unrest the disciples feel when Jesus begins the discourse should give way to confidence in the Father who does the work to complete their salvation.

The Crucifixion

According to my thesis, the focus of the Fourth Gospel turns to the work of the Son in 18–21. Jesus's role as a king offering a kingdom comes center-stage, with very little reference to the Father (18:33, 36 [3x], 37, 38; 19:3, 12, 14, 15, 19, 21 [2x]). Those to whom Jesus has come have missed the Father [via Jesus]. All concerns now turn to Jesus—the "Father" that they can see (cf. 1:18; 14:8)—who will be crucified because the revelation of the Father is complete (and missed).

Yet, the distinction between the persons of the Father and Son remains significant. One cannot imagine that the writer of John would suggest that anyone could flog the Father or call the Father "King of the Jews." Such concepts are reserved for the incarnate Christ only. The same

---

22. Also within the discourse, Jesus speaks of "my Father" (14:1, 20; 15:1, 8, 15, 23), "the Father" (14:12, 13, 16, 24, 26, 28, 31; 15:9, 16, 26; 16:3, 10, 15, 17, 23, 25, 26, 27, 28 [2x], 32), and "him who sent me" (15:21; 16:5).

23. "Whereas the other 'I am' sayings refer to Jesus, this one refers to both Jesus and the Father. One cannot help but sense that the close association repeatedly stated between Jesus and the Father in chap. 14 has had an important impact upon the appearance of this varied form of the saying in this core chapter. What is interesting to note is that after v. 2 the Father is not mentioned as intimately involved in the metaphor of the vine. Nevertheless, the Father, as the ultimate focus of glory and the ultimate source of the commandments, does reappear in the discussion at vv. 8 and 10." Borchert, *John 12–21*, 138.

24. "The role of the Father in 15:2 is that of a master gardener who is responsible for removing/trimming/cleansing the branches, both positively and negatively . . . The task of the master gardener, therefore, was one of distinguishing between productive and unproductive branches and dealing appropriately with them in both cases" (Borchert, *John 12–21*, 140).

would seem to hold true for John's portrayal of Jesus (and not the Father) as one being pierced.

The Father's Heart for Women

Although Jesus's words to Mary at the wedding in Cana of Galilee seem harsh,[25] it is evident that Jesus acts caringly and tenderly toward women throughout the Gospel of John. For example, Jesus gradually leads the Samaritan woman to a place of faith (4:26, 28, 42). The episode of John 4 portrays the woman's response to Christ as the initiative for some Samaritans coming to faith (4:42). Her initial words with Jesus and her history of divorce, remarriage, and adultery (4:17–18)—which show disregard for God's law—stand in stark contrast to her zeal to introduce her townsfolk to the one she now perceives to be the Messiah (4:42). The portrayal of the woman's change in character and attitude is positive, as are the portrayals of other characters who come to faith and/or have changes in their responses to Jesus (cf. 1:46–50; 3:1–9 with 19:39–40; 11:21, 39 with 12:2).

The positive change in the woman at Samaria rests on her encounter with Jesus. That is, Jesus' treatment of the woman is not off-putting, but inviting, leading her to faith. If read in light of Jesus completing the work of revealing the Father, the woman is experiencing the kindness of the Father toward a Samaritan, a woman, a lawbreaker, and maybe even one with disregard for the Jewish people (4:9). If there is a question about God's care, concern, or kindness toward such persons, the Fourth Gospel seems to answer the question with the revelation of the Father in Jesus.

The Father's love for a woman would be evident in Jesus's love for Martha (11:5) and sympathy for Mary (11:33). The writer depicts Mary as a worshiper of Jesus, and as one whose act of worship Jesus receives (12:5–7)—whose act of worship the Father, therefore, receives (cf. 13:20).

Differently, in 19:26–27, the reader views a scene that centers on Christ in his completion of the work of redemption. The Son of God takes particular care for his earthly mother, portraying cosmic salvation as having earthly concerns—concern for the care of a woman in particular.

---

25. Whitacre explains the nature of Jesus's rebuke with balance: "The word *woman* does not necessarily connote coldness, but the idiom 'what [is there] to me and to you?' does express either a harsh rejection or a mild form of detachment, depending on the context. Here it expresses distance but not disdain. It is part of the larger theme that Jesus is guided by his heavenly Father and not by the agenda of any human beings, even his family (cf. Jn 7:1–10; Mk 3:33–35; Lk 2:49)" (Whitacre, *John*, 78–79).

How We Teach Greek Grammar

Finally, if the aorist of NT Greek always is perfective, we need to rethink the way we are teaching Greek grammar. Upcoming grammars need to give great weight to the aspect of verbs, and all previous ideas of the aorist communicating simple punctiliar action or an action viewing a full scope and/or without reference to the completion of an action should be revised.

Bibliography

Akala, Adesola Joan. *The Son–Father Relationship and Christological Symbolism in the Gospel of John*. Library of New Testament Studies 505. London: T. & T. Clark, 2014.
Akin, Daniel L., ed. *A Theology for the Church*. Rev. ed. Nashville: B&H Academic, 2014.
Anderson, Paul N. "The Having-Sent-Me Father: Aspects of Agency, Encounter, and Irony in the Johannine Father-Son Relationship." *Semeia* 85 (1999) 33–57.
Aquinas, St. Thomas. *Commentary on John*, 17. Albany, NY: Magi Books, 1980. http://dhspriory.org/thomas/SSJohn.htm.
Augustine. "Tractate 105." *Tractates on the Gospel of John*. Translated by John Gibb. From Nicene and Post-Nicene Fathers, First Series, 7. Edited by Philip Schaff. Buffalo, NY: Christian Literature Publishing, 1888. http://www.newadvent.org/fathers/1701105.htm.
Balz, Horst Robert, and Gerhard Schneider, eds. *Exegetical Dictionary of the New Testament*. Grand Rapids: Eerdmans, 1990–1999.
Barnard, Jody A. "Is Verbal Aspect A Prominence Indicator? An Evaluation of Stanley Porter's Proposal with Special Reference to the Gospel of Luke." *Filología Neotestamentaria* 19 (2006) 3–29.
Baugh, Steven M. *Introduction to Greek Tense Form Choice in the Non-Indicative Moods (PDF Edition)*. Morrisville: Lulu, 2009. https://dailydoseofgreek.com/wp-content/uploads/sites/2/2015/09/GreekTenseFormChoice-Baugh.pdf.
Beasley-Murray, George R. *John*. Word Biblical Commentary 36. Waco: Word, 1987.
———. *John*. 2nd ed. Word Biblical Commentary 36. Waco: Word, 1999.
Becker, Jürgen. "Aufbau, Schichtung und theologiegeschichtliche Stellung des Gebetes in Johannes 17." *ZNW* 60 (1969) 56–83.
Bedard, Stephen J. "The Johannine Creation Account." *AJBT* 12 (2011). http://www.biblicaltheology.com/Research/BedardSJ03.pdf.
Berkhof, Louis. *Systematic Theology*. Grand Rapids: Eerdmans, 1938.
Berkouwer, G. C. *Faith and Justification*. Studies in Dogmatics. Grand Rapids: Eerdmans, 1954.
———. *The Return of Christ*. Studies in Dogmatics. Grand Rapids: Eerdmans, 1972.
Berry, Everett, and Winston Hottman. "Baptists and Ecumenism: A Discussion with Timothy George." The Center for Baptist Renewal (April 6, 2017). http://www.centerforbaptistrenewal.com/blog/2017/4/6/baptists-and-ecumenism-a-discussion-with-timothy-george.

Blomberg, Craig. *Matthew*. New American Commentary. Nashville: Broadman & Holman, 1992.

Boogart, Ronny, and Theo Janssen. "Tense and Aspect in Geeraerts and Cuyckens." In *Oxford Handbook of Cognitive Linguistics*, edited by Dirk Geeraerts and Hubert Cuyckens, 803–28. Oxford: Oxford University Press, 2010.

Borchert, Gerald L. *John 12–21*. New American Commentary 25B. Nashville: Broadman & Holman, 2002.

Braaten, Carl E., and Robert W. Jenson. Introduction to *Church Unity and the Papal Office: An Ecumenical Dialogue with John Paul II's Encyclical Ut Unum Sint*. Edited by Carl E. Braaten and Robert W. Jenson. Grand Rapids: Eerdmans, 2001.

Brannan, Rick. "Writing a Systematic Theology? You Must Discuss These References." The Logos Academic Blog, (June 5, 2017). https://academic.logos.com/writing-a-systematic-theology-you-must-discuss-these-references/.

Bratcher, Robert G. "What Does 'Glory' Mean in Relation to Jesus? Translating *doxa* and *doxazo* in John." *BT* 42 (1991) 401–8.

Bray, Gerald. *God is Love: A Biblical and Systematic Theology*. Wheaton, IL: Crossway, 2012.

Brenton, Lancelot C. L. *The Septuagint Version: Greek*. London: Bagster, 1851.

Bromiley, Geoffrey, ed. *The International Standard Bible Encyclopedia*, Rev. ed. Grand Rapids: Eerdmans, 1979–1988.

Brookins, Timothy. "A Tense Discussion: Rethinking the Grammaticalization of Time in Greek Indicative Verbs." *JBL* 137 (2018) 147–68.

Brown, Christopher Boyd, ed. *Luther's Works: American Edition, vol. 69. Sermons on the Gospel of St. John Chapters 17–20*. St. Louis: Concordia, 2009.

Brown, Francis, Samuel Rolles Driver, and Charles Augustus Briggs. *Enhanced Brown-Driver-Briggs Hebrew and English Lexicon*. Oxford: Clarendon, 1977.

Brown, Jeannine K. "Creation's Renewal in the Gospel of John." *CBQ* 72 (2010) 274–75.

Bultmann, Rudolf. *The Gospel of John: A Commentary*. Translated by G. R. Beasley-Murray. Philadelphia: Westminster, 1971.

Burge, Gary. *John*. NIV Application Commentary. Grand Rapids: Zondervan, 2000.

Buth, Randall. "Participles as Pragmatic Choice: Where Semantics Meets Pragmatics." In *The Greek Verb Revisited: A Fresh Approach for Biblical Exegesis*. Edited by Steven E. Runge and Christopher J. Fresch, 275–306. Bellingham, WA: Lexham, 2016.

Caird, G. B. "The Glory of God in the Fourth Gospel: An Exercise in Biblical Semantics." *NTS* 15 (1969) 265–77.

Calvin, John. *Calvin's New Testament Commentaries: John 11–21 and 1 John*. Grand Rapids: Eerdmans, 1994.

Calvin, John, and William Pringle. *Commentary on the Gospel According to John*, vol. 1. Bellingham, WA: Logos Bible Software, 2010.

———. *Commentary on the Gospel According to John*. Vol. 2. Bellingham, WA: Logos Bible Software, 2010.

Campbell, Constantine R. *Advances in the Study of Greek: New Insights for Reading the New Testament*. Grand Rapids: Zondervan, 2015.

———. *Basics of Verbal Aspect in Biblical Greek*. Grand Rapids: Zondervan Academic, 2008.

———. *Verbal Aspect, the Indicative Mood, and Narrative: Soundings in the Greek of the New Testament*. Studies in Biblical Greek 13. New York: Lang, 2007.

———. *Verbal Aspect and Non-indicative verbs: Further Soundings in the Greek of the New Testament*. Studies in Biblical Greek 15. New York: Peter Lang, 2008.

Carson, D. A. "An Introduction to the Porter/Fanning Debate." In *Biblical Greek Language and Linguistics: Open Questions in Current Research*, edited by Stanley E. Porter and D. A. Carson, 21–25. JSNTSup 80. Sheffield: Sheffield Academic, 1993.

———. *The Gospel According to John*. Pillar New Testament Commentary. Grand Rapids: Eerdmans, 1991.

Carver, Daniel E. "A Reconsideration of the Prophetic Perfect in Biblical Hebrew." PhD diss., Catholic University of America, 2017.

Chrysostom, John. "Homilies of St. John Chrysostom, Archbishop of Constantinople, on the Gospel of St. John." In *Saint Chrysostom: Homilies on the Gospel of St. John and Epistle to the Hebrews: A Select Library of the Nicene and Post-Nicene Fathers of the Christian Church, First Series* 14. Edited by Philip Schaff. Translated by G. T. Stupart. New York: Christian Literature Company, 1889.

Coleman, Lucien E. "*Doxa* and the Passion in the Fourth Gospel." PhD diss., Southern Baptist Theological Seminary, 1958.

Coloe, Mary L. "Theological Reflections on the Creation in the Gospel of John." *Pacifica* 24 (2011) 1–12.

———. "The Structure of the Johannine Prologue and Genesis 1." *Australian Biblical Review* 45 (1997) 54–55.

Conti, Marco, and Joel C. Elowsky, eds. *Commentary on the Gospel of John*. Downers Grove, IL: InterVarsity Press, 2010.

Cook, W. Robert. "The 'Glory' Motif in the Johannine Corpus." *JETS* 27 (1984) 291–97.

Cowan, Christopher. "The Father and Son in the Fourth Gospel: Johannine Subordination Revisited." *JETS* 49 (2006) 115–35.

Crellin, Robert. "The Semantics of the Perfect in the Greek of the New Testament." In *The Greek Verb Revisited: A Fresh Approach to Biblical Exegesis*, edited by Steven E. Runge and Christopher J. Fresch, 430–57. Bellingham, WA: Lexham, 2016.

Crowe, Brandon D. *The Last Adam: A Theology of the Obedient Life of Jesus in the Gospels*. Grand Rapids: Baker, 2017.

Culver, Robert Duncan. *Systematic Theology: Biblical and Historical*. Fearn, UK: Mentor, 2013.

Cyril of Alexandria. *Commentary on John*. Library of the Fathers, vol. 48, Book 11.2. Translated by T. Randall, 453–588. http://www.tertullian.org/fathers/cyril_on_john_11_book11. htm#C3.

Cyril of Alexandria, Joel C. Elowsky, and David R. Maxwell. *Commentary on John*. Vol. 2. Downers Grove, IL: InterVarsity, 2015.

Dana, H. E., and Julius R. Mantey. *A Manual Grammar of the Greek New Testament*. New York: Macmillan, 1927.

D'Angelo, Mary Rose. "Intimating Deity in the Gospel of John: Theological Language and 'Father' in 'Prayers of Jesus.'" *Semeia* 85 (1999) 59–82

Decker, Rodney J. *Temporal Deixis of the Greek Verb in the Gospel of Mark with Reference to Verbal Aspect*. Studies in Biblical Greek 10. New York: Lang, 2001.

———. "The Poor Man's Porter: A Condensation and Summarization of *Verbal Aspect in the Greek New Testament, with Reference to Tense and Mood*, by Stanley E. Porter." NT Resources (website). October 1994. http://ntresources. com/blog/documents/porter.pdf.

"Decree on Ecumenism: Unitatis Redintegratio: La Santa Sede, September 21, 1964." Rome: Vatican Publishing House, 1964. http://www.vatican.va/archive/hist_councils/ii_ vatican_council/documents/vat-ii_decree_19641121_unitatis-redintegratio_en.htm.

Dekker, Jim. "Generativity, Covenant Witness, and Jesus' Final Discourse." *ExAud* 28 (2012) 147–59.

Dodd, C. H. *Historical Tradition in the Fourth Gospel*. Cambridge: Cambridge University Press, 1963.

———. *The Interpretation of the Fourth Gospel*. Cambridge: Cambridge University Press, 1968.

Downing, Henry. *Short Notes on St. John's Gospel*. London: Parker, 1861.

Eckman, George P. *Studies in the Gospel of John: Chapters 13–21*, vol. 2. New York: Jennings and Graham; Eaton and Mains, 1908.

Ellis, Nicholas J. "Aspect-Prominence, Morpho-Syntax, and a Cognitive-Linguistic Framework for the Greek Verb." In *The Greek Verb Revisited: A Fresh Approach for Biblical Exegesis*, edited by Steven E. Runge and Christopher J. Fresch, 122–60. Bellingham, WA: Lexham, 2016.

Ellis, Nicholas J., Michael G. Aubrey, and Mark Dubis. "The Greek Verbal System and Aspectual Prominence: Revising Our Taxonomy and Nomenclature." *JETS* 59 (2016) 33–62.

Ellis, Wesley Gene. "An Investigation into the Meaning of DOXA in the Fourth Gospel." PhD diss., New Orleans Baptist Theological Seminary, 1968.

Elwell, Walter A., and Barry J. Beitzel. "Shekinah." In *Baker Encyclopedia of the Bible*. Grand Rapids: Baker, 1988.

Ensor, Peter. "The Glorification of the Son of Man: An Analysis of John 13:31–32." *TynBul* 58 (2007) 229–52.

Erickson, Millard J. *Christian Theology*, 3rd ed. Grand Rapids: Baker Academic, 2013.

———. *The Word Became Flesh: A Contemporary Incarnational Christology*. Grand Rapids: Baker, 1991.

Fanning, Buist M. "Approaches to Verbal Aspect in New Testament Greek: Issues in Definition and Method." In *Biblical Greek Language and Linguistics: Open Questions in Current Research*, edited by D. A. Carson and Stanley E. Porter, 46–62. JSNTSup 80. Sheffield: JSOT Press, 1993.

———. "Greek Presents, Imperfects, and Aorists in the Synoptic Gospels: Their Contribution to Narrative Structuring." In *Discourse Studies and Biblical Interpretation: A Festschrift in Honor of Stephen H. Levinsohn*, edited by Steven Runge, 157–90. Bellingham, WA: Logos Research Systems, 2011.

———. "Greek Tenses in John's Apocalypse: Issues in Verbal Aspect, Discourse Analysis, and Diachronic Change." In *The Language and Literature of the New Testament: Essays in Honor of Stanley E. Porter's 60th Birthday*, edited by Lois Fuller Dow, Craig A. Evans, and Andrew W. Pitts, 328–53. Leiden: Brill Academic, 2016.

———. *Verbal Aspect in New Testament Greek*. Oxford: Oxford University Press, 1990.

Fesko, J. V. "John Owen on Union with Christ and Justification." *Them* (2012) 7–19.

Fisher, Matthew C. "God the Father in the Fourth Gospel: A Biblical Patrology." PhD diss., Southeastern Baptist Theological Seminary, 2003.

Frame, John M. *Salvation Belongs to the Lord: An Introduction to Systematic Theology*. Phillipsburg, NJ: P&R, 2006.

Frey, Jörg. *The Glory of the Crucified One: Christology and Theology in the Gospel of John*. Translated by Wayne Coppins and Christopher Heilig. Waco: Baylor University Press, 2018.

Furnish, Victor P. *II Corinthians*. Anchor Bible 32A. New Haven: Yale University Press, 2005.

Garland, David E. *2 Corinthians*. New American Commentary 29. Nashville: Broadman & Holman, 1999.

Gentry, Peter J. "'The Glory of God'—The Character of God's Being and Way in the World: Some Reflections on a Key Biblical Theology Theme." *SBJT* 20 (2016) 149–61.

George, Timothy. "Ecumenism After 50 Years." *First Things* (website). December 1, 2014. https://www.firstthings.com/web-exclusives/2014/12/ecumenism-after-50-years.

Gill, John. *An Exposition of the Gospel According to John*. Springfield, IL: Particular Baptist Press, 2003.

Giannakis, Georgios K., ed. *Encyclopedia of Ancient Greek Language and Linguistics*, vol. 1. Leiden: Brill, 2014.

Godet, Frederic Louis. *Commentary on the Gospel of John*. Vol. 2. Grand Rapids: Zondervan, 1969.

Good, Roger. *The Septuagint's Translation of the Hebrew Verbal System in Chronicles*. VTSup 136. Leiden: Brill, 2010.

Govett, R. *Exposition of the Gospel of St. John*. Vol. 2. London: Bemrose, 1881.

Greene, Joseph. "Did God Dwell In The Second Temple? Clarifying the Relationship Between Theophany and Temple Dwelling." *JETS* 61 (2018) 767–84.

Grudem, Wayne. *Systematic Theology: An Introduction to Biblical Doctrine*. Grand Rapids: Zondervan, 1995.

Guthrie, Donald. "The Importance of Signs in the Fourth Gospel." *VE* 5 (1967) 72–83.

Haenchen, Ernst. "Der vater, der mich gesandt hat." *NTS* 9 (1963) 208–16.

Harris, Murray J. *Exegetical Guide to the Greek New Testament*. Nashville: B&H Academic, 2015.

Hastings, James, et al. eds. *A Dictionary of the Bible: Dealing with Its Language, Literature, and Contents Including the Biblical Theology*. Edinburgh: T. & T. Clark, 1911–12.

Hatav, Galia. "Review of Alleged Non-Past Uses of Qatal in Classical Hebrew." *HS* 45 (2004) 302–04.

Hays, Richard B. *The Conversion of the Imagination: Paul as Interpreter of Israel's Scripture*. Grand Rapids: Eerdmans, 2005.

Helm, Paul. "Calvin and the Covenant: Unity and Continuity." *EvQ* 55 (1983) 65–81.

Hengel, Martin. "The Interpretation of the Wine Miracle at Cana: John 2:1–11." In *The Glory of Christ in the New Testament: Studies in Christology in Memory of George Bradford Caird*, edited by L. D. Hurst and N. T. Wright, 83–122. Oxford: Oxford University Press, 1987.

———. "The Old Testament in the Fourth Gospel." In *The Gospels and the Scriptures of Israel*, 380–95. JSNTSup 104. Sheffield: Sheffield Academic, 1994.

Hengstenberg, E. W. *Commentary on the Gospel of St John*. Vol. 2. Edinburgh: T. & T. Clark, 1865.

Hilary of Poitiers. "On the Trinity (Book 4)." http://www.newadvent.org/fathers/330206.htm.

Hodge, Archibald Alexander. *Outlines of Theology*. New York: Carter, 1863.

The Holy Bible: Authorized King James Version. London: Oxford University Press, 2008.
Hovey, Alvah. *Commentary on the Gospel of John*. Philadelphia: American Baptist Publication Society, 1885.
Huffman, Douglas S. *Verbal Aspect Theory and the Prohibitions in the Greek New Testament*. Studies in Biblical Greek 16. New York: Lang, 2014.
"Interfaith Relations and the Church: The Ecumenical Challenge: A Resource of the Interfaith Relations Committee of the National Council of Churches in Christ in the USA." New York: National Council of Churches in Christ in the USA, n.d.
Jin, Soo Keum. "DOXA and Related Concepts in the Fourth Gospel: An Inquiry into the Manifestation of DOXA in Jesus' Cross." PhD diss., University of Pretoria, 2007.
Johns, Loren L., and Douglas B. Miller, "The Signs as Witnesses in the Fourth Gospel: Reexamining the Evidence." *CBQ* 56 (1994) 519–35.
Käsemann, Ernst. *The Testament of Jesus: A Study of the Gospel of John in the Light of John 17*. Minneapolis: Fortress, 1968.
Keener, Craig S. *The Gospel of John: A Commentary*. Vol. 2. Peabody, MA: Hendrickson, 2003.
Kelly, William. *An Exposition of the Gospel of John*. London: Weston, 1898.
Kidner, Derek. *Psalms 1–72: An Introduction and Commentary*. Downers Grove, IL: InterVarsity, 1973.
Kim, Stephen S. "The Christological and Eschatological Significance of Jesus' Miracle in John 5." *BSac* 165 (2008) 413–24.
Kittel, Gerhard, and Gerhard Friedrich, eds. *Theological Dictionary of the New Testament*. Translated by Geoffrey W. Bromiley. 10 vols. Grand Rapids: Eerdmans, 1964–1976.
Klink, Edward W. *John: Zondervan Exegetical Commentary on the New Testament*. Grand Rapids: Zondervan, 2016.
Koehler, Ludwig, Walter Baumgartner, and Johann Jakob Stamm, eds. *The Hebrew and Aramaic Lexicon of the Old Testament*. Leiden: Brill, 1994–2000.
Kohler, Kaufmann. "Shekinah." In *The Jewish Encyclopedia* (website). http://www.jewish encyclopedia.com/articles/13537-shekinah.
Kok, Jacobus. "The Healing of the Blind Man in John." *Journal of Early Christian History* 2 (2017) 36–62.
Köstenberger, Andreas J. "The Glory of God in John's Gospel and Revelation." In *The Glory of God*. Edited by Christopher W. Morgan and Robert A. Peterson, 107–26. Wheaton, IL: Crossway, 2010.
———. *John*. Grand Rapids: Baker Academic, 2004.
———. "John's Appropriation of Isaiah's Signs Theology: Implications for the Structure of John's Gospel." *Them* 43 (2018) 376–86.
———. *The Missions of Jesus and His Disciples According to the Fourth Gospel: With Implications for the Fourth Gospel's Purpose and the Mission of the Contemporary Church*. Grand Rapids: Eerdmans, 1998.
———. *A Theology of John's Gospel and Letters: The Word, the Christ, the Son of God*. Grand Rapids: Zondervan, 2009.
Köstenberger, Andreas J., and Scott R. Swain. *Father, Son, and Spirit: Trinity in John's Gospel*. Downers Grove, IL: InterVarsity, 2008.
Kruse, Colin G. *John*. Grand Rapids: Eerdmans, 2003.

Kysar, R. "Rudolf Bultmann's Interpretation of the Concept of Creation in John 1, 3–4: A Study of Exegetical Method." *CBQ* 32 (1970) 77–85.

Lamb, Gregory E. "Verbal Aspect, *Aktionsart*, and the Greek New Testament: The Approaches of Constantine R. Campbell and Stanley E. Porter." *Presb* 43 (2017) 95–130.

Lange, John Peter, and Philip Schaff. *A Commentary on the Holy Scriptures: John*. Bellingham, WA: Logos Bible Software, 2008.

Lee, Dorothy A. "Beyond Suspicion? The Fatherhood of God in the Fourth Gospel." *Pacifica* 8 (1995) 140–50.

———. "'Signs' and 'Works:' The Miracles in the Gospels of Mark and John." *Colloq* 47 (2015) 89–101.

———. "The Symbol of Divine Fatherhood." *Semeia* 85 (1999) 177–87.

Lenski, R. C. H. *The Interpretation of St. John's Gospel*. Minneapolis: Augsburg, 1961.

Levinsohn, Stephen H. *Discourse Features of New Testament Greek: A Coursebook on the Information Structure of New Testament Greek*. 2nd ed. Dallas: SIL International, 2000.

Liddell, Henry George, and Robert Scott., eds. *A Greek-English Lexicon*. Oxford: Clarendon, 1996.

Lincoln, Andrew T. *The Gospel According to Saint John*. Black's New Testament Commentaries 4. London: Continuum, 2005.

Lindars, Barnabas. *The Gospel of John*. New Century Bible Commentary. Grand Rapids: Eerdmans, 1982.

Lindgren, Caleb. "Sorry, Old Testament: Most Theologians Don't Use You." *Christianity Today* (June 13, 2017). http://www.christianitytoday.com/news/2017/june/old-testament-systematic-theology-top-100-verses-logos.html.

Louw, Johannes P., and Eugene Albert Nida, eds. *Greek-English Lexicon of the New Testament: Based on Semantic Domains*. New York: United Bible Societies, 1996.

Machen, J. Gresham. *New Testament Greek for Beginners*. Toronto: Macmillan, 1923.

Mahoney, Jack. "The Glory of God in St John's Gospel." *The Way* 50 (2011) 21–37.

Malatesta, Edward. "The Literary Structure of John 17 (Two Folding Charts)." *Bib* 52 (1971) 190–214.

Manton, Thomas. *The Complete Works of Thomas Manton, D.D. Volume 10: Containing Several Sermons Upon the Twenty-Fifth Chapter of St. Matthew; also, Sermons Upon the Seventeenth Chapter of John*. London: Nisbet, 1872.

Marlowe, Michael D. "The Semitic Style of the NT." Bible Researcher (website). http://www.bible-researcher.com/hebraisms.html.

Marshall, I. Howard, A. R. Millard, J. I. Packer, and Donald J. Wiseman, eds. *New Bible Dictionary*. Downers Grove, IL: InterVarsity, 1996.

Mathews, K. A. *Genesis 1—11:26*. New American Commentary 1A. Nashville: Broadman & Holman, 1996.

Matson, Mark A. "The Glory of God: Echoes of Exodus in the Gospels." *Leaven* 21 (2014) 86–90.

McCann, J. Clinton, Jr. "The Book of Psalms: Introduction, Commentary, and Reflections." In *The New Interpreter's Bible*, edited by Leander E. Keck, 4:870–74. Nashville: Abingdon, 1996.

McColl, Mary Ann, and Richard S. Ascough. "Jesus and People with Disabilities: Old Stories, New Approaches." *JPC&C* 63 (2009) 1–11.

McKay, K. L. "Aspect in Imperatival Constructions in New Testament Greek." *NovT* 27 (1985) 201–26.

———. *Greek Grammar for Students: A Concise Grammar of Classical Attic with Special Reference to Aspect in the Verb.* Canberra: Australian National University, 1974.

———. *A New Syntax of the Verb in New Testament Greek: An Aspectual Approach.* Studies in Biblical Greek 5. New York: Lang, 1994.

Merkle, Benjamin L. "Abused Aspect: Neglecting the Influence of a Verb's Lexical Meaning on Tense-Form Choice." *BBR* 26 (2016) 57–74.

———. "Response to Porter." *BBR* 26 (2016) 83.

Metzger, Bruce Manning. *A Textual Commentary on the Greek New Testament, Second Edition: A Companion Volume to the United Bible Societies' Greek New Testament.* 4th rev. ed. New York: United Bible Societies, 1994.

Metzner, Rainer. "Der Geheilte von Johannes 5—Repräsentant des Unglaubens." *ZNW* 90 (1999) 177–93.

Meyer, Heinrich August Wilhelm. *Critical and Exegetical Handbook to the Epistle to the Romans.* Translated by John C. Moore and Edwin Johnson. New York: Funk & Wagnalls, 1884.

Meyer, Paul W. "'The Father:' The Presentation of God in the Fourth Gospel." In *Exploring the Gospel of John: In Honor of D. Moody Smith*, edited by R. Alan Culpepper and C. Clifton Black, 255–73. Louisville: Westminster John Knox, 1996.

Michaels, J. Ramsey. *The Gospel of John.* New International Commentary on the New Testament. Grand Rapids: Eerdmans, 2010.

Milewski, Douglas. "Nos Locus Dei Sumus: Augustine's Exegesis and Theology of John 17 in the Light of in Evangelium Iohannis Tractatus CIV–CXI." PhD diss., Pontificia Universitas Lateranensis, 2000.

Moloney, Francis J. *The Gospel of John: Text and Context.* Leiden: Brill, 2005.

———. *Johannine Studies, 1975–2017.* Tübingen: Mohr Siebeck, 2017.

———. *Love in the Gospel of John: An Exegetical, Theological, and Literary Study.* Grand Rapids: Baker Academic, 2013.

Montanari, Franco. *The Brill Dictionary of Ancient Greek, α—χ.* Edited by Madeleine Goh and Chad Schroeder. Leiden: Brill, 2015.

Moore, George Foot. "Intermediaries in Jewish theology: Memra, Shekinah, Metatron." *HTR* 15 (1922) 41–85.

Morris, Leon. *The Gospel According to John.* Rev. ed. New International Commentary on the New Testament. Grand Rapids: Eerdmans, 1995.

Moulton, James Hope. *Prolegomena.* 3rd ed. Vol. 1. *A Grammar of New Testament Greek*, 4 vols. Edinburgh: T. & T. Clark, 1908–76.

Moulton, James Hope, and George Milligan. *The Vocabulary of the Greek Testament Illustrated from the Papyri and Other Non-Literary Sources.* London: Hodder & Stoughton, 1914–29.

Mounce, William D. *Basics of Biblical Greek: Grammar.* 3rd ed. Grand Rapids: Zondervan, 2009.

Mullins, Edgar Young. *The Christian Religion in Its Doctrinal Expression.* Philadelphia: Roger Williams, 1917.

Naselli, Andrew David. "A Brief Introduction to Verbal Aspect in New Testament Greek." *DBSJ* 12 (2007) 17–28.

Nielsen, Jesper Tang. "The Narrative Structures of Glory and Glorification in the Fourth Gospel." *NTS* 56 (2010) 343–66.

Nolland, John. *The Gospel of Matthew: A Commentary on the Greek Text*. New International Greek New Testament Commentary. Grand Rapids: Eerdmans, 2005.

O'Day, Gail R. "Show Us the Father." *Semeia* 85 (1999) 11–17.

The Orthodox Presbyterian Church, *Larger Catechism*, https://www.opc.org/lc.html.

Ortlund, Dane. "Inaugurated Glorification: Revising Romans 8:30." *JETS* 57 (2014), 111–33.

Owen, John J. *A Commentary, Critical, Expository, and Practical, on the Gospel of John*. New York: Leavitt & Allen, 1861.

Paddison, Angus. "Engaging Scripture: Incarnation and the Gospel of John." *SJT* 60 (2007) 144–60.

Painter, John. "The Signs of the Messiah and the Quest for Eternal Life." In *What We Have Heard from the Beginning: The Past, Present, and Future of Johannine Studies*, edited by Tom Thatcher, 233–56. Waco: Baylor University Press, 2007.

Pamment, Margaret. "The Meaning of *Doxa* in the Fourth Gospel." *ZNW* 74 (1983) 12–16.

Park, Hoseok. "Discourse-Analytic Significance of the Use of 'Father' as God's Title in John's Gospel." PhD diss., Dallas Theological Seminary, 2014.

Paterson, Andrew. *Opening Up John's Gospel*. Leominster: Day One Publications, 2010.

Peterson, Robert A. *Salvation Accomplished by the Son: The Work of Christ*. Wheaton, IL: Crossway, 2012.

Picirilli, Robert E. "The Meaning of the Tenses in New Testament Greek: Where Are We?" *JETS* 48 (2005) 533–55.

Pictet, Benedict. *Christian Theology*. Translated by Frederick Reyroux. London: Seeley, 1834.

Pilch, John J. "Jesus as Healer." In *Christian Reflection: A Series in Faith and Ethics* by The Center for Christian Ethics at Baylor University. Edited by Robert B. Kruschwitz. https://www.baylor.edu/ifl/christianreflection/HealthArticlePilch.pdf.

Poole, Matthew. *Annotations upon the Holy Bible*, vol. 3. New York: Robert Carter and Brothers, 1853.

Pope, William Burt. *A Compendium of Christian Theology: Being Analytical Outlines of a Course of Theological Study, Biblical, Dogmatic, Historical*. Vol. 3. London: Beveridge, 1879.

Porter, Stanley E. *Idioms of the Greek New Testament*. 2nd ed. Biblical Languages: Greek 2. Sheffield: Sheffield Academic, 1999.

———. "Prominence: A Theoretical Overview." In *The Linguist as Pedagogue: Trends in the Teaching and Linguistic Analysis of the Greek New Testament*, edited by S. E. Porter and M. B. O'Donnell, 45–74. NTM 11. Sheffield: Sheffield Phoenix, 2009.

———. *Verbal Aspect in the Greek of the New Testament, with Reference to Tense and Mood*. 3rd ed. Studies in Biblical Greek 1. New York: Lang, 2003.

———. "What More Shall I Say? A Response to Steve Runge and Benjamin Merkle." *BBR* 26 (2016) 75–79.

Rahlfs, Alfred. *Septuaginta: With Morphology*. Electronic ed. Logos Bible Software. Stuttgart: Deutsche Bibelgesellschaft, 1979.

Reinhartz, Adele. "Introduction: 'Father' as Metaphor in the Fourth Gospel." *Semeia* 85 (1999) 1–10.

Rhodes, Ben. "Signs and Wonders: Disability in the Fourth Gospel." *JCID* 5 (2016) 53–75.

Ridderbos, Herman N. *The Gospel of John: A Theological Commentary.* Translated by John Vriend. Grand Rapids: Eerdmans, 1997.
Riedl, Johannes. *Das Heilswerk Jesus nach Johannes.* Freiburger theologische Studien 93. Freiburg: Herder, 1973.
Robertson, A. T. *Grammar of the Greek New Testament in the Light of Historical Research.* 3rd ed. New York: Hodder & Stoughton, 1919.
Robertson, Paul E. "Glory in the Fourth Gospel." *TTE* 38 (1988) 121–31.
Rogland, Max. *Alleged Non-Past Uses of Qatal in Classical Hebrew.* Assen: Van Gorcum, 2003.
Runge, Steven E. *Discourse Grammar of the Greek New Testament: A Practical Introduction for Teaching and Exegesis.* Lexham Bible Reference Series. Peabody, MA: Hendrickson, 2013.
———. "Markedness: Contrasting Porter's Model with the Linguists Cited as Support." *BBR* 26 (2016) 43–56.
———. "Response to Porter." *BBR* 26 (2016) 81–82.
Runge Steven E., and Christopher J. Fresch, eds. *The Greek Verb Revisited: A Fresh Approach to Biblical Exegesis: Proceedings from the Linguistics and Greek Verb Conference, Cambridge University, 2015.* Bellingham, WA: Lexham, 2016.
Salier, Willis Hedley. *The Rhetorical Impact of the Sēmeia in the Gospel of John.* WUNT 186. Tübingen: Mohr Siebeck, 2004.
Shedd, William Greenough Thayer. *Dogmatic Theology.* Edited by Alan W. Gomes. 3rd ed. Phillipsburg, NJ: P&R, 2003.
Silva, Moisés. *New International Dictionary of New Testament Theology and Exegesis.* 2nd ed. Grand Rapids: Zondervan, 2014.
Simeon, Charles. *Horae Homileticae: John XIII to Acts.* Vol. 14. London: Holdsworth & Ball, 1833.
Smith, Ralph Allan. "Trinitarian Covenant in John 17." *Global Missiology* 3 (2005) 1–13.
Spence-Jones, H. D. M. ed., *St. John, vol. 2: The Pulpit Commentary.* London: Funk & Wagnalls, 1909.
St. Bonaventure. *Commentary on the Gospel of John: Introduction, Translation and Notes.* Edited by Robert J. Karris. New York: Franciscan Institute Publications, 2007.
Styler, G. M., and Buist M. Fanning. *Verbal Aspect in New Testament Greek.* Oxford: Oxford University Press, 1993.
Swete, Henry Barclay. *The Old Testament in Greek: According to the Septuagint.* Cambridge: Cambridge University Press, 1909.
Tabb, Brian. "Jesus's Thirst at the Cross: Irony and Intertextuality in John 19:28." *EvQ* 85 (2013) 338–51.
Tasker, R. V. G. *The Gospel According to John.* Grand Rapids: Eerdmans, 1960.
Terrien, Samuel. *The Psalms: Strophic Structure and Theological Commentary.* Grand Rapids: Eerdmans, 2003.
Tholuck, A. *A Commentary on the Gospel of St. John.* Translated by A. Kaufman. Boston: Perkins & Marvin, 1836.
Thomas, J. C. "Healing in the Atonement: A Johannine Perspective." *JPT* 14 (2005) 22–39.
Thompson, Marianne Meye. *The God of the Gospel of John.* Grand Rapids: Eerdmans, 2001.
———. "The Living Father." *Semeia* 85 (1999) 19–31.
———. *The Promise of the Father: Jesus and God in the New Testament.* Louisville: Westminster John Knox, 2000.

———. "Signs and Faith in the Fourth Gospel." *BBR* 1 (1991) 89–108.
Thompson, Robin. "Healing at the Pool of Bethesda: A Challenge to Asclepius?" *BBR* 27 (2017) 65–84.
Tolmie, D. Francois. "The Characterization of God in the Fourth Gospel." *JSNT* 20 (1998) 57–75.
Tresham, Aaron. "Aspect and *Aktionsart* in Greek Grammars." Academia (website). https://www.academia.edu/5886132/Aspect_and_Aktionsart_in_Greek_Grammars.
Turner, Nigel. *A Grammar of New Testament Greek*. Vol. 3: *Syntax*. Edinburgh: T. & T. Clark, 1963.
———. *Grammatical Insights into the New Testament*. Edinburgh: T. & T. Clark, 1965.
Usher, James. *A Body of Divinity: Or, the Sum and Substance of Christian Religion*, 8th ed. Sacramento: Creative Media Partners, 2018.
Uzukwu, Gesila Nneka. "The Disabled in the Gospel of John: An Exegetical Study of John's Account of Jesus' Healing in John 5:1–47 and 9:1–41, and its Implications for Contemporary African Society." *Sapientia Logos* 5 (2012) 39–67.
Van der Merwe, D. G. "The Glory-Motif in John 17:1–5: An Exercise in Biblical Semantics." *Verbum et Ecclesia* 23 (2002) 229–31.
Van der Watt, Jan G. "Double Entendre in the Gospel According to John." In *Theology and Christology in the Fourth Gospel: Essays by the Members of the SNTS Johannine Writings Seminar*, edited by Gilbert van Belle, J. G. van der Watt, and P. Maritz, 463–81. Bibliotheca Ephemeridum Theologicarum Lovaniensium 184. Leuven: Peeters, 2005.
Van Dyke, Blair G. "Miracles of Jesus in the Gospel of John." *Religious Educator* 9 (2008) 15–30.
Van Eerden, Brad L. "John's Depiction of God as Father: Analysis of the God Language in the Fourth Gospel." PhD diss., Dallas Theological Seminary, 2003.
VanGemeren, Willem A. "Psalms." In *The Expositor's Bible Commentary*, Edited by Frank Gaebelein, 5:3–880. Grand Rapids: Zondervan, 1991.
Voelz, J. W. "Present and Aorist Verbal Aspect: A New Proposal." *Neot* 27 (1993) 153–64.
———. "Semitic Influence on the Greek of the New Testament." *Concordia Journal* 20 (1994) 115–29.
von Wahlde, Urban C. "Faith and Works in Jn 6.28–29: Exegesis or Eisegesis?" *NovT* 22 (1980) 304–15.
Wallace, Daniel B. *Greek Grammar Beyond the Basics: An Exegetical Syntax of the New Testament*. Grand Rapids: Zondervan, 1996.
Waterson, A. P. "The Miracles of Healing in the Fourth Gospel." *Chm* 71 (1957) 21–26.
Wellum, Stephen. *God the Son Incarnate: The Doctrine of Christ*. Wheaton, IL: Crossway, 2016.
Westcott, B. F. *The Gospel According to St. John: The Authorized Version with Introduction and Notes*. London: Murray, 1896.
Whitacre, Rodney A. *John*. Downers Grove, IL: InterVarsity Press, 1999.
Whitelaw, Thomas. *The Gospel of St. John: An Exposition Exegetical and Homiletical*. New York: Dutton, 1888.
Winer, G. B. *A Treatise on the Grammar of New Testament Greek: Regarded as A Sure Basis for New Testament Exegesis*. Vols. 1–2. Translated by W. F. Moulton. Edinburgh: T. & T. Clark, 1882.

Witsius, Herman. *The Economy of the Covenants between God and Man: Comprehending a Complete Body of Divinity*. Vol. 1. Translated by William Crookshank. London: Tegg, 1837.
Wong, Corinne Hong Sling. "The *Doxa* of Christ and His Followers in the Fourth Gospel: An Inquiry into the Meaning and Background of *Doxa* in John 17.22." PhD diss., University of Pretoria, 2005.
Wynn, Kerry H. "Johannine Healings and the Otherness of Disability." *PRSt* 34 (2007) 61–75.

www.ingramcontent.com/pod-product-compliance
Lightning Source LLC
Chambersburg PA
CBHW050846230426
43667CB00012B/2172